# WELCOME TO
# FAIRYLAND

D1546407

# LAND

*Queer Miami before 1940*

## JULIO CAPÓ JR.

THE UNIVERSITY OF NORTH CAROLINA PRESS    CHAPEL HILL

Cover illustration: John Singer Sargent, *The Bathers*. Courtesy Worcester Art Museum (MA), Sustaining Membership Fund, 1917.91.

Library of Congress Cataloging-in-Publication Data
Names: Capó, Julio, Jr., author.
Title: Welcome to fairyland : queer Miami before 1940 / Julio Capó Jr.
Description: Chapel Hill : University of North Carolina Press, [2017] | Includes bibliographical references and index.
Identifiers: LCCN 2017020580 | ISBN 9781469635194 (cloth : alk. paper) | ISBN 9781469635200 (pbk : alk. paper) | ISBN 9781469635217 (ebook)
Subjects: LCSH: Sexual minorities—Florida—Miami—History—19th century. | Sexual minorities—Florida—Miami—History—20th century. | Miami (Fla.)—History—19th century. | Miami (Fla.)—History—20th century. | Miami (Fla.)—Race relations. | Caribbean Area—Emigration and immigration.
Classification: LCC HQ76.3.U62 M5315 2017 | DDC 305.8009759/381—dc23
LC record available at https://lccn.loc.gov/2017020580

TO ANNETTE,

WHOSE EXAMPLE I ALWAYS SEEK TO FOLLOW.

I WILL ALWAYS DANCE

PIMPINELA'S "HERMANOS" WITH YOU.

———

# Contents

# Figures, Maps, and Table

MAPS

TABLE

# Acknowledgments

Writing a book is a lot of work. Despite warnings that it's an exercise in solitude, I never felt alone. My heartfelt gratitude to Alex Lichtenstein, whose unmatched generosity, support, and sharp mind has taught me so much over the years. While this book is not a revision of my doctoral dissertation, which covered Miami's post-1945 queer history, I owe my professors at Florida International University, especially Lichtenstein and Darden A. Pyron, much gratitude for their support and encouragement and for helping me first conceptualize Miami's queer past. Sherry Johnson, Aurora Morcillo, and Alex Stepick also showered me with a perfect mix of care, tough love, feedback, and insight. Please know that I will forever pay it forward and that I do my very best to emulate your dedication and commitment now that I have students of my own.

This book greatly benefited from the insight of scholars who elevated my analysis of the material and made this a stronger work. I am especially grateful to Marc Stein for generously offering me extensive comments on this manuscript and an early draft of my second book project on Miami's post–World War II period. Thank you for being so gracious and engaged, and for your ability to explain even the most difficult matters. Thank you, too, to the folks at UNC Press for their help seeing this work through. I especially would like to thank my editor Mark Simpson-Vos for his undying support of me and my work and his critical eye and mind. I owe a great deal of thanks to so many others who read either the whole draft or parts of this work: Mark Philip Bradley, Michael Bronski, Nathan Connolly, María Cristina García, Timothy Gilfoyle, Richard Godbeer, David K. Johnson, Laura Lovett, Ana Raquel Minian, Kevin Murphy, Melanie Shell-Weiss, and Naoko Shibusawa. Of course, any faults or limitations in this book are entirely on me.

Several others have forever shaped the way I think and my relationship to scholarship. I first made the decision to revisit the archives and write a new book that began with Miami in the 1890s during my postdoc in the American Studies and the Ethnicity, Race, and Migration programs at Yale University. For their continued support, guidance, and warmth, I am especially grateful to Jafari Allen, P. Sean Brotherton, Alicia Schmidt Camacho, George Chauncey, Walter Foery, Joanne Meyerowitz, Stephen Pitti, and Birgit Brander Rasmussen. I also hold the short time I spent with the late Patricia Pessar dear to my heart.

I am incredibly fortunate to have so many generous and caring colleagues at the University of Massachusetts, Amherst. My history department chair, Joye Bowman, made my transition to faculty member seem seamless. Thank you for your open door, open mind, and open heart. Similarly, I can never express how much joy and inspiration Jessica Johnson, Jennifer Nye, Priyanka Srivastava, and Heidi Scott bring me on a daily basis. While there are simply too many people to mention (an embarrassment of riches, really), I would like to specifically express my gratitude to Audrey Altstadt, Laura Briggs, Brian Bunk, Richard Chu, Sarah Cornell, Tanisha Ford, Jennifer Fronc, David Glassberg, Dan Gordon, Jennifer Heuer, Barbara Krauthamer, Laura Lovett, Johan Mathew, Alice Nash, Brian Ogilvie, Sigrid Schmalzer, Libby Sharrow, Anna Taylor, Joel Wolfe, and Kevin Young. I am similarly grateful to my colleagues in the Commonwealth Honors College for their encouragement, support, and camaraderie. Thanks to Alex Deschamps, Gretchen Gerzina, and Tim Lang. I am also indebted to the late Priscilla M. Clarkson, whose warmth and positive outlook I will always carry with me. Others across campus, such as Sonia Alvarez, Genny Beemyn, Adeline Broussan, Gloria Bernabe-Ramos, Mari Castañeda, Julie Hayes, Anne Moore, Susan Shapiro, and Manisha Sinha also offered me support and collegiality.

This book would not have been possible without the assistance and guidance of many talented and knowledgeable librarians and archivists. Thank you to the incredibly warm and expedient folks at the UMass Interlibrary Loan office. I am indebted to the talented staff at the UMass Image Collection Library: Michael Foldy, Brian Shelburne, and Annie Sollinger. Miriam Spalding at the State Archives of Florida helped me countless times in Tallahassee and over the phone or e-mail. Thank you for that, and the many laughs we had along the way. The staff at the National Archives of the Bahamas was incredibly generous in assisting me with locating records and sources. Emily Gibson and Alex Privee, both formerly at the Vizcaya Museum and Gardens Archives, shared their knowledge of the sources and depositories with me. HistoryMiami has always felt like a second home to me. I am indebted to Dawn Hugh and Ashley Trujillo for their continued support, assistance, and camaraderie over the years. Many thanks, too, to John Shipley at the Miami-Dade Public Library, whose knowledge of southern Florida's history is unmatched. I am also grateful to Joe Clein for sharing with me his private collection of *Miami Life*, a source that would otherwise be lost to us.

Over the years, several organizations and institutions have generously offered me financial support to conduct research on Miami's queer past more broadly and allowed me to conceive of this book and my other research projects. In addition to my position at Yale upon my graduation, I benefited greatly from a visiting fellow position at the United States Studies Centre at the University of Sydney five years later. Earlier in my career, I was the recipient of two major financial awards as a graduate student at FIU, the Doctoral Evidence Acquisition and Dissertation Year fellowships. During that time, I also received the Joan Heller–Diane Bernard fellowship from the Center for LGBTQ Studies (CLAGS). More recently, the Department of History, Commonwealth Honors College, and the College of Humanities and Fine Arts at UMass Amherst offered me financial and professional support over the past five years. A Mellon Mutual Mentoring Team Grant on "Transnational Feminisms and Sexualities" I coreceived with Tanisha Ford, Laura Lovett, and Priyanka Srivastava similarly helped shape this work. Words cannot convey how grateful I am to these organizations and institutions for making this research possible and for their faith in me to conduct it and tell these long forgotten histories.

Whether we swapped stories, presented on panels together, or discussed and shared ideas, I would like to thank the many colleagues I have yet to mention who offered emotional support and brought me much joy in the profession. Thanks to Llana Barber, Katie Batza, Kathleen Belew, Jonathan Bell, Nan Alamilla Boyd, Jennifer Brier, Gerry Cadava, Margot Canaday, Chris Capozzola, Javier Corrales, Ben Cowan, LaToya Eaves, Erika Edwards, Kevin Fogg, Gill Frank, Marcia Gallo, James Green, Rachel Guberman, Ramón Gutiérrez, Kwame Holmes, Ryan Jones, Aaron Lecklider, Ian Lekus, Amanda Littauer, Víctor Macías-González, Jen Manion, April Merleaux, La Shonda Mims, Kym Morrison, Barbara Posadas, Dan Royles, Jason Ruiz, Andrew Sandoval-Strausz, Laurie Shrage, Megan Springate, Timothy Stewart-Winter, Hadassah St. Hubert, Amy Sueyoshi, Nick Syrett, and Chantalle Verna. A separate and heartfelt token of gratitude to John D'Emilio, who agreed to meet with and counsel a young journalist he had never met before at a Chicago coffee shop a decade ago. This book, and my choice in careers, wouldn't exist without that meeting.

I also want to thank those who trained and shepherded me through the difficult work of broadcast news writing and producing before I entered academia. My time at WSVN and WPLG shaped me as a writer and thinker in most productive ways. I am especially grateful to Jennifer Benitez-Golfen, Jacey Birch, Hannah Jane Corsa, and Richard Lemus.

It's hard to write acknowledgments knowing several people who shaped and influenced me over the years are no longer with us. Abuelo Nono, you helped raise me and taught me that nothing mattered more than family and those we let into our lives. You risked everything to give me the life I lead today. Thank you just doesn't seem like enough. Yurena Rivero-Osorio, I feel your presence every day. Because of your example, *prima*, I learned to embrace every aspect of myself, especially those I was once ashamed or afraid of. Horacio N. Roque Ramírez, your confidence in me, *jotería*, and *chispa* helped me find my voice at a most critical time of my journey. Little did you know then, you forever changed me.

I think of "family" as an expansive concept that includes both my blood relatives and my "queer" kin; that is, the special bonds we form with others that extend well beyond sharing bloodlines. Ana Raquel Minian: you will always (read: *alllwaaaays*) be my *media naranja*. Thank you for your friendship, sharp wit, and brilliant mind. My work and life are no doubt better because of you. Thanks, too, to Sitela Alvarez, Victor Capó, Michael Chunyk, Stephanie Cramer, Liam Crowley, Luis X. Davila, Paul Evans, Ashley Mateiro, Harley Matthews, Orlando Moreno, Keith Paul, Michael Perry, Morgan Stone, Darryl Toppins, and Jen and Brad Turner for their undying support and friendship. My love and gratitude to Erin and Bob Edge, too, for so generously welcoming me into the family.

I have the most extraordinary blood family, too. My parents, Anna and Julio, have always encouraged me to pursue the advanced degrees they, because of life's circumstances, did not. Along with my grandparents, Aida and Manolo, they constantly reminded me that alongside all the things one can lose in life, love and knowledge would always be permanent fixtures. Thank you for believing in me and giving me countless opportunities, often through your many sacrifices. My sister Annette first opened my eyes to questions of social justice and forged my early feminist consciousness, even though she didn't necessarily know it. Nana, you are my everything and I love you more than I could ever explain. As I write this, you are pregnant with Hannah, whom I haven't met yet, but already love oodles and oodles. Hannah, I know you'll read this one day and not be at all surprised that your mother's love was the source of constant inspiration, joy, and encouragement.

At the risk of sounding cliché, I truly can't find the words to thank Eamonn Edge. When you came into my life several years ago you brought me a level of happiness I didn't know existed. No one has ever made me feel the way you do. Thank you for always believing in me. It means more to me than you know. You shower me with love and joy every single day and remind me why I write and research, among other things, forbidden loves. Like the title of Lige and Clarke's memoir, "I have more fun with you than anybody."

WELCOME TO

# FAIRYLAND

# INTRODUCTION

n 1941 gay socialite and national columnist Lucius Beebe attempted to put into words his view of Miami as a fairyland. He called it "the last Gomorrah, the ultimate Babylon, the final Gnome-Rhone-Jupiter-Whirlwind, superdeluxe, extra-special, colossal, double-feature and Zombie-ridden madhouse of the world."[1] Beebe captured the national and transnational influences that had earned Miami its wide-open reputation. Like the fallen cities of Gomorrah and Babylon—and even Sodom—Miami had come to represent unrestrained carnal pleasure, vice, and sin. Just a few decades prior, white wealthy families constituted the vast majority of those able to indulge in the exclusive resort city's fairyland. The area had since become much more accessible. Visitors boarded modern airplanes with the whirlwind engines of the "Gnome-Rhone-Jupiter" variety and mobile tourists drove "superdeluxe" trailers. Over the years, Miami had become a hub for pleasure, the unthinkable exhilarating magic beyond the exclusive grasp of an elite class.

Miami's fairyland appeal had long drawn inspiration from the sorcery U.S. imperialists attributed to "uncivilized" lands in the Caribbean. In this way, Miami as fairyland had also become a "Zombie-ridden madhouse of the world."[2] In fact, the zombie as a U.S. cultural phenomenon had entered the national imagination less than a decade prior to Beebe's musings as a metaphorical representation that helped justify U.S. military forces' regulating of "backward" Haiti.[3] Much like the United States had tamed Haiti's so-called savagery through occupation, capital, cultural dominance, and the subjugation of native and racialized communities, a mix of northern, midwestern, and southern investors had converted Miami into an "exotic" tropical fairyland linked to the Caribbean and available for purchase.

Beginning in the early 1900s, travelers and residents alike referred to Dade County (modern-day Miami-Dade County) as fairyland. While fairyland, a marketing strategy crafted by urban boosters, meant different things to a diverse group of people, its dominant sense was that of a place where leisure and entertainment were central to every aspect of life. A visit to fairyland could suspend reality and the rules of the "real world." Miami became a "veritable Fairyland" where one could escape the busy life of the big industrialized city, indulge in paradise, and live out a fantasy.[4] One man called Miami Beach a "combination of Heaven, the Garden of Eden, and Fairyland all rolled into one shell."[5] Like a siren's song, the area's lure made women and men do things that appeared unimaginable in their hometowns. In Miami, they could shuck the social graces and propriety that had long constrained them, even if only temporarily. As another early visitor noted, "It is just as well we didn't know beforehand just how like fairyland 'Mecca, U.S.A.' really is ... or our impatience would surely have far surpassed the danger point," resorting to turning "the fire extinguisher on each other to quell the flames of wrath."[6]

Not everyone enthusiastically accepted the wide-open reputation Beebe and others associated with Miami, nor did they experience fairyland in similarly fantastical ways. One journalist took Beebe to task, observing how "very few people wrote about, read about or even talked about the other Florida" that served as "a haven of the sane which boasted none of their expensive fantasies."[7] A Florida-based journalist concurred, adding that "columnists and magazine writers are most interested in the whirling night life of Miami. But ... the real backbone of the Florida tourist business is the hundreds of thousands of *substantial persons* who come down here to fish and loaf in the sun and live quiet, happy, social lives."[8] According to these perspectives, the majority of Miami's residents understood and at times even accepted that their city had come to represent a site that permitted and encouraged multiple forms of transgression and vice. By no means did that marketing ploy reflect their moral values, however, and they maintained that the "real" Miami was the opposite of the fairyland Beebe described.

For many of Miami's racial and ethnic minorities and working-class residents, fairyland represented something else entirely. From Miami's earliest days, urban planners designed the area by consolidating the city's black neighborhoods with its red-light district. Miami's sexual economy proved critical to the nascent city's success. White "slummers" frequently sought sexual thrills in these racialized spaces. Urban designers were keen on physically quarantining—but not purging—this thriving sexual economy. In 1918, the Dade County Grand Jury recommended to a circuit court judge that "the county and city authorities maintain a proper house of refuge for the care of prostitutes and unfortunate women and girls who may express a desire to reform and lead a proper life."[9] It also maintained that it could not "abate this evil entirely, for many women of lewd character would never" be fully reformed and would "continue their nefarious work against the good morals of the community." Its members recommended that women suspected of being irredeemable "be segregated outside the barred zone prescribed by the government, and be kept under strict surveillance." They would be physically relocated to spaces where prostitution was made legal. In Miami, as elsewhere, such proposals had eugenicist origins wherein "quarantining those who challenged the nineteenth-century ideal of female sexual purity would allow civilization to progress."[10] While this plan was ultimately rejected, the sentiment was clear: Miami residents wanted easy access to a segregated and regulated sexual demimonde in which the exploitation of these laboring women would neither reproduce new "unfit" progeny or impede civilization. Sexually transgressive women made fairyland work.[11]

So too did Fred Symonette, a black Bahamian who worked as a common laborer in Miami. Although conflicting accounts obfuscate whether he was born in Miami or the then-British colony of the Bahamas, it is certain he and his family made their way to and from both sites in the early 1900s. It seems they settled in Miami in 1922, shortly after U.S. immigration laws more stringently restricted such travel. Black Bahamians like Symonette built much of the early city and were the pillars of its urban growth. Despite his contributions to the fairyland, as both a black and migrant man living in the Jim Crow South, Symonette soon found himself in trouble with the law.[12]

In assessing Symonette's perceived criminality, Miami police and state medical officials fixated on his relationships with other men. Police arrested him for unknown reasons in 1927. Given his limited financial means and perceived deviant and criminal personality, law enforcement sought to purge him from the city. As with others before him, police made the case before a judge that Symonette should be transferred to the Florida State Hospital in Chattahoochee in the northwest part of the state. His medical file reveals he suffered from syphilis, which caused a sore on the foreskin of his penis that "swelled and [he] was immediately circumcised and put in jail." Perhaps the pain or mental anguish of the disease caused him to act erratically. Or perhaps police noticed him because he was an unemployed "loafer" or "vagrant," or maybe he was cruising the streets for sex. It is certain police viewed him as suspect and had him committed; his circumcision was thought to alleviate his pain, but also possibly to dampen his sexual urges. In their medical diagnosis and assessment, examiners observed that Symonette "likes men better than women." They elaborated on his unnatural preference: "Patient talks incessantly; seems impossible for him to talk on any subject" without "referring to men." The fact that he was an unmarried, black migrant further led to his uncontested commitment in the state asylum.[13]

Symonette's Bahamian family in Miami, which also had limited resources, had no idea what happened to him after his commitment. Symonette died in that asylum in 1944, seventeen years after being committed. In 1952, the institution received a letter from a man identified as Symonette's friend who wrote on behalf of the deceased's mother in Miami. They wanted to know how Symonette was doing and if they could retrieve him, completely unaware that he had died nearly a decade prior. Regrettably, only the county judge who adjudicated him mentally deficient had been alerted of his passing.[14] Although men like Symonette found willing sex partners—both women and men—in the fairyland, their black, migrant, and working-class statuses often rendered Miami much more a nightmare than a recreational playground.

Meanwhile, for their part, many conservative residents and transplants resisted Miami's wide-open reputation. In 1926, Bertie Charles Forbes, founder of *Forbes* magazine, wrote about an "ex-sailor who wouldn't be licked" and who established the "ideal" city. Forbes profiled Joseph W. Young Jr., credited with founding Hollywood, Florida—roughly twenty miles north of Miami. In his story, Forbes noted how Florida's "nearness to Cuba [made] it easy for Florida to continue wet" and to maintain its access to alcohol during Prohibition (1920–33). The area had become the "playground of the rich" who "gamble ... heavily." In this way, Florida seemed "modern," rather "than Puritan." This was an important distinction, as the latter critiqued the antiquated in an era of significant cultural and social change. Forbes suggested that Hollywood, incorporated in 1925, represented a healthy balance of modernity and morality. Young built "a progressive city" with "no gambling clubs, no speakeasies, no entertainments featuring nudity," and "no drinking dens." It was instead "clean, decent, the kind of place one would like to have his children grow up in." Hollywood stood in stark contrast to Miami, which had earned a national and international reputation as a fairyland run amok. In fact, Miami's reputation as a wide-open tourist resort only escalated in the mid- and late-1930s.[15]

In defending Young's "wholesome" vision for the city of Hollywood, especially as juxtaposed to Miami, Forbes clarified that the founder was "not of the feminine, goody-goody type. . . . He is very much of a he-man." By no means was he a "mollycoddle," a term used to mark those read as feminine or politically soft. Measured against "red-blooded" masculinity, the "mollycoddle" gained currency just as contemporaries came to identify an emerging homosexual prototype.[16] Forbes went to great lengths to describe Young's "physical and mental force" to explain his perceived rejection of the vices associated with cities like Miami. The writer knew his readers might now question Young's masculinity because he favored the "wholesome" over vice, pleasures of the flesh, and crass entertainment, which were standard in Miami.[17]

While not necessarily the dominant understanding of the playful moniker, many of Miami's visitors and settlers joined Beebe in viewing fairyland as a site where one could transgress gender and sexual norms. Many came to know the area as a place where such acts were permitted, encouraged, and expected. In this way, an expansive understanding of fairyland's dominant meaning—at least as crafted by urban boosters and marketing campaigns—resonated with fairies and other queers who pushed the boundaries of acceptable gender and sexual norms. As one journalist lamented in 1935, "During the rapid growth of a city such as Miami whose primary fame is that of a pleasure center, it is inevitable that many sordid chapters must be written in its history." In this case, he specifically referred to the existence of nightspots that catered to gender and sexual transgressives seen as "degenerates" and "perverts." He conceded, however, "Some offerings are liked, some disliked, others merely tolerated."[18] Indeed, at different times in Miami's relatively short urban history—it was only incorporated as a city in 1896—residents and boosters fought hard to both combat and capitalize on the capricious image that facilitated numerous acts of transgression, including same-sex intimacies, interracial encounters, commercialized sex, and gender-bending expressions.

This book reveals the many textured meanings and origins of Miami as fairyland and chronicles the complex ways queer women and men negotiated their own space, role, and understanding of themselves in this budding international city from the 1890s to 1940. While *Welcome to Fairyland* contextualizes the city's place in the larger narrative of U.S. history, it also encourages a break from the geopolitical restrictions placed by national barriers. It reinterprets queer history by maintaining a transnational perspective and by providing an intersectional analysis that factors in how gender and sexuality influenced constructions of class, race, ethnicity, age, and (dis)ability. As such, it highlights the influence of migrants and immigrants who proved critical to shaping this fairyland. Beginning with the migration of Bahamian laborers in the 1890s, both temporary and permanent settlers from the nearby Caribbean proved instrumental to shaping gender norms and sexual desires, as well as who constituted an outsider in the city. This book interprets tourism, trade, and manifestations of U.S. imperialism as central to these processes in Miami.

*Welcome to Fairyland* unearths the forgotten history of how competing visions for the early city paved particular spaces for queer women and men from throughout the United States and abroad, especially the Caribbean. In viewing queer as an analytic tool, it expands the scope of the urban space's own understanding of who subverted and defined what constituted normative expressions of gender and sexuality, as well as concepts of "normalcy" and "deviancy" more generally. Miami's early designers and politicians negotiated civic, conservative values with the profitability of the land. Unlike the popular narrative of the U.S. urban frontier, Miami was *not* a mining town fueled by a gold rush. Instead, its source of gold proved to be its sun-kissed climate and its reputation for excess and unmatched leisure. Miami's fairyland, however, was not necessarily made available to all who wished to play there. Some who found themselves in Miami were deemed undesirable or unfit for the area and were encouraged to leave, forcefully relocated, or made to live in the city's margins.

*The Parameters and Many Faces of Fairyland*

Miami has several sources of distinction that challenge existing narratives of the years 1890 to 1940, including the fact that it existed at the intersection of several contested colonial spaces: borderland, frontier, and city. This book "queers" these phenomena, noting how the uneven power structures produced by these statuses have imposed, shattered, and renegotiated understandings of gender and sexuality. Some scholars have observed how conquest narratives mandated a particular set of gender and sexual structures that demarcated the physical and figurative depths of the borderlands.[19] Scholars have increasingly started to explore how gender and sexual transgression was not only possible but constituted a significant component of life on the frontier, particularly in the U.S. West.[20] While this study takes these leads as formative to Miami's development as a fairyland, it also notes how Miami's distinct establishment, demography, and geopolitical realities reveal different historical trajectories.

In particular, *Welcome to Fairyland* expands the scope—in its geography, methodology, and investigation of race and power structures—of the "community study" that has, since the early 1990s, proven instrumental to shaping our understanding of queer history. This book builds on past queer urban histories that have revealed the textured formations of communities, identities, and later, social movements.[21] This study joins a handful of studies that center the lives and experiences of smaller or less amply populated cities prior to World War II.[22] The U.S. South, however, remains a seriously understudied and poorly misunderstood region in the field of queer history. Although a few scholars, such as John Howard, have greatly enriched our understanding of queer experiences in the U.S. South, this history remains largely reduced to provocations of a conservative bastion and cultural backwater that sought to oppress, disassociate itself, and eliminate queer expressions and individuals, a narrative Miami's history certainly disrupts.[23]

Indeed, while this study contextualizes Miami's southern influences and identity, the city's relative youth and social makeup also separate it from most major metropolitan areas in the U.S. South. Adopted "southerners" also learned and exploited the sociopolitical customs of the day, particularly Jim Crow racial segregation. One Miami resident noted the need to curb the city's racial and ethnic ambiguities, which found "negroes taking more and more liberties in this county." While he believed this was a product of "northern influence and sentiment for this equality," these southern transplants from the North largely shared his view. Despite that, he believed, "Miami and the Beach are not wholly Northern as yet and I am a Southerner and do not believe in social equality with negroes."[24]

More forcefully, this book answers historians' persistent call to employ a transnational lens in the recovery of queer voices, lives, and experiences.[25] In this way, *Welcome to Fairyland* is representative of the "next urban history" that expands the scope of the urban center by employing a transnational methodology and approach.[26] Scholars such as Daniel Rodgers paved the path to recover the transnational origins and influences of urban spaces, although surprisingly few scholars have taken his lead.[27] As a contested colonial space shaped by uneven regional and transnational forces, it is important to remember that Miami is geographically situated in the U.S. South and tucked in the northern section of the Caribbean Basin. Its labor and service sector was largely made up of blacks from the U.S. South and migrants and immigrants from the British, Spanish, and French Caribbean. As this suggests, the trans*national* turn is further complicated in this study in part because so much of the Caribbean remained under colonial and neocolonial dominion. This book destabilizes both the nation-state and the empire-state and draws on the works of scholars who have explored the nuances of the transnational colonial state that is bound by the metropole and yet frequently operates independent of it. It also distinguishes the sense of belonging and community attributed to the nation despite the multiple forms of exclusion from the nation-state.[28] Altogether, this book shifts urban history's focus outward and away from the insular.

This book also pushes the field of transnational history—queer or otherwise—to broaden the scope of what we stand to learn from this methodology by challenging the nation-state and empire-state and the power relations embedded in other modes of exchange, including tourism, capital, trade, empire, subjectivities, and knowledge production.[29] With a particular focus on recovering the gendered and sexualized nature of migration flows, scholars have helped decenter modes of power and privilege generally ascribed to particular nation-states or ideologies.[30] *Welcome to Fairyland* similarly uncovers the major implications inherent in migratory politics for states of belonging, citizenship (political and cultural), and the permeability and mobility of bodies, ideas, and modes of exchange. This book uncovers some of the queer "routes" and "roots" brought on or disrupted by imperialist forces.[31] Following the lead of other scholars, this book is mindful of the ways empire has historically informed and regulated everyday people's most intimate and personal matters and experiences.[32]

This book stresses how, as a resort city dependent on satiating tourist demands and desires, Miami's urban space regularly permitted and encouraged gender and sexual difference, if only temporarily. *Welcome to Fairyland* injects a queer analysis into the growing, but still rather limited, work on Miami. In recent years, N. D. B. Connolly complicated meanings of liberalism through Miami's real estate markets and Chanelle N. Rose explored the city's distinct brand of "Jim Crow tourism." While Connolly urges readers to think beyond one-dimensional images of racist capitalists in juxtaposition to radical reformers, Rose blurs the lines between blackness and whiteness in this southern and Caribbean setting.[33] Although this book positions itself in this scholarly milieu by interpreting their works as fighting against established binaries, it stresses the centrality of gender and sexuality in such interpretations. It also highlights the queer as a critical lens in which to understand contested meanings of nation, race, belonging, and citizenship.

Just the same, *Welcome to Fairyland* positions tourism to and from Miami as both a domestic and a transnational experience. As the field of tourism studies continues to grow, scholars have increasingly paid notice to the peculiar economic, cultural, and social settings of "resort towns." Several works have turned their attention to the distinct economies of resort towns and cities from coastal Europe, Winnipeg Beach, and Atlantic City.[34] Their tourist-dependent economies required powerbrokers to live up to their advertised amenities. In Miami, boosters promised outsiders a fairyland that operated on the provisional allowance to transgress racial, gender, and sexual norms. One contemporary recalled, for instance, that in Miami, "owners of hotels, motels, night clubs, restaurants and other places open to the public do not consider themselves censors of their customers' morality."[35] As such, this book is particularly informed by the literature that illuminates these queer expression and interactions.[36]

Scholars have similarly uncovered the queer histories of slumming and racialized sex tourism in urban settings. In large part because of its reliance on molding fairyland as a tropical extension of the Caribbean, this form of urban tourism took shape on a much wider scale in Miami. In many ways, visiting Miami *was* a form of "slumming." *Welcome to Fairyland* interprets such occurrences through the lens of imperialism, which heavily informed normative expressions of gender and sexuality in large part due to the racialized nature of such exploits.[37] Miami's fairyland tourism operated on the premise of marketing several forms of colonial conquest. As one woman's letter to the governor stated, "In my estimation, Miami is at present a veritable hotbed of vice, hell's hole, and a devil's caldron where missions and missionaries are more needed than in the wilds of Africa, or the South Sea Islands."[38]

*Welcome to Fairyland* begins with the decade that saw Miami proper's municipal incorporation *as well as* the greater expansion of the United States into the Caribbean with the "Spanish-American War," a nomenclature that all but erased the plights of the colonized peoples who had been fighting for independence for decades.[39] By positioning Miami's autonomous incorporation within the narrative of heightened U.S. imperialism, this book demonstrates how the "conquering" of the city's frontier developed alongside imperial machinations articulated through the language of gender and sexual difference.[40]

By the early 1900s, a strong white, male, and Protestant establishment—particularly within the Baptist and Methodist traditions, as with much of the U.S. South—had taken root in all forms of local power in Miami. This included urban politics, law enforcement, newspapers, schools, and trade boards. As Thomas Tweed has argued, within a few years of its municipal incorporation, a firmly entrenched Protestant establishment dominated Miami. The area's initial "frontier egalitarianism"—or the limited power afforded to some women, Jews, and Catholics during Miami's nascent days—receded through the consolidation and exertion of power and influence in the urban center. Most of Miami's Native American and black communities were never afforded a space in the city's power equation.[41] It is true that a limited number of blacks made significant social and economic gains in the early years, but that was largely a product of the needs of the white male Protestant-capitalists who relied on black labor and bodies to maintain power. John Sewell, a Baptist from Georgia who served as Miami's third mayor, joked that he called on his "black artillery" whenever he needed to influence or manipulate a local election. That included having "one hundred ... negroes registered and qualified to vote." He maintained he "held them in reserve for emergencies," or when he needed to squash any threat to his vision for the city.[42] This white, male, and Protestant establishment dominated urban politics for decades.

This does not mean, however, that this power went uncontested or that marginalized communities did not resist these structures. Blacks, migrants and immigrants, laborers, sex workers, and other queers took claim of their lives and self-expressions despite the urban authorities' insistence that their primary function and tolerability in the fairyland was connected to their ability to provide labor and entertain tourists and residents. Their stories are told through the reconstruction of the saloons, beaches, immigration inspection sites, bars, nightclubs, streets, parks, apartments, and brothels, and by their transit in cars, planes, and sea vessels. Instant cities like Miami were, by definition, made up of transplants with diverse views, cultures, expectations, and visions. They "lacked traditions of their own and learned to adapt to their immediate needs the customs and components of the disparate life styles brought by the first settlers with them from distant lands. Thus the cities pieced together a mosaic of practices, largely borrowed from the past, but reflecting in their immediacy and usefulness the creativity of the new cities."[43] While this "traditionlessness" did, in fact, consolidate white civic control, its less cohesive identity allowed marginalized communities to carve out spaces for themselves and create rich subcultures and counterpublics.[44]

Early urban promoters and designers initially marketed this fairyland to a white, moneyed, and modern clientele that wished to take pleasure in the area's balmy temperatures (fig. I.1). One contemporary joked, "The way they coddle the rich and the famous in Miami is enough to make a socialist weep!"[45] This strategy initially proved effective and lucrative, increasing Miami's profile as a desirable place for wealthy women and men from the Midwest and Northeast to visit, build a seasonal residence, or permanently settle. These early snowbirds often articulated Miami's so-called enchantment as an expansion or mirror of the Caribbean. While this added greatly to its appeal, it also, by association, helped promote Miami as a "respectable" site for wealthy travelers and residents to safely experience the vice culture in the Caribbean, one largely made available through U.S. empire.

This book's use of the terms "promoter" and "booster" is expansive. It includes those who were paid to market Miami as a tourist destination and a desirable place for permanent settlement. It also includes those who sought to increase and protect their investments in the early city by promoting this attractive image. This analysis also takes seriously, however, the effects of inadvertent promoters and boosters who may not have directly capitalized on such an enterprise but nonetheless wrote about their experiences—both good and bad—in visiting the area. In that capacity, they too helped direct attention and traffic to southern Florida. Boosters staged Miami as a fairyland through "spectacular attractions, intense promotional activity, a land boom, and what was seen as a feverish pace of life accentuated [by] a uniquely modern style of urban engagement."[46]

As this book argues, such imagery was textured with gender and sexual meanings. These professional and unofficial promoters and boosters rep-

FIGURE I.1. A group of wealthy travelers on the pier waiting to enter Fairy-Land in Miami Beach, c. 1909. Image no. RC03719, courtesy of the State Archives of Florida.

resented a powerful force that marketed Miami as a fairyland where those who could afford the trip could sow their oats. Boosters used monikers such as "fairyland" and "magic city" to promote the city as special, unique, and ephemeral. These terms also nodded to Miami's status as an "instant city" that had appeared as if by magic. They also held social and cultural currency, designating a space where women and men could transgress social norms, including gender and sexuality.

In addition to its moneyed visitors and investors, from its earliest years, Miami attracted migrants, workers, and visitors from the nearby Caribbean whose presence in the city further complicated existing racial categories. If these Caribbean people represented a sort of crack in the color line, Miami's white settlers were sure to keep them in check and re-cement their own position on top of the sociopolitical hierarchy. Some scholars have noted Miami's distinct urban transformation and origins, emphasizing the city's ethnic and racial demographics and power structure.[47] As Miami has received more attention, some scholars have urged us to interpret the city's Caribbean origins as central to its nascent character and identity.[48] Like *Welcome to Fairyland*, these works push back against the idea that Miami's checkered relationship to the Caribbean greatly began with the influx of Cubans fleeing the 1959 revolution. In following this lead, this book complicates the narrative of "Cuban exceptionalism" that heavily informs fields in Latina/o/x, immigration, and Latin American and Caribbean history. While this book certainly acknowledges the significance of Cuba in creating Miami's fairyland, the evidence shows that the Bahamas were equally influential on the city—if not more so—during this earlier period, as was a greater imperial ethos that helped market the city as "exotic" to white visitors and "slummers."

As this reveals, Miami's queer past raises significant insights that provide a window through which to consider how Progressivism took shape through delayed and fragmented urbanization and in the absence of industrialization. Rooted in the Protestant notion of conversion, Miami's early powerbrokers were imbued with a vision of both a figurative and literal "rebirth," starting anew in this urban frontier. By the turn of the century, fueled by a form of "social Christianity," privileged Progressives tasked themselves with serving and reforming their symbolic wards. During this era, most Protestants regarded the urban center as a problem, associating it with moral and physical decline. Protestantism survived and thrived in the "spiritually fearful" urban setting.[49] In part, this was because Protestant powerbrokers employed the basic tenets of their faith to society's ills. As T. J. Jackson Lears has argued, "American seekers merged Protestant dreams of spiritual rebirth with secular projects of purification." This included "reasserting elite power against restive farmers, taming capital in the name of the public good, reviving individual and national vitality by banning the use of alcohol, granting women the right to vote, disenfranchising African-Americans, restricting the flow of immigrants and acquiring an overseas empire."[50] In this Progressive vision, Miami provided white settler-pioneers a terrestrial tabula rasa on which to start anew.

Unlike well-established, populated, and industrialized cities like New York or Chicago, Miami appeared overnight. As John B. Reilly, the city's first mayor, recalled in 1917, "We were never a town, you know, but were incorporated first as a city."[51] Surely, Miami shared some characteristics with other "instant cities" in the United States, such as San Francisco and Denver—even though they were incorporated as autonomous municipalities and populated several decades earlier. These urban spaces transformed from wilderness to metropolis, their populations increasing exponentially with each passing year, rather than reaching formal maturation and development from settlement to town over the span of several decades. As Gunther Paul

Barth has demonstrated, technological advancements made these built environments habitable and manageable to man's will.[52]

Miami was also an "urban frontier" molded by transience, speculation, boosterism, and the "conquering of the wilderness."[53] While these features were central to Miami's identity, this book's employment of a queer and transnational lens also reveals how transgressive gender and sex threaded these phenomena. Miami's 1896 incorporation occurred three years *after* historian Frederick Jackson Turner bemoaned, "The frontier has gone, and with its going has closed the first period of American history."[54] While the windfall promises that helped populate the U.S. West proved disappointing for most and dried up, it turned out the frontier was still alive just "south of the [U.S.] South."[55] As a minister remarked in 1912, "This lusty young city of Miami may be called the newest and most extreme frontier town in the United States, for even San Diego in California and Port Townsend in Washington are old in comparison."[56] Miami's later urbanization, its nonindustrial economy, and its entrenched relationship to the Caribbean separated it from most of the nation's urban spaces.

Even into the late 1930s, despite boosters' efforts to shake off the image of the urban frontier in favor of a sophisticated and modern city, parts of Miami remained undeveloped and uninhabitable. In many respects, this checkered "urban maturity" could be attributed to Miami's exponential growth, which municipal and county governments could not keep up with.[57] While only 1,681 people resided in Miami proper in 1900 (four years after it was incorporated), the city boasted 29,571 residents by 1920. Its population further expanded with the land and real estate boom of the 1920s, growing 274 percent by 1930, when 110,637 people called the city home. Similarly, while Miami Beach had fewer than 650 residents in 1920, its population grew a whopping 980 percent by 1930, when its population was 6,494.[58] The figures for all of Dade County are similarly astronomical (table I.1). Urban boosters' ambitious plans for Miami were debilitated by bloated speculations, dwindling demand, and other major economic offsets. During the height of its land boom in the early 1920s, the county included 275 residential subdivisions, and property sales gave the impression that construction might challenge tourism as the area's dominant industry. The city encompassed two square miles in 1900 but had grown to forty-three square miles by the mid-1920s.[59] Indeed, as it had done in 1913 with bordering neighborhoods, the City of Miami annexed nearby towns in 1925 to expand its municipal limits and meet the higher real estate demands boosters foresaw. In 1925, Miami annexed the towns of Coconut Grove, Allapattah, and Lemon City, among several others. By 1926, a real estate crash and a devastating hurricane set

TABLE I.1. Population growth of Dade County, 1880–1950

| YEAR | POPULATION | % INCREASE |
|------|-----------|-----------|
| 1880 | 257 | |
| 1890 | 861 | 235 |
| 1900 | 4,955 | 476 |
| 1910 | 11,933 | 141 |
| 1920 | 42,753 | 258 |
| 1930 | 142,955 | 234 |
| 1940 | 267,739 | 87 |
| 1950 | 495,084 | 85 |

Source: *Data from U.S. Bureau of the Census.*
Note: *Land from Dade County was used to establish neighboring Palm Beach and Broward Counties in 1909 and 1915, respectively.*

Miami back, and much of its newly acquired land would be abandoned or left only minimally developed for years. The economic downturn even saw the City of Miami "deannex," or relinquish control over, some of its recently acquired municipal lands in 1932.[60] Despite Miami's massive overnight growth, vestiges of the urban frontier thus endured for decades.

Indeed, Miami's urban history has also been fraught with questions and disputes over the area's *geographic* parameters. Like many other metropolitan areas in the United States, the space generally associated with "Miami" is often imprecise or misleading. To this day, it remains common for films, TV shows, and news reports to show pastel-laden, Art Deco visuals of South Beach to represent "Miami," even as Miami Beach has constituted a distinct municipality for over a century that both competed with and capitalized on its neighboring city's success. In actuality, the metropolitan area of Miami represents a constellation of distinct municipalities, including Miami Beach, Coral Gables, Hialeah, and many others. *Welcome to Fairyland* explores the history of *Greater* Miami, cognizant that municipal limits were porous, contested, and in flux, to say nothing of how many people, then and now, viewed these distinct municipalities and unincorporated county areas as constitutive of the fairyland promoted throughout the nation and beyond. This book distinguishes Miami, the expansive area in southern Florida, from Miami the distinct municipality. Similarly, as Kenneth T. Jackson has demonstrated, the term "incorporation" can allude to either the formation of an autonomous municipality or the consolidation of territory through the process of municipal annexation.[61] For clarity, this book uses the word "incorporation" to refer to the former and "annexation" for the latter.

In addition to challenging dominant meanings and understandings of

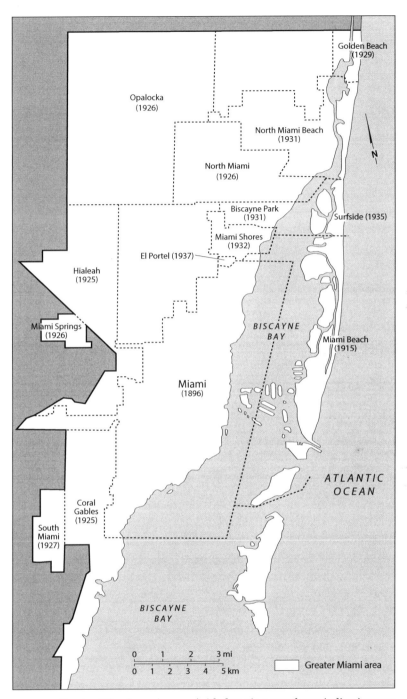

Golden Beach
(1929)

Opalocka
(1926)

North Miami Beach
(1931)

North Miami
(1926)

Biscayne Park
(1931)

Surfside (1935)

Miami Shores
(1932)

El Portel (1937)

Hialeah
(1925)

BISCAYNE
BAY

Miami Springs
(1926)

Miami Beach
(1915)

Miami
(1896)

ATLANTIC
OCEAN

Coral
Gables
(1925)

South
Miami
(1927)

BISCAYNE
BAY

N

| 0 | | 1 | | 2 | | 3 mi |
|---|---|---|---|---|---|---|

| 0 | 1 | 2 | 3 | 4 | 5 km |
|---|---|---|---|---|---|

☐ Greater Miami area

MAP I.1. Greater Miami area in 1940 (with dates in parentheses indicating year municipalities were autonomously incorporated).

urbanity, the frontier, and the U.S. South, *Welcome to Fairyland* offers other alternative periodizations by emphasizing the textured and transnational influences of Miami's queer past. It dates the centrality of the Caribbean in shaping Miami's identity to before its municipal incorporation. It also encourages scholars to rethink the era of nativism and immigration restriction in the early twentieth century as interconnected to gendered, sexualized, and racialized concepts of "desirable" and "undesirable" entrants. In focusing on the policing of *colonial* subjects' gender and sexuality at the Miami-Caribbean border, this book encourages new understandings of *limited* permeability, even in the absence of numerical quotas for the Western Hemisphere prior to the 1965 Immigration Act. Similarly, in shifting attention to black Bahamian migrants, early Cuban exiles, and others, such as seafaring Greek spongers, this book shows that colonial and imperialist forces did not produce a static immigration process that necessarily entailed patterns of assimilation and settlement. Rather, these experiences reveal cyclical patterns of migration deeply in tune with the lives and experiences of hometowns and communities of origin.[62]

Similarly, in addition to the distinct trajectories of Progressivism and economic depression traced above, Miami's transnational, queer past offers alternative meanings and catalysts to classify social and cultural change in the 1920s and 1930s. Miami's entrenched relationship with the Caribbean provides a radically different narrative to the Prohibition era in the United States. While some historians have shown how the repeal of Prohibition either curbed, relocated, or even escalated queer visibility in different urban spaces, Miami's transnational formation urges us to similarly look outside the United States to better understand these shifts or developments.[63] Instead of solely viewing 1933 as the year of Prohibition's repeal, for instance, this study shifts attention to the concurrent revolution in Cuba that ousted dictator Gerardo Machado, and it argues that this event played a similarly instrumental role in shaping Miami's gender- and sexually transgressive culture well into the late 1930s and early 1940s.

This study concludes with 1940, or just before the city experienced a new era of social, cultural, political, and economic change. From the 1890s to the 1930s, the very promotion of Miami as fairyland was interwoven with the area's distinct political economy, particularly tourism. It also depended on the economic and social exchanges of transnational laborers, trade (both legal and illicit), and ideas. Several economic crises in the 1920s prompted urban boosters to further expand Miami's tourist markets rather than diversify its economy. By then, as one publication observed, Miami had been "given over to the entertainment of tourists and the cult of the sun."[64] By 1945, Miami earned its badge as "the least industrialized metropolitan district in the United States." Before World War II, only 3.3 percent of Dade County's laborers worked in factories. Even then, much of that labor remained connected to the success of Miami's king industry: tourism.[65] In Miami, World War II brought major changes in urban politics and culture that had profound effects on the city's gender and sexual transgressives. As such, this study explores Miami's queer past before inchoate sexual behaviors and desires more formally crystallized into distinct identities, for example. A future study will further explore how new gender and sexual networks and communities navigated these changes in Miami, uncovering new challenges, backdrops, and transnational forces that took shape during the Cold War era.

### Queer as Method and Archive

*Welcome to Fairyland* views "queer" as a category of analysis and primarily works in two modes. This book is not explicitly a history of homosexual acts, same-sex desires, or transgender expressions in Miami. Although those manifestations do constitute much of the material in subsequent pages, this book applies a more expansive queer lens to investigate disruptions to normative gender and sexuality, including what we today understand as heterosexuality and patriarchy.[66] This book does not privilege a static identity-informed category and instead advances, as Colin R. Johnson and many others have done, a "queer historicism" that moves beyond essentialist concepts and identities.[67] Although several historians have unearthed localized usages and etymologies of the term "queer," there is limited evidence to support the notion that it had a singular or dominant meaning in Miami prior to World War II.[68] Although this may ease the decision to use "queer" as a critical lens of analysis (rather than as a noun), it underscores that, as Jafari S. Allen has argued, "no term, even those that may seem self-evidently local, indigenous, or autochthonous, is perfectly stable or synchronous with dynamic self-identification on the ground."[69] This book acknowledges the subversive and radical intonations of "queer." As Jack/Judith Halberstam has stated, "the queer 'way of life'" encompasses "subcultural practices, alternative methods of alliance, forms of transgender embodiment, and those forms of representation dedicated to capturing these willfully eccentric modes of being."[70]

This study contextualizes the fluidity, permeability, and shifting meanings of normativity and transgression that are similarly not reducible or beholden to identities and do not necessarily have currency with us today. *Welcome to Fairyland* places the man caught performing oral sex on another man, for example, alongside the trousered lesbian, the female and male impersonator, the mannish woman, the sex worker, the brothel-visiting slummer, the woman donning a scandalous two-piece bathing suit, the thrill-seeking tourist, the interracial and intergenerational couple, the surveilled migrant and immigrant, and the vagrant, hobo, and transient. Put another way, this book views them as queer, too, even if they might not have seen or labeled themselves as such.

As all of this suggests, this book employs queer analysis as a method that can be used to explore the intersecting formulations of norms and transgressions through the matrix of gender, sexuality, class, race, ethnicity, nationality, age, and (dis)ability. Through textured and nuanced readings of these multiple categories and their intersections, it lays bare how articulations of normalcy and deviancy, more broadly, have been historically organized. It follows the lead of scholars such as Siobhan B. Somerville, who invite readers, through historical readings of turn-of-the-century "racialization" and state formation projects, to explore the connectedness of race and sexuality and the dominant systems they produced and reproduced: whiteness and heterosexuality.[71] As this book shows, these "queer" processes are inherently informed by racialized and exoticized processes in their collective efforts to produce hegemonic cultures that seek to differentiate "us" from "them."

The queer method used in this book highlights the lived experiences of those on the "margins" to provide a window into the "queer politics" that scholars like Cathy J. Cohen have set forth to challenge systemic attempts "to normalize our sexuality, exploit our labor, and constrain our visibility."[72] Even though the period covered in this study has been described as "prepolitical" because no social or political movement directly addressed gender transgression or same-sex sexuality, it certainly yielded multiple forms of daily resistance that must indeed be read as political.[73]

Altogether, this approach both facilitates the greater recovery of voices that, at best, appear in the margins of the archive and traces broader epistemological questions about how and under what historical circumstances norms get shaped, are bifurcated, and become hegemonic. While the historical record, for instance, is limited on women who engaged in same-sex sexual relations during Miami's early period—especially gender normative or feminine women—this queer approach uncovers other subjects whose marginal lives helped shape the articulation of deviance more broadly. This also permits us to foreground fractures and breaks outside of binary manifestations: black/white, migrant/native, deviant/normative, and rural/urban, among many others.[74]

It is important to explain the book's use of sources, too. *Welcome to Fairyland* is the product of years of research from a broad range of sources housed in numerous archives and depositories. This includes contemporary newspapers, films, short stories, paintings, songs, correspondence, the minutes of city boards, judicial hearings, arrest records, medical and commitment files, commission reports, and immigration logs, among others. As other historians of feminist, gender, and sexuality studies have had to do for decades, this book built its own "queer" archive. To speak plainly, one of the greatest challenges remains how to recover voices the state systematically sought to suppress, eradicate, or overlook, a process the late Michel-Rolph Trouillot called "silencing the past."[75] Accepting this as a foregone conclusion, however, is an evasion of our task.

We must "queer" the archives by paying equal notice—if not giving *greater* emphasis—to the archive's silences and voids.[76] This book reads both with and against the grain in its interpretation of "official" sources, such as police records and commission reports, which did not see queer preservation or visibility as their objective. In this process, it is critical that we break down power hierarchies that privilege particular, "legitimate" sources over others. This book gives equal weight to numerous modes of production, whether paintings, poetry, or staged sketches. Over the years, I have personally collected historic ephemera, including souvenir programs, piggy banks, postcards, and matchbook covers, featured in this book. It is significant to nod to the visceral and affect responses these sources provide and how they too queer the archives. This is what Martin F. Manalansan IV calls "disarrangements," or the very chaotic nature of queer experiences that also constitute the archive.[77]

It is significant to note that, in large part because of its late incorporation and its incipient "traditionlessness," Miami simply did not develop a uniform or formalized regulatory body to monitor or promote the city's moral fabric. This stands in stark contrast to the vice commissions established in larger, more established cities such as New York and Chicago. While Dade County Grand Jury reports often carried out similar tasks, they are hardly equivalent in their influence and effectiveness, and their deliberations were either undocumented or have since been lost. Indeed, most individual criminal records for this period have been destroyed, a problem further compounded by the fact that Miami does not have a proper municipal or county archive of such records.

After much searching, I uncovered the intact General Index to Criminal

Cases for Dade County. It appears to be a complete or near complete record of Dade County's two highest courts during the early twentieth century, the Circuit Court and the Criminal Court of Record. The latter was created in 1907 to help relieve the former of its increasing caseload. In fact, as historian Paul George has observed, the rapid and sometimes checkered evolution of the area's judiciary reflected Greater Miami's "meteoric growth," all of which further complicates the retrieval and archiving of local criminal records.[78] In my search, I also uncovered select files from a separate, lower county tribunal, the Judge's Court, that heard both criminal and civil cases. While at least two cases charging a defendant with either sodomy or the crime against nature appeared in the Judge's Court docket for the period in study, the county judge who served as the presiding officer at the Judge's Court had two options in that tribunal: discharge a defendant from arrest or send the case to the higher county court. Although the defendant's name should have theoretically been added to the General Index in at least the latter scenario, it is also possible that, in a few circumstances, some cases simply went unrecorded in that record.[79] Indeed, it is possible that some charges documented in this index may have been dropped, reduced, or modified and ultimately not recorded at all, or perhaps not as sodomy or a crime against nature. Certain clues suggest that most of these would have been recorded too, however. For example, the clerk tasked with writing a suspect's information by hand often relied on known nicknames, the phonetic pronunciation of the person's name, or descriptive—and often offensive—characteristics. Suspect names written into the index include "Blackie," "Rambling Kid," "Sid the Mouse," and "Jew Kid."[80] These names could have been retroactively corrected, but they weren't. This suggests the index likely documented some information from the arresting officer's initial report, including original understandings of a particular crime or suspect. I read these records as reflective of many of the cultural assumptions of the era, as well as indicative of some of the "coded" language that sought to criminalize and define Miami's marginal communities.

While the absence of some records often makes it difficult to re-create the social worlds of Miami's most marginalized individuals, *Welcome to Fairyland* pieces together many aspects of these people's lives and experiences through a tapestry of other available sources. When available, criminal and legal records provide a rare look into whom the law targeted. The most complete of these records were those that reached higher courts, particularly the Florida Supreme Court. In the absence of detailed criminal files, however, I paired the available information with other existing documentation, such as immigration logs and census records, to more fully reconstruct the queer lives the archives sought to eradicate. Just the same, local and state laws often reflected certain tensions and concerns about what constituted criminality, including vagrancy, disorderly conduct, operating a house of ill fame, and cross-dressing. Cultural sources, such as newspaper and magazine reports, films, paintings, postcards, memoirs, and literature similarly helped fill some archival voids and supplemented this study's understanding of the biases that informed the selective enforcement of laws, judicial process, and the crafting of legislation. Even more so, these sources offered significant insight into how queer spaces were created, who traversed them and why, and the desire, love, insecurity, fear, sense of belonging, or loneliness they experienced along the way. Indeed, as Cynthia Blair has cautioned in her work on African American women's sexuality, we must work tirelessly to distinguish the silences of the archives from our *own* silences. In reconstructing the worlds of those living on the margins, we must not erase or diminish sexual pleasure and desire, for instance, in fear that it contribute to narratives of sexual pathology and lust.[81]

Lastly, a significant part of this archive-building and voice-recovering project requires transnational sources and efforts. Transnational subjects and processes often exist outside of particular nation-states and their respective archives. For this book, I relied on archives in both the United States and the Bahamas. My research on Miami more broadly, including the post–World War II period, additionally relied on archives in Cuba and Haiti. All of this informs *Welcome to Fairyland*. After all, the uneven processes are not beholden to particular national narratives, or uniform languages or cultural experiences. If Miami's history proved dependent on the Caribbean, so too do its archives.

### Fairyland's Contents

The book's first two chapters unearth the queer origins of the urban frontier and its connection to the seasonal migrants from the Caribbean who proved instrumental in building it. In tracing the social, cultural, economic, and political circumstances that led to Miami's municipal incorporation in 1896, chapter 1 reveals how the establishment of Miami's sex and vice district was a product of conscientious, albeit uneven, urban design. It reveals how Miami's queer frontier took shape through the prism of competing colonial exchanges, transgressive sex acts, interracial encounters, and working-class vices. Chapter 2 shifts attention to Bahamian migrants in Miami, at the borders, and the archipelago. It uncovers the gendered migrations that found Bahamian men living in "bachelor" societies in Miami's urban frontier. Similarly, several Bahamian islands became female-dominated, homosocial spaces. These processes broke down traditional family models and facilitated multiple forms of gender and sexual transgression in both the Bahamas and Miami.

Chapters 3 and 4 explore the makings of fairyland as a white, moneyed tourist destination that permitted challenges to gender and sexual norms. As chapter 3 shows, tourists and boosters often articulated Miami's so-called enchantment as directly connected to the racialized tourism available in Cuba and the Bahamas. This chapter specifically traces the lives of some of the queer women and men who helped tailor the fairyland as a site of nonconformity that lacked the rigidity ascribed to larger, industrial urban spaces. It unearths the significance of the area's queer artists, investors, settlers, and imperial architects in fashioning the modern fairyland. Chapter 4 takes seriously boosters' framing of Miami as a fairyland. It pays particular attention to the ways the city was "staged," both literally and figuratively, in the U.S. imagination. It notes how theatricality, spectacle, and publicity collided in the urban center to help sell the fairyland to outsiders. It also explores the way the literal stage—in both theater and film—associated Miami as a racialized site for gender and sexual fluidity.

While chapter 5 uncovers how queers, primarily those the historical record listed as men, traversed Miami's public and semipublic spaces, chapter 6 turns to the formation of normative women's sexualities in the city. The former chapter focuses on the ways mostly working-class, transient men transgressed gender and sexual norms in Miami's beaches, borders, outlying areas, apartments, and other temporary housing accommodations, streets, and parks. It explores how state and local laws criminalized gender transgression and homosexual acts, as well as the uneven prosecution of such activities based on judicial interpretations of class, race, ethnicity, age, and (dis)ability. Chapter 6 turns to the queer origins of what became normative heterosexuality. In particular, it locates fairyland's distinct promotion of transgressive, white, and predominantly middle-class women's bodies in the 1920s and 1930s. The modern and scantily clad "Miami mermaid" became a commodity in Miami that permitted boosters to continue promoting the area as a fairyland for gender and sexual renegades.

Chapter 7 and the book's epilogue examine the transnational and local influences that, despite the visibility of a commoditized *hetero*sexuality in the fairyland, further allowed queer folk a visible space in Miami. Chapter 7 traces major conservative residents, institutions, and organizations that sought to curb Miami's growing reputation as a wide-open fairyland during and after 1933, the year that saw the repeal of Prohibition *and* a Cuban revolution. Local moral reformers unsuccessfully fought Miami's dependence on tourism, which had expanded significantly in response to Cuba's own tourist boom. Miami became notorious as a "wet" city, primarily because of illicit trade from the Bahamas and tourist travel to Cuba. Many Miami power-brokers began incorporating vice, queer entertainment, and sexual tourism to the city's list of offerings. In this way, queer women and men became central characters in Miami's renewed transnational, urban tourist economy. Finally, the epilogue introduces the changes that came about after World War II. It unveils some of the major factors—including the diversification of Miami's economy, which moved the city further from its tourism dependency—that contributed to a major crackdown on queer individuals and communities in the early Cold War era.

It is now time to enter fairyland. When the *Philadelphia Record* wrote a scathing editorial in 1933—as many other periodicals of the era had done and would continue to do—titled the "Moral Collapse of Miami," it sought to mobilize reformers to clean up the city.[82] While this account seemed to offend Florida's governor and several Miami residents, most celebrated this kind of free publicity. One source posed: "Do you realize that if Miami were to capitalize and promote our notoriety we would get EIGHTY times as much front page newspaper space as we can ever get from publicity?"[83] This was the fairyland most people wanted. As the following pages reveal, queerness proved central to this world.

# QUEER FRONTIER

We never had an arrest oftener than about once a month. All the
disturbances occurred in the north Miami section where the only
saloons were.

—JOHN B. REILLY, MIAMI'S FIRST MAYOR, 1917

Florida had been looked upon as a semi-invalid resort, not a
pleasure ground, but the construction of these houses started
Florida as a playground for the Nation, and railroad construction
and the construction of other large and beautiful hotels followed
the success attending upon Mr. [Henry] Flagler's developments.

—JOHN SEWELL, MIAMI'S THIRD MAYOR, 1933

In late 1908, municipal judge John C. Gramling commended
"vigilant" Chief of Police Frank B. Hardee for his role in making Miami respectable. Gramling, a native Alabamian, had moved to southern Florida
just a decade prior, when Miami was incorporated as a city. Hardee also
settled in Miami in those years, leaving Georgia to become the city's first
police chief. Hardee received Gramling's praise for zoning Miami's segregated, black neighborhood, "Colored Town," as the area's site for deviant sex,
crime, and vice. "Through his efforts," Gramling claimed, "several resorts of
questionable character have been completely broken up and the inmates [of
the houses of ill fame] made to seek legitimate employment or leave the City."
He also applauded Hardee for "put[ting] the gambling places out of business." Because of Hardee's work, the judge argued, "Miami is given credit
for having the most respectful and law abiding class of negroes as any city
in the south."[1]

Chief Hardee had visited all the saloons in Miami a few months before
to inspect whether they complied with a new ordinance passed that May
regulating those spaces. Miami's city council responded to residents' complaints over the area's vice culture and passed a law that literally shed light
on saloons and made them visible, especially from the outside.[2] This law also
sought to police the discreet sexual encounters, often interracial, that took
place within the establishments. The saloon's poorly lit backrooms, sometimes furnished with beds, made quick sexual flings convenient. The local
ordinance prohibited the placement of screens on front doors to allow more

light in and greater transparency. The ordinance banned women and minors not just from purchasing alcohol in saloons but even from entering them.[3]

Efforts to purge red-light districts from Miami proper advanced the city's segregation efforts. Hardee expressed concern over the presence of saloons outside of Miami's black district. Like many of Miami's other white urban designers and powerbrokers, Hardee believed racial mixing could lead to sexual urges deemed unnatural.[4] From the early 1890s through World War I, Progressive reformers throughout the United States launched campaigns like this to suppress or tame urban red-light districts. As Mara Laura Keire has observed, "They wanted to separate residence from commerce and respectable from disreputable, but they never expected to eliminate completely one side of the divide."[5] They negotiated the virtues of disciplining the city's vice culture or making it less visible, with the "imperative" of keeping the races apart. Into the early twentieth century, a "segregated district" was not a concept that necessarily corresponded to racial division in U.S. cities. Rather, the phrase served as a euphemism for a city's red-light district.[6] This also occurred in the "instant city" of Miami, which, unlike established metropolitan areas, had not yet "matured" from its status as an "urban frontier."[7]

Like the very concept of an urban frontier, Miami was bursting with paradoxes connected to city boosters' efforts to establish boundaries, turn a profit, and maintain social order—all of which helped carve out distinct spaces for gender and sexual subversives to exist and even thrive. Incorporated as a city in 1896, Miami was built from ambitions dreamed up by wealthy, white pioneer-settlers. They, along with a growing middle class, were transplants from the U.S. South, Midwest, and Northeast. But calling Miami a city did not make it so. Its urban center did not develop as a product of industrialization, nor did its red-light districts mature organically. Miami took shape through countervailing forces.

For instance, Miami's developer-pioneers played a juggling act between designing and promoting the area's built and natural environments, or marketing all sides of the area's urban frontier. Even before Miami became a city, boosters touted the area's tropical environment as a health resort where moneyed women and men could gain better mental and physical vigor away from the confines and ills of urbanity and industrialization.[8] "Conquering" Miami's untamed wilderness provided an opportunity to reclaim white masculinity during an era of widespread urbanization and immigration.

Miami's identity and traditions were constantly in flux, imbued by numerous effects from the area's colonial past, its roots in the U.S. South and North, and a multitude of Caribbean influences. After centuries of colonial transfers of power among European states, the U.S. federal government waged violent wars in Florida to purge and regulate indigenous communities and cultures. Indeed, empire proved critical to building Miami, a frontier just south of the U.S. South. Early Miami capitalists also banked on the 1898 U.S. war against Spain in the name of Cuban independence. In addition to using federal funds to help develop the city, U.S. control of the island opened new markets for sexual tourism. This was often linked to Miami's own burgeoning tourist economy.

Once the area's "backwardness" had been tamed—whether by subduing the Seminoles, advancing U.S. imperialism, or draining swamplands—Miami boosters got to work building a "model city" that was also modern. Modernity, however, came at a price. Many early boosters believed saloons, houses of ill fame, opium dens, and gambling houses represented "a ubiquitous symbol of urban life," even as they often decried their existence.[9] This necessary evil, they believed, would make Miami appear modern at a time when people increasingly sought pleasure through vice, sex, and "slumming."[10]

As Hardee's efforts demonstrate, Miami's urban designers initially zoned the city in such a way that areas of vice, crime, and sexual exploration were relegated to just *outside* Miami's borders. These "interzones" remained within reach, and many respectable white residents crossed city lines to explore this "dangerous," yet appealing, underworld.[11] When powerbrokers contained and pushed these operations into a northwest district that became known as Colored Town, Miami's black residents became sitting ducks for local law enforcement officials, who could arrest them on any number of charges. Even in the early twentieth century, Miami lacked a cohesive and stable economy, remained sparsely populated, and was in great need of better transportation and roads. These police roundups helped solve the latter problem in particular, as the working-class, ethnic, and black residents caught up in police raids became a free labor force that helped build the city and enrich its white powerbrokers' pockets.

Miami's queer frontier took shape through the prism of these colonial exchanges, transgressive sex acts, interracial encounters, and working-class vices. When Miami became an instant city, boosters negotiated the promotion of numerous countervailing visions: the natural environment and the urban landscape, the traditional and the modern, and the respectable and the subversive. In this urban frontier rife with paradoxes, residents and visitors could explore the frontiers of their own inhibitions by physically venturing outside the white and respectable city limits to experience subversive expressions of gender and sex. Criminal records help re-create this demimonde and the experiences of women and men police targeted for crimes such as prostitution, sexual assault, and vagrancy. Miami's early interracial sexual economy thrived despite policing efforts. It grew in spite of—or as a result of—the fact that the black, ethnic, and working-class residents who lived in the neighborhoods that provided these services combated crime, poverty, and discrimination.

### The Frontier Just South of the U.S. South

In many ways, Florida's colonial past helped shape concepts of gender, sexuality, race, and nation in what became the City of Miami in the late nineteenth century. Prior to being admitted as a U.S. state in 1845, parts of what we today know as Florida passed through the hands of numerous colonial powers, including Spain, France, and Great Britain. Despite many border disputes and colonial transfers of power, Spain claimed dominion over Florida for most of the period between 1565 and 1821, when it ceded control to the United States. Although frequently designated a backwater of the Spanish Empire, Florida's cultures, traditions, peoples, and resources had been linked to the Caribbean for centuries.[12] Although this relationship evolved and changed over time, it has never ceased.

Not only did the acquisition of Florida increase U.S. territory, it also factored into the nation's larger imperial ambitions, which increasingly turned to the Caribbean. U.S. politicians cautiously negotiated the acquisition of Florida from Spain. Prior to the formal 1821 cession, President James Monroe's administration balanced the U.S. desire to obtain Florida with the imperative of trading with new Latin American republics that waged war against Spain. Once Florida had been secured, the United States recognized several of Spain's previous colonies as independent nations, and in 1823 Monroe articulated a new cornerstone in U.S. foreign policy. The "Monroe Doctrine" asserted the U.S. sphere of influence in the Americas that anticipated the nation's territorial expansion across the continent and beyond.[13]

The growing U.S. empire had immediate and long-term effects on regional concepts of race, gender, and sex. Under Spanish rule, African slavery in Florida constituted a condition that could also prove temporary through manumission. These policies were, in part, a product of Spanish Catholic teachings and several economic and political circumstances, such as the need for homesteaders and militiamen.[14] This stood in stark contrast to the rigid two-caste system of race institutionalized in the 1820s when Florida became a U.S. territory. Florida's territorial council passed numerous laws targeting free blacks that decade, including prohibiting them from giving seditious speeches, selling alcohol to slaves, voting, testifying against whites, and carrying firearms.[15] Regulating gender and sex proved similarly important. By 1832, Florida outlawed interracial marriage and invalidated any such existing unions, which, in effect, bastardized and robbed progeny of their inheritance. The legislative council also criminalized white men who fornicated or committed adultery with black women.[16] When southern planters migrated to Florida's panhandle after 1821, they clashed with the masculine ideals and traditions of the area's nonplanter "countrymen." Economic and social pressures soon facilitated new alliances between these two classes, which helped forge a mythologized narrative of a unified Old South that reified rigid racial codes and consolidated political power for years to come.[17]

Meanwhile, as a frontier, Florida largely "remained Indian country" until the early nineteenth century, which contributed to the preservation of multiple forms of gender and sexual difference among the area's indigenous peoples.[18] Sixteenth-century Spanish and French explorers made numerous references to what their colonial eyes interpreted as "hermaphroditic" behavior. While the Spanish explorer Álvar Núñez Cabeza de Vaca observed "a devilish thing" of "one man married to another," Frenchman René Goulaine de Laudonnière documented the presence of "many hermaphrodites."[19] Detailed reports of gender and sexual difference into the nineteenth century are scant, but it is clear that indigenous peoples "lived in semi-autonomous villages that routinely disregarded the interests of Spain, Great Britain, and then the United States."[20] Colonial prejudices regarded them as transgressive in multiple ways: as harborers of runaway slaves, polygamists, and practitioners of miscegenation.[21] By the eighteenth century, Anglo-colonial sources referred to diverse tribes from modern-day Florida, Georgia, and Alabama as "Creeks." The Seminoles—the multiethnic Creeks who migrated to Florida—resisted numerous policies of removal and extermination once the land became a U.S. territory. While the nineteenth-century "Seminole Wars" resulted in the forceful relocation of thousands of indigenous peoples to Creek territory west of the Mississippi River, hundreds retreated to Florida's southern frontier, particularly the Everglades.[22] Even though most of Florida was a frontier until 1860, when the United States surveyed the land, the area encompassing present-day Miami remained an untamed frontier for several more decades.[23] In this way, the Seminoles maintained a culture of gender and sexual difference into the twentieth century that was "considered normal and socially acceptable for certain members of the community."[24]

In part, it was this frontier status and the perceived masculine virility associated with the uncivilized wilderness that attracted many of Florida's and Miami's late nineteenth-century visitors and settlers. After the U.S. Civil

War, Floridians aggressively marketed their state as a health resort, whose unmatched tropical climate made it an ideal place for people in the Midwest and Northeast to live in or visit. Travel books and guides promised that the warm temperatures and tropical breezes could "cure" the invalid suffering from the bitter cold and confines of man-made environments such as the urban center.[25] The Florida climate, so went these claims, served as a natural remedy for maladies such as bronchitis and asthma. One guide written in 1869 cited a doctor who believed Miami had the "nearest model climate for consumptives." No other place could "compare with this for salubrity."[26]

Incidentally, 1869 was also the year Dr. George Beard identified a new malady, neurasthenia, which gained cultural currency as a form of femininity or masculine regression linked to middle-class comforts and the urban setting. Symptoms included fatigue, tension, and depression.[27] Beard maintained neurasthenia was "part of the compensation for our progress and refinement."[28] If manliness was in crisis, perhaps it could be regained by rejecting civilization, the comforts of urbanity, and the perceived femininity of professional work. For many, masculinity could be asserted and reclaimed by conquering the Miami frontier.

Florida still seemed a natural habitat for the gender difference and the "sexual inversion and perversion" associated with "primitive" and "uncivilized" cultures.[29] In the 1870s, U.S. author Constance Fenimore Woolson spent considerable time in the South, including St. Augustine. Originally published in 1876, her short story "Felipa" reflects, as she described, the "real impressions" of her time in the area. In this story, Woolson introduced the narrator, Catherine, as one of Florida's nineteenth-century health tourists. Her beautiful friend Christine, along with Christine's beau Edward, joins her on this trip to Florida's east coast. While there, they become acquainted with Felipa, an eleven-year-old Minorcan girl living in a salt marsh. Woolson describes Felipa as a young immigrant ignorant of the path of womanhood and femininity. She dresses in boy's clothing and becomes enamored of Christine, whom she often wants to kiss. When Edward asks for Christine's hand in marriage, Felipa's jealousy turns violent and she stabs him. Felipa's grandparents worry the young girl's actions signal a form of same-sex sexual depravity. When Catherine consoles them that "it will pass; she is but a child," Felipa's grandfather adds: "You are right, lady; she does not know. But *I* know. It was two loves, and the stronger thrust the knife." Throughout the short story, the narrator describes Felipa as distinctly primitive: "She was a small, dark-skinned, yellow-eyed child, the offspring of the ocean and the heats, tawny, lithe and wild."[30] Gender and sexual transgression not only seemed possible; it ran rampant in Florida's "uncivilized" wilderness.

Boosters carefully balanced marketing southern Florida's natural environment with the imperative of advancing "civilization," often to the detriment of the area's indigenous cultures. An 1894 observer noted that Seminole "squaws are models of womanly virtue and industry," while one of their men was "a vigorous specimen of aboriginal manhood." Their "race remains pure," he claimed, "notwithstanding the inroads of 'civilization.'" This, he believed, was a consequence of the "severity of the punishment of those of either sex who are guilty of a breach of the law, for chastity is prescribed by their religion." With this prescription in place, the Seminoles' sexuality could be regulated and tamed. Miscegenation would not create a problem for white settlers. The writer maintained, "Seminoles do not think much of white women."[31] In addition to contrasting significantly with portrayals of blacks harboring an uncontrollable lust for white women, this perspective erased the sexual violence white men inflicted on native women during conquest.[32]

The writer observed other instances of gender difference among the Seminoles. "I was informed that their own women are not forced to perform *all* the work, with a hint that many New England farmers' wives are more in slavery."[33] Under this logic, Seminole men were inherently weaker and less manly than their white counterparts because they did not subjugate "their own women" in the same manner or degree. Rather than complete subordination, which the writer likened to slavery, Seminole women shared "women's work" with men. A new form of masculinity would soon be asserted in southern Florida. In her short story, Woolson suggested that Felipa's gender inversion was at least in part due to her lack of proper female role models. Felipa had met only three women in her life and, as described by the narrator, none was properly equipped to teach her the ways of womanhood or femininity. This included a Seminole woman.[34]

This process was both cause and effect of the violence and subjugation Seminoles endured in the name of white modernity. While the observer claimed that Seminoles were "not quarrelsome," he believed all bets were off when they were "under the influence," or inebriated. Even then, any subordination would be short-lived, "for they usually become limp in a very short time, and are unceremoniously tumbled into . . . their canoes by the squaws, and taken home to sleep it off."[35] The writer infantilized and effeminized Seminole men, portraying them as "limp" and easily overpowered by tribal women. This articulation of white masculinity helped rationalize the subjugation of indigenous cultures and peoples. It operated under a logic in which white male masculinity could be reasserted by conquering the racialized Other.[36] This control helped prove that "despite being civilized, white

men had lost none of the masculine power which had made their race dominant in the primeval past."[37]

By 1896, the *Miami Metropolis* published an editorial justifying this civi-
lizing brand of white masculinity. It argued that although it was true that the
Seminole "redskin" now "uses a sewing machine in his home, and cooks in
pots bought from the white hardware merchant, he seldom wears the garb
of the pale face and he is as much a savage as he ever was."[38] Foreshadowing
what was to come, one of the area's first resort hotels was built in 1897 on
top of a village and burial ground belonging to the Tequesta—an indigenous
tribe that predated the Seminoles.[39] Early city designers exerted their white
masculinity to bring about a profitable form of "progress" to the area. There
was no turning back.

The efforts of Cleveland native Julia Tuttle particularly helped populate and bring capital to Miami, as limited accessibility had kept it from
being "one of the most popular tourist resorts in Florida."[40] She became acquainted with southern Florida in 1875. Tuttle soon inherited and purchased
significant landholdings there and sought to develop the area after her husband died in 1891. She courted the money and ambition of Standard Oil
tycoon Henry Flagler and the development he could bring with his Florida
East Coast Railway (FEC). He had built an empire laying tracks on Florida's
Atlantic coast, making the terrain more accessible and attractive to northern travelers. Before 1895, the tracks ended in Palm Beach—at least seventy
miles north of Tuttle's properties. Thus, one either had to enter Miami by sea
or by a long stagecoach ride from Palm Beach.[41]

Tuttle helped convince Flagler to add a stop in Miami to his railroad empire, which helped lead to Miami's incorporation as a city. Florida citrus
farmers counted their losses following destructive freezes in 1894 and 1895.
Foreshadowing the moralist attitude that would soon trickle down and be
refashioned in Miami, Tallahassee-based Reverend Josephus Anderson argued that the state's "manifold sins" caused the freeze.[42] Tuttle seized this
opportunity to pitch Miami's desirability. She sent Flagler a package of fresh
orange blossoms from her freeze-immune Miami property, evidence of the
sound investment the area represented. The plan worked. The FEC first
blazed through Miami in April 1896.[43] Shortly after, on July 28, 344 men
voted to incorporate Miami as a city.[44] Once he agreed to expand the FEC
southward, Flagler quickly built a new luxury hotel, the Royal Palm, along
Biscayne Bay. This signaled the focus on leisure that soon transformed the
area. A new city was born.

It would be wrong to think of this frontier as ending in Miami, as the
"closing" of the U.S. West helped spark new campaigns abroad. Buttressed

by the principles of the Monroe Doctrine, the U.S. frontier expanded in the form of empire beyond the continent. The United States understood Cuba's third and final war of independence against Spain as its responsibility and potential gain. With this in mind, U.S. politicians carefully watched Cuban insurgents wage war against Spain from 1895 to 1898, providing the much-anticipated opportunity for the island to enter the realm of U.S. influence.[45]

The height of this U.S. imperialism occurred at the turn of the century and thus coincided with Miami's incorporation. While Cuba's war against Spain raged a short boat ride away, Miami pioneers searched for lucrative endeavors to attract new people and capital. The United States entered the war in the summer of 1898, swiftly defeating the Spanish forces already severely crippled by Cuban insurgents. The United States then occupied the newly "freed" Cuba and pressured its Constitutional Convention to ratify the Platt Amendment in 1901. This stood as a testament to U.S. ambitions to ultimately control the island. Under the Platt Amendment, the Republic of Cuba could not enter into a treaty with another foreign power without U.S. approval. The law also allowed the United States to intervene and occupy the island and permitted the establishment of Guantánamo Bay as a U.S. naval base. The gendered implications of this were massive, especially as the U.S. press and policymakers constructed a metaphor of Cuba as a "damsel in distress" in need of a heroic Uncle Sam to break her free from the shackles of Spanish tyranny.[46]

Miami powerbrokers initially opposed the war. The mysterious explosion of the USS *Maine* on February 15, 1898, shifted public opinion on the war throughout the country and silenced most antiwar voices.[47] Miami, however, lagged. Even in late March, Miami's *Metropolis* wrote that, "Speaking from a local standpoint, we do not long for war." In its early days, Miami's first newspaper was an unofficial extension of Flagler's enterprise, as well as a booster and public-opinion shaper for many of the city's seasonally absent capitalists.[48] The *Miami Metropolis* emphasized the danger war posed to the new city. If Cuba was in the United States's backyard—a powerful metaphor often deployed by prowar forces—nowhere was this truer than southern Florida.[49] Perhaps one of Spain's "gunboats could stand off the shore and the . . . hotels would make pretty but easily battered targets," quipped the newspaper.[50] Urban leaders perceived the war as a threat to the prosperity Florida experienced in the 1890s. The thought of the United States's annexing Cuba particularly troubled them, as it would create a worthy competitor in agriculture and for tourist dollars and pesos.[51]

The tide in Miami changed when the city's pioneer-entrepreneurs came to understand the war as an opportunity to further develop the city and stimulate sales and travel to the area. Miami powerbrokers realized the desolate city could gain from the war, on Uncle Sam's dime no less. They applied great pressure on the federal government—emphasizing Miami's proximity to Cuba, its fresh water, and its climate—to open a camp for soldiers in the city. After much hesitation, the federal government agreed. By April 1898, nascent Miami was home to roughly 2,000 residents. Imagine the local response when more than 7,000 army volunteers arrived in the city that June. Miami proved ill prepared. Countless soldiers got sick from drinking contaminated water, while several others fell ill or even died of malaria or typhoid fever. A newspaper from New Orleans, where many of the camp's soldiers came from, lamented the passing of "men sacrificed at this so-called health resort."[52] This was no paradise. Instead, the men referred to it as "Camp Hell." Within six weeks, the men were ordered to pack up.[53]

Poor reputation and tragedy notwithstanding, the men's short stint in Miami forced the clearing of more land, the paving of additional roads, and the building of new warehouses, all of which stimulated business.[54] Many interpreted Flagler's insistence on making Miami a key site for the war as part of his capitalist ventures. Eleanor "Nellie" Kinzie Gordon, who opened a hospital for the sick soldiers in Miami, observed, "Bringing troops here . . . is what has been a really criminal piece of jobbery to fill Mr. Flagler's pockets."[55] Troops who suddenly found themselves clearing Miami's backwoods were sarcastically called the FIC squad, or the "Flagler Improvement Company."[56]

Some soldiers also visited Miami's sexual demimonde. In addition to disease, soldiers on the camp complained about supply shortages and boredom. Although the sparse Miami community attempted to entertain them—by opening the pool at the Royal Palm Hotel or finding a space to play games, for instance—many of the men made their own form of leisure and recreation in the frontier city. It was not unusual for the men to swim nude in Biscayne Bay or congregate by the beach.[57] These men experienced a great deal of freedom and privacy in this largely undeveloped "jungle." One day, a group of soldiers from Texas saw "a big, burly negro" who they claimed did not allow two white women full access to a sidewalk. Consequently, "they grabbed this negro, gave him a good beating and started to string him up to a pine tree." Although police stopped them from lynching him, the men went into "Negro town" later that night. They fired shots and burned down parts of the neighborhood. The same group later traveled outside the city limits to North Miami to drink alcohol and visit a saloon.[58] Another man recalled how a "company of soldiers . . . invaded the colored settlement and terrorized the negroes who scattered in all directions for safety."[59] These black and working-class spaces served as the city's main site for vice, prostitution, and transgressive sex.[60]

All the while, the sexual politics of empire reared its head among the enlisted soldiers serving under the U.S. Military Government of Cuba during the post-1898 occupation. While U.S. forces suppressed acts associated with "Spanish backwardness"—such as lotteries, cockfights, and bullfights—official policy was to preserve sex work on the island. As Tiffany A. Sippial has argued, this "spoke volumes about U.S. priorities in Cuba."[61] In July 1901, U.S. officials reported that "about one-eighth of soldiers on the sick reports are victims" of syphilis and other venereal diseases. U.S. Army surgeon Major Valery Havard wrote, "Were it possible to examine all prostitutes and subject them to treatment when necessary, these diseases would be much less prevalent; but in several garrison towns there is no law requiring examination, or else it is so loosely applied … that it fails of its purpose." Treatment did not reach "clandestine prostitution nor the many women living in a state of concubinage."[62]

In blaming Cuban women—and their sexual proclivities or family arrangements, such as "concubinage"—as the source of the enlisted men's infections, the U.S. Military Government also consolidated its power and influence over the island. "It has been proposed," Havard wrote, "to apply the remedy inside instead of outside, and subject all enlisted men to a weekly examination." Havard claimed, however, that "the objections against" this plan were "so strong that it never extended beyond a few posts."[63] The policy placed the charge on the "outside," or the "diseased" Cuban women. The enlisted men's power over the occupied women rendered them largely immune from accountability.[64]

Similarly, U.S. officials reported three cases of sodomy by enlisted men from November 1900 to July 1901, suggestive of how sexual anxieties took shape alongside an expanding empire. While it is unclear whether the men engaged in same-sex acts—or perhaps even cross-sex sodomy—with other enlistees or with Cubans, it is certain that they were all soldiers and not commissioned officers. In this context, military officials expressed concern about protecting the "peaceable inhabitants of any foreign state, territory, or country" that the United States occupied. This suggests Cuban nationals had somehow been implicated in these accusations.[65] Just a few years prior, debates surfaced in Cuba concerning the feared prevalence of homosexuality among male bachelor laborers on the island.[66] Meanwhile, it is important to note that U.S. reports from occupied Cuba observed that offenses violating the Articles of War applied only to "an army serving within the United States" and therefore urged an expansion of military jurisdiction to make allowances "for an army occupying the extended field that we are now called upon to operate in."[67] While such jurisdictional parameters remained subject to "very liberal construction[s]" of existing provisions for several years, other revisions to the Articles of War in 1916 expanded "the field" to include more than just the immediate "theater of military operations."[68] In this way, U.S. empire in Cuba helped justify extending the geographical reach of the state's policing of sex the United States deemed undesirable or unnatural.

## Miami (Anti)vice

For its part, while Miami inherited Florida's criminal statutes targeting deviant sex, local law enforcement didn't always enforce them. In 1822, Congress created a territorial government in Florida. That same year, Florida's legislative council enacted "the common law of England which is of a general nature," as well as certain British statutes that were "not inconsistent" with the U.S. Constitution. While common law included the crime of sodomy, it had not been distinctly articulated among the territory's criminal offenses. The 1822 council did criminalize "illegal marriages" such as bigamy, as well as fornication and adultery, however.[69]

Florida's legislative council made new specifications—with an eye to controlling class and race relations—to this criminal code a decade later. In 1832, it further elaborated on bigamy, adultery, fornication, and other forms of "unlawful intimacy" and first specified the illegality of incest. It also distinctly targeted "open lewdness," which included "any notorious acts of public indecency, tending to debauch the morals of society." This banned "tippling houses" where illicit liquor was sold along with vice and pleasure dens such as "lewd houses," "disorderly houses," and "gaming houses." Other offenses, such as those targeting nuisance and vagrancy, were also written broadly enough to include deviant and transgressive expressions of gender and sex. Vagrancy, for instance, criminalized those who did not support themselves "in a respectable way, or [led] an idle, immoral, or profligate course of life."[70] These laws particularly targeted black, ethnic, and working-class communities. Lest we forget, it was this legislative session that specifically added racialized prohibitions to the crimes of fornication and adultery, as well as prohibited intermarriage.[71]

Tracing the selective enforcement of such offenses in Dade County reveals how race, gender, and class helped dictate what forms of deviant sex would be tolerated. Ruby Norwood, a young, single white woman who boarded with a family in North Miami, the vice district, was arrested three separate times between 1906 and 1909 for fornication (i.e., sexual intercourse between unmarried persons) and lascivious conduct.[72] Bertha Salter was first arrested in 1907 for visiting an opium den and twice the following year on vagrancy charges. Police arrested a black cook named Gertrude Miller, who was boarding with several other working-class black women and men in the city, for both lascivious conduct and unlawful cohabitation in 1909.[73] In Florida, unlawful cohabitation could either refer to any "negro man and white woman, or any white man and negro woman, who are not married to each other ... and in the night time occupy the same room," or the separate "lewd and lascivious behavior" law. The latter statute criminalized those who "cohabit together" outside of legal wedlock.[74] Another clause in that statute was broad enough to possibly cover a number of sex acts outside of marriage, both cross-sex and same-sex. Police could charge "any man or woman, married or unmarried," who engaged in the vague crime of "open and gross lewdness and lascivious behavior."[75] Police in Miami frequently charged both women and men with "lascivious conduct" during this period.[76]

The case of a married, mixed-race cook named Eugenia Collins is particularly revealing, in part because Miami police charged her with several sex crimes. She was arrested at least four times between 1910 and 1915 on charges ranging from vagrancy, fornication, and carnal intercourse.[77] Police arrested Collins for carnal intercourse even though, by the twentieth century, the law targeted "whoever has unlawful carnal intercourse with any unmarried female ... under the age of eighteen."[78] While it is possible that Collins had been charged with having a same-sex encounter with a younger girl, future reiterations of the offense limited potential perpetrators to men.[79] Police may have expanded the purview of the law in charging Collins with that offense. The evidence more heavily suggests Collins was implicated for her role in the sex trade. She may have also been paid for sex. Either way, she seems to have been married at the time, which placed her at odds with the charge. More likely, police may have charged her with *facilitating* the carnal intercourse of a young woman, perhaps in her capacity as a madam at a brothel.

Miami arrest records reveal that black women were more likely to be charged with operating a house of ill fame. Mamie Walker, a black washerwoman who lived with her husband, daughter, and father, was charged with that crime in 1917.[80] Other women—like Maude Mitchell, Ruby Monson, Pinkey Shamrock, and Lila Lois Albury—were also no strangers to the police. Mitchell was arrested twice in 1912, once for operating a house of ill fame and another time for aggravated assault. Monson was arrested three separate times in 1918 for fornication while also facing charges connected to running a brothel. Shamrock, a black domestic, was brought into the station at least four separate times in a span of two years.[81] Two of those charges, filed in 1921, were for operating a house of ill fame.[82]

The repeat offenses suggest several things. Fear of the law didn't seem to deter many black and mixed-race women from conducting their businesses. This sexual economy represented a steady and reliable source of income for these women and, when applicable, their families.[83] Attached to that is a common thread: law enforcement selectively raided and surveilled black and working-class spaces. Police and other urban powerbrokers zoned these spaces as part of the new city's underworld. Indeed, a thriving sexual economy existed just outside Miami's white middle- and upper-class neighborhoods.

Although men were legally implicated in Miami's sex trade, the evidence strongly suggests women generally oversaw the business. Men, especially those who were black, ethnic, and working class, were often charged with "enticing [a] female for immoral purposes." Police also arrested women for solicitation, however. Zita Powers and Zettie White were both charged in 1909 with "enticing female for prostitution." While this too could represent a same-sex proposition, the law was crafted to punish women who worked as a brothel's madam and got caught recruiting new employees.[84] White was a widowed black woman who otherwise worked as a laundress.[85] Although exceptions existed, the majority of those charged with this crime in Miami's early days were black and working-class women.[86]

Deemed unredeemable and immoral, black, ethnic, and working-class women stood outside of the social confines of respectability the law sought to defend.[87] The law qualified that enticing a woman for immoral purposes also meant taking the woman in question away from a previously "chaste life and conversation." The law generally didn't protect most women of color, who were already believed to be inherently sexual and vice-driven, or "unchaste."[88] Similarly, Florida's statute criminalizing coercive sex ambiguously left open a judicial interpretation that "unchaste" women were excluded from its purview. It was not entirely clear whether the court would hold that a prostitute, for instance, could be raped.[89]

Some offenses could potentially criminalize same-sex intimacies among women, but the law's defense of white femininity and the family, marriage, and reproductive intercourse likely helped women who desired women avoid detection.[90] For instance, judicial interpretation of Florida's lewd and lascivious cohabitation law clarified that it targeted cross-sex couples "dwell[ing] together as if the conjugal relation existed between them." In this way, "a transient or single unlawful interview," or more casual sexual affairs, would not qualify. The court also made clear it was meant to "prohibit the public scandal and disgrace of such living together by persons of *opposite sexes*, and unmarried to each other, to prevent such evil and indecent examples."[91] While it appears that queer black women particularly socialized in private spaces such as residences, the law seemed nearly oblivious that such intimate encounters could be sexual.[92] The law's patriarchal myopia helped immunize most women from arrest for homosexual intimacy, while also exposing the limitations of criminal records capturing the sexual lives of all women. Other forces, such as families, churches, and aggressive or forceful men, may have policed women's same-sex desires more effectively or privately than even the law.

Meanwhile, men who had sex with other men could be arrested under Florida's sodomy and crime against nature laws, even though these charges proved difficult to establish and appeared infrequently in Miami's dockets during this period. In 1842, two decades after Florida passed its rape law, Florida's legislative council formally wrote sodomy into the state's criminal code. Based on English common law, the state's first and most draconian sodomy law punished those "who shall commit buggery or sodomy with either human being or beast." The perpetrator would "be adjudged guilty of felony and shall suffer death." This also partially amended the criminal code pertaining to the application of common law, which had implicitly covered sodomy for years, that limited punishment to a $500 fine or a twelve-month imprisonment. This reveals that the council understood that sodomy had been criminalized in its statute for twenty years, while also affirming a desire to drastically increase the stakes for committing the offense.[93] In 1845, lawmakers excluded those convicted of sodomy or buggery "from being a witness, or from giving evidence" in any civil or criminal case.[94] Florida legislators amended the state's sodomy law in 1868. While the crime could no longer be punished by death, it remained a felony, and the amendment included harsher language. "Whoever commits the abominable and detestable crime against nature, either with mankind or with any beast, shall be punished by imprisonment ... not exceeding twenty years," read the law.[95] By invoking the common law "crime against nature" taxonomy, the law particularly defined sodomy—which primarily targeted homosexual acts between men and, in Florida, was limited to anal sex until the 1920s—as unnatural and contrary to normal and traditional feelings or behaviors.[96]

The General Index to Criminal Cases for Dade County listed only *one* person as having been charged with committing sodomy or a crime against nature in Miami from 1896 to 1909, as Miami police simply did not enforce these laws with any regularity until at least the 1940s.[97] Police charged a man named C. R. Whitehurst with the crime in 1896, the year Miami became a city.[98] Unfortunately, the case file did not survive and the *Miami Metropolis* seems to have been silent on the matter. It is uncertain, then, whether

Whitehurst was convicted or if he had been accused of committing same-sex or cross-sex anal intercourse or bestiality. While the law covered all those acts, "in both practice and popular understanding, sodomy was a crime that involved males."[99]

In addition, Florida law construed rape as a cross-sex crime until 1974, which helped consolidate sodomy as a crime males committed and submitted to.[100] Miami police frequently charged men with the "carnal knowledge" offense, which covered either rape inflicted on a woman who resists sexual penetration or sexual contact with a girl of ten or younger whose age invalidated consent.[101] This law was more legible and accessible to those filing charges for cross-sex anal penetration—coercive or otherwise. While judicial interpretation had increasingly gestured toward requiring that the "male organ actually penetrated the genitals of the female" to convict, the law did not altogether preclude the possibility that coercive anal sex might also fall in its purview.[102]

More specifically, the evidence suggests that in Miami, at least through 1940, the sodomy law primarily targeted intergenerational same-sex acts among men that were also, at times, described as coercive. Almost all other reports of these offenses, such as court hearings and newspaper reports, dealt with men accused of having sexual relations with young boys or adolescents. Youths often testified to some form of assault or coercion. Sex with beasts also appeared in the record, though sparsely. The prevalence of adult-juvenile homosexual acts in Miami's fairly slim charges for sodomy in this period may suggest, as Peter Boag has demonstrated, that these were mostly working-class pairings in outlying areas of the city.[103] Other evidence certainly suggests this was the case with other sex offenses, wherein black, ethnic, and working-class neighborhoods were the primary targets of police surveillance and legal recourse.

Whitehurst's 1896 charge stands out as the *only* time sodomy or the crime against nature was specifically listed in the Dade County General Index to Criminal Cases as an "assault," at least through 1930. It is possible, then, that Miami's first crime against nature or sodomy charge was nonconsensual, or that anal intercourse was understood as an assault in and of itself. In listing his charge as a "crime against nature *assault*," the recorder anomalously qualified the offense as a coercive, physical attack.[104] This complements William Eskridge's broader findings on sodomy laws in the nineteenth century, wherein they "filled a regulatory gap" for nonconsensual sex because rape charges were strictly defined by vaginal penetration by the penis and the court could not convict on the testimony of an "accomplice," or a willing sexual participant, alone. Sodomy laws served as "instruments to regulate sexual assault" during this period.[105] Courts and law enforcement paid particular attention to cases that appeared to be "flagrant" and "notorious." This does not seem to have been the case with the accused Whitehurst, since the *Metropolis* did not address it and the case does not appear in the Dade County Grand Jury Report.[106]

It is also important to remember that Miami was a frontier burdened with difficult terrain, limited access, and scarce resources that further complicated the regular policing of sex crimes. For instance, two male suspects charged with rape and murder in 1896 could not be confined in Miami and were instead transported to a jail in Juno, roughly eighty-five miles north.[107] During Miami's earliest days, the only nearby jail was a boxcar under the authority of Flagler's Royal Palm Hotel.[108] Miami developers built the city's first jail that December.[109] Even with that new space, by early 1897, Miami's city clerk complained that the new jail was too small and lacked "conveniences." It would only hold *city* prisoners.[110] In addition, Miami only had one police officer until 1898, and he also served as a building inspector, street superintendent, sanitary inspector, and tax collector.[111]

Physical distance, local bureaucracy, and overworked municipal officials further complicated the efficiency of policing during Miami's early years. Prior to 1899, the lone court in the immediate area was Miami proper's Police Court, which "met only briefly and sporadically."[112] The city charter granted this court jurisdiction over offenses listed in the city code and over state-outlined misdemeanors committed in Miami proper, then still a relatively small area. Part of the problem was that the Dade County seat had been moved to Juno, which had more voters than Miami, in 1889. City designers succeeded in bringing the seat back to Miami in 1899.[113] After that, county tribunals would also be heard in Miami. The need for a more efficient process quickly grew along with the city's population. Miami's Police Court, for instance, was better known as the Mayor Court because the city mayor, who already had many official and unofficial duties, served as its judge in compliance with the municipal code. In 1905, a new court, the Municipal Court, replaced that tribunal system and had a full-time elected judge presiding.[114] Early obstacles and inefficiencies were indeed part of the area's growing pains.

Effectively policing and prosecuting people scattered throughout the area proved challenging, if not impossible. John Sewell, Miami's third mayor, recalled that because "the crooks and gamblers were a good distance from the Court House and out of the city," they were able to run "things with a high hand." Things did not immediately improve once the county seat moved back to Miami. In 1905 police waited hours for a bloodhound to be sent from West

Palm Beach to help sniff out a sexual assault suspect on the run.[115] By 1918, civilians tasked with serving on the Dade County Grand Jury—an adjunct of the Circuit Court that investigated crimes, made indictments, and proposed urban improvements—observed the difficulty in policing the frontier-in-transition. They maintained that "it would call for a veritable army of officials to cope with the conditions of affairs" in the city, a reference to the many sources of commercial and transgressive sex that were taking place in public and remote places throughout the area.[116]

It would be erroneous, then, to interpret a dearth of sodomy charges as evidence of absence of same-sex desires and behaviors in early Miami. All the other evidence suggests the contrary. That there was any charge at all in an urban frontier with a population of no more than 2,000 by the end of 1896—and barely 500 residents just a few months prior—is telling.[117] Because of the difficulty of prosecuting sodomy charges, law enforcement could try to convict with other crimes on the books such as vagrancy, lascivious conduct, indecent exposure, fornication, disorderly conduct, and prostitution. In addition, the applicability of the crime against nature charge to criminalize oral sex on men remained ambiguous in Florida until the 1920s, and it would take another two decades after that for the courts to debate cunnilingus as an act, much less a punishable crime.[118]

Broader charges such as disorderly conduct and vagrancy proved more effective at policing sexual acts, which often occurred in public spaces such as streets, parks, docks, and beaches. Police often accused Miami residents of disorderly conduct when the available evidence was scarce, unreliable, or circumstantial. Take the 1920 case of a white man named A. H. Bouldin, who was charged with two counts of disorderly conduct in Miami. At first, police charged him with disorderly conduct for allegedly inviting a twelve-year-old girl playing on her bike on the street to take a ride in his vehicle. Witness testimony claimed that after the girl declined his offer, Bouldin made several other attempts to pass by her in his car. He only stopped, one female neighbor testified, when she asked him what he wanted. The city attorney argued Bouldin's actions constituted "an insulting and indecent proposal to a person of the opposite sex in a public place." Bouldin denied the accusations. The judge agreed and tossed out that charge because there was "insufficient evidence ... to convict ... beyond a reasonable doubt or to show criminal intent." The attorney then made a separate disorderly conduct charge: "offensive conduct calculated to provoke a breach of the peace." On the same grounds, the judge also dismissed that charge.[119]

The case reveals the legal maneuvering employed by the city's law enforcement, attorneys, and judicial system. For instance, the attorney's charge that Bouldin's actions constituted "a proposal to a person of the *opposite sex*" may suggest the court's acknowledgment of similar same-sex propositions. Also, we learned about this case, in part, because the accused happened to be a successful white man connected to the city's real estate business. Most people accused of such charges likely couldn't afford a lawyer and feared a case would incite public humiliation or harassment. Their options were limited and generally resulted in serving time, often in the form of hard labor. The city attorney tried his case before the municipal court, even though the court could not agree on what crime—if any—Bouldin had committed.[120]

When trying to prove before the judge that Bouldin had made offensive or insulting remarks to the girl, the city attorney tried to associate the accused man with perverse and interracial sex. When the judge ruled against admitting evidence from Bouldin's past to make the new charges stick, the city attorney rebutted anyway: "I am not attacking his character; I am attacking his habits." To do that, he maintained, it was necessary for the court to know whether Bouldin had ever been "convicted with reference to accosting a negro woman." If Bouldin had accosted or solicited a black woman in the past, inviting the young girl to his vehicle may have been understood as malicious. Bouldin's lawyer then accused the city attorney of "attempting to try this case on public sentiment." He too understood that evidence linking him to interracial sex and perhaps prostitution baited him as unnatural and deviant. Similar dubious tactics emerged when the judge tossed out the final charge that Bouldin's acts provoked a breach of the peace. The city attorney angrily told the court, "I say most assuredly ... that if she [the young girl] had told it to a man instead of a woman there would have been a breach of the peace." Any reasonable *man*, he maintained, logically would have responded to the report with violence. These courts operated in ways that further ostracized, stigmatized, or even criminalized those whose gender and sexuality were read as suspect or abnormal. While Bouldin's race and class helped save him from conviction, most others would have had very different experiences with the law.[121]

Florida's broad antivagrancy laws similarly criminalized those the state read as deviant, suspect, or undesirable. The Florida legislature initially passed antivagrancy laws in the 1860s as part of the "black code" that sought to limit and control blacks after the U.S. Civil War.[122] When slavery was abolished, vagrancy laws provided another route to coercive labor. In arbitrarily criminalizing blacks, immigrants, and working-class people, the law mandated retribution in the form of hard labor. In 1868, Florida law criminalized "rogues and vagabonds, idle and dissolute persons who go about begging." It regulated labor by targeting "persons who neglect their calling or employment, misspend what they earn and do not provide for themselves or … their families." It targeted those who "misspent" their earnings on drink, vice, or maybe commercial sex. The law's reach was so wide it also criminalized "fiddlers," "runaways," "common drunkards," "common night-walkers," and "pilferers."[123]

This charge proved an effective way for Miami's white powerbrokers to police the city's black and ethnic communities, while also securing a steady and free and coercive labor force. In 1896, the Dade County Grand Jury noted that "County roads and bridges" needed immediate attention. It recommended "the employment of County prisoners" to build new structures, just "as soon as there are enough of them in custody to make it profitable to use them."[124] Within a few years, the discriminatory efforts of local law enforcement guaranteed there would be ample convict manpower. In 1903 a Georgia man named B. B. Tatum, who owned the *Miami Metropolis* for several years, blamed saloons and the "manufacturers and dealers in liquor" for the violent crimes associated with the city's black communities. "One suggestion as to the negroes who in Miami as elsewhere are hanging around the [vice] dives and doing nothing is to put them all to work. Arrest every one of them on the charge of vagrancy and put them on the county roads.... There is no excuse for an idler to live and the man who loafs around a saloon and will not work should be taken charge of by the officials and courts."[125] Convict labor was used for one of the city's more ambitious projects that made Miami more accessible to outsiders: the building of the Tamiami Trail connecting Tampa and Miami.[126] Perceived as naturally inclined to drink and commit crimes, so-called vagrants—both women and men—were among those targeted for this kind of exploitative labor.

Transgressive sexuality had long been linked to transients, tramps, hoboes, and vagrants.[127] Perhaps the Florida antivagrancy law's most direct attack on gender transgression, illicit sex, and homosexuality was its inclusion of "lewd, wanton, and lascivious persons in speech or behavior." Adding further to its vagueness and its ability to criminalize sexual subversives, the legislation included those who "neglect all lawful business and misspend their time by frequenting houses of ill-fame, gaming houses, or tippling shops."[128] In 1909, the *Miami Metropolis* observed that city police were preoccupied with "the hauling in of drunken extension laborers—distorted hulks of humanity, who are probably more deserving of pity than censure."[129]

Criminal dockets throughout the county soon ballooned. Florida's legislature conceived of a Criminal Court of Record for Dade County in 1907 to help the overworked Circuit Court. Although it only heard 120 cases its first year of existence, the following session saw the court dispose of "nearly

700 cases, from misdemeanors to homicides." This trend escalated further over the years. The busiest local tribunal, however, remained the Municipal Court. "By 1915, it was deciding 3,000 cases annually and its fine ... total had reached $12,000."[130] This represented a substantial source of revenue for the city coffers. It ruled on the alleged infractions relating to nearly every municipal ordinance. This included laws that targeted gender- and sexual-transgressive people, especially those living in black, ethnic, and working-class neighborhoods, in Miami proper.[131]

The area's law enforcement and tribunals worked together to implement a punitive approach to regulating vice that capitalized on the social and political vulnerability of Miami's black, ethnic, and working-class residents. In November 1906, Municipal Court Judge James T. Sanders, a native Georgian who was also the first person in the city to preside over that tribunal, announced that if the "police will arrest the vagrants, he will do the rest." The *Miami Metropolis* endorsed this position, noting that vagrancy was covered by one of the "most explicit of the State statutes." Cracking down on this "menace and ... nuisance to the community" would help guarantee that "labor will be less scarce" in Miami.[132]

In the midst of the Great War, when anxieties over prostitution and the spread of venereal disease helped squash red-light districts throughout the country, vagrancy was even more directly linked to the city's sexual underground. Sheriff Durward W. Moran, another Georgia native, followed through with his promise to "rid Miami and Dade county of negro vagrants and prostitutes." He and his deputies arrested several black women and men on vagrancy charges. Judge Sanders then took over and gave them "stiff fines or alternatives of long jail sentences," namely, hard labor building or repairing local roads. Judge Sanders maintained, "In this time of war ... it behooves every man and woman to do their part."[133] Two years later, another municipal judge made good on this antivice campaign and promised to "impose maximum fines on prostitutes who came before his court."[134] Thus, the policing of the city's blacks and sexual subversives proved critical to the steady flow of free, coercive labor.

The broad nature of these laws also left open the possibility of criminalizing Miami's sexual subversives into at least the mid-twentieth century. The direct association with "houses of ill-fame" and "gaming houses," which were specifically zoned outside of Miami proper, further located the city's sexual underground in Miami's black and ethnic neighborhoods. The zoning of the city's red-light district in these working-class neighborhoods was the product of careful urban design, conceived with an eye to achieve maximum profit for mostly white entrepreneurs and investors. A new city was being built on the backs of those who were excluded from calling it home.

### Making a City Respectable while Making Room for Pleasure

Contrary to popular images of life in Miami today, the city was *not* founded with an eye to liberal or lax moral attitudes. Many of the powerful white pioneers in the city mandated a conservative and strict standard for a moral "model city." They launched campaigns to make the city respectable for its white residents and visitors. Whereas members of Miami's upper and aspiring middle class won some of the initial battles on the pretense of keeping the city chaste, this was but a Pyrrhic victory. Vice easily seeped into Miami's culture. The city soon transformed from a frontier model city into the playground of the nation.

Representative of this tension, Tuttle only agreed to sell land to Flagler and others under the stipulation that Miami remain "dry." Early land deeds included clauses that prohibited the "buying, selling, or manufacturing" of liquor.[135] This was the growing popular sentiment among moralists that would culminate in national Prohibition two decades later. The *Miami Metropolis* defended Tuttle's position. It reminded critics: "If she has dreamed of a model city and has confidence in her ability to make it.... Who has the right to criticize her judgment?"[136]

An exception was made, however, for Flagler's new hotel, anticipating a distinct brand of contradictory politics that heeded the ambitions of wealthy white developers. Tuttle and William and Mary Brickell, another early settler-developer family from Ohio, allowed Flagler to serve alcohol in the Royal Palm Hotel during tourist season.[137] Prior to Miami's incorporation, Mary Brickell even secured a county license to sell tobacco in the area.[138] This sent a mixed message. The *Miami Metropolis* reported that although "the gentlemen who compose the Board of Aldermen are mostly business men with private interests of their own," "they are devoted to the welfare of the city."[139] It was clear that this remained true insofar as it was *their* city. This caused a great deal of friction among other less powerful landowners who also wanted to capitalize on the tropical frontier by building a paradise for elite travelers.[140]

Petitions written to the Dade County Board of Commissioners reveal how elite pioneers united to keep certain Miami residents from opening saloons. In September 1899, ten Miami residents wrote a letter to the commissioners to "emphatically protest against the granting of a liquor license" to a man named P. J. Stephenson. They argued his application was a "scheme" on behalf of the Woods' Saloon in North Miami, an establishment in the black neighborhood notorious for its "murders and robberies," to expand its enterprise within city limits. The residents maintained that Stephenson had frequented and even worked at Woods' Saloon, "a disorderly place."[141] This meant he was "not a man of good character," a requisite for obtaining a license. Applications also required several sworn witnesses to attest to the applicant's age, sobriety, and status as a "law abiding person."[142] These processes demonstrate how some Miami residents, usually of lesser means, were vilified and marked as criminal or suspect within the community. All the while, barriers kept particular individuals from profiting from the city's growing vice enterprise.

The *Metropolis* clearly presented the ongoing dilemma: these early decisions would dictate what type of city Miami would become. "The career of Miami has been too brief for any one to predict what kind of city it is to be, or what manner of people will compose its population," the newspaper explained. It believed these conservative pioneers were not "temperance cranks" but strategic urban designers "determined ... to make the place a model city, to make it attractive to the higher class of well-to-do, law-abiding people."[143] In a separate piece, the Miami newspaper reported the growing tension: "It is said by some visitors, we might say by many of them, that ... [the deeded prohibitions on the sale of alcohol] are unreasonably restrictive."[144]

When Tuttle died in September 1898, the executors of her estate were faced with a massive decision: whether to enforce her commitment to remaining a "dry" city. They chose not to. By 1899, the deeds to properties sold in Miami proper no longer contained an antiliquor clause.[145] With this, Prohibition in Miami had ended, at least for a few years. Immediately, "saloons opened up in all parts of the city."[146] By 1910, Miami proper was home to eight saloons, with many more just outside its borders.[147] Competing visions for Miami, marked by ideas of race, class, gender, and sexuality, drew new city borders.

The moral antiliquor sentiment and language also became an effective way to segregate the city along racial and class lines. Tuttle's conditions for land sale included "provisions for residences being placed at least twenty-five feet back from the street lines" and "the confining of factories and colored people in certain localities."[148] Flagler tapped into existing moralist anxieties to argue against including either Lemon City or Coconut Grove within Miami's limits, citing the presence of "saloons" in these areas.[149] Racial and class divides dictated these restrictions. The Freedmen's Bureau chose Lemon City as a relocation site for former slaves. A few dozen displaced Seminoles also remained throughout the area.[150] Meanwhile, homesteaders largely settled Coconut Grove shortly after the U.S. Civil War. Its population consisted mostly of settlers from Great Britain and black and white residents from the British West Indies, namely, the Bahamas. The vast majority of the "local" blacks had migrated to Miami in search of work from north and central Florida, Georgia, and South Carolina.[151] The area between Miami and Lemon City, or "North Miami," was similarly segregated. It housed many of the black laborers who built the railroad. Reports show that the "indecent bathing" of black workers equally became a source of anxiety for those seeking to upholding white respectability. Miami's outskirts became home to several saloons and brothels forcibly pushed out of the city limits.[152]

Even before Tuttle died, the sale of alcohol and the vice associated with it quickly found its way into Miami proper. By March 1897, a man who already operated a saloon in North Miami purchased a plot of land on the south end of the Miami River in Coconut Grove. The Brickells had initially sold that property to a separate man prior to the consensus that added the restrictive liquor clause to deeds. This issue proved to be of great interest to "those who do not wish saloons" and "those who dislike to go . . . to North Miami for a night-cap or an eye opener."[153] This controversy inadvertently acknowledged that "respectable" men often crossed city lines to visit and experience the vice culture associated with Miami's black and working-class neighborhoods.

Although this sexual underground flourished in ethnic and racialized spaces just beyond the city limits, it is clear that white middle- and upper-class Miamians were frequent visitors and craved access to this world. Anti-miscegenation laws in Florida and throughout the U.S. South served as an instrument to uphold white male social and political control. The enforcement of such miscegenation laws most frequently targeted more formal and public liaisons and relationships. In this way, "Southern whites generally enforced an intimacy color line rather than a sexual color line."[154] This belief was further sustained by southern Progressives, who believed that briefer, interracial sexual encounters lacked mutual care or respect. They did not suggest that the two sexual partners were social equals and still allowed for the social perception of black inferiority. This made interracial sex, particularly commercial sex between a white man and a black woman, permissible.[155] Miami's antivice campaigns helped draw the city boundaries and established the area's red-light district within a distinctly racialized sexual subculture. With this as a sort of map, curious residents and travelers alike could easily identify and visit local sites for sexual exploration.

This "slumming" enabled pleasure seekers to satiate their own curiosities and perhaps even experiment with their carnal appetites beyond the security and safety of their neighborhoods. Slummers engaged in titillating behavior by venturing beyond the familiarity of the city limits and into the nearby dark spaces that lacked the restrictions, laws, or even "public morals" they had grown accustomed to. All the while, because such perceived depravity occurred "over there," it allowed these visitors to retain a pretense of chastity and respectability. Chad Heap documented similar findings on slumming in New York and Chicago. He noted that, although "reform-minded middle- and upper-class whites eventually forced the closure of the red-light districts and slum resorts that attracted affluent thrill seekers, . . . attempts to police these areas and to regulate the behavior of their inhabitants often served to reinforce their appeal."[156]

Unlike New York or Chicago, however, Miami remained a frontier. These spaces were still relatively ill-defined. This was the tension at play when, in 1896, the *Miami Metropolis* tried to cultivate more white investments in Lemon City. It assured its readers, "You are safe. Come up."[157] Miami's fron- tier status made it easier for white urban designers to specifically carve out which spaces would be zoned as respectable (i.e., white, middle, and upper class) and which would serve as the city's playground (i.e., black, ethnic, and working class). The irony is that *all* of Miami would soon be marketed as the nation's playground, or a "fairyland," where visitors were invited to consume all forms of recreation and leisure—including the transgression of gender and sexual norms.

Slumming in Miami involved far more than voyeurism and helped give shape to the public's sexual behaviors and inchoate understandings of their desires. Sewell admitted, "Some saloons were built within *twenty feet* of the city limits, as they wished to be just as close to the city as possible."[158] The proximity made a brief visit not only tempting but also feasible. Shortly after Miami became a city, the *Miami Metropolis*—which had been a staunch advocate of temperance—proposed the public and legal endorsement of the area's saloons. Upon citing North Miami's notoriety as a cesspool for vice and sin, it proposed two options: either Miami annex North Miami, or the latter too should become an independent municipality. The newspaper even came clean, as "the owners of the *Metropolis* have personal interests as property owners in the North Miami territory."[159] Like many others, the voices behind the *Miami Metropolis* understood that North Miami's unsavory reputation would also be the source of Miami's success, particularly in light of the alco- hol restrictions placed on the city proper. It suggested that a North Miami municipality could raise revenue by collecting "a town license of $250 per year from each saloon."[160] If the original "founders of the city" instead "de- sire[d] to publish to the world the fact that there are no saloons in the City of Miami (which they can not do if North Miami is annexed)," the newspaper noted it would regretfully respect that decision. Either way, the newspaper understood it was just a matter of time before saloons made their way into the city. The founders were fighting a losing battle.[161]

Many of the city's urban designers understood a sequestered red-light district as a *necessity*—or a much-needed outlet for release or revenue—for Miami's own success and modern development. This can be gleaned when a local sheriff called North Miami's vice culture the "so-called necessary evil." He offered an alternative view: "I do not believe ... that such resorts as North Miami are a necessity." The sheriff admitted his opinion was contrary to public and official positions that claimed North Miami and later, Colored Town, were necessary outlets that could be used, abused, and exploited intermittently by white, respectable visitors. In order for Miami proper to exist as a respectable space, it needed a place of disrepute to exist by its side. The "chaste" or "pure" required the presence of a "whore" alongside her to visually offset and define what is "normal." The sheriff argued, "I am ... aware that sin and vice are always with us, and always will be but I know that it can be checked in a marked degree by activity and open-eyedness on the part of the authorities."[162] Miami residents and officials understood the desirability of a "vice" outlet just outside city borders and designed it close enough for comfort. Miami *needed* the red-light district in black neighborhoods for the city to fully thrive, develop, and grow.

The fact that this practice was known as slumming was, of course, not incidental. Situated in the city's margins, these racialized spaces were in fact the slums.[163] They also became a major source of profit for local slumlords—both black and white, although predominantly the latter. As N. D. B. Connolly has argued, "under Jim Crow's folk wisdom, 'niggers' seemed to be natural impediments to the making of moral communities."[164] Thus, these sexualized and racialized processes solidified capital gains for mostly white middle- and upper-class residents at the expense—lived out through incarceration, surveillance, poverty, and discrimination—of the city's working-class black and ethnic communities.

Evidence reveals how local law enforcement policed illicit economies that thrived among the area's remaining indigenous peoples connected to North Miami, particularly its saloons. In 1909, the Miami sheriff cracked down on "saloon keepers in the city and in colored town" selling liquor to the Seminoles. In perpetuating the belief that the Native Americans were inherently prone to drunkenness and disorderly behavior, he maintained, "These Indians know no law and get drunk every time they come to the city."[165] In 1914, authorities arrested a local Seminole man named Teeth Pull Tiger for selling wild bird feathers in Miami.[166] This informal economy prospered in

North Miami. Seminoles frequently crossed the Miami River on canoes and sold contraband—such as bird plumes and animal hides—to North Miami saloonkeepers who then resold them at a profit. In return, Native Americans received either gold or whiskey.[167] This economy operated in ways that financially benefited white residents while further stigmatizing and criminalizing Native Americans as drunks, disorderly, and immoral.[168] White settlers could both profit and retain their respectability at the Seminoles' expense.

This is a local manifestation of the varied ways state and federal legislation sought to control Native American and black populations, even as the latter—through a state politics of exploitation and turning a blind eye—particularly became the perceived source of "immorality" for cities like Miami in the early twentieth century. While the law regarded both Native American and black communities as inherently prone to savagery, immorality, and drunkenness—albeit to varying degrees and under different circumstances—lawmakers distinctly prohibited the sale of alcohol to Native Americans until a federal law repealed existing bans in 1953.[169] Conversely, blacks in Florida could drink alcohol without breaking state law after the 1860s. That was when the post–U.S. Civil War Florida legislature enacted new state constitutions in 1865 and 1868 to comply with the federal regulations mandated by Reconstruction.[170] Coupled with segregation, these laws ensured that black neighborhoods became sites of so-called immorality and vice. The state both facilitated and necessitated the creation of these spaces.

So while the state policed the so-called immorality of Native Americans by legislatively prohibiting the sale of alcohol to indigenous people, it controlled black communities through multiple forms of surveillance and exploitative labor. When police arrested Julia Holman in 1915 for accepting two dollars from a group of people and promising to secure them contraband alcohol, they described her as "the negress so well known in police trouble."[171] Black residents were zoned to live in areas such as Colored Town that were defined by the nonregulation of alcohol and vice for all, black or white. In addition to zoning these areas as sex and vice districts where communities of color lived, the evidence in Miami supports the claim that engaging in underground economies—which placed them at odds with the law and therefore vulnerable to sporadic raids—proved one of the more successful avenues for economic survival, particularly for women of color.[172]

Racial segregation helped carve out a space where the city's early sexual underground could thrive, particularly in North Miami. Sewell recalled the development of the city's sexual geography in his memoir. In response to the restrictions landowners found in Miami, "whiskey men opened up barrooms just north of the city limits on Avenue D and called it North Miami." There,

FIGURE 1.1. An early 1900s photograph of Miami's Avenue D (modern-day Miami Avenue) captures the heart of Miami's retail district. A sign for "Majestic Saloon" is visible on the right. The city's Colored Town was farther north. Image RC06688, courtesy of the State Archives of Florida.

one found "all the vices ... that were ever in the worst frontier town." This too was rife with race and class tensions. To visit "the night after pay day," one could find "the workmen spending their money getting drunk, fighting, shooting and killing." In particular, "the gambling bunch did most of the devilment," which helped make "North Miami ... notorious for its vices all over the country."[173] In 1896, the *Miami Metropolis* maintained, "The majority of the criminal cases were from that suburb. Something will have to be done to control matters at North Miami."[174] At the northern end of Miami proper's limits, one could find "a number of saloons, gambling houses and kindred evils." That space grew in notoriety, both in and outside the city, as the "unsavory district" *just* outside of Miami.[175]

The white "tramps" and black men who frequented or lived in these areas were often depicted as violent and sexually transgressive. In part because of their lack of community ties, so-called tramps, hoboes, and vagrants were often associated with sex crimes. One woman accused "three or four white men" thought to be "tramps" on the fringes of Coconut Grove of attempted sexual assault.[176] In October 1896, Asbury Duckett, described by the newspaper as a "bad 'Nigger,'" was found guilty of stabbing and killing the pool table attendant "in the negro section" of Woods' Saloon "just at the north edge of town in North Miami." The incident reportedly took place after the victim "offended him by demanding pay for a pool debt."[177] In another instance, residents pondered whether a North Miami black man named Moses McQueen would soon be "dancing on a wind platform with a hempen accompaniment, or at least to a long period of years in the chain gang." Charged with raping an eleven-year-old black girl, it appears the only evidence against him was that both suffered from a "loathsome" venereal disease.[178]

Black men were believed to be the primary assailants who threatened the white woman's virtue and chastity. Several discourses, including medical literature, offered testimony to the "sexual peculiarities of the [southern] negro," alluding to his "physical and moral degeneracy." This operated on a logic in which the black man's perceived primitive nature rendered him incapable of controlling his "animal impulses," including sexual violence.[179] The "black rapist" narrative in the post-Reconstruction and turn-of-the-century U.S. South was produced alongside sexology reports that diagnosed the disease of "perverted" sex acts—including a sensationalized 1892 "lesbian lover" murder in Memphis.[180]

To be sure, the building of Miami—like modernity itself—would unfold through a kaleidoscope of popular accounts of racial violence, sexual perversion, and gender difference as a means to define normalcy. The *Metropolis*'s Tatum expressed this racist anxiety in an editorial concerning the "assault upon a respectable white woman ... by a fiendish black brute." He asked, "What can be done with these black sons of hell?" He demanded retribution and a means of curbing the sexual depravity he believed came naturally to black men. "All kinds of remedies have been resorted to including hemp, tar and torch and yet it seems that it is all of no avail, and occasionally the demon in human form breaks loose, fearing neither God nor man, bent upon the commission of a crime worse than the foulest murder." He maintained, "No wonder that lynchings and roastings are resorted to" in Miami and beyond. In the end, he saw such violence against blacks in Miami as imminent and necessary, so long as "these devilish attempts upon the virtue and lives of white women are made."[181] Two years later, the town mourned the sexual assault and murder of a white woman named Dora Suggs in Coconut Grove. This brutal act "aroused every one to the fact that action of an extreme kind is necessary to protect life and womanhood in this city and state." Police brought in "two negro suspects."[182] With scant and circumstantial evidence, one of them met his end at the city gallows.[183]

The regulation of Miami's vice and sex trade took form alongside the defense of white respectability, particularly the virtues associated with white womanhood and the nuclear family. In the early 1900s, dozens of Miami residents signed their names to a petition addressed to the Board of Dade County Commissioners requesting that a "Club ... situated in Coloredtown" be relocated farther away from Miami proper. In addition to being a "public nuisance," they claimed, the club served as a "rendezvous for vagrants." There, "profanity and vulgarity" were regularly used, causing great "discomfort" to the "families living near and the ladies who must pass that way." This establishment had to be relocated, they insisted, as it was "a disturber of the peace at night," "a destroyer of the morals of the youth," and "a robber of innocent wives and children."[184]

City residents sometimes expressed great concern that the saloons, and the sexually suspect characters who frequented them, would corrupt Miami's youth. In 1907 one woman noted that schoolchildren often felt pressured to enter saloons and drink. Many, she claimed, were successful. Those who were "game" exuded a "feeling of manliness," while those who had to be convinced were effeminate "coward[s]." In this way, the presence of the saloon—not just for the young boys, but also for the adults in the community—helped define gender norms in the city. While the expression of a healthy masculinity—even among younger boys—was of great importance, many worried about the dangers that lurked in these spaces. The primary threats appeared to be alcohol and crime. At least one woman suggested that the saloon would introduce vulnerable boys to deviant sex with older men. She noted that two schoolboys who snuck into a Miami saloon reported "a dandy fellow in town who stands a treat of beer any time you meet him." The young boys, she added, "spent almost all one Saturday cleaning his wheel for him and 'boozing.'" This was reason enough, she suggested, to prohibit alcohol in the city and shut down the saloons.[185]

With such anxieties mounting, city reformers launched a moral crusade to contain and sequester the crime, vice, and illicit sex in the name of Miami's white, respectable residents. Powerful figures like Tuttle and Flagler, several clergymen, members of the Women's Christian Temperance Union (WCTU), the Anti-Saloon League, and even the *Miami Metropolis* represented a powerful coalition that sought to purge undesirable elements from the city. Although often fostering different motives and visions, these forces collectively applied great pressure on Miami's city council, which passed laws aimed at curbing the accessibility and profitability of alcohol.[186]

The *Miami Metropolis* became a powerful voice in this battle. A native Alabamian named Simpson Bobo Dean took over major responsibilities at the newspaper in early 1905. With Dean at the helm, the newspaper aggressively sought to disassociate itself from accusations that it was a mouthpiece for Flagler's railroad empire and the special interests of other capitalists. With the newspaper as his platform, Dean also waged a war against vice, gambling, and the sale and consumption of alcohol in Miami.[187]

Local and national Protestant women and their organizations also proved critical to this moral crusade. In March 1908, Miami's WCTU invited national "saloon smasher" Carrie Nation to help clean up the city. Originally from Kentucky, Nation was a leading temperance advocate. Her visit was the product of the organized and mobilized efforts of Miami's chapter of the WCTU, particularly the work of a northern Methodist named Ida E. Nelson.[188] One young woman called Nelson "Miami's Carrie Nation."[189] In addition to the WCTU, two other local women's organizations were central to this crusade: the Ladies' Afternoon Club and the Baptist Ladies' Aid Society.[190] These efforts culminated from a broader Protestant and Progressive vision of being "reborn" and doing away with the evils that plagued society's moral fabric, particularly in the urban center. Indicative of this, Nation delivered a fiery public speech condemning Miami's "crime and corruption."[191] The *Miami Metropolis* endorsed her message, noting that those in attendance were "imbued with the spirit of order, good government, the abolishment of the open saloon and the purifying of public morals." According to the newspaper, they were "fighting the greatest evil in the world."[192]

Nation's crusade in Miami reveals how a "morality" strongly predicated on racial and class divisions demarcated the city lines. During her trip, she visited a North Miami brothel, where she "found a number of women lounging around in loose attire, smoking and using profane and vulgar language."[193] She also caught an unmarried couple secluded in a darkened room and later found a few men smoking. Nation knocked the cigars from their mouths and yelled, "You tobacco-saturated loafers, why don't you go home to your wives?"[194] Despite the conservative nature of Nation's crusade, she was part of a powerful movement that challenged gender norms by asserting a woman's place in public and political debates.

The growth of the moral crusade against Miami's saloons, vice, and flourishing sexual economy was particularly the result of efforts by a new sheriff: Dan Hardie. Originally from Ohio, Hardie served as the chief of Miami's early fire department. He ran for Dade County sheriff in 1908 on an ambitious campaign to clean up the area. His candidacy statement clearly laid out his objective and modus operandi: "I am for arresting suspicious characters first, and letting them explain afterwards. The lower element in Dade

County, more especially the inhabitants of the North Miami district, are against my principles, and for my part, the feeling is mutual."[195] His message resonated with voters, who elected him that year. He served in that post until 1916, and again in the 1930s.

Hardie's efforts were in large part a response to the reevaluation of land once deemed undesirable to white settlers who, once faced with the city's exponential growth, sought to reclaim it. Real estate prospectors, pioneers, boosters, and other capitalists sought ways to expand their investments and encroached farther north of Miami's limits. As early as 1896, the *Miami Metropolis* advertised North Miami as a "desirable place for residence." This desirability seemed connected to the fact that land deeds there contained "no restrictive conditions," or that it remained legal to consume liquor.[196] In this case, the newspaper marketed land in North Miami as a good investment because it *permitted* saloons to operate freely. Interestingly, the newspaper made a reverse argument when advertising the desirability of Lemon City, an area north of the center and just south of North Miami. Saloons thrived there before Miami became a municipality, which led many to associate the area with crime and violence.[197] By 1896, the *Miami Metropolis* reported, "The removal of all the saloons of our village to Miami is an accomplished fact, significant of the fact that there are not topes," or drunks, "enough left to insure to one a decent living in that business." The correspondent claimed, "The saloon is *dead*. There is not even a 'blind tiger,'" a term used to refer to either a seller of illegal alcohol or the place in which the contraband was sold, "lurking around the hotels."[198] Once vice had been purged from Lemon City, that land had the potential to be a valuable investment. In both instances, saloons proved central to measuring an area's desirability. In order for them to be deemed wholly desirable, however, they could not remain associated with the city's blacks, immigrants, tramps, and vagrants. These communities would have to be forcefully relocated.

Once elected, Hardie got to work redistricting—not purging—Miami's "blind tigers, gambling dens, and so-called necessary evils."[199] Hardie launched numerous raids and campaigns in North Miami, maintaining he would resign before seeing "North Miami ... exist as it used to" or if he proved incapable of keeping it "from being a den of vice."[200] The *Miami Metropolis* frequently praised Hardie and his efforts, elevating him to hero status in higher echelons of society.[201] During a "gambling dive" raid in 1912, Hardie "noiselessly made his way up rickety stairs and suddenly made his presence known in the room by plunging in through a trap door."[202] The raids grew in frequency, intensity, and even theatricality over the years, and by the time

FIGURE 1.2. Cartoon featured in *Miami Metropolis* that coincided with Carrie Nation's visit to the city and anticipating Dan Hardie's election in the coming weeks. Business depended on law enforcement's ability to round up Miami's undesirables. *Miami Metropolis*, March 12, 1908, 1.

he completed his term, Hardie seems to have succeeded in shutting down most of the operations in North Miami and, at times, those in Miami proper. These spaces had been reclaimed for white, respectable residents.

The chronology here is essential to understanding what came next: Miami's 1913 annexation of the "suburb" of unincorporated North Miami. Several civic forces believed Miami's founders had erred in limiting the city boundaries. Some believed it hurt their investments to advertise property outside of the city limits, especially as saloons seeped their way into Miami proper. A 1905 Florida law required that two-thirds of voters from both the existing municipality and the area under consideration approve annexation. These guidelines favored the wishes of the existing municipality, which generally had more voters who could either approve or reject proposals, potentially against the will of the majority of a township or unincorporated area.[203] In this instance, however, wealthy landowners in North Miami were swayed by the promise of higher returns on their investments, particularly Miami proper's promise to help fund new roads, sewers, parks, and a fire station.[204] The purging of vice, crime, and commercial sex from North Miami just *be-*

*fore* this decision was both necessary and of the greatest urgency to seal the deal.

In fact, that same year, residents voted to prohibit alcohol altogether. Debates about whether Miami should go "dry" centered on how such actions would affect investor and city profits. At first, many prominent businessmen believed Miami, increasingly referred to as a fairyland, could coexist with the prohibition of alcohol. In late 1913, a city merchant argued, "A town that has to depend upon the saloon to regulate its real estate values, isn't much of a town."[205] This sentiment did not last very long. After all, would anyone really want to visit a dry fairyland? Several businessmen, particularly those connected to the saloon, petitioned Miami politicians to consider the financial consequences for not only individual operations, but the city at large. Despite the arrival of Prohibition in Miami that year, the city's proximity to the Caribbean guaranteed it was never dry.

All the while, those opposed to the "wets" saw other opportunities in closing down Miami saloons. In particular, Prohibition provided new opportunities for real estate sales, further entrenchment upon the "segregated" districts, and codifying desirable residents in terms of class and race. One Miami investor believed, "Few people will stay away [from Miami] because of the lack of saloons." He maintained, if going dry discouraged some from going to Miami, "in their place will come many *desirable* people." Yet another similarly suggested that if going dry "simply cleans up Avenue D and makes it the fine retail street it ought to be, it is worth" any money the city might lose out on.[206]

These concerted efforts led to the proper development of Miami's redlight district: Colored Town. Of course, North Miami had existed previously and had served as a site for vice since at least 1896 and until Miami annexed it. As the *Miami Metropolis*'s advertisements on the "desirability" of North Miami and Lemon City suggest, however, there was significant debate concerning how that space would best be used. Moral reformers dismantled North Miami's association with vice and crime, as well as the Jim Crow segregation that zoned it as the city's black neighborhood. The vice dens—such as gambling joints and brothels—did not disappear. Rather, they were forcibly relocated. Hardie's efforts pushed these operations—as well as Miami's black, immigrant, and working-class communities who lived in those spaces—away from North Miami and into "the northwestern section of the city adjoining colored town." Many often referred to that district as "Hardieville," in homage to the sheriff who herded and consolidated the city's unsavory spaces away from respectable residents.[207] While Hardieville was ambiguously understood as the northwest area of Colored Town, amorphous borders and existing associations helped consolidate the two sites more generally. Indeed, this red-light district was intentionally zoned and confined within Miami's segregated, black neighborhood, just as urban designers had done several years prior with North Miami. The Municipal Court's criminal dockets reveal a preponderance of arrests in Miami's black neighborhoods, including Hardieville or Colored Town.[208] Miami's black community was inextricably marked by crime, violence, vice, and sexual deviancy.

The white claim to moral authority often helped create physical borders demarcated on racial lines in the city. By summer 1913 Miami mayor John Watson Sr., a North Carolina native, informed the city council of a new ordinance passed in Atlanta that "designate[d] a place for white and a place for colored people to live." He believed Miami's councilmen should consider passing a similar law.[209] It is no coincidence that these efforts were heightened following the widening of Miami's city limits to include land formerly occupied by black residents. A few years later, in 1917, Louis Seitlen, a naturalized Russian immigrant and merchant, pleaded that "a stationary color line" be established, with "a street as a division, instead of an imaginary line." He argued that his property was losing value because several houses east of his lot were being "rented ... to negroes." Seitlen's complaint produced a committee to overlook the curtailing of "certain blocks for white people," so as to "not mix the races." The city council acknowledged that while ordinances meant to segregate the area had been proposed in the past, none had ever been adopted. They acknowledged, however, that a de facto color line— particularly along Avenue I—had been observed for years.[210]

This social and sexual regulation encouraged some blacks, especially within the aspiring middle class, to repudiate Miami's underworld. In 1913, the city council heard a petition "from the colored people of colored town ... requesting ... to take some action of getting rid of a certain white settler in their midst." Although it is unknown why they felt so averse to this man, the record shows they did not deem him "a desirable settler."[211] Other black residents aggressively fought the zoning of their segregated neighborhood as the city's red-light district. One man noted how, following "years of protest," "the decent element of the colored population" had finally managed to purge this "incubus" from its neighborhood.[212]

FROM ITS EARLIEST DAYS, Miami's thriving red-light district proved central to the city's development and success. When saloons opened up throughout Miami, those in Colored Town did not close their doors. Sex, class, and race continued to divide Miami's urban geography, thus giving shape to this budding city's identity as a segregated "model city," with its easy access to transgressive pleasures. The marginalized people who engaged in "unnatural" sex would come to understand their own sexual desires in these terms. Their sexual expressions took shape alongside the formation of the instant City of Miami and its status as an urban frontier with porous margins. This socially and geographically diverse matrix of urban power came to rule Miami in distinct ways, particularly through the exploitation and subjugation of the city's black, ethnic, indigenous, and working-class communities.

Many of the city's white powerbrokers capitalized on this enterprise. This was evident when the owners of the *Metropolis* admitted they had vested interests in building and cleaning up North Miami to protect their property investments there. Similarly, upon completing his term in 1916—a period defined by the coercive relocation of Miami's black community from North Miami into Colored Town—Sheriff Hardie amassed a fortune investing in Miami Beach real estate.[213] Gramling, the municipal judge who commended the police chief's segregation efforts, later became one of the city's most aggressive boosters and the main proponent for securing federal housing in Miami. In many ways, the latter effort was an extension of his earlier visions for the city: racial segregation. As the city grew, Gramling and other urban leaders used New Deal federal funds to push out black communities from the areas of Colored Town near the center of Miami. Like so many others, Gramling profited from the displacement and criminalization of the city's black communities.[214]

Miami developed through complex and often competing permutations of U.S. empire, urban frontierism, and the proliferation of a segregated, sexual underground, all of which fattened the city's pioneer-capitalists' pockets and constituted key ingredients in the formation of a distinct queer frontier. Urban designers would later chip away at the vision of a pure, model city by reinventing Miami as a "fairyland." Pioneer moralists gave way to city promoters hell-bent on "selling" Miami as a site of indulgence and exploration, albeit specifically designed for the enjoyment of a moneyed, white clientele. Miami's urban identity also took shape alongside diverse geographical traditions and histories. Transplants from the U.S. Northeast, Midwest, and South populated the area, where they exploited many of the cultural and social customs of the day, such as Jim Crow segregation. Miami was also a contested colonial space at the intersection of the United States and the Caribbean. Many of Miami's other residents—who also complicated racial hierarchies in the city—hailed from the Caribbean, particularly the then-British colony of the Bahamas. Their presence in Miami helped construct distinct queer erotics in the city.

# BAHAMIANS AND MIAMI'S
# QUEER EROTIC

There is evidently a desire to prevent Miami from becoming a sort
of *refugium peccatorum.*
—BAHAMIAN OBSERVER, 1911

Florida continues to call for our men. It is making special overtures
to get them.
—BAHAMIAN COLONIAL OFFICIAL, 1920

Miami police arrested a twenty-eight-year-old Bahamian migrant named Sam Carey in 1912, accusing him of committing a crime against
nature. This offense was predominantly used to criminalize same-sex acts
between men, especially those like Carey whose race, ethnicity, and class
fueled white mythologies of inherent immorality and criminality. Although
criminal records like Carey's have not survived, other evidence heavily suggests that Carey—like other Bahamian men in Miami's early days—had been
linked to homosexuality and other forms of "sexual perversions."[1]

Although it is unknown whether Carey was ultimately convicted and it
is uncertain if police arrested him for committing a homosexual act, immigration and census records are rich with information that help re-create
the social, cultural, political, and economic circumstances that shaped his
experience in both Miami and at the border. Carey seems to have first migrated to southern Florida in 1909, after having saved enough money to
board an overcrowded schooner from the Bahamian capital of Nassau. Once
in Miami, Carey, then twenty-five, found work on a section gang that tended
and maintained the new railroad tracks along the Florida Keys. He and five
other men lived together in small, intimate quarters stationed along their
given "section," or a track space covering several miles. Carey and four of the
other male laborers—all of whom were also black Bahamians—lived there
as boarders and likely shared beds. The sixth man, the "head" or foreman,
also lived among them. Unlike the laborers he supervised, the foreman was
white and a native Floridian. Although it is unknown whether police arrested Carey for committing sodomy while living in these quarters, it is certain he often found himself in such intimate, male-dominated spaces. Carey

temporarily left Miami for the Bahamas sometime after he was arrested in 1912. He reentered Miami looking for new work in 1914.[2]

While it is possible Carey's trouble with Miami law enforcement prompted his temporary departure, it much more likely reflected Bahamian migratory patterns sparked by the early city's labor demands. His arrest did not prohibit him from reentering the United States two years later. Considering that the modern bureaucratic state was being formalized during this period, it seems most unlikely that Miami police would have shared arrests records with immigration officials. Just the same, U.S. immigration officials, like most people during the era, did not register those who committed homosexual acts as a type of person, or as a trait corresponding to a distinct *sexual* identity. Normalcy was, instead, predominantly measured by one's gender comportment, or whether women appeared feminine and men appeared masculine, which was similarly informed by preconceptions of race, ethnicity, class, and (dis)ability. At times, border inspectors flagged those with anatomical irregularities and those charged with committing acts of moral turpitude.[3]

What became of Carey is uncertain, although the temporary work Miami offered him kept him in the city for at least a few more years. The 1920 census listed him as a Miami resident—unnaturalized—who was not only still single but also still renting a space on his own. He still worked as a laborer, but now in the "cold storage" industry that shipped refrigerated goods. Carey's social stability seems to have slightly improved since he first arrived in Miami.[4]

While settlers populated the urban frontier, Miami's borders proved mostly permeable in the early twentieth century for male migrants like Carey. This was partly because city politicians faced several problems: inadequate infrastructure, a growing population, and an ill-defined local economy. In response to these urban needs, city employers relied heavily on cheap yet experienced labor available in the Bahamas, then a British colony. They particularly looked to the seasonal male migrant.

This black male laborer proved fundamental to the articulation of queer erotic desires in Miami. Historian John D'Emilio has traced the centrality of capitalism—in particular, the tenets of the "free labor" system and the radical transformation of the nuclear family—to the eventual formation of distinct homosexual identities. Bahamians certainly contributed to the free labor system by migrating to Miami. These processes also broke down their household economies, as well as their traditional family models. This, along with greater economic independence, helped disassociate sexual acts from their previous defining core: procreation.[5] Similarly, as Jennifer Ting has suggested, it is critical to interpolate the "sojourner mentality" to make room for, among the migrants' many statuses and experiences, the economic utility of their decisions. Indeed, capitalism's demand for cheap labor heavily produced these "bachelor societies."[6]

This is just a fraction of the story, however. White middle- and upper-class employers hired and often disciplined Bahamian migrants who left their hometowns on the islands to find work building Miami's early infrastructure and growing and harvesting produce. This process not only commodified the migrants' black bodies but also centered a white male gaze on the Bahamians' physicality—which was often described as chiseled and muscular as a result of their intense physical labor. If Miami's labor needs seem to have made its borders largely porous for these Bahamian men before 1924, local law enforcement closely policed them once they entered. This is manifest in the criminal records, which reveal Miami police disproportionately arrested Bahamians for numerous crimes. This included local police's selective enforcement of state laws that criminalized sexual acts between men, namely, sodomy and "crimes against nature."

Miami's labor needs commodified the black male body in critical ways. First, the Bahamians were regarded as ideal workers in building the city's infrastructure and in its growing agricultural industry. Miami stood apart from many other metropolitan areas in the United States during this period in that it did not attract a lot of European immigrants to fill its labor shortages on the cheap. In an era when anti-immigrant and nativist debates escalated in other parts of the country, such anxieties were at least partially muted at Miami's borders because Bahamians were willing to come to the city for just months or years at a time. Initially, most had little or no interest in staying permanently. This was further demarcated by the belief, which proved largely true, that male Bahamian migrants rarely entered the United States with their wives or children. Perhaps more critical was the fact that Miami's labor shortage immediately trumped—but, as we shall see, by no means eradicated—nativist anxieties. Meanwhile, as the British colony struggled with problems such as drought and fiscal recession, seasonal migration to Miami seemed like the most viable option for employment for many Bahamian men.

This transnational backdrop dictated every aspect of the Bahamians' lives, and it contributed greatly to the formation of male-dominated spaces in Miami and female-dominated spaces throughout the Bahamas. Carey's ability to reenter Miami stands in stark contrast to the experiences of many unaccompanied Bahamian women whom immigration officials deemed undesirable and sent back to the islands. Despite the absence of laws that specifically targeted sexual acts between women, their sexualities were policed in other ways. As Eithne Luibhéid has argued, "the policing of immigrant women on the basis of sexuality . . . enabled the discursive production of exclusionary forms of nationalism that took concrete shape in immigration laws and procedures, but extended well beyond the border to produce particular visions of the U.S. nation and citizenry."[7] Indeed, immigration officials and medical inspectors in Miami often deemed Bahamian women morally suspect and turned them away at the port. Viewing these migration patterns through a transnational lens, however, reveals the breakdown of traditional family models that helped alter gender roles on the islands, at the borders, and in Miami. The homosocial spaces similarly increased opportunities for extramarital sex, including prostitution and homosexuality.

With Bahamian women policed at the borders and excluded from entering Miami, a powerful discourse surfaced surrounding the abundance of unaccompanied or single men who were often valued or imagined as fit and able-bodied. As the Bahamian male migrant-laborer became a commodity in Miami, a white upper- and middle-class male gaze centered on his body. This gaze helped give shape to a queer erotic that served as a building block for diverse expressions and subjectivities—and perhaps, in years to come, identities—of gender and sexuality. This took shape alongside understandings of black, ethnic, and working-class cultures and aesthetics. The black Bahamian's availability and vulnerability in Miami and at the border helped solidify which desires and behaviors would be understood as normal, and which would be read as deviant.

The development of this queer erotic found release in the hyperpolicing of Bahamians in Miami's streets, fields, and public and semipublic spaces. Like Bahamian women at the borders, as both black and migrant, Bahamian men bore the brunt of the local law enforcement's surveillance. Although the Bahamians' labor rendered the men desirable under U.S. immigration law prior to 1924, by no means does this suggest that their presence in Miami went uncontested. Nativist sentiments proved to be alive and well in the city. White and black "native" residents alike quickly condemned the Bahamians as immoral and lazy. It is critical, then, to place in this context the Bahamians' overrepresentation among those charged in the city with sodomy and crimes against nature. This greater representation is, in part, a reflection of local law enforcement's greater vigilance and policing of Bahamians more generally. It was also, however, a product of the queer erotic discourse's collision with actual same-sex behaviors.[8] That is, the discourse of the sexually available and able-bodied Bahamian man informed the policing of same-sex acts, while evidence of same-sex acts buttressed the belief that unaccompanied Bahamian men were more sexually "perverse."

## The Gendering of Bahamian Migration

Much like they did in clearing Native American land and the 1898 conclusion of Cuba's war against Spain, Miami entrepreneurs exercised imperialist power to capitalize on tourism, travel, and labor to and from the Bahamas. The lucrative empire that venture capitalist Henry Flagler built went farther south than Miami. He understood that Miami's proximity to the Caribbean would be one of its greatest selling points to wealthy travelers. According to one magazine, Flagler "looked about him and he discovered Florida." After all, "the United States had then no tropical possessions—no Puerto Rico, no Hawaii, no Tutuila, no Philippines, no Guam. Florida was our nearest approach to a tropical resort."[9] A few months after Miami became a city, Flagler hosted the Bahamas' governor-general at his Royal Palm Hotel, thus allowing colonial officers to sample the opulence and modernity he could bring to Nassau by way of Miami. To further Flagler's cause, upon the governor-general's arrival, "the American flag was hauled down and the British flag run up."[10] These efforts proved effective. With the railroad blazing through Miami, Flagler made sure travelers could board a steamship from Miami to Nassau and Key West. Flagler then struck a deal with the Bahamian colonial government that provided him with an annual subsidy for his enterprises. In return, he provided the Bahamas—and Miami—regular mail and freight service through his steamships. To round it up, he built luxury hotels in Nassau, including the Royal Victoria and the Colonial.[11]

Considering that the Bahamas was "not well equipped for providing the many and varied wants of the capricious and exacting tourist," it became dependent on its northern neighbor. In Nassau, one man maintained, "nearly everything that a hotel requires must be imported from the United States or manufactured on the hotel ground."[12] In Bimini, the Bahamian district nearest to Miami, colonial officials noted that "all the foodstuffs imported direct came from Miami." Similarly, in 1922, a resort hotel in Bimini even imported its water from Miami; the government observed that Bahamians "in the good grace of the Hotel management . . . enjoy the luxury of a good drink of water."[13]

The cultures and economies of Miami and the Bahamas were indelibly linked. Miami brought "modernity" to the Bahamas and stimulated travel to the islands. Meanwhile, travel to the Bahamas attracted visitors to Miami and provided it with a steady flow of laborers. Nassau became Miami's "sister city."[14] Travel to the Bahamas, Cuba, and other Caribbean destinations was so critical to the tourist economy of Miami—the "logical mainland port for the near West Indies"—that in 1920 the Miami Chamber of Commerce petitioned the U.S. State Department to waive passport requirements for travel from the city to the Bahamas and Cuba.[15]

While some Bahamians boarded these steamships for tourism and to visit family, they more frequently used them to find work.[16] The Miami area had long housed a sizeable Bahamian population. For Bahamians in the late nineteenth and early twentieth centuries, traveling to and from southern Florida proved no more difficult than crossing from one island in the archipelago to another. Like the thousands of Europeans and Asians who entered Ellis and Angel Islands before restrictive immigration laws curbed their passage, economic opportunity attracted the Bahamians to Miami. Just as Cubans had historic ties with Florida cities such as Key West and Ybor City in the nineteenth century, Bahamians had long frequented the Florida Keys as fishers, spongers, and turtlers.[17]

Bahamians specifically looked to Miami after municipal incorporation in 1896. British West Indians were particularly mobile during this period largely due to the construction of the Panama Canal and other U.S. operations throughout the Americas that provided steady work.[18] Unlike most other British West Indians, Bahamians primarily found work in Florida. Those from the northern islands, such as Abaco, Bimini, Cat Island, and Eleuthera, especially traveled to Miami.[19] Roughly one-fifth of the entire Bahamian population left for Florida between 1900 and 1920.[20] There they earned significantly higher wages and cordoned off West Indian competition. Some Bahamians told stories of Miami as the "young Magic City where money could be 'shaken from trees.'"[21]

Their gravitation toward Miami was further impelled by the deterioration of local economies. In particular, the global market saw prices plummet for the Bahamas' key exports: pineapples and sisal. A colonial backwater, the Bahamas suffered from lack of transportation, wireless communication, paved roads, and technological advancements in agriculture.[22] The Bahamas also intermittently endured both shortages and deluges of water, as the islands were often plagued with drought and pummeled by tropical storms or hurricanes.[23] Bahamians sought to counteract their economic dependence on agriculture by developing their sponging industry and working more aggressively to attract tourists.[24] During the first two decades of the twentieth century, however, seasonal work in Florida offered Bahamians higher wages and relief from hunger and poverty. In turn, Bahamians proved instrumental to the expansion of southern Florida's agribusiness.[25]

Bahamians responded to Miami's desperate call for labor and built much

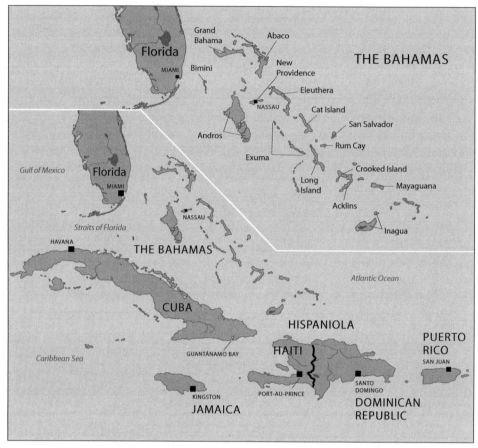

MAP 2.1. Greater Antilles and the Bahamas in the Caribbean in relation to southern Florida. Map by Eamonn Edge.

of its early structures. The sparsely populated yet ambitious city quickly outgrew its limited workforce. South Florida pioneer-developer and Pennsylvania native George Merrick recalled how all of Miami's "heavy laborers were Bahaman negroes" during the late nineteenth century. After all, "Georgia negroes did not come in any volume until after 1900," or after the completion of the railroad Bahamians built. Merrick singled out the Bahamian's proven "skill in masonry building" that could withstand Atlantic hurricanes.[26] The Bahamians' familiarity with the area's tropical climate and agriculture helped make them indispensable.

The construction and agricultural jobs that attracted Bahamian men to Miami created homosocial spaces that facilitated queer expressions, desires, and acts. Prior to 1905, or when Miami's port remained largely inaccessible,

Bahamian patterns of migration to southern Florida were largely family-oriented. This quickly changed as Miami's labor needs shifted and the port became cheaper and easier for Bahamians to access.[27] After that, Bahamian migration to Miami was largely male. Bahamian men entered Miami as seasonal or temporary migrant workers for a few months at a time. The colonial secretary's report on migration patterns for 1912 reveals that 1,909 men left the Bahamas for Florida that year, while 1,922 returned to the islands. The migration of Bahamian women was noticeably smaller: 719 left for Florida and 626 returned to the Bahamas.[28] Other estimates for these early years suggest that the number of male migrants was higher.[29]

Considering the gendered labor division that interpreted this type of intense physical work as masculine, it is no surprise that younger Bahamian men represented the largest group of migrants who entered Miami. Census records from the Bahamas indicate the population on the islands aged forty-five and over increased about 10 percent from 1911 to 1921. Meanwhile, those aged five to thirty-four—as even the youngest in that category would be able-bodied and deemed prime for such physical labor in the next decade—*decreased* nearly 11 percent during that same period. Most of those younger men found themselves in Miami.[30]

The onset of the Great War in 1914 further altered the islands' demographics and facilitated transnational homosocial spaces. Hundreds of Bahamians volunteered for the British West India Regiment or joined as regulars in other forces during the war.[31] Far more, however, had already left for Miami. When a U.S. journalist asked an older Bahamian if he had sons serving in the war, the man simply responded: "No'm; dey's all in Miami, my sons is, all in Miami."[32] The Bahamian census reveals a decrease in the colony's population, dipping from 55,944 in 1911 to 53,031 ten years later.[33]

Meanwhile, southern Florida's drain on Bahamian male labor created new anxieties on the islands, including the breakdown of the family and the dearth of male laborers. In early 1913 Nassau's *Tribune* presented "a matter that for some time past has given us great concern." It noted that despite aggressive labor recruitment in the Bahamas, workers gravitated toward Florida and caused "a scarcity of labour in these islands." Higher wages pushed Bahamians to Miami. "It seems ... useless to offer men 2s.[shillings] per day when they can take a night's run and find themselves where they can earn 6s. per day.... If they go, can we blame them?"[34] A Bahamian commissioner stationed in the Long Island district complained that "most of the able-bodied men ... are now in Miami."[35] By 1920, the Bahamian government lamented the scarcity of men in Watling's Island, or San Salvador: "The Island is almost denuded of young men. I regret to report that ... there is not a single man on the whole island.... If something out of the ordinary doesn't turn up soon, the district will be menless, because the married as well as the single are going."[36] These fears were not just expressed by colonial sources. One Bahamian fieldworker wrote to a Nassau newspaper that the mass exodus was devastating the islands: "Some people dun no what a hard time we is gwine to have dis ear all of the sponger is lefin the colony gwine to Miami to work."[37]

Despite the relative ease in migrating to Miami during this period, most Bahamian men did not leave their lives and families behind lightly. Evidence suggests that Bahamians paid close attention to a given season's wages and opportunities, thus making family separation less predictable. In some recorded years, such as 1912, the net migration was considerably closer to zero. Just the previous year, 1,266 more Bahamians left the islands than came back. After 1912, net migration further mirrored this higher number, suggesting that the 1911–12 season was anomalous.[38] If wages in southern Florida did not seem competitive and the men could secure good employment in the Bahamas, they often stayed put. This seems to have been the case in 1915 and 1917, for instance, when Bahamians observed "decreased rates of wages in Florida" and more departed the state than left the islands.[39]

### Bahamian Women and the Sexually Suspect

While these migration patterns created homosocial male spaces in Miami, they similarly created female-dominant spaces in the Bahamas. The emigration drained so many young men and their manual labor from the islands that by 1921 the male-to-female ratio of those aged twenty-five to thirty-four in the Bahamas reached 1.3:2. That is, among this age group, the population of women in the Bahamas was nearly double that of men.[40]

These gender-imbalanced migration patterns placed new burdens on women left behind on the islands that challenged traditional gender norms in the Bahamas.[41] A Bahamian colonial official recalled an instance in the Watlings Island district when the community mourned the death of one of its residents. Because the settlement was "denuded of men," "women had to be the pall-bearers," a role generally associated with masculinity.[42] Another Bahamian expressed concern that "women have to do all the farm work to maintain themselves and their children, for in the majority of cases in which the men have emigrated, the remittances to their families do not compensate for moral and financial losses."[43]

Evidence suggests transnational anxieties about other "moral ... losses" in the Bahamas resulting from these predominantly male migrations, such as the breakdown of traditional family models and multiple forms of women's sexual transgression.[44] Most Bahamian women remained on the islands with any children a couple may have had. The men's prolonged and disruptive absence from the islands seems to have caused several women to turn to other men for intimacy. This was not unlike what some of the Bahamian men did in Miami with other men or new women. In some instances, both parents migrated to Miami, abandoning their children altogether.[45] The men who made the trip to Florida, Bahamian colonial officials claimed, "leave their families to punish." "The wife or mother endures these hardships for a time" but later decides to go to Miami as well, "leaving . . . little children in care of her old parents who are not able to look after themselves." This practice led to "scores of children . . . strolling over the District, with no proper care or correction." Local governments worried this would breed "thieves and vagabonds."[46] In Miami and the Bahamas, many expressed concern that these circumstances might create a new generation of idle laborers and vagrants— a recipe, they believed, for undesirable behaviors and transgressions.

Women and children left behind on the islands made do in the absence of able-bodied husbands, lovers, fathers, and brothers by discarding some traditional roles dictated by patriarchy and seeking new trades, including sex work. Bahamian women entered new industries, including the service industry and others connected to tourism. Some employed existing skills to perform work at home. Women from Rum Cay who were largely abandoned on the islands by their male counterparts started using unsold sisal to make hats, for instance.[47] Others attempted to sell sharkskin as a substitute for cowhide leather.[48] While evidence does not specifically reveal that married or partnered women turned to prostitution during these times, colonial sources certainly indicate increased anxieties over the pervasiveness of brothels and sex work during this period. Whether these women were single or abandoned wives, by 1917 the Bahamian colonial government proposed an act to regulate sex work, particularly in the capital, from which most schooners headed to Florida departed.[49] These "moral . . . losses," colonial officials worried, had also led to an increase in venereal disease. While sex work in the Bahamas no doubt contributed to this, colonial sources saw the greatest increase in infection among "seamen returning from their voyages abroad." The breakdown of morals and the family, they believed, was widespread and occurring in both the Caribbean and Florida.

These gendered migration patterns—and, perhaps, the social circumstances they produced—also contributed to the belief among U.S. immigration officials in Miami that unmarried Bahamian women might be prostitutes and therefore undesirable entrants. In order to get to Miami, Bahamians boarded small schooners "so crowded with people that there was barely standing room on their decks."[50] Many complained that vessels were "over-crowded" and equipped with "absolutely no comforts, not even a latrine."[51] Some Bahamian officials suggested that the voyage was particularly troublesome for women passengers traveling alongside many unaccompanied men. They could not imagine how anyone would "take passage on such boats unless compelled to by necessity."[52] They believed any woman who made the voyage to Miami under such precarious conditions did so in desperation—which rendered her vulnerable to immoral influences—or would otherwise be read as suspect for undergoing a passage unbecoming of a decent woman.

Once Bahamians arrived at the Miami port, they were met by U.S. immigration officials, who included a physician and quarantine officer. These authorities boarded the vessel and conducted medical inspections of the incoming migrants, weeding out those deemed undesirable. According to one Miami source, 10 percent of the Bahamian migrants had been "sent back for one reason and another, in failing to meet the requirements of the immigration laws." Those "who appeared to be in such a condition as to perhaps become a public charge" and "persons of questionable character" were "immediately returned from whence they came."[53] The inspectors at the port of entry were charged with identifying and reporting "all insane persons, idiots, persons suffering from a loathsome or a dangerous contagious disease, and all persons whose mental or physical condition will affect their ability to earn a living."[54] While most male Bahamian migrants seem to have had little problems entering through Miami's ports, the city's borders were by no means impermeable. A 1916 U.S. immigration report noted a "smuggling" operation that sought to bring "approximately 35 negroes" from the Bahamas into the United States. These Bahamians were caught and deported. These anxieties often crossed with questions of "immorality."[55] It is likely that women were among these intercepted Bahamians.

Upon arrival, the quarantine officer conducted "a veritable quiz" on the Bahamians wishing to enter the United States that served as a means of excluding undesirables, particularly women suspected of being prostitutes. The questions asked of these women, one Bahamian believed, were "too personal and embarrassing." He maintained that there was "evidently a desire to prevent Miami from becoming a sort of *refugium peccatorum*," or a refuge for sinners.[56] In addition to these interrogations, it seems likely that, as Luibhéid has shown with the surveillance of Chinese women at the U.S. borders, immigration officers also policed Bahamian women by making individual assessments of their bodies and clothing, which were thought to offer "possible clues about 'inner character,'" or sexual propriety.[57] One Bahamian observer believed the quarantine officers' "praiseworthy . . . effort[s]" had "sternly closed the doors to questionable characters that have not come to seek a living by *bona fide* means," at least in part a reference to Miami's sexual economy.[58] This represented one of the main factors that made Bahamian men more mobile and why far fewer single women made Miami home during this period.

At the Miami-Caribbean border, a single, Bahamian woman seeking work became cause for alarm, her gender comportment and sexuality immediately suspect. "It is useless for any unmarried woman of the working class to seek admission," noted one man, "unless she have there some married female relative, known to be living a respectable life, to come forward and stand sponsor for her." This gave both the medical and emigrant officers in Miami a great deal of power and discretion when making these decisions. The Bahamian observer described the emigrant officer as "vigilant as the fabled Cerberus," a reference to the hellhound guarding the underworld in Greek myth. He told the story of one young Bahamian woman who tried to enter Miami. A man met her at the port with a marriage license in hand hoping to change her status to that of a respectable married woman and thereby eligible to disembark and settle in Miami. It did not work. The "obdurate" officer did not allow the ceremony to take place on the vessel nor could the "distressed young woman" set foot on Miami soil. The captain was ordered to take her— at that point, in "tears and sobs"—back to the Bahamas.[59]

The gender imbalance this created greatly contributed to cultural perceptions that Bahamians on the islands remained attached and under the watchful eyes of women and traditional families while those who ventured to Miami had greater access to sexual experiences outside the traditional family unit, including extramarital and sometimes commercialized cross-sex and same-sex intimacies. In 1909, a colonial official from the Andros district maintained that several of the migrants returning from Florida were inclined to "what is called a sporting life," often a euphemism that included paying for sex and suggesting that Bahamians had grown accustomed to idleness and vice more generally in Miami.[60] It was also difficult to ignore that the Bahamians in Miami had more income available to them. Instead of working again in Bahamian fields or finding work at sea, those who had traveled to Miami "more fully develop[ed] what in their natures appeals to the lower creation," believed one Bahamian official.[61]

In stark contrast to the majority of the available employment in Miami, several plantation jobs on the islands catered to entire Bahamian families. A 1913 ad in Nassau's *Tribune* promised "employment for every and any one and all the time on our sisal plantations down west." The company offered "small cottages for men and their families" on the plantation.[62] Most seasonal jobs in Miami, however, attracted younger men who sent much of their wages to their families in the Bahamas. These remittances helped sustain entire communities on the islands and became a critical component of the Bahamian economy.[63]

The single or unaccompanied women who did manage to make it past the "fabled Cerberus" at the border were frequently met with suspicion by Miami law enforcement and residents alike, who associated them with transgressive behaviors. Some of these Bahamian women became lodgers in others' homes. Unaccompanied women and those who traveled with their children in the absence of an adult man leased boarding spaces with families, many of whom were U.S. African American. In these intimate spaces, Bahamian women often met other female or male lodgers. While tensions certainly existed between Bahamians and U.S. African Americans, who often competed for work and were pitted against each other by Miami nativists, they also often intermarried and united in the face of tightening racial codes that targeted them as blacks. As Melanie Shell-Weiss has shown, Bahamian women were much more likely to marry U.S. African American men than Bahamian men were to find U.S. African American wives.[64] One possible explanation may be that these women, many of whom were deserted in some way back in the Bahamas, found comfort in their new and perhaps liberating circumstances in Miami. Some Bahamian women did not marry at all. Indeed, numerous transnational effects heavily informed how their lives unfolded. In this regard, interethnic marriages and the sharing of intimate spaces with others represented another way they became transgressive. Police frequently targeted Bahamian women for a variety of offenses, including vagrancy, disorderly conduct, and fornication.

### Bahamian Men as a Source of Queer Erotic Desire

Meanwhile, the oversaturation of single, able-bodied Bahamian men in Miami helped forge a queer erotic focused on the black laborer's perceived masculinity and hypersexuality. As his body and the labor it produced became a valued commodity in the new city, a white male gaze centered on the Bahamian man and its physical possibilities. Often erotic and sensual, this gaze inventoried and made legible his physical strength, vigor, subservience, and ability to be disciplined.

Some cultural observances, delineated through class and gender divisions in both the Bahamas and Miami, marked Bahamian men and their bodily comportments as transgressive and outside the norm. Returning Bahamians often showed off the newfound "fame and fortune" they had procured in

Miami, or the "'promised land,'" by dressing "flashily" back on the islands. "The splendid appearance of those boys from the States stood out in striking contrast to us ill-fashionably clad country lads," remembered one man. Oftentimes, this consumerist seduction spurred first-time sojourners to make the trek to Miami.[65] Another observer noted how returning migrants brought "some extraordinary clothes (and it is now *de rigeur* [*sic*] to change three times on Sunday)."[66] Those who returned to the islands, claimed a government official from Eleuthera, spent their time "in idleness, lounging from place to place, airing their acquired ill-manners and fantastically made clothes."[67] In the early 1910s, an official from the Exuma district complained about disturbances of the peace and cited the returning migrants as the cause. Their exodus forced Bahamian officials to apply "firm measures" to restore order.[68] British colonial officers believed Miami, as well as the greater access to capital found there, had corrupted Bahamian migrants.

Conversely, once the Bahamians entered the United States, local whites and blacks marked them as different and outside the norm by taking note of the Bahamian's accent, "loose-fitting" clothes, shorter pants, and hairstyle. Several observed that West Indians did not "slick back" their hair as was then customary in many parts of the United States. They were "not one of the *city boys*."[69]

Gender-imbalanced migration patterns found hundreds of young, able-bodied Bahamian men unaccompanied in Miami and thus created bachelor societies in the city. This was not unlike much of the rest of early Miami, including early white Miami, where male-dominated spaces with little to no regular access to women were the norm. Early settler John Sewell recalled that "one of the most striking things about Miami ... was that our new citizens were all men—and mostly young men. They came from everywhere." He claimed that Julia Tuttle's Miami Hotel—which he dubbed the "headquarters for all the newcomers"—housed "only one lady" at first.[70]

Both skilled and unskilled laborers, thus including the Bahamians, similarly found themselves in homosocial environments. "Some boarded at regular boarding houses, some lived in tents and some built small board houses that we called shacks," observed Sewell. It was common for men without families "to get together and build a shack, and these shacks were scattered everywhere." Emotions and tensions could easily come to a boil in these intimate and transitional spaces. Sewell recounted a quarrel between two workers who shacked together. One of the men, a carpenter, decided to saw the shack in half and move his partial home elsewhere.[71] These men often shared a bed, too.[72] While these circumstances could easily turn sexual, they more generally facilitated an intense closeness among men, what Nayan

Shah calls "stranger intimacy."[73] Miami's Bahamians often lived in these homosocial environments, which facilitated the construction of a distinct queer erotic in the city.

One particularly vivid account of the homoeroticism bred by the intimate and homosocial spaces of the urban frontier took place in the opulent winter villa Vizcaya. In the early 1910s, a white tycoon from Chicago named James Deering chose Miami as the site for his new home. He welcomed famed painter John Singer Sargent, also white, to his estate in 1917. Sargent delighted in its tropical atmosphere, where he found "a mine of sketching."[74] Although Sargent is best known for his portraits of the upper classes in Europe and the United States, he produced numerous provocative watercolors of Miami's working class. This included the villa's black laborers.

Scholars who have analyzed these works have assumed the black men Sargent painted in Vizcaya were U.S. African Americans, but the evidence heavily suggests otherwise.[75] Bahamians who worked the fields and built past structures in the city—including streets, railroads, and even the Overseas Railway that extended the railroad to Key West—were more likely Sargent's inspiration.[76] Unlike black Bahamians, "native" blacks throughout the United States were disproportionately overdrafted and represented a greater proportion of draft evaders during the Great War.[77] When registration was mandated for the draft in June 1917, a Miami newspaper reported that "in the negro precincts many of those who registered were Bahamans and declared themselves British subjects." That these men did not know "whether they would be subject to draft in this country" and that they "preferred to serve in the British army" bought them extra time to find temporary work in Miami, such as completing Vizcaya.[78]

Sargent's watercolors of these men provide a rare glimpse into the homosocial world of early Miami and the elite's gaze and fetishization of the black laborer's body. Like much of early Miami, Vizcaya remained a male-dominated space with few women during its construction.[79] In one of Sargent's paintings (fig. 2.1), three black men rest in the sandbar of Biscayne Bay under some mangrove trees. They can be seen cooling down and taking a break from the intense physicality and heat they endured at work. All three men are stripped naked and appear to be only partially aware of the painter's presence. Sargent captured their exposed and muscular bodies in surprising detail for a watercolor. In a separate canvas (fig. 2.2), Sargent painted another black man straddling a fallen tree trunk on the beach. This worker is aware of Sargent's gaze and is, in fact, posing for him. Not only is he staring directly at Sargent, his pose is suggestively inviting. There are two major perspectives here: the subject and the artist. In many ways, Sargent's perspec-

FIGURE 2.1. John Singer Sargent, *The Bathers*, 1917, watercolor and gouache on off-white wove paper, 40.1 × 53 cm. Worcester Art Museum, MA, Sustaining Membership Fund, 1917.91.

tive is more revealing, as his eye for the erotic is palpable. His brush captured the ripples in the worker's muscular shoulders, forearms, pectorals, abdominals, buttocks, and legs. In yet another watercolor (fig. 2.3), Sargent used his craft to capture a muscular and naked black bather exposing his penis, which is possibly painted as erect.[80] These paintings are among a handful of works Sargent produced in Miami featuring naked black laborers.[81] One art historian noted how "exoticism ... played a role in the allure of the figure, the intimate bowerlike setting, and the sense of a voyeuristic peek into a more carefree world." Indeed, Sargent's "images present a vibrant, forceful realism while subtly projecting emotions, desires, and intuitions as their visual subtext."[82]

These artworks suggest a white middle-class and elite heightened awareness of the black male body as a source of eroticism and hypermasculinity. Historians have shown that working-class and immigrant cultures of this period did not yet organize or understand their sexual practices as either

FIGURE 2.2. John Singer Sargent, *Man and Trees, Florida*, 1917, watercolor, gouache, and graphite on white wove paper, 53.3 × 39.7 cm. Gift of Mrs. Francis Ormond, 1950, acc. no. 50.130.59, Metropolitan Museum of Art, NY. www.metmusuem.org.

FIGURE 2.3. John Singer Sargent, *Bather, Florida*, 1917, watercolor on white wove paper, 40 × 53 cm. Gift of Mrs. Francis Ormond, 1950, acc. no. 50.130.60, Metropolitan Museum of Art, NY. www.metmusuem.org.

homosexual or heterosexual. They remained "normal" by way of their masculinity; that is, they did not transgress gender norms and were less likely to be (or admit to being) the "passive" or receptive partner in a same-sex encounter, usually with a "fairy" or effeminate man, or with an adolescent or younger man.[83] Evidence suggests the Bahamian migrants in Miami shared this form of sexual fluidity, too. In addition, there is a long history of a white male eroticization of the black male's body that dates back to slavery in the Americas.[84] At least part of this black erotic stemmed from the workers' servitude and the white employer's power over him. Suggestive of this is the fact that Sargent's Miami subjects were lounging naked in what was known as "servants' beach."[85]

As a lifelong bachelor, Sargent's own sexual proclivities have been the subject of debate—both during his lifetime and posthumously—suggesting that these experiences articulated a form of eroticism that later coincided with emerging sexual subjectivities and possibly identities.[86] Sargent's oeuvre demonstrates he had an affinity for the working-class male body and his perceived stalwart black masculinity. In particular, he had a penchant for making "non-Caucasian people" the subjects of his art, even though this often did not prove a lucrative enterprise. This produced a tension between his "repression and self-expression."[87] As Trevor Fairbrother has suggested, "If Sargent suffered through sexual inhibition or socially induced shame about homosexuality, he may have been able to express this part of his personality" through his art.[88] Sargent also kept an album of male nudes—not unlike those of the black laborers in Miami—in his personal collection.[89]

The erotic quality evident in Sargent's paintings parallels the works of contemporary watercolorist Winslow Homer, who traveled to the Bahamas, Cuba, and Florida beginning in 1884. In Nassau, he captured the rugged musculature and masculinity of black conch and coral divers. As with Sargent, many have speculated about Homer's sexual appetites. Homer had an intense and devoted relationship with his flatmate, Albert Kelsey, whom he drew in the Bahamas riding the back of a turtle in the nude. That is, Sargent was not alone in identifying a queer black erotic in the Bahamian worker.[90]

Another vantage point to this phenomenon is evident in a 1910 short story, "Shark," by the white U.S. author Richard Washburn Child. One literary journal called it "fantastic to the verge of absurdity."[91] The story is set in southern Florida with the Caribbean plainly in sight. The author relays the story through a conversation between a white watchman and a "rum smuggler, a real 'Conch'"—a common nickname for Bahamians, usually white or light-skinned.[92] The two men discussed a black man named "Jim" Hutten who one day encountered a massive shark, described as "she," who became enamored of him. The female shark grew jealous of a petite black woman Jim had been courting and killed her in the water. Jim ultimately took revenge on the love-struck fish by knifing her. The New York Times applauded Child's "unusual love story."[93] Another critic, however, called it "unthinkably unclean, and an offence against good taste."[94] In fact, the author didn't shy away from queer storylines. A few years later, Child published another short story titled "The Feminist" that addressed anxieties over the "New Woman," including suggestions of the female "invert" or lesbian.[95]

In addition to portraying Jim's affections and circumstances as perverse and unnatural, Child's story also points to the construction of a black male erotic, particularly in his descriptions of the Bahamian body. Although Jim is described simply as a "Florida nigger," several descriptions reveal he is of Bahamian descent. The watchman noted that years before when Jim worked "on the docks at Miami," he caught him "singing and grinning like a mainland nigger." He believed, "No island niggers can point up to happiness like 'em. There's more joy in a minute in a Florida nigger than all there is in Nassau or the Barbados. There's too much philosophizing in an island nigger." The narrator also referred to the other man conversing with the watchman as the *real* "Conch," suggesting that despite Jim's Bahamian heritage, he was now more Floridian than West Indian (the fact that he was "blacker than the rest of 'em" likely also contributed to this distinction).[96] Contemporary readers also understood Jim as Bahamian. One critic summarized the plot as "the affection of a female shark for a West Indian negro."[97]

In his "tale of the West Indian seas," the author painted a vivid picture of Jim's stalwart physicality, almost always in the nude and exposed to both the reader and other characters.[98] The reader first meets Jim as a "giant negro, stripped" of his clothing. The watchman describes him as statuesque: "Look at the size of him! Look at his arms, as big as my legs! And a neck like a windlass!" The watchman is so taken by his appearance that he ponders if it is even possible for Jim to have ever been a "little nigger." He posed, "They're pretty—black velvet, eh?"[99] In this and other descriptions, the men gaze at Jim's muscular body in utter amazement of its massive size, constructing it as a distinct erotic aesthetic.

Much like the Bahamians who built Miami's railroads and early structures, Jim attained his muscular aesthetic by performing arduous physical labor for white employers. The reader learns that earlier in his life, Jim "went to work in them phosphate camps," likely in central Florida. While there, the foreman whipped him. Jim grew in size through his work. This physical labor "put them hunks of meat below his arms and that upholstery of muscles below his chests." When Jim finished his work there, he returned "to the East Coast a silent nigger."[100] He had been violently disciplined, his strengthened body, a consequence of that discipline, now toned for his white employer. These men understood that the erotic images of Jim's engorged biceps and chiseled abdominal muscles were in fact a direct consequence of his violence-induced physical labor. Similarly, the numerous observations the men made of how Jim "pulled off his clothes and stood up, stripped and black" help locate the construction of the laboring black body as a source of erotic desire, one simultaneously defined by its strapping masculinity and its disciplined subservience.[101] To several white contemporaries, Jim's black skin meant he was able-bodied and perfectly suited to and capable of performing demanding manual labor. Jim's blackness also rendered him vulnerable to corporal and legal discipline and punishment.

This permutation served as the crux of the black Bahamian's eroticism—and homoeroticism, in particular—in Miami. Many contemporary U.S. Americans interpreted urbanization and cities as "breeding grounds of 'luxury' and 'effeminacy.'" This helped cement the romantic view and desire for the "natural," which would have included Miami's unindustrial tropical landscape. It would have also included the manual labor performed by the Bahamians, as well as the Bahamians themselves, who were believed to be closer to nature and farther removed from civilization.[102] One of Miami's wealthy white pioneer-entrepreneurs boasted that he had found "the most wonderful Bahama negroes you ever saw." Bahamians throughout Miami were often hired in the growing service industry, where they tended to white visitors as wait staff, bellhops, and hotel maids. As an added attraction for the city's white visitors, these migrant-laborers were also hired to steer gondolas at one of the swankiest hotels in Miami Beach. The white entrepreneur who hired them observed how these Bahamian men would "be stripped to the waist" and made to "wear big brass rings." This distinct aesthetic sought to construct the Bahamian in Miami as innately primitive, atavistic, inherently sexual, and subservient to white desires. Further resonating with the frontier aesthetic that sought to associate the "exotic" Bahamians with the rawness of savagery and nature, the wealthy businessman also noted how his black migrant-employees might also be forced to wear "necklaces of live crabs or crawfish."[103] As N. D. B. Connolly has noted, this colonial experience proved integral to cementing Miami's early image as a place of leisure for white consumers: "At practically every site of white leisure, nonwhite servitude proved integral to the everyday theatrics and comforts of seaside recreation."[104]

Evidence also supports that, in at least some instances, the rendering of the muscular black Bahamian man may have also been the work of a distinct *white* fiction—perhaps even a fantasy—developed in Miami. One U.S. African American man who resided in Florida in the early 1920s recalled that Bahamians in Miami "didn't know much about vegetables" and that "many looked small and undernourished."[105] Other sources similarly suggested that the malnourished Bahamian was, in part, a product of his deprived diet. Studies during this era revealed that the U.S. South was plagued by pellagra, a vitamin deficiency disease that often left sufferers looking gaunt and sickly. A 1914 pellagra study of the Bahamas observed that "local conditions seem to be ideal for the disease." In addition to a poor diet, exposure to bacterial infection was high among the islands' black populations.[106] Colonial reports from the Bahamas and some contemporary photographs substantiate claims that many of the islanders were malnourished and, at times, even starving.[107]

All this suggests the possibility that contemporary renderings of the muscular black Bahamian physique may not have been completely accurate but rather a white erotic construction informed by the powerful race and class relations that subjugated the migrants as both desirable and disciplinable.

Surely, it is possible that those Bahamians who worked in Vizcaya may have simply been better nourished, particularly compared to those remaining on the islands or who only entered the United States for a short period of time. It is also possible that these men attained a more chiseled physical musculature through the demanding manual labor their employment required. Whether fiction or surreal representation, the black Bahamian body as object and distinct aesthetic was, in part, defined by its *labor* potential—and therefore, its greater desirability. That is, the Bahamian's body was readily available, cheap, and subject to white discipline and fetishization.

Such erotic imagery is suggestive of a local articulation of the era's pathologization of the black man as sexually perverse by way of his very "nature." Although some scientific or pseudoscientific studies predated it, what we now understand as Anglo-European sexology emerged as a distinct field by the late nineteenth century. It was that discursive field that put sexual "inverts" and homosexuals under the microscope, thereby constructing them as pathologized individuals and communities.[108] Sexology was in conversation with contemporary discussions of eugenics and "scientific racism" invested in identifying the devolution and atavism of blacks in the United States.[109] Some sexologists sought to "naturalize" the black man's sexuality as animalistic and savage. The narrative of the "black rapist" bent on violating the white woman's chastity was probably the most popular manifestation of this.[110] An 1894 editorial published in a medical journal noted, "The brutal and uncontrollable passion of the negro has been traced to a variety of causes, the chief of which has been referred to [as] a perversion of his sexual instincts and ungoverned sexual passion."[111] To this end, forms of discipline and punishment, including lynching, proved ineffective and did not curb recidivism. It was this belief that led some to endorse "preventative" measures to contain the black man's uncontrollable lust, including circumcision and castration.[112]

Under this logic, the black man in Miami naturally acted out on his sexual appetites, defined as both perverse and insatiable. This was evident in Jim's relationship with the shark, which recalled a form of sodomy in Miami. After all, that same state felony also criminalized acts of bestiality. "Shark" also reveals the white man's gaze on the Bahamian's body, regardless of whether his muscled physique was real or an idealized fiction dreamed up by a white imaginary.

The construction of the black man's sexuality and body, especially he who resided in the U.S. South, as perverse and animalistic served a much greater purpose: the curtailment of his liberty. This is why the West Indian still living in the islands was deemed less attractive. *That* West Indian was too preoccupied with "philosophizing" for the white man, who preferred the "joy" and physicality found "in a Florida nigger." Although nineteenth-century sodomy laws largely served as "regulatory gap" for nonconsensual sex, this gradually shifted as such same-sex sexual behaviors became more directly associated with a pathologized individual.[113] Scholars have documented that sodomitic rape, particularly anxieties over boys and young men as "rape victims," permeated discussions of immigrant "perversion" into the 1920s.[114] The image of the immigrant as "perverse" and the black man as "rapist" thus converged with the Bahamian.

Even though U.S. immigration law had not yet conceived of a distinct category of exclusion for homosexuality, border officials and police understood certain immigrants as sexually perverse. In the absence of a discernible understanding of the "homosexual" individual, immigration law "lumped together aliens who exhibited gender inversion, had anatomical defects, or engaged in sodomy as degenerates." The latter "was a racial and economic construct that explained 'the immorality of the poor.'" "Perversion" was associated "with 'primitive' races and lower classes, and poor immigrants and nonwhites were believed to be especially inclined."[115] As one contemporary wrote, "It scarcely needs to be mentioned that Americans frequently blame one or the other ethnic group for homosexuality."[116]

Although Bahamians were never excluded as aggressively, there are parallels between their experience and that of Chinese migrants. Chinese women were restricted by U.S. immigration law as early as 1875 as a result of their perceived deviant sexualities, the belief that they were being brought into the United States for "lewd and immoral purposes." Along with the 1875 Page Law, other immigration laws, such as the 1882 Immigration Act, the 1882 Chinese Exclusion Act, and the 1885 Contract Labor Law, further restricted their admission and codified exclusions under a rubric of those likely to become a "public charge." As early as 1875, U.S. immigration law privileged the reunification of the traditional nuclear family, which was measured against those who challenged the heterosexual and patriarchal social order. Restrictions at the border based on one's nonnormative sexuality—real or imagined—were further strengthened by the 1917 Immigration Act's ban on those with a "constitutional psychopathic inferiority." In the era of sexual pathology, this could include those suspected of having "abnormal sexual instincts."[117]

As Margot Canaday has argued, however, women and men who engaged in same-sex and other transgressive sexual acts were more likely to be excluded at the border as liable to become a "public charge" to the state, or restricted or deported on a "moral turpitude" charge. This further cements the need to understand the exclusion of black Bahamian women from entering

Miami through a queer lens, as this policy effectively promoted the formation of a "straight state" that privileged entry into the United States those who were white and married.[118] Ironically, in promoting the desirability of admitting seasonal black Bahamian male labor in Miami, this imperative facilitated queer expressions and desires in the nascent city. If early U.S. immigration policy promoted a "straight state," migrants challenged it every step of the way. A colloquialism in the modern queer world jokes, "Even spaghetti is straight until it gets wet." Perhaps a similar analogy can be made with early U.S. immigration policy, as it too was perceived as shaping a "straight state" until arriving migrants and immigrants confronted—and queered—the system.

All the while, the new restrictive measures of federal immigration law operated under an imagined racial hierarchy that privileged "old immigrants," namely, whites of British and northern European heritage.[119] Census data confirmed fears of the "general shift from 'old' to 'new' immigration, and the recent increases in south European and Mexican, West Indian, and Spanish-American immigration."[120] These "new" immigrants, including the Chinese and Bahamians, were labeled "inferior stock." In 1919, one writer argued that this shift meant "murder, rape and sex immorality are becoming more common than our former predominating crimes of burglary, drunkenness and vagrancy."[121]

Both migrant groups faced towering nativist sentiments and forms of discrimination, but the Bahamians' blackness and residence in Miami—with its Jim Crow codes—helped define their experience. The immigration laws that barred Chinese women from entering the United States proved effective. Just before the enforcement of the 1882 Exclusion Act, 39,579 Chinese entered the United States. Only 136 of them were women.[122] When their homosocial circumstances coupled with nativist sentiments, Chinese migrants were frequently labeled "feminine." That they often found work as domestics, in part *because* of this association, only strengthened this belief.[123] "Women, like the Chinese," noted one journal, "will work for low wages."[124] As Shah has shown in his research on Asian male migrants in the Pacific Northwest during this period, such racialized gender and sexual constructions were largely manipulated and exaggerated "in order to assert white male victimization and exclude consensual sexual relations."[125] In Miami, the Bahamians' labor and skin color designated these migrant men as not only "masculine" but hypermasculine. Like the Chinese, they too found themselves in male-dominated environments. But unlike the Chinese, contemporaries did not read Bahamians as "feminine." Their blackness distinguished them in this respect. The Bahamians' circular migration pattern placated U.S. immigration law's imperative of privileging the heteropatriarchal family. Although the border proved porous for most of these men, local police read them as suspicious once they entered Miami.

## Policing Immigrant Sodomites

All these sexually transgressive associations complicated the Bahamians' admissibility, desirability, assimilation, and reception in Miami. The city's law enforcement was responsible for a different type of gaze, as Bahamian men became prime targets for arrest, including for offenses such as sodomy and crimes against nature. Indeed, police also took notice of the city's saturation of robust, young migrant men.

In the early twentieth century, urban powerbrokers seemed to prefer Bahamian laborers to U.S. African Americans. Some believed Bahamian male sojourners in Miami had less immediate familial obligations, which made them more laborious, even as that logic erased how such circumstances could also free up time for vices such as gambling or visiting a brothel. Some businessmen, particularly those connected to agriculture, saw Bahamians as cheaper laborers and less likely to organize. Others placed a value on the distinct experiences and skill sets Bahamians had from living in a similarly tropical climate, while some connected to the service industry appreciated the "exoticness" these workers provided white tourists. Racist and anti-immigrant sentiments in Miami soon crystallized in the hyperpolicing of these Bahamians, who were now described as immoral, lazy, and criminally suspect.

Dade County's General Index for criminal cases lists only fourteen men who were arrested on sodomy or a crime against nature charge—whether same-sex or cross-sex anal intercourse—from 1896 to 1924, the year Bahamian migration to the city largely ceased. Coupling this information with other available records, it appears that *at least* five of the men arrested for this crime before 1924 were Bahamian. The origin of several others who were arrested cannot be identified for certain using either census or immigration records. It is possible, then, that the number of Bahamians arrested for these charges was even higher. Even though Bahamians made up less than one-fifth of Miami's population in 1920, they represented at least 36 percent of the arrests for sodomy or crimes against nature before 1924.[126]

John Delancy was one of these Bahamians. He was working as a farm laborer when Miami police arrested him on a sodomy charge in 1910.[127] Delancy left Miami—most likely to visit his wife and family—and returned several times between then and 1920. Immigration records heavily suggest that Delancy had no intention of permanently settling in Miami and that his travel there was to find temporary work. In 1913 Delancy, then twenty-five, reentered Miami alone. Immigration officials at the port admitted him into Miami upon first inspection.[128]

While Bahamian men accused of having same-sex sexual relations in Miami were not kept from entering the country to work, women had very different experiences as travelers, migrants, and subjects under U.S. immigration law. For instance, several Bahamian women aboard Delancy's schooner—including four widowers and one unmarried woman, all of whom reported working as washers—were detained and only discharged once relatives claimed them.[129]

The Delancy family's experience also sheds light on the social circumstances that separated traditional family models and granted men greater opportunities to engage in homosexual acts in Miami. John Delancy's wife, Victoria, visited Miami for a few months in 1920, identifying herself as a farm laborer. She brought along her three-year-old daughter. They too were detained at the port until John Delancy claimed them. Victoria Delancy and her daughter soon returned to the Bahamas, without John, only to sail back to Miami in 1922 and again in 1923. The latter time, Victoria also brought her other daughter to the city. As before, they told immigration officers that they did not intend to stay in Miami or the United States and that they estimated their stay would be no longer than six months.[130]

The record yields several things about the family's conditions. It suggests that John Delancy accrued enough money to pay for his family's many travels to and from the Bahamas and Miami. It also suggests that Victoria Delancy also came to Miami to work as a farm laborer—albeit on an even more temporary basis than her husband. All the while, it appears John Delancy often found himself alone and detached from his family and working in male-dominated spaces throughout southern Florida. The labor needs of Florida's growing agricultural business commodified Delancy's body. They also disrupted his family life both in the Bahamas and Miami, while also creating space for him to engage in extramarital sexual acts, including homosexuality.

Other Bahamian men arrested for sodomy intended to stay in Miami for longer periods of time and made new lives in their adoptive city. Miami police arrested migrant Philemon Roberts in 1917 for committing a crime against nature.[131] Like so many of the migrants who entered Miami, he was born on Cat Island. It seems he first entered Miami in 1913 to work on the farms and made several trips back to the Bahamas. He reentered Miami twice in 1916 and one more time in 1919, that is, two years *after* being arrested for the crime. As with the others, the charge was not enough for immigration officers to keep him from reentering. It is not known whether

Roberts was found guilty of committing a crime against nature, or perhaps a lesser charge. It is certain, however, that Roberts reported his intention to stay in Miami early on to immigration officials.[132]

While it is impossible to know whether men like Roberts hoped to make Miami their permanent home, it is clear that labor needs helped establish Miami as a desirable destination for many men who, once separated from their traditional families, engaged in sodomy—likely with men or male youths who shared their intimate spaces.[133] Roberts's case suggests that the temporary bachelorhood created by the city's labor needs facilitated same-sex intimacies. In the absence of their families and distinct homo- or heterosexual identities, these men could partake in sexual acts with women and men far more fluidly.[134]

Roberts's circumstances changed significantly after World War I, when he reunited with his Bahamian family in Miami. Still unmarried in 1920, Roberts had found a job breaking stones to build city streets and roads. Presumably the highest wage earner, he had also become "head" of his rented residence. He welcomed several members of his extended family to live with him. This included his older uncle and three cousins—two of whom had arrived the year before and the other, just a few months old, who was born in Miami. It seems that Roberts returned to the Bahamas shortly thereafter and married a woman named Elizabeth on Cat Island. He made the trip back to Miami in November 1923. This time he told immigration officers that he only intended to stay in Miami for four months, enough time to find agricultural work during the harvest. His request for a four-month sojourn represents a significant shift from the much longer periods of time Roberts had requested in the past. As they had done before, officials listed him in good mental and physical health and allowed him to enter.[135]

While some of this may suggest that men like Roberts at least partially found the city attractive because it permitted them greater opportunities to engage in homosexual acts once away from their families, the available evidence does not substantiate such speculation. Roberts's experiences do suggest that temporary, free market labor in Miami—as a disruption of heterosocial and traditional family models—proved central to facilitating same-sex and extramarital acts in the city. Once these disruptions ceased or were halted by a return to the islands, a heterosexual marriage and traditional family could once again take precedence. This does not mean, however, that they always did or that they viewed this as the most desirable result.[136]

Miami's sodomy arrests were at least part of a white "corrective" that insisted Bahamians remember their "place" in Miami. Their overrepresentation in the criminal records does not necessarily suggest that Bahamians were more likely to engage in same-sex acts than other ethnic groups. Although it seems that several Bahamian men did have sexual relations with other men, the record reveals that they were also monitored much more closely and read as naturally suspect. This reflects patterns in many other U.S. cities, wherein black and immigrant men were more likely to be arrested for committing same-sex acts.[137] This corrective operated on three major levels, as the Bahamians were surveilled and criminalized for their status as blacks in the U.S. South, migrants or immigrants in the midst of escalated nativist fervor, and colonial subjects with little recourse to petition such abuses.

While immigration inspectors at the border permitted these men to enter Miami without hindrance, local law enforcement heavily policed them, as black subjects, once they arrived.[138] Bahamians in Miami disrupted, complicated, and inadvertently helped tighten the area's racial codes. In 1908, a municipal judge commended the chief of police for his regulation of the area's black community. He argued that this was a massive achievement because of "the great number of Nassau negros who live here." After all, he believed, "upon their arrival" in Miami, Bahamians "consider themselves the social equal of the white people."[139]

Once in Miami, Bahamians experienced a radically different set of racial codes from the ones they had grown accustomed to in the West Indies. The bifurcated black-white backdrop of the U.S. South marked them as racial inferiors in Miami and was manifested in local law enforcement's hyperpolicing of them. One U.S. observer noted in 1922 that "under the British colonial policy the natives are placed on an equal footing with the white, which is quite a contrast to one having lived in the South."[140] Similarly, a Bahamian recalled that in Savannah Sound off of Eleuthera "the Negroes are masters and white people servants." Another noted that while in the Bahamas "colored men were addressed as gentlemen," they became "niggers" in Miami. In one instance, a Bahamian recalled riding in a carriage driven by a local black man following his immigration and customs inspection. The driver took him to "'Nigger Town,'" or Colored Town. "It was the first time I had heard that opprobrious epithet employed, and then, by a colored man himself," recalled the newly arrived Bahamian.[141]

If Bahamians represented a crack in the color line, Miami's white law enforcement was quick to clarify that they would not be equals. Actor Sidney Poitier recalled hostile moments in Miami. His parents were tomato farmers from the Bahamas' Cat Island who traveled to sell their produce in Miami, where Sidney was born. At one point, Poitier worked as a delivery boy in Miami and a woman became "screamingly hysterical" because he "brought a package to her front door rather than the rear"—an often-mandated practice in the Jim Crow South. Although unsuccessful, several "angry white men" passed by his house "bent on teaching him a lesson." In another instance, Miami Beach police searched, harassed, and threatened a young Poitier at gunpoint when he asked them for a ride to town.[142] Poitier's experiences were by no means anomalous.[143]

In addition to experiencing racism as blacks in the U.S. South, the Bahamians combated strong nativist sentiments as migrants in Miami. By the early 1910s, Miami nativists responded to the migrants' presence in the city by charging black Bahamian students whose parents had not been naturalized in the United States $1.50 per month as a tax for attending the city's public schools.[144] Nativists cast them as immediate outsiders by emphasizing their so-called immorality, inability to read or write (which, in many cases, proved untrue), affiliation with "the Church of England," and the fact that they were "almost as hard to understand as the people of other tongues."[145] Some dismissed them as lazy workers and drunks.[146] An administrator connected to Flagler's Key West Extension complained that the Bahamians they hired "were likely to quit whenever they had a few dollars coming to them." He suggested that like other transient "skid-row" employees, they would eventually "sober up and return to work" when they ran out of money.[147] Such popular beliefs not only depicted Bahamians as vagrants but also helped cement the idea they were prone to city vice. As one U.S. African American man was quoted as saying, "Dhey cusses 'foe de ladies an' does all kinds a things what nobuddy else would do."[148]

Meanwhile, although many in the agricultural industry saw them as skilled farmhands, many Miami nativists viewed them as "Nassau niggers." Some nativist sources even suggested that, despite the push to recruit them for agricultural work, Bahamians disappointed. "The farmers in and around Miami declare that they would rather have two native negroes work for them than a dozen Nassau negroes."[149] While many attached to the city's agribusiness fought to protect their source of cheap labor, it seems they did little or nothing to shield the Bahamians from the discrimination they experienced once they were in the city.[150]

As Philemon Roberts's case suggested, the question of citizenship—or lack thereof—became a subject of great debate among both Bahamians and nativists in Miami. This was one of the issues at stake when many Bahamians chose not to register for military service in Miami and reminded enlistment officers that they were British subjects. Several Bahamians opted to fill out a new alien card every year and resisted becoming U.S. citizens, often "because of the way white people" treated them in Miami. Other Bahamians—perhaps like Roberts—likely only applied for citizenship to retain or secure a job in agriculture or construction. Similarly, many who entered Miami intent on making it their home changed "their minds . . . to remain among their kind." As the tone suggests, a white nativist made this observation.[151]

The Bahamians' presence in Miami and cheap labor often caused much friction—albeit often exaggerated to advance white nativist goals—with Miami's U.S. African American communities. Labor rivalries stood at the center of much of this antagonism. Bahamians often competed with local blacks for many of the same jobs in the construction, agriculture, and service sectors, and as servants or domestics. Miami's "native" blacks even had a nickname for the Bahamians: "Saws" (most likely a shortened version of Nassau). This served to isolate and distinguish them in the local arena. One white source in Miami claimed: "The native negroes do not associate with the Nassau negroes to any great extent, and the better element of the native negroes keep strictly apart from the Nassaus." He continued, "They believe the Nassau negroes are a shiftless, undesirable class, and give them a wide berth." While this suggests that local blacks kept their distance from the Bahamians, it perhaps more accurately captures how white nativist forces pitted the two against one another. This is evident in the source's racialized quoting of a U.S. African American man in Miami: "Nobody whot is ennybody over our way don't have nuffin' to do with them kinder fokes. Dhey don't do nuffin', 'cept wunct in a wile."[152]

Despite the fact that the historical record suggests growing tensions between local blacks and Bahamians during this period, there is ample evidence that members of the two communities often intermarried, shared intimate spaces as lodgers, and joined forces to fight racism. This included joining Miami's chapter of the Universal Negro Improvement Association (UNIA), the black organization established by Jamaican-born pan-Africanist leader Marcus Garvey.[153] Similarly, Bahamian migrant H. E. S. Reeves, who once worked at the *Nassau Guardian*, was instrumental to the founding of Miami's first black newspaper, the *Miami Sun*, of which he was also the first editor. The *Sun* was "published specially for the coloured folk" in Miami, including the Bahamians.[154] Police reports also show examples of solidarity. In late 1918, a police officer apprehended a local black man. A Bahamian man in the vicinity believed the arrest unjust and meddled with the officer's arrest. "I'm a 'Sau' [a Bahamian], but I am not going to stand here and see an American negro beaten," he told the officer. In the end, he too was arrested.[155]

The migrants' racist and nativist reception in Miami also served colonial interests back in the Bahamas, as some government sources exploited the discrimination their subjects experienced in Florida as a means to recruit them back to the islands at a considerably cheaper rate—one largely set by the colonial government. "We do not think that our workmen expect to get ... the wages paid in Florida," one colonial officer maintained. "On the contrary, we believe they would not leave our shores if they could earn at home one half of the American wages, as they are better treated and have many more privileges under their own flag than under the American."[156] In 1922, a representative from Eleuthera also observed how "racial troubles in Florida have discouraged emigration."[157]

Colonial and imperialist concerns labeled black West Indians immoral, undesirable, and lazy. The 1911 edition of the *Encyclopedia Britannica* maintained, "The West Indian negro, as a labouring class, has frequently been condemned as averse from regular work, apathetic in regard to both his own and his colony's affairs, immoral and dishonest." It attributed this to "tendencies inherited from the period of slavery." Similarly, it stated, the "drafting of large numbers of labourers" to the Panama Canal "exercised a moral effect on the natives by enlarging their horizon."[158]

The Bahamians' move to Miami also represented an expansion of the West Indian's horizon—both physical and moral. A Miami source matter-of-factly stated that, "morally, the native negro is considered a degree better than the Nassau negro."[159] Similar beliefs emanated from the Bahamas, where colonial forces speculated that the trip to Miami had indelibly corrupted the Bahamians. One Bahamian official lamented, "After once living in Miami," the migrants were no longer "satisfied to live in a place cut off from everything that goes to make life worth living." Miami, and the glitz and glamour associated with the city's perceived modernity, changed them. For many Bahamians, colonial officials worried, there was no turning back.[160]

Meanwhile, waves of new immigrants led to moral anxieties in the United States over West Indian "black magic" and its transgressive possibilities. More West Indians entered the United States when empire-building projects, such as the building of the Panama Canal, altered local economies. For Bahamians, the spiritual practice of obeah—Caribbean manifestations of African-derived faiths that call on the supernatural and spiritual worlds for strength and support in the material world—particularly fed into this image of them as "haughty, immoral," and "accustomed to vagrancy."[161] With such associations, broad vagrancy laws became tools in which to criminalize immigrants and migrants and any of their actions interpreted as transgressive, including expressions of gender and sexual difference.[162]

Considering the Bahamas became an independent nation within the British Commonwealth only in 1973, Bahamians' long history as British subjects left many feeling like outsiders in their Caribbean homeland and across diasporic communities, including Miami. The growing stigma of Bahamians as immoral and lazy—and the city's hyperpolicing of them as such—grew so strong that local Bahamian governments felt they needed to warn those emigrating of the dangers of Miami's law enforcement. "In Miami the black man has to be extremely careful as to how he conducts himself, otherwise his liberty and even his life are endangered." For this reason alone, an Eleutheran source optimistically claimed, the Bahamian in Miami "abstains from liquor, saves his money and remits to his people at home."[163]

Several Bahamians wrote to British officials complaining about Miami police's abuse and violence against them. One man wrote about another Bahamian who was constantly harassed by Miami law enforcement. The man he wrote about was eventually killed, shot in the back by a police officer.[164] In Miami, it was reported, Bahamians "had been beaten in jail or compelled to furnish bond money when they had committed no offence."[165] As early as 1906, Bahamian migrants sent letters to the British Embassy in the United States "praying for the appointment of a British Consul" in Miami. They hoped such a move might help protect them from the violence and discrimination they experienced. The British Colonial Office opened no such office there, however. Bahamians learned that their pleas to the British colonial government largely fell on deaf ears. The British embassy in Washington, DC, acknowledged "that in such States as Florida … coloured people are not treated with much consideration." Colonial officials accepted this as an unfortunate truth they could do little about. After all, the colonial source lamented, "the evidence of negroes is never reliable and they are apt to misrepresent facts and contradict themselves, when cross examined."[166]

Although British colonial forces privately expressed contempt for the discrimination their black subjects experienced, they largely left them to fend for themselves on U.S. soil. This was evident in 1907, when a white man named William McClellan murdered a Bahamian named Joseph Saunders. At 4:00 a.m. Saunders left his house to work as a sponger. Upon opening the door, he saw McClellan—described as a "Cracker, or a man who was ready to use his gun, when necessary"—waiting for him with a rifle. McClellan shot and killed Saunders on his own doorstep. McClellan claimed Saunders had publicly stated he would "take charge of" McClellan's seventy-year-old wife a few hours prior. Jurors accepted that the murderer "vindicat[ed] the honour of his wife," or the defense of white women's honor against the black rapist mythology, and acquitted McClellan.[167] With no effective form of recourse in either Miami or the islands, many Bahamians suffered deeply the transnational consequences of racism, nativism, and colonialism.

## Closing the Border

While several forces succeeded in depicting Bahamians as immoral and lazy, many employers continued to recruit the cheap labor they provided. Federal immigration policy, however, soon curtailed that. As southern Florida's agribusiness fought to keep its regular flow of Bahamian farmhands, it strengthened a discourse on the commodification of the black male body.

In 1921, the U.S. Congress introduced a quota system that used claims of perceived assimilability as measures for exclusion. It limited the "number of aliens of any nationality who may be admitted" to 3 percent of the number of foreign-born people from that country, as listed in the 1910 census. Exceptions were generally made for those in the Western Hemisphere. Those from the British Caribbean were exempt from the new restrictions and instead subject to the "remote control" system, or a case-by-case evaluation conducted by U.S. consuls.[168] In early 1921, a representative from the Florida East Coast Growers' Association (FECGA) pleaded before the U.S. Senate's Committee on Immigration that it make an exception for the "Bahama Islands." Nodding to the long-standing immigration policy that favored skilled labor, he argued that without this "expert labor," Florida's agribusiness would fail. Conveniently, in this discourse the Bahamians became docile workers and "law-abiding people." They proved ideal workers, he argued, because "they do not sympathize with the unions" and "there are no radicals among them."[169] Or, as Bahamian colonial officers observed, Bahamians were different from the "ethnic revolutionaries" the United States sought to keep off its shores during this period, namely, those from eastern and southern Europe.[170] Local law enforcement aggressively policed Bahamians and, by the nature of their arrests, labeled them a key source of crime—including sodomy and crimes against nature.

While those in the Bahamas remained concerned over the effects of this migration on their communities, several people attached to Miami's agribusiness still touted the male-heavy wave of labor as an ideal pattern in the face of restriction and the closing of U.S. borders. In 1921, G. S. Fletcher of the FECGA tried to convince the U.S. Senate's Committee on Immigration that Bahamians were seasonal migrants—not *im*migrants—and overwhelmingly male. Fletcher maintained that when their work in Miami "is finished, 99 per cent of them go back." In explaining this pattern to the Immigration Committee, Fletcher argued that Bahamian men "come without their families." So few Bahamian women entered the United States, Fletcher argued, that "I have never seen two dozen Nassau women on the east coast of Florida." These workers "leave their women home."[171]

Fletcher's argument was misleading, however, as several changes had since altered Bahamian migration patterns. The "Miami Craze," or the mass Bahamian exodus to southern Florida, had reached its peak a decade prior. The push was caused by both the nadir of the Bahamian economic downturn following severe droughts and stories of success told by past sojourners. Those in the Bahamas and Miami paid close attention to the statistics that suggested Bahamians were increasingly making their trips to Miami permanent settlements. This ultimately helped spur a change in the Bahamians' migration patterns. Although some Bahamian women worked in Miami early on, particularly as domestics and in the budding service industry, they came in larger numbers—or numbers closer to those of male migrants—after World War I. As Miami grew, so too did its need for service labor, a void Bahamian women helped fill.[172]

Women, children, and whole families increasingly joined Bahamian men in Miami. In 1920, one Bahamian on Cat Island wrote to the *Nassau Guardian* lamenting that the "steady stream [of migration to Florida] has already accounted for nearly four-fifths of our strongest men." By that point, the writer maintained, when the men returned to the island it was "merely to take their families back with them."[173] This shift was also, in part, a product of a U.S. immigration policy that favored heteropatriarchal family reunification. More than before, many families attempted to make their stays permanent.[174] They worked alongside other working-class Bahamians and U.S. African Americans as maids, hotel porters, bellmen, cooks, waiters, dishwashers, servants, and domestics.[175] Even then, many of the Bahamians who managed to settle in Miami did not feel safe there, or sought a return back to their native island. One British traveler overheard a black Bahamian woman who worked as a maid in the city discuss fears of being deported while in Miami and state that "she considered Nassau infinitely superior to Florida."[176]

Indeed, the Bahamians' circumstances changed yet again by the early 1920s, when the effects of new immigration restrictions curtailed Miami's regular flow of West Indian laborers and led to the repatriation of some already in the city.[177] The 1917 Immigration Act included a prohibitive measure that determined immigrants' eligibility to enter the United States based on their literacy. This measure greatly concerned some pro-emigration Bahamian officials, as they had come to rely on the regular flow of remittances to sustain the islands' unstable economies.[178] By 1922, a colonial official noted that only the "young men who possessed the means and were able to pass the literacy test emigrated to Florida."[179] It appeared that "most of the labouring class ... able to read and write" went "regularly to Florida," while the rest were forced to stay behind.[180]

Other U.S. immigration policies squeezed Miami's regular flow of migrants from the Bahamas. Working on the foundation of the 1921 Emergency Quota Act, the U.S. Congress passed the Johnson-Reed Act in 1924. It included the National Origins Act, which further restricted immigration from Asia and southern and eastern Europe. The Western Hemisphere was generally exempt again, although, certainly, the gender and sexual policing at the borders offers some challenges to that narrative. Immigrants under British colonial rule were included in a 2 percent "cap" based on the percentage—now determined by the 1890 census—of immigrants from the metropole living in the United States. As a dependent colony, the Bahamas was neither given a separate quota nor exempt. It was instead included in the numerical restrictions afforded to Great Britain. This sealed the fate for Bahamians and other West Indians, who were all but excluded in this system that privileged white immigrants in the mother country.[181] By July 1924, Miami commissioners passed a resolution seeking an amendment to the immigration law to allow "more laborers from the Bahama Islands ... to come into this country and relieve the labor question, especially applicable to Miami."[182] Under pressure from Florida's agribusiness, these Miami politicians unsuccessfully petitioned against the restrictive quota system and literacy tests.[183] These policies effectively doomed the legal flow of Bahamians to Miami.

Interestingly, significant changes to the criminalization of homosexual acts on the islands also occurred that year. Much like Florida, the Bahamas had historically followed British common law, which criminalized the "abominable crime of Buggary, committed either with mankind or with any animal." Since at least 1868, anyone found guilty of buggery, or sodomy, could face "penal servitude for life, or for any term not less than ten years."[184] This all changed when the Bahamas Legislative Council and Assembly passed its own Penal Code on May 15, 1924—the same year and month the Johnson-Reed Act was enacted.[185] Although the Bahamian Penal Code did not take effect until 1927, now "any two persons" or "any person guilty of unnatural connection with any animal" would be liable "to imprisonment for ten years."[186] Bahamian men who engaged in physical relations with other men in Miami but returned back to the Bahamas could no longer serve a life sentence for committing a homosexual act on the islands. Although it appears that no flagrant cases of sodomy were reported in Bahamian criminal records at the height of the "Miami craze," reports from colonial officials suggest that most "crimes" went undocumented by local governments. Rather, "all serious matters are either hushed up or turned over to the Obeah man to avenge the cause of the aggrieved parties in some mysterious way known only to the initiated."[187] Considerable evidence, including the increased reporting of venereal disease and prostitution, suggests Florida migrations significantly affected the sexual lives of Bahamians both on and off the islands.

DESPITE THE MANY challenges they now faced, the 1924 migration freeze could not have come at a better time for Bahamians. The Bahamian tourism industry had further developed and brought new jobs throughout the islands, especially in Nassau. The Bahamas also started to reap the benefits of a new underground economy connected to Miami: bootlegging alcohol during U.S. Prohibition. This new trade brought more work and capital into the British colony. As the *New York Times* reported, Prohibition "created ... an opportunity such as rarely has come to a sleepy British colony ... since piracy went out of style."[188] The bootlegging business replaced many Bahamians' need to find seasonal agricultural work in Miami. In fact, this also started new trends. The onset of Prohibition prompted new formal and informal economies in the Caribbean just as U.S. immigration law became more restrictive. The smuggling business Bahamians engaged in soon expanded, as Cuban smugglers began trafficking through southern Florida people (mostly from China and southern and eastern Europe) who could not enter the United States legally.[189]

The Bahamians significantly changed Miami's social and cultural landscape. The men's commodified labor helped give voice to new desires—at times erotic—in the city while also altering life back on the islands. Black Bahamian men, described or imagined as physically fit and chiseled by their manual labor, became a major source of the area's growing understanding and articulation of queer desires and behaviors. A significant part of this formulation rendered Bahamian women who managed to enter the city susceptible to multiple forms of regulation and surveillance in the Bahamas, at the Caribbean-U.S. borders, and in Miami. Altogether, the Bahamians' migration and sometimes settlement in Miami coincided with—and proved instrumental to—numerous changes in the city and the United States at large. Indeed, these shifts preceded other developments throughout the United States in coming years, including the emergence of a homo-heterosexual binary that would come to organize sexual practices and the consolidation of race and "whiteness" as new immigrants entered the country.[190] The promotion of Miami as a leisure destination within the confines of white upper-class respectability further cemented these changes.

# MAKING FAIRYLAND REAL

In this winter fairyland you will find health, freedom, happiness and Utopia all mixed up together.
—MIAMI BEACH VISITOR, 1927

There is something magnetic about Miami. Once you get some of Miami's sand in your shoes it seems impossible to shake loose from it.
—NEWSPAPER EDITORIAL, 1929

No one will molest you if you are bringing money into town.
—FLORIDA CLERGYMAN, 1929

In 1934, white New York–based journalist Lowell Thomas noted that he dreaded leaving Miami Beach. He described his time there as "a delightful teaser and just long enough to fill me full of enthusiasm for . . . [the] tropical fairyland."[1] Thomas, who popularized the story of T. E. Lawrence of *Lawrence of Arabia* fame, was all-too-familiar with the fairies and pansy craze of New York—that is, the popular entertainment and public displays of gender and sexual transgression. Thomas had even defended Lawrence from accusations of homosexuality.[2] By then, although fairyland's dominant meaning remained its association with leisure and recreation, more broadly, to some it also represented other queer possibilities. For instance, that same year, one of Harlem's most popular attractions was "Clara Bow and *His* Fairyland Revue," which featured a black performer in drag.[3] While this may suggest that fairies were primarily understood as cross-gender performers or feminine men who might or might not seek sexual intimacy from other men, evidence suggests the term encapsulated a variety of gender-bending folks and sexual nonconformists.[4]

Indeed, Thomas also intimated the sexual possibilities southern Florida could provide its visitors. "From now on," Thomas told a group of Miami Beach elites, "I'll do my best to act as the New York John the Baptist for you and your fellow Ponce de Leons." As John the Baptist, Thomas would preach the good word of what awaited visitors—or explorers, like the Spanish conquistador Juan Ponce de León—in Miami. A more literal reading of Thomas's words suggests that in addition to leading others in search of Ponce de León's "fountain of youth," he would "baptize" travelers into Miami's sinful "fairyland" in his capacity as the "New York John the Baptist."[5]

City boosters marketed fairyland as a space for white leisure and recreation, particularly among the upper class and aspiring middle class. This marketing strategy has much in common with and, in fact, was inspired by efforts in many other, more established coastal resort towns and cities throughout the eastern United States, such as Provincetown, Fire Island, Coney Island, and Atlantic City.[6] They foregrounded tourism, recreation, and the feeling of being transported to a place where reality could be suspended, even if only temporarily. Boosters emphasized what was possible there, sprinkling just enough elements of risk and danger in their marketing schemes. In this way, fairyland meant different things to different people. As Thomas's words demonstrate, one such interpretation allowed those "in the know" to take a step further, often through subtle wordplay and subterfuge. For some, fairyland represented a space where one could more overtly transgress gender and sexual norms.

This chapter portrays some of the elite women and men who helped shape the fairyland to which Thomas referred. It demonstrates how these figures' wealth, status, and whiteness licensed them to tailor Miami as a space where gender and sexuality could, in fact, be challenged, renegotiated, and subverted. These people proved influential in molding the image of southern Florida Thomas described. Many of these elites were in some way connected to a growing artists' colony recruited to the nascent city. Their artistic visions, modes of self-expression, and broader defiance of social conventions helped form that fairyland image and early understanding of queer desires and expressions.[7]

As influential powerbrokers in the city, several of these queers crafted Miami's lucrative image as fairyland through the tentacles of U.S. imperialism, casting the city's offerings as an extension of the vice and pleasure available in the nearby Caribbean. In supporting and contributing to an imperial ethos that exploited and opened up foreign markets, through U.S. capital, investment, cultural dominance, and even occupation, these elite queers also helped cement Miami's intimate ties to the Caribbean for decades to come.

Before we enter the queer fairyland elite travelers and settlers fashioned in and around Miami, it is important to explore the concept of the "open secret" that helped define their experiences and affectations in the city. For many of these queer women and men, everyday life played out inside a sort of "glass closet," a space for the clandestine and the veiled. This is the closet from which today's lesbians and gays "come out" to publicly reveal themselves. Eve Kosofsky Sedgwick has shifted our attention to the glass closet, or open secret, that operates outside of—while also being constitutive of—the confines of existing binaries.[8] This particularly resonated in Miami, where the cultural politics of the U.S. South and the Caribbean frequently collided. As John Howard and Carlos U. Decena have shown in their works on these regions, respectively, "tacit" knowledge was often coded as a private affair that was known but never explicit.[9] For instance, most of Miami's early queer women and men navigated their sexual feelings through dualities such as knowledge and ignorance, the private and the public, the seen and the unseen, and disclosure and secrecy. They traversed the glass closet where their transgression—including gender expressions and sexual desires and behaviors—were both concealed and in plain sight, or at least tacitly legible to those in the city. That these women and men were privileged through their whiteness and upper- or middle-class status afforded them greater fluidity and helped protect them and their open secret from the law.

*The Early Guest List*

Moneyed settlers and those aspiring to greater wealth from the U.S. Northeast and Midwest came to Miami in search of *something*. In addition to economic opportunity and balmy weather, they often sought a counter to the mundane rhythm and ills of urban life—perhaps inspiration, recreation, or perspiration. Artist John Singer Sargent represents this trend. What exactly did he think he would find in the swampland? We know he found heat and humidity along with a source of artistic inspiration, if not sexual temptation. By and large, what tied the vast majority of these early Miami stories together was whiteness and social status. Those who marketed Miami as a fairyland specifically classified it as an elite space where the world's finest could take a load off.

While travel to and trade with the Caribbean proved critical to Miami's fairyland image, in its most literal incarnation, this marketing tool was largely connected to the municipal incorporation of Miami Beach in 1915. Before it became a winter resort and an autonomous city, Miami Beach was a swampland populated almost entirely by mosquitoes and reptiles. Following failed efforts to farm either coconuts or avocados in the area, northern, white entrepreneurs—particularly John Collins and Carl Fisher—saw the potential in Miami Beach's tropical climate and enviable sandbar and revamped it as a pleasure destination.[10] In 1909, Connecticut entrepreneurs Avery C. Smith and James Warr formed the Biscayne Navigation Company that developed boardwalks, wharves, and bathhouses in Miami Beach. They originally dubbed one of their more successful ventures, a pavilion-turned-casino located at the southern tip of South Beach, Fairy-Land. It is possible that the name was a play on the double-decker ferries operated by the Biscayne Navigation Company that visitors boarded to cross Biscayne Bay from the mainland.[11] Fairyland then became known as Smith's Casino.[12]

Such casinos, which predated Miami Beach's incorporation, proved popular among Miami's white well-to-do residents and visitors. Casinos were beachfront structures—not gambling joints—offering a wide range of amenities: dancing, entertainment, restaurants, swimming, changing rooms, massage parlors, and bathhouses. The latter three were among Miami's first sex-segregated spaces moneyed women and men used to explore bodily pleasures, as they changed into bathing suits, relaxed in a steam room, or undressed for a massage.[13]

While most who employed the moniker "fairyland" were not referring specifically to Miami as a haven for gender- or sexually transgressive behavior, many would have understood it as such. In a literary sense, fairyland represented the "imaginary land of the fairies."[14] Fairyland colloquially referred to a myth-like fantasyland of hedonism and indulgence. Monikers like "Mecca," "Eden," "playground," "enchantment," "Eldorado," and "paradise" similarly helped describe the transcendent and pleasure-seeking aura urban designers strategically sought to associate with Miami. In this vein, fairyland represented another way of effectively marketing Miami to white outsiders, especially those seeking to flee the bitter winters of the Northeast and Midwest. The slogan that proved most effective, or at least the one that outlived the others, "the Magic City," similarly conveyed a sense of ethereal pleasure. As one magazine noted in 1914, Miami "became 'The Magic City' at a touch of the wand of American enterprise."[15] Years later, another source observed that "Miami, the Magic City … grew up as it were, over night, with two flourishes of the fairy's magic wand."[16] This association was also a reference to Miami's "instant city" status.[17]

Some claimed Miami was the only place in the United States with a "real tropical climate," which helped sell the city as a prime destination because of its relative nearness to the North—compared to California, Hawaii, or even the Caribbean, for instance—just as war broke out in Europe.[18] As a 1916 piece reminded its readers, "Let this winter be a revelation to you that the world's best winter climate is not abroad and far away, but right here at home, 'Made in America.'"[19] By late 1921, several entrepreneurs who built Miami Beach and subsequently served on its Chamber of Commerce chipped in to create a monetary prize for the person who came up with a slogan that best marketed the city. They hired an associate editor from *National Geographic* magazine to review the entries. While the editor preferred the slogan "Miami Beach—Florida's Fairyland," he ultimately did "not recommend that." Other proposed slogans included "Pacemakers for the Tropics," "The City That Made Out-Doors Famous," "Where the Pulse of Pleasure Never Slows," and "The Fairy City of Florida."[20]

Make no mistake, many travelers understood that this fairyland *did* permit and facilitate transgressions of gender and sexuality. While it is unclear why the editor rejected "Miami Beach—Florida's Fairyland," the slogan he cited as his favorite, this campaign coincided with the rise in visibility of the effeminate fairy in some of the major U.S. metropolitan areas, places many of Miami's residents and tourists would have been familiar with.[21] Like the entrepreneurs who opened up the casinos in Miami Beach, many who visited were wealthy travelers from the Northeast. In January 1922 boosters paid for a big electric sign over New York's intersection of Forty-Second Street and Broadway advertising that it was "June in Miami."[22] By that point, Times Square had become a well-known gay cruising spot for those in search of "fairy prostitutes."[23]

Miami boosters also had great familiarity with—and often tried to emulate—New York's nightlife, including the pansy craze. In the early 1920s, a New York–based entrepreneur bought one of the Miami Beach casinos and spruced it up with a tea garden, water polo, and musical revues from New York.[24] In 1932, the *Miami Daily News* printed a review of the New York night scene announcing that "scenery-eating actors have given away to pansy performers."[25] Nothing was more indicative of this familiarity or the tacit understanding that fairyland permitted and facilitated gender- and sexual-transgressive acts and expressions than the presence and daily activities of many of its elite residents.

After all, this fairyland was specifically designed to cater to the tastes of a white elite clientele. While some Miami Beach casinos were technically open to the public, these were exclusive, white clubs that required money and status for admission. Getting to the casinos was not easy, as crossing Biscayne Bay—either by ferry or bridge—was an extra expense. Before June 1913, when New Jersey native and entrepreneur John Collins connected Miami to the islands of Miami Beach with the Collins Bridge, one had to take a ferry or private boat to enter Miami Beach.[26] Pedestrians and those riding bicycles, motorcycles, horse buggies, or other vehicles were charged a toll to use the bridge, further restricting access to fairyland.[27] In 1921, a Miami Beach casino owner insisted, "This will be a high-class amusement place for high-class people."[28] Later that decade, casino operators even used their influence to urge lawmakers to have the city pay for lifeguards at their establishments to "encourage bathers to use the private bathing places rather than public beaches," where no such protection could be found.[29]

Meanwhile, one of the most significant changes in this era was the local realization that homosexuality was not limited to black, immigrant, or working-class cultures.[30] Rather, it pervaded every social circle in Miami. While this included the "vagrants" and "drifters" local law enforcement continued to criminalize, elite white women and men also publicly transgressed gender and sexual norms in the city. This became a critical feature in marketing Miami. City boosters aggressively promoted Miami as a fairyland that permitted such expressions and behaviors, particularly among its white and well-to-do visitors.

The casinos in Miami Beach were not the only elite spaces that made the area a veritable fairyland. The building of the Italian-style palazzo Vizcaya, located on the shores of Biscayne Bay, also represents Miami's status as an elite paradise. James Deering, a Chicago agricultural equipment tycoon whose father was one of the founders of the company that became International Harvester, built his winter villa in Miami. "In four years what was a strip of waste and marshy woodland on the shores of the Bay of Biscayne has become Alladin's [sic] palace," observed Deering's architects.[31] Deering lived in Vizcaya from late 1916 until his death in September 1925. The property defined extravagance and excess. In addition to its fine tropical gardens, "the interior of Villa Vizcaya is the repository of a wonderful collection of art objects, antique statuary, brocades, velvets, carpets, and hangings, which centuries ago were precious possessions in Venetian palaces."[32]

Unattached white men of means, like those connected to Vizcaya, tried to turn the urban frontier into a new "city of bachelors," where they could indulge in the wealth and excess they had accumulated. This period saw the development of a distinct bachelor culture tied to the recreations and vices modern cities offered, a subculture that soon inspired anxieties about homosexuality and the breakdown of the family.[33] Contemporary newspapers often emphasized Deering's "bachelor" status. In 1922 a Missouri newspaper noted that Deering's "house has 39 guest rooms and as he is a bachelor of 59, it is said that although every room is kept in readiness for company, he has never had a guest."[34] In fact, he hosted several guests. One of his contemporaries noted that "there were many lovely ladies [who] wanted to marry him … but, he sidestepped them."[35] This narrative soon evolved and took on a life of its own. By 1961, a report referred to then-deceased Deering as "the prissy bachelor who preferred bourbon to women."[36] One of his Vizcaya guests recalled: "He certainly wasn't interested in women. But, he wasn't interested in men either."[37] Although no evidence seems to suggest that Deering engaged in homosexual acts, his sexuality became a subject of speculation and even legend that persists in Miami to this day.[38] As for the Bahamian migrants who worked in Vizcaya, this was a bachelor space that, especially in its earliest days, very few women visited.

Unlike with the Bahamians, however, white elite men's power and influence helped them adapt the frontier's tabula rasa into a queer space tailored to their distinct tastes without the contempt—and even with the tacit approval—of law enforcement. Deering chose white artist, interior decorator, architect, and New York native Paul Chalfin "to plan, buy and arrange his superb home at Miami." Chalfin's work on the estate, one contemporary observed, was a "monument to the perfection of American taste and the period of American Renaissance."[39] Chalfin and Deering traveled the world together "buying all of the things that went into the house." Deering never bought "anything until he had Paul's advice." Chalfin even designed a secret passage from Deering's bedroom to an adjoining bedroom to ensure his privacy, a known feature Deering was often teased about.[40] There was similarly a lot of speculation and intrigue about Deering's den in Vizcaya. People wanted to know what it looked like and, perhaps, who might have been sharing the "lounging room" with the "master of the house."[41] Many others interpreted his much-talked-about bachelorhood, as one houseguest recalled, as indicative of Deering simply not being a "romantic." In this way, Deering appeared queer in his asexuality. Several jokingly wondered whether he "ever took off all his clothes ... even to bathe."[42]

On the other hand, Chalfin lived openly with his male lover in Miami, where he expressed himself as a gender-transgressive pansy (fig. 3.1). Like Deering, Chalfin was a "well known bachelor."[43] One of Deering's employees referred to Chalfin as a "funny fellow," while Vizcaya's Colombian-born landscape architect Diego Suarez remembered him as "a man with very peculiar tastes."[44] He was "absolutely the worst pansy I have ever known," Suarez claimed. Chalfin was "remembered as having been unusually effeminate." He always kept his male partner and "secretary," Louis Koons, close. "He used to kiss him goodbye—he was always kissing his hand," Suarez recalled. To his mind, Koons "simply hung around Chalfin," with no purpose other than to keep his lover company.[45]

In Miami Chalfin and Koons partook in and mimicked the gay and gaudy lifestyle popularized in cities like New York and Chicago, flaunting their open secret to those in the city. While Talbot S. Hanan of the shoe manufacturing fortune was probably best known for hosting extravagant balls in Narragansett Pier, his family also built a winter home in Miami known as the "Hanania."[46] Much like the "Hawaiian Ball" he threw in Rhode Island, Hanan presented the "A Night in Japan" ball in Miami on March 8, 1917. This event was representative of the remnants of wealth and excess of the Gilded

FIGURE 3.1.
Paul Chalfin in Miami
in the early 1910s,
likely in or around
Vizcaya. Photograph
by Alice Woods.
Arva Moore Parks
Vizcaya Photograph
Collection, Vizcaya
Museum & Gardens,
Miami, FL.

Age and reveals the upper-class fetishization of the exoticized "Other." For his Miami ball, Hanan promised "beautiful silver cups" awarded for the "best costumes."[47] Many of the area's social elite attended and contributed to the event. Deering, for example, donated $250.[48] Feminist and *Miami Herald* columnist Marjory Stoneman Douglas described the ball's lavish nature and its attendees' costumes. Not all the costumes recalled Japan; several attendees—including Chalfin and Koons—dressed in Chinese-inspired clothes. "Among the Chinese costumes, those of Mr. Paul Chalfin and Mr. Louis Koons attracted much attention," reported Douglas. In addition to suggesting they attended the ball as a couple, Douglas meticulously detailed their extravagant and ornate outfits: "The former wore an embroidered coat in soft blue and rose, with rose pongee trousers, carefully folded in at the ankle, while the latter was resplendent in a coat of dull blue and gold embroidery, cream trousers and gold embroidered scarf." Her description stands out, as it more closely resembled costumes worn by women at the dance, even as the white elite's obsession with the "exotic" may have diminished, or made more permissible, any feminine associations.[49]

The area's elite tacitly tolerated and accepted the male lovers and their open secret. This also reflects Deering's attitude toward Chalfin. His relationship with his employee and confidant seems to have never been compromised by Chalfin's homosexuality or effeminate behavior. Similarly, the crowd welcomed the coupled Chalfin and Koons to the ball and celebrated their dress. The ball judges even awarded Koons "the gentleman's cup."[50]

This white queer attraction to the "exotic," particularly connected to the Caribbean, similarly helped shape the fairyland. In August 1914 the *Miami Metropolis* announced that Chalfin and Koons had just "returned from a pleasure trip to Cuba" together.[51] With the island so nearby, the two lovers, like so many others in Miami during this period, could easily travel there. Once there, they could partake in Cuba's pleasure market, which included vice, gambling, and "deviant" sex. Although we do not know whether these men took part in the vice and sex available in Cuba during their visits, most people of their means were aware of the island's "anything goes" reputation.[52]

### The Sins of Speculation

While real estate had long dominated conversations about Miami's future, market speculation reached new heights as the city grew in the post–World War I era. By the mid-1920s, Miami boosters who dreamed of a new "big city" look for Miami could see a modest skyscraper skyline featuring sixteen buildings. These boosters depicted Miami, which was sparsely populated compared to major metropolitan areas, as an ambitious and modern city that could still be shaped.[53] Miami real estate and speculation sales peaked in the early 1920s, when the city had more forcefully entered the national imaginary as a desirable place for moneyed visitors and settlers.

Postwar economic prosperity, further swamp drainage, and a 1924 amendment to the Florida Constitution that barred state inheritance and income tax helped pave the way for Miami's land boom. One realty advertisement from 1922 claimed, "Nothing can stop the increase of property values at Miami Beach."[54] Many subdivisions in Miami sold out on the first day they became available to investors. Frequently, the buyer would merely see a blueprint of the lot of land embellished with drawings of boulevards, parks, and coconut trees before making a purchase. Many failed to realize that some of these plots of land were as far as thirty miles from Miami proper.[55] In March 1925, the *New York Times* reported, "Much of [Miami was] in the hands of men who have made good elsewhere, and who, coming to Florida for a brief Winter vacation, have been fired with the possible future of this great Winter garden."[56] Many interpreted the land opportunity in Miami as a get-rich-quick scheme. "In many cases it has taken no more than four years to spell the difference between poverty and affluence" in Miami, where many "have become rich through the sale and resale of land."[57] Although those with financial means made the investments, the boom involved nearly everyone in Miami. "The butcher, the baker, the candlestick maker, and their wives, will buy a lot for you, or sell you one."[58] Many capitalized on this venture, if only for a few years.

Miami's heavily inflated real estate market burst by 1926, contributing to the early arrival of economic depression in the city. Limited means of transportation, fraud, inflation, and speculations and prospects that failed to materialize or yield a profit in the early 1920s bankrupted many investments. By 1925, several Miami firms had already filed paperwork to foreclose mortgages on liquidated hotels, buildings, and residences. In 1927 Harvard professor Homer B. Vanderblue noted that money invested in these boom speculations, "notably . . . skyscrapers in Miami," "has probably been lost exactly as though it had been sunk in drilling dry holes in an oil field."[59] As a result, the area was already in recovery mode when the stock market crashed in 1929 and ushered in the Great Depression.

Coupled with that, a hurricane with winds over 125 miles per hour pummeled the city in September 1926. Following the disaster, a local newspaper published an editorial on Miami's economic recovery and its foreseeable impact on the real estate boom. It stressed that "only the death cannot be undone," as 370 fatalities were estimated.[60] Survivors needed to "rebuild Miami at any cost in time, money and labor. . . . Too much money is invested here to permit of a desertion of an entire city." The newspaper emphasized Miami's gendered virility and resilience. Wherein the "adversity might have discouraged weaker men and women," Miami's men would laboriously rebuild with "axes and hammers and saws and riveters."[61] The estimated fiscal damage caused by the hurricane reached $76 million. Even that number excluded losses incurred to personal property or the economic nightmare caused by the real estate burst.[62]

Despite such setbacks—or, because of them—investors continued to sell the image of Miami as a fairyland and the "nation's playground" where anything was possible. In the midst of national economic depression, one New York businessman noted the "peculiarities of local behavior" in Miami. While the Great Depression in New York found "only 'mile-long' faces worn by people who ... haven't yet grown reconciled to the change," those in Miami were "walking about dead broke and smiling."[63] This image intensified to advance economic recovery. One wealthy temporary Miami Beach winter resident claimed that "since leaving Miami Beach" in June, he and has family had "spent three weeks in Atlantic City, and nearly two months enjoying ... Vermont and the Adirondacks of New York." His experiences only "confirmed" his "convictions that Miami Beach is America's playground."[64]

Investors also cemented this image through contemporary songs. In 1926, a team of composers wrote "Along Miami Shore." The song relayed that "someone waits alone for me" in Miami, a "paradise in someone's empty arms."[65] Love in Miami seemed both possible and certain. Similarly, Italian composer Caesar LaMonaca—who performed throughout southern Florida nightclubs and parks through the 1980s—released a fox-trot in 1929 titled "Miami, Playground of the U.S.A.!" With lyrics such as "Here's where we cheat Father Time" and "Miami calls the world to come and play," the song helped establish the city as a recreational paradise where wealthy white outsiders could sow their oats.[66]

## Miami's Free Spirits

Several influential white queers helped the city grow during this period, lured by the fairyland's je-ne-sais-quoi identity. One such man was socialist, radical philanthropist, and architect Alden Freeman (fig. 3.2). Born in Cleveland, Freeman moved to Miami in 1923, when he was in his early sixties, and immediately became a "prominent figure in ... civic and social circles."[67] This was, in large part, a result of the massive fortune he inherited from his father, Joel Francis Freeman, who served as the first treasurer of the Standard Oil Company. He epitomized high society in Miami. Freeman traced his lineage to the Mayflower and belonged to some of the most exclusive social clubs and orders in the nation.[68]

As with Chalfin and Koons, the evidence suggests that the elite social circles Freeman belonged to in Miami were keenly aware of his homosexuality and seem to have tacitly accepted his gender- and sexually transgressive behavior in the tropical fairyland. As Will Durant, a contemporary "free love" lecturer and later historian, recalled, Freeman was "a homosexual, ill at ease in the heterosexual society that gathered about him as the son of a Standard

FIGURE 3.2.
Portrait of a young
Alden Freeman.
Printed in *American
Biography: A New
Cyclopedia*, vol. 4.

Oil millionaire."[69] His obituary in a Miami newspaper similarly made reference to his "colorful" personality and the fact that "he never married."[70] As this nudge-nudge-wink-wink language suggests, Freeman's homosexuality was an open secret city residents understood and at least tacitly accepted.

Even before moving to Miami, Freeman constantly found himself in elite social circles that acknowledged and coded him as deviant. Local and national press often used euphemisms to describe him, including adjectives such as "eccentric" and "peculiar."[71] One newspaper all but called him an effeminate, overly sensitive queer by poking fun of the fact that he fell physically ill after New York police prohibited his friend, anarchist-orator Emma Goldman, from speaking in 1909.[72] About a week later, Freeman surprised members of the Mayflower Descendants, an exclusive group he belonged to in East Orange, New Jersey, when he brought Goldman to one of the group's luncheons. Club members were not amused. Best known for her radical and anarchist lectures, Goldman was also a staunch defender of free love and homosexuality in the early 1900s. In fact, many anarchists in the early twentieth century came to the defense of same-sex love and expressions, interpreting attacks on homosexuality as the state's encroachment on individual and collective liberties. In part, Oscar Wilde's 1895 criminal trial in England for sodomy prompted many anarchists in the United States to demand that no outside authority regulate intimate or romantic matters.[73]

This worldview was part of what attracted Freeman to Goldman. After all, Freeman sought out "freedom from tradition" and "sympathized with other rebels."[74] Police alerted the two radicals that Goldman's lecture would not take place in East Orange. Rather than accept defeat, the idealist Freeman alerted all who had shown up to hear the talk that they were welcome to his New Jersey mansion. Goldman's lecture was held on the lawn of his property.[75] The whole nation learned about the incident, associating Freeman with Goldman. Those in Miami were aware of Freeman's radical inclinations and his well-established reputation as a sexual renegade. As one newspaper noted, "Freeman is as fond of the notoriety he is getting as are the anarchists."[76]

Freeman's open secret morphed into something more coherent and legible during his time in Miami's fairyland, which was, from the start, directly linked to real estate and investment speculation. While Freeman roused controversy in his home in East Orange, he seems to have had a different experience in Miami. In 1930, Freeman, who already owned real estate in Miami, built a new property in the center of Miami Beach's Ocean Drive: Casa Casuarina. Today, the house is best remembered as the mansion of fashion designer Gianni Versace. Because the openly gay Versace was killed just outside the property in 1997, it has maintained its queer nexus for many decades.[77] In addition to paying for its construction, Freeman was listed as one of the architects of the ornate three-story apartment complex. This was a particularly welcome addition to the city, as several boosters panicked that there were not enough accommodations to cater to the growing tourist economy. Like Vizcaya, Casa Casuarina was built in the Mediterranean revival style. It featured "murals representing kings, queens and other notables of nearly every country in the world."[78] It similarly housed antiques from throughout the world, further demonstrating contemporary and elite efforts to transplant the high culture of the old world into their fairyland. An Englishman trained as a landscape architect named Charles Daniel Boulton was listed as one of Casa Casuarina's two builders. Freeman's relationship with Boulton is perhaps one of the greatest indications that Miami residents were clued in to the former's open secret. According to several Miami reports, Freeman adopted Boulton—who was thirty-four years his junior—when the latter was an adult.[79]

Although the record is unclear about the nature of the men's relationship, we can glean several things about the way Freeman bent social conventions in Miami due, in large part, to the privilege his wealth and whiteness afforded him. It is possible Freeman adopted an adult-aged Boulton to help the foreigner obtain U.S. citizenship. Boulton married a woman named Nora Hattie in New Jersey in 1927. Considering she was a U.S.-born citizen, Freeman's sponsorship may have no longer seemed necessary, although it could have certainly strengthened his case before U.S. immigration officials, especially in an era of rigid quotas—even for England.[80] It is also entirely possible that Freeman never formally adopted Boulton. Neither Freeman's last will and testament from 1936 nor Boulton's naturalization records from 1938 suggest a formal adoption.[81]

It is likely Freeman made such claims as a means of supporting the Boultons. Freeman's will listed the Boulton children as beneficiaries to his estate.[82] It was not unheard of for one to "adopt" an adult of the same sex to legally protect the adoptee in the same way a legal marriage would. Many queer women and men did this in subsequent decades as a tax avoidance strategy. Freeman's past and free love perspective certainly supports this as a possibility. His radical leanings heavily support this act as a defense of his right to privacy, his greater distrust or contempt for government oversight on personal matters, and legal restrictions that prohibited two consenting and competent adults from entering such a relationship.[83]

While these are all plausible explanations, the evidence yields no definitive answers as to whether theirs was a sexual or even romantic relationship. In fact, it is even possible Freeman's loyalties may have been to Boulton's wife, who was also from New Jersey. The nature of the men's relationship appears secondary, however. The public knowledge or belief that Freeman had adopted Boulton only added depth to the unconventional ways this "eccentric" and "peculiar" bachelor conducted his personal and business matters in the city.[84] The men's unusual relationship both confirmed and added greater intrigue to Freeman's open secret in Miami. Boulton and his biological family lived alongside Freeman in Casa Casuarina. In fact, evidence seems to suggest that Freeman built the property *for* Boulton. It is certain that Boulton was an heir to Freeman's estate, including Casa Casuarina.[85] When the property opened up to tourists in December 1930, several local businesses dedicated space in the *Miami Daily News* to congratulate the partner-owners: Freeman *and* Boulton.[86]

Other major gestures Freeman initiated in Miami, and which made local and national headlines, similarly coded him as a sexual rogue. Just as Casa Casuarina was being constructed, Freeman read a book in which the author, Nan Britton, claimed she had had an affair with U.S. president Warren Harding, by then deceased, and that he was the biological father to her child. Many quickly labeled Britton a liar and immoral woman. In 1931, Britton filed a libel suit against a man who called her a "degenerate" and "sex pervert." This national news resonated with Freeman, who could have been branded a "degenerate" and "sex pervert" all these years for his own sexual behavior. He seems to have largely dodged that, however, because of his wealth and privilege. In 1932, newspapers throughout the country revealed that Freeman had written Britton's daughter into his will.[87] In that document, Freeman called Britton "a most devoted mother and one of the noblest and most unselfish of women."[88] Freeman also wrote a letter to Britton in which he further revealed his queer affinity for her. He noted how her daughter's "love is the solace, consolation and reward for the suffering and anguish through which this wonderful mother has passed in her efforts to secure justice not only for President Harding's daughter but for all other wronged and disinherited children of unmarried mothers."[89] If any of Miami's residents had not yet caught on to Freeman's open secret, his public commitment to Britton and the cause of sexual freedom changed that.

Indeed, Freeman seems to have playfully flaunted the queerness made available in this fairyland to Miami's elite, at times through hidden messages or innuendo. Freeman commissioned impressionist artist Henry Salem Hubbell to capture the construction of Casa Casuarina on canvas. Hubbell, like so many others, moved to Miami in the early 1920s during its real estate boom. In Hubbell's painting, five young white men hoist a heavy beam in front of Casa Casuarina's arcade (fig. 3.3). This painting served as a metaphor for the City of Miami at large: development, progress, hope, and idealism. There appears to have been a more tacit message of masculine virility. Four of the men in the painting go about their work bare-chested, and all the men have bulging and well-defined muscles. In reality, the four shirtless Adonises were models recruited from the football team at the University of Miami, which was founded in 1925 and held its first classes in 1926. This is not to suggest that this was a *gay* painting. Rather, men like Freeman, who commissioned the painting and planned to hang it by the interior stairway of Casa Casuarina, associated Miami's urban development with a strapping, virile masculinity that made it possible. That the embodiment of that hypermasculinity was often a working-class laborer—or here, a *modeled* performance of a construction worker—who was often made available to elite men like Freeman is manifest in Hubbell's painting.[90] All the while, there are significant parallels here with the black physical aesthetic John Singer Sargent found in the working-class Bahamian laborers in Vizcaya.

As this suggests, Miami's early boosters recruited an active artists' colony to the city that proved critical to diverse gender and sexual expressions that

FIGURE 3.3. Henry Salem Hubbell, *Building of the House*, 1930, oil on canvas, 162 × 114 inches, Collection of Michael A. Mennello, Winter Park, FL.

preceded identities. Several urban investors believed artists would help convert the frontier from wilderness to a progressive and modern resort for the wealthy. This was a sound investment, as the artists' work served as some of the most effective boosterism for the growing fairyland. This included a wide range of artistic professions, such as painters, sculptors, architects, photographers, writers, fashion designers, actors, performers, dancers, and singers, as well as collectors and patrons of the arts. As a local newspaper boasted, "Being the Magic City, it did not take years for Miami to develop ... centers of culture."[91]

As beacons for cultural, social, political, and even economic progress, these artists helped define this fairyland as the nation's playground. As scholars such as Daniel Hurewitz and Karen Christel Krahulik have shown, artist communities wielded great cultural power in defining and developing urban and resort centers.[92] The artists' collective works and creativity advanced progressive concepts of individuality and self-expression that became a voice and social conscience for the city at large. As these artists questioned the world around them and the role of art and the artist in society— reflected in movements such as modernism and aestheticism, which defied rigid definitions of beauty and art—their artistic renderings conveyed the possibilities of self-expression outside of what was conventional or socially acceptable. These early articulations of self-expression matured over time into multiple gender and sexual subjectivities and identities in the city.

Many of Miami's artists promoted the idea that gender and sexual norms could easily be subverted in this fairyland. This does not necessarily imply that all these artists fostered liberal ideas concerning gender and sexuality, that conservative artists did not exist, or that all artists had wealth or power. Some were conservative and poor. "Bachelor" men like Deering, Chalfin, Koons, Sargent, and Freeman did have great influence, however. They joined several other prominent artists in the area, such as Hubbell, who helped articulate that vision, even as they did not seem to engage in homosexual sex or forgo acceptable gender norms. Other such artists included Louis Comfort Tiffany, a New York native who became best known for his multicolored, floral lamps, and G. Howard Hilder, a British painter who captured the area's scenic beauty.[93] These, and many others, helped create the fantasy that was fairyland to outsiders as well as those living in Miami.

Several of these artists helped redraw the lines of what was acceptable in society and subsequently challenged established gender norms. Such was the case with Freeman and his fashion choices. In an era of much greater formality and conservatism in dress, Freeman shocked many throughout the country with his flashy and bright apparel. He had become "a familiar character about Greater Miami clad in shorts, sandals and pith helmet."[94] He fashioned a sort of tropical and casual aesthetic—a tropical dandyism— that became associated with Miami. By dressing smartly, in bright hues, and appropriately for the tropical climate, Freeman helped define the fairyland's permissiveness. Others throughout the country seemed bewildered by his expressive style, which seemed utterly queer outside of Miami. In summer 1931, for instance, he boarded a plane in Dallas wearing "the latest in blue shorts, a blue shirt and striped necktie." When Freeman deplaned in Los Angeles, photographers snapped pictures of him wearing "a light flannel robe and black and white pajamas" for the slightly "cooler" weather. Observers seemed fascinated by Freeman's wardrobe change, especially since he told them he still had his flamboyant tropical attire on underneath. Freeman's tropical dandyism helped link his "sensible hot weather outfit" with the permissive fairyland.[95] In so doing, Freeman and others with comparable power and influence challenged social conventions.

Interestingly, Freeman found himself in trouble with the law while visiting Washington, DC, a few years later, exposing the complexities of his "open secret" to public speculation in Miami and elsewhere. The front page of the *Miami Daily News*'s January 18, 1936, issue reported that Freeman, then seventy-four, had been taken into custody in a Washington "psychopathic ward." The police had not charged the "Miamian" with a crime, and the article did not elaborate on the nature of his arrest. In fact, other than reveal he was taken into custody, the report only detailed Freeman's charitable works, prestige, and accolades.[96] In reality, however, he had been sent to the ward "for observation at the request of police" after they had "picked [Freeman] up at a downtown Turkish bath."[97] While it is unclear what exactly police caught Freeman doing at the bathhouse, it is possible he may have been caught seeking to be sexually intimate with other men at a common site for homosexual cruising. He was taken to the psychopathic ward at Gallinger Municipal Hospital, where patients suspected of mental instability were held. If they did not improve, they were then sent to St. Elizabeth's Hospital, where many "sexual psychopaths," which included those attracted to the same sex who were believed to have a psychological maladjustment, were regularly treated.[98] It also appears that Freeman may have been suffering from dementia. According to reports, sometime in the 1930s Dade County Judge W. Frank Blanton declared Freeman "mentally incompetent" and named his "relative" Charles D. Boulton as his guardian.[99] While it appears Freeman may have been mentally ill, it is also possible psychiatrists and judges read his "eccentric" behavior as representative of a sickness. It seems likely that any understanding of his "sickness" may have also been informed by his queer behaviors. All the while, it is hard to ignore the Miami newspaper's failure to mention that DC police took him into custody after he was found in a bathhouse. It seems possible Freeman's "open secret" was safer, so to speak, in Miami.

Women also played integral roles in forging this modern fairyland. Those of influence cultivated a queer elite, often artistic, culture in Miami. This included recruiting opera divas of international acclaim with great queer followings, such as Amelita Galli-Curci and Mary Garden, to perform in the city.[100] Freeman personally hosted these women. In part to inaugurate and celebrate the opening of Casa Casuarina, in February 1931 Freeman hosted Garden for a concert in Miami.[101] Garden, who never married, had earned a reputation for her sexual ambiguity and gender-bending characters and became a lesbian icon. For instance, she created the lesbian role of Chrysis in Camille Erlanger's 1906 opera *Aphrodite*. In 1913, a nineteen-year-old girl in Philadelphia committed suicide because of her uncontrollable—and unrequited—infatuation with the opera singer, whom she had never met. "The young girl had become imbued with the idea that Mary Garden was Queen Cleopatra, and that she was her slave," noted one report.[102] It appears Garden's queer aura also resonated with men like Freeman.[103]

From Miami's earliest days, women spearheaded the formal establishment of strong literary and artistic circles in the city. Even before its autonomous incorporation, many of Miami's women longed to bring their talents and enthusiasm to the public sphere, which frontier life both permitted and required. They often expressed the solitude that came from the confines of the home and sought the companionship of other women to help bring culture and progress to their new city, even if this was initially articulated through the language of domesticity and embodied through their public role as "social mothers." One pioneer woman, Mary Barr Monroe, recalled "the great loneliness of the early days," when women "longed for other women from the great outside world."[104] By 1900, they came together to form a literary club they called the Married Ladies' Afternoon Club, which changed its name in 1906 to the Miami Woman's Club to reflect the fact it permitted "spinsters" and widows to join. A similar club also emerged in Coconut Grove. These clubs worked to advance the cause of art and culture in the fairyland. In particular, they established the city's library system. By the 1920s, the Miami Woman's Club was hosting art classes, lectures, and exhibiting local artwork. In this capacity, it proved central to the advancement of art and culture in the early city, much of which promulgated the club's tropical home as fantastical in nature.[105]

One female artist and civic leader, Dewing Woodward (fig. 3.4), particu-

FIGURE 3.4.
Dewing Woodward,
c. 1925. Folder 3,
Box 11, University
of Miami Historical
Photograph
Collection, University
Archives, University
of Miami Libraries,
Coral Gables, FL.

larly helped shape the fairyland image, all while challenging established gender and sexual mores. Although her life has been largely erased from our history books, she was a well-known pioneer-artist with great influence— in Miami and elsewhere. Born in Williamsport, Pennsylvania, Woodward (née Martha Dewing Woodward) was the daughter of a prominent northern family. She worked as an art instructor in the United States and, at age thirty-six, moved to Paris. There she found inspiration, exhibited her work, and had a studio. After eleven years in France, Woodward, by then a well-established artist of considerable fame, moved back to the United States. In the late 1890s, she started one of the first—if not *the* first—artists' colonies in Provincetown, Massachusetts, which became a site for artists and sexual and gender nonconformists by the early 1900s.[106] In 1905, Woodward and her companion, Louise Johnson, visited the Bearsville hamlet in Woodstock, New York, similarly in search of inspiration. Drawn by its "pictorial surroundings," the two women bought several acres of land in the nearby hamlet of Shady, also in Woodstock, and built a home and artist studio there. They established an artists' colony that became the Blue Dome Fellowship, where "a group of artists and students affiliated for mutual benefit" studied

"the figure in the landscape."[107] The two women soon ran into serious financial trouble and, in 1919, decided to move to Miami, where they hoped to
find similar inspiration in the area's tropical climate and wilderness. They
too were lured by the idea of fairyland, and they brought their Blue Dome
Fellowship along with them.[108]

Unconventionality characterized Woodward's personal life and career;
her aesthetic and influence helped define the public image of Miami as fairyland. Her family was not pleased with her decision to move to Paris, her
claims to independence, and her rebellion against male control. Woodward,
who never legally married, embodied many aspects of the autonomous and
"mannish" woman, which later proved instrumental to the development of
sexual subjectivities and identities. At one point in her career, her artwork
received the highest mark and was set to win a grand prize. The selection
jury, however, learned that the artist was a woman and questioned whether
she had received any "professional" (i.e., male) assistance. The evidence suggests that the misogyny and chauvinism she habitually encountered led to
her decision to drop "Martha" from her name. That she only identified herself with the androgynous, if not masculine, name of "Dewing" for the rest
of her life is representative of the way she defied traditional feminine conventions in her pursuit of male privilege. She set up shop with Johnson and
headed a bohemian artists' colony. The two women scandalized the Catskills
community by painting nude female models *en plein air*.[109] Census records
reveal that in Woodstock and Miami, Woodward and Johnson headed
their household together and permitted other women artists to board with
them. When Johnson left Miami, Woodward continued this tradition without her.[110] Years later, Johnson reflected fondly on their time together and
their intimate partnership.[111] While there may be a modern impulse to label
Woodward a "lesbian," the imposition of such an identity cannot be substan-
tiated by the available evidence.[112] Insofar as she transgressed the era's conventional gender norms, however, Woodward contributed greatly to Miami's
queer and fairyland ethos.

Much like Freeman, Woodward rose to prominence in spite of, or perhaps because of, her own open secret of unconventionality. Just a few years
before she moved to Miami, she published a largely autobiographical text
titled *Some Adventures of Two Vagabonds* under the pseudonym Wealthy
Ann York, York being her mother's maiden name. In this work, she not only
flaunted her transient and gender-transgressive lifestyle but also coded it
with an unfamiliar name, albeit one that could easily be deciphered. And so
it was. A newspaper from her native Williamsport soon "outed" her as the
writer.[113] In that text, she described her queer family: "We are not precisely a

'family'; we are only 'two old maids 't gits th'er livin' skitchin', two dogs and a cat."[114] She mastered the art of self-expression and individuality, significant characteristics for the nascent shaping of sexual identities in the city. One art critic noted that Woodward "leans to the 'freedom of the individual,' standing between the rigidly classical and the ultra modern." Rather than follow established patterns, "her technique is her very own and … she paints what *she* sees."[115] Indeed, her work and personal life embodied the very essence of self-expression so critical to the formulation of an identity—lesbian or otherwise.

Woodward's free spirit and bohemian lifestyle not only transgressed gender norms but also secured her positions of power and influence in Miami. She was asked to paint numerous canvases and murals for the growing fairyland. With her modern aesthetic and technique, she produced works featuring landscapes, birds, portraits, and nudes. Her work gave shape to the lure and enchantment of the city. One of her most popular works, *Morning Song of the Pines*, features sensual nymphs. She donated the piece to the Miami Woman's Club.[116] Woodward continued to paint and contribute to the city's culture until her death in 1950. She also helped start the art program at the University of Miami, served as president of the Florida Federation of Arts, and, during the New Deal, was hired by the Works Progress Administration to embellish local public buildings. Despite her influence, she constantly ran into financial trouble. It appears she was often uncompensated or undercompensated for her work. This stands in stark contrast to the experiences of male artists and reveals the prevailing sexism she combated all her life.[117]

Part of what made these women and men, particularly the latter, so influential in shaping Miami as a fairyland was their privilege. They were able to live outside of social conventions largely because of their wealth, whiteness, status, or fame. As a woman who often found herself undermined by misogyny, Woodward seems to have struggled a lot more than most of the men. She remained influential, however, in part due to her acclaimed artistry and prominent family.

Freeman is perhaps the best example of how some queer elites could exert their influence in Miami—and shape it as a fairyland—through wealth and status. When Freeman got into trouble for inviting Emma Goldman to speak in East Orange, one of the prominent organizations he belonged to reluctantly requested his resignation, "realizing that Freeman's father is a man for whom every member holds the greatest respect." The letter asking for his resignation even included an apology to Freeman's father.[118] Goldman similarly recalled that their confrontation with law enforcement prohibiting her public lecture was Freeman's "first experience with the police." She suggested that Freeman, unlike her, appeared naïve to censorship and the oppressive and discriminatory arm of the law. The authorities allowed Freeman to host Goldman's speech at his mansion because they recognized that "it was private ground, and the police knew that their authority stopped where property rights began."[119] This was a concept Freeman both understood and cherished. Unlike Miami's working-class laborers and migrants who lived in shared spaces, men like Freeman had much greater access to privacy.

For law enforcement, Freeman's status, race, and wealth put whatever he did—and with whom—at Miami Beach's Casa Casuarina outside their jurisdiction. During his summer 1931 visit to Dallas that attracted much attention because of his flamboyant attire, Freeman showed up to a local restaurant wearing "sandals, bright purple shorts, a polo shirt and a necktie"—attire reflecting the tropical dandyism he displayed in Miami. The maître d'hôtel "remonstrated and insisted that diners must wear more clothes." Freeman simply responded, "I am a privileged character."[120] Men like Freeman proved influential in shaping the fairyland image, and received at least tacit indulgence of their open secrets, because their privilege gave them license to operate outside of traditional conventions.

### Tropical Queers and the U.S. Imperial Ethos

Influential queer men exerted their power in both the urban center *and* the transnational markets tied to Miami's fairyland, at times advancing a U.S. imperial ethos. The word "imperialism" can carry many meanings and, at times, imprecise definitions. It can include foreign armed intervention and occupation, capital investment and penetration, nation-building projects and interference in internal political affairs, and cultural saturation and imposition. The United States carried out all of these imperialist projects in Cuba during these years. Miami pioneers and investors often capitalized on this. More broadly, "imperialism" denotes exercises in power that "enable and produce relations of hierarchy, discipline, dispossession, extraction, and exploitation."[121] Empire's relationship to gender and sexuality is more than incidental. They are interwoven and intimately tied to empire's execution.[122] This particularly resonated in a new city like Miami, where investors and powerbrokers grappled with simultaneously marketing the area's lack of urbanity (i.e., a sun-kissed return to one's more basic needs and joys) and its modern image. In addition to acknowledging that U.S. empire could advance Miami's prospects, early city investor-residents were particularly motivated and committed to bringing civilization to the backward and barbaric Caribbean because this mirrored the work they were doing to build and promote the fairyland back in Florida.

This imbalanced power relationship strengthened over the years, particularly as new markets opened in the Caribbean. Travel to Cuba and the Bahamas from Miami dominated the early city's marketing relationship to the Caribbean and thus contributed to the development of the fairyland image. Surely some travelers found their way to other ports in the Caribbean via Miami, but this was on a much smaller scale. Until at least the late 1920s, Miami's port and tourist industry could not accommodate regular traffic to many Caribbean destinations. It is similarly critical to stress the significance of geographical proximity in establishing these sites as an extension of southern Florida's fairyland. Miami is, of course, physically nearest to Cuba and the Bahamas, which made sea travel shorter and more pleasant, and Havana and Nassau the focus of Miami's tourism industry.

Travel from Miami to British colonies other than the Bahamas, such as Jamaica, was much less frequent during this period. Miami did not offer regular sea travel to Jamaica until the 1930s.[123] Jamaica only shifted its attention to tourism as a means of salvaging its postemancipation economy. Initially, like southern Florida, Jamaica heralded itself as a health resort. Reports of disease and discomforts, such as sweltering heat and crawling insects, delayed the successful marketing of Jamaica as a destination, or as an extension of Miami's own playground.[124]

Other sites in the Caribbean yielded less traffic to and from Miami largely due to the interworking of U.S. imperialist policies. Puerto Rico did not factor greatly in Miami's designs for leisure travel until about the 1930s. As with Cuba, the United States occupied the island during the 1898 war. Unlike Cuba, Puerto Rico became an official colonial possession. Puerto Ricans did, however, constitute a significant portion of Miami's workers in its small but growing manufacturing sector. Since all Puerto Ricans received U.S. citizenship after 1917, workers were not excluded as immigrants, as Bahamians had been after 1924.[125]

Farther west in the Caribbean, U.S. empire had a very different impact. In 1915, U.S. Marines occupied Haiti. The following year, the U.S. government also occupied the Dominican Republic, thereby exerting its presence on the whole island of Hispaniola. These subjugated states became sites of contestation and violence rather than destinations for leisure and recreation. The United States maintained a physical presence in the Dominican Republic until 1924 and in Haiti through 1934. The United States argued that its occupation of these sovereign nations was necessary to correct internal political strife and instability. It only agreed to end its occupation once it had made these nations ready for U.S.-approved governance that favored foreign investment and capital. Tellingly, the deoccupation of Haiti coincided with the establishment of that country's National Tourism Office.[126] These occupations also helped consolidate and centralize the state's power in ways that facilitated the rise of populist dictators in both Haiti and the Dominican Republic.[127] Years later, these processes affected Miami in very different ways as Haitians, in particular, fled to the city seeking refuge from tyranny.[128]

While these factors limited extending Miami's fairyland to the rest of the Caribbean and Latin America, the rise of the aviation industry beginning in the late 1920s quickly changed that. Air travel was also an effective move to combat the economic depression. By 1929, a Miami newspaper informed its readers that "every manjack of us must prepare to become air-minded, or else to be air-muddled."[129] When Pan American World Airways was founded in 1927, it secured a coveted contract to carry mail to Havana from Key West. Within a few months, the airline moved its base to the Miami area, and passenger flights to Havana began departing from the city later that year.[130] Other routes often combined train and plane service. This meant that New Yorkers could take a train to Miami and then board a three-hour flight to Havana. This brought "Cuba within 39 hours of New York" in 1928.[131] As the name of the airline suggests, these changes also reflected Pan-Americanism, or the contemporary movement that purported and promised greater cooperation and equality among the Americas.[132]

Although Cuba and the Bahamas remained central to Miami's tourist industry, the development of aviation created new markets throughout the Caribbean and Latin America. By the late 1920s, new routes connected Miami to Nicaragua, British Honduras, Panama, Costa Rica, Mexico, the Dominican Republic, Haiti, and Puerto Rico.[133] In 1929, the *Miami News* boasted, "An air-minded Miami, with new maps, new meanings ... means a mightier Miami." One must "learn how to finance the fact that Nassau and Havana are no farther off than Palm Beach used to be, that presently the New York post office will be but a night's flight away ... and that ... the Canal Zone" was "within three day's distance." Miami was "no longer land's end, but the central gateway of the now consciously-connected Americas."[134] In March 1932, the president of the Greater Miami Airport Association informed the city's businessmen that the previous year had seen 26,000 passengers fly out of Miami to several Latin American countries. In all but three months that year, "more people entered by air than by steamer." The future had arrived in Miami. "You can travel on regular lines from Alaska to Argentina—and Miami is in the center of this picture."[135] By the late 1930s, Eastern Airlines and National Air Lines had moved to the city, cementing Miami's dominance of the Latin American aviation market.[136]

This new industry challenged established gender and sexual norms in the city. Pan Am's inaugural flight to Havana from Key West carried its first flight attendant: a Cuban American man named Amaury Sanchez. The creation of the flight attendant profession in the late 1920s was steeped in gender and sexual conjecture. The early profession required attendants to meet the safety and comfort needs of a sophisticated and wealthy white crowd. While this made a perceived masculinity essential, the profession soon associated male stewards based in the city with femininity. Meanwhile, many of the elite women and men who traveled on these early flights partook and were familiar with the "gay" nightlife in cosmopolitan areas such as New York and Chicago. This included gender-transgressive expressions in fashion, grooming, dancing, and perhaps even same-sex desires.[137]

Miami's early queer residents boarded these Pan Am flights to places such as Havana and Port-au-Prince in search of more tantalizing tropical recreation. Perhaps Freeman best represents this queer, elite fetishization of the Caribbean, one accomplished through the cozy embrace of U.S. imperialism. In 1929, a Miami newspaper reported that "Mr. Freeman spends much time flying between the south Atlantic islands, using Miami as a base."[138] In fact, he was often described as a jetsetter and Caribbean-trotter who would fly to a place like Havana for lunch and catch a flight back to Miami in time for dinner.[139]

While Freeman frequented Cuba regularly under circumstances largely amenable to U.S. interests, it was his fascination with Haiti that best demonstrates how he contributed to the expansion of U.S. power in the Caribbean. Freeman's fascination with colonial history—and Hispaniola, more specifically—was evident in his design for Casa Casuarina. He boasted that the property was a "modern adaptation" of the Alcázar de Colón, the sixteenth-century palace built by Christopher Columbus's family in Santo Domingo.[140] Freeman even flew in the Dominican Republic's prominent politician and archbishop Adolfo Alejandro Nouel y Bobadilla to bless his Miami property.[141] By the time he built Casa Casuarina, he was making regular trips to Haiti. Although travel to Haiti was limited and deemed less desirable during the U.S. occupation, the popularization of air travel and the domination of Haitians by U.S. Marines had slowly opened the country to tourism.

During this period, Freeman maintained a close relationship with Faustin Wirkus, the "white king of La Gonâve." Wirkus was one of the U.S. Marines who served in Haiti during the occupation. He claimed Haitians had crowned him king of La Gonâve, the island northwest of Port-au-Prince. As one report noted, Wirkus's "ability and the superstitions of the natives combined to give him almost complete control of the island."[142] Freeman clearly admired this about Wirkus. In fact, Wirkus hosted Freeman in La Gonâve in

1929. There, among the "blacks, many almost savages," Freeman witnessed firsthand the racialized oppression of the occupation. One newspaper joked how Wirkus introduced Freeman to "the beauties of the island (terrestrial)." This seemed to make light of Freeman's open secret, while simultaneously noting that Haitian "beauties" were, in fact, made available to U.S. visitors. Freeman later invited Wirkus to Miami, a prospect local newspapers celebrated.[143]

Freeman wielded his wealth and influence to secure both his and Miami's close ties to Haiti. In 1930, Freeman attended the Bal Bohème at the Arts Club in Washington, DC, dressed as Christopher Columbus, and he and his friends reenacted the discovery of Hispaniola.[144] At the lavish costume party many of the country's most prominent elites joined artists and bohemians for what one newspaper called the "gayest of the gay," gesturing to how it departed from gender and social norms.[145] Similarly, it is difficult to ignore that Freeman's relationship to Wirkus and U.S. empire yielded him greater social status and recognition in Miami. Although it is unclear who designated him such, several reports referred to Freeman as Miami's "Honorary Consul General for Haiti" (the city did not yet have a Haitian consulate).[146] It is possible Freeman self-appointed himself to that position, or perhaps Wirkus bestowed him with the title. Freeman became a sort of spokesperson for Haiti, often giving impromptu and sensational lectures of its history in Miami and elsewhere.[147]

As this suggests, much of Freeman's relationship with Haiti played out through power differentials that strengthened the U.S. imperial ethos. Freeman believed his "benevolence" had earned a special place in Haiti's history. In his last will and testament, he "bequeath[ed]" his "heart to the People and Government of the Republic of Haiti." He requested that his heart be placed in a silver casket and "deposited in the ... tombs of Dessalines and Petion [sic]," two of Haiti's founding fathers. Although his will claimed that two Pan American Airways officials had "been fully instructed" on how to carry out his final wishes, it seems his body was ultimately sent to New Jersey.[148] That Freeman believed the tombs of Haiti's revolutionary heroes should be disturbed to make room for him speaks volumes about the unequal power and influence he exerted on the nation.

Miami investors appreciated the city's intimate relationship with Haiti, largely brokered by Freeman, because the opening up of that tourism market—long deemed a mysterious forbidden fruit—only strengthened southern Florida's fairyland image. Some evidence even suggests that the U.S. occupation of Haiti temporarily branded the Black Republic a new fairyland for U.S. American visitors.[149] In 1930, a U.S.-appointed Haitian president sought to send to Miami, via Freeman, an anchor thought to belong to one of Columbus's ships as a "gesture of friendship." The anchor was to join "a collection of Haitian and other West Indian relics and products" housed in Miami.[150] In the midst of the U.S. occupation, items the marines procured and confiscated from the Haitians were prominently displayed in Miami exhibits. Freeman obtained Haitian basketwork, artwork, sandals, and a banned vodou drum. This was part of a city effort to "arouse greater interest in international trade relations" and promote opportunities for travel to the Black Republic. In fact, "Pan American air officials" reminded "Miami and visitors in the city" that they could take "a morning plane from here" and arrive in Haiti "for a 3 p.m. luncheon, such as is popular among residents here."[151] In 1935, the year after marines deoccupied Haiti, Freeman and several others hosted an event in Miami they called "A Night in Haiti." It featured dancers, art, and a film that purportedly represented Haitian culture.[152] This proved critical to building Miami's reputation as a gateway to the so-called enchantments awaiting U.S. visitors in the Caribbean.

ONE OF THE GREATEST contradictions and tensions of this fairyland image is that most people in the city did not experience life in Miami in such fantastical ways. This imperialist culture is representative of a greater trend in which sentiments of racial uplift and paternalism served as vehicles to justify the oppression of those in foreign nations. Because of the racialized nature of imperialism, it also helped justify the discrimination and subjugation of black, immigrant, and working-class communities in the United States, including Miami. As Mary Renda has argued, sensational accounts of a barbarous Haiti being subjugated by white forces and "benevolent" U.S. paternalism carried over and entered the U.S. imagination in real and meaningful ways. Or, put differently, "once the violence of imperialism had done its work, the literature of empire would invite others to such imaginings."[153] This overseas affair particularly helped renegotiate ideas of race and gender that reified whiteness and masculinity in Miami. Jim Crow was alive and well in the city. When Sténio Vincent, the Haitian president in power when U.S. forces evacuated, came to Miami in 1939, all white hotels refused the black leader a room. If the president of Haiti experienced this level of bigotry and discrimination, Miami's black residents knew they would only fare worse.[154]

So while Miami's well-to-do residents and visitors helped shape and came to understand Miami as a fairyland, many of the city's black, queer, immigrant, and laboring communities experienced violence, surveillance, poverty, and crime with far greater frequency. In fact, it is no coincidence that—rather than "fairyland," which conjured up warm images of unrestricted pleasure—the city's marginal communities often called Miami "Sodom" or "Gomorrah." Like "fairyland," these monikers recalled immorality. *Unlike* "fairyland," they evoked the forbidden, unwelcome, dangerous, and repulsive.

This chapter has documented the textured and multilayered ways Miami became a fairyland for the nation's white elites, particularly during the interwar years. Both real and imaginary, this marketed image offered wealthy and powerful residents and visitors both hedonistic pleasure and the safety net of respectability. The fairyland represented numerous things to different people. For many, it was an elite, tropical playground detached from the anxieties associated with urban life in older cities, as well as the bitter winters endured farther north. Miami was also marketed as distinctly modern. These renderings permitted and made available the temporary violation of traditional gender—and at times, sexual—norms. Indeed, many would come to understand the fairyland as a space where such transgression could be expected. Urban boosters spent much time and money staging the city in ways they believed would enhance that image, as well as tourists' expectations of a trip to fairyland.

# MIAMI AS STAGE

The truth is, we don't want a town that hasn't any raciness about it. If people want to bring up their children in a Sunday School atmosphere, let 'em hunt up Sleepville and when the kids are grown, bring 'em to Miami to wake 'em up.
—MIAMI VISITOR, 1920

Miami is a stage actress among cities, beautiful in her makeup of colored floodlight and neon, frowsy in the morning light over her slums, mercurial and temperamental in her private life, equally capable of excesses of virtue and vice, playing before the nation in a drama which has included among the male leads such dissimilar actors as a Carl Fisher and an Al Capone.
—MIAMI NEWSPAPER, 1953

In September 1916, the Miami Chamber of Commerce received an anonymous letter urging urban promoters to make the city more presentable to wealthy white tourists and out-of-towners. The tourist, who had spent a year in Miami, implored city managers to trim the dead or limp fronds of the city's coconut palm trees. The "well wisher" employed the metaphor of Miami as a lady in need of a "shave," emphasizing the need to "wash up and clean up" the city before rolling out the welcome mat to "winter tourists." Chamber of Commerce president Everest George Sewell agreed, and chimed in, "We're spending a lot of money advertising Miami, but I declare I don't like this idea of making a sideshow out of her and advertising her as a bearded lady."[1]

While Sewell's derisive response advanced the metaphor of a feminine city in need of some tidying up, it also paid tribute to the representation of gender transgression in Miami. This included the visibility of the "mannish" woman in Miami. Her presence played a significant role in the marketing of fairyland, particularly because she signaled the arrival of modernity, even as new gender and sexual anxieties started to surface. While Sewell wanted to welcome tourists to the modern and gender-transgressive fairyland, he made clear that he did not want the city to become a sort of "sideshow" or "bearded lady." What the city needed was a good polish. Both literally and figuratively, this meant taming the city's image as a space of disrepute. While urban designers marketed the city as a modern space where gender noncon-formity was possible, new tensions pertaining to what that transgression might entail—including *sexual* deviancy—gradually increased.

This metaphorical conjuring was by no means anomalous; the very essence of fairyland operated on both a literal and figurative level. Louis A. Pérez Jr. has demonstrated the significance of taking seriously the distinct metaphors U.S. media, politicians, and citizens have historically employed to make sense of Cuba. He has observed the evolution of Cuba as metaphor—whether of ripe fruit, damsel in distress, whore, or racialized child—in re-sponse to particular sociopolitical moments and how they advanced U.S. imperialism. Drawing on a rich literature on language and metaphor, Pérez argues that metaphors create new forms of knowledge and moral systems that have serious consequences in shaping social and political thought.[2] At face value, early boosters' articulation of Miami as an elite, white fairyland proved a lucrative enterprise. It also had real-life consequences for how publics and counterpublics understood their sense of self, urges, desires, and worth.[3] If fairyland proved real for several white elite settler-residents, what drew them there in the first place? What forces facilitated their ability, along with that of other booster-investors, to shape the nascent city as a site for gender, sexual, and racial transgression and experimentation?

One metaphor, in particular, proved central to this permutation: Miami as stage. Christopher Krolikowski and Graham Brown have implored schol-ars to explore how the staging of urban sites for tourism influences visitors' behaviors and experiences. "Tourism precincts are performed, as their space is inhabited, given meaning and thus transformed into place by fleeting groups of visitors," they argue.[4] Indeed, urban boosters staged and helped create a "mental geography" of the city for tourists and would-be tourists.[5] While a handful of scholars have observed the performative role constitutive of the tourism industry—both in catering to outsiders and playing the role of the leisured outsider—very little attention has been given to the way boost-ers' staging of the urban landscape helped script tourists' performances of gender, sexuality, race, ethnicity, and nationality.[6]

Both figurative and literal, these performances played a social, cultural, and political role in Miami. No discussion of performativity—particularly as it relates to gender—is complete without the influential arguments set forth by Judith Butler. Her major thesis that gender is not an inherent or given force that "is" has helped destabilize dominant understandings of gen-der's "naturalness." She argues that gender is something one *does*. In this way, "acts, gestures, enactments, generally construed, are performative in the sense that the essence or identity that they purport to express are fabrications manufactured and sustained through corporeal signs and other discursive means."[7] Relying on Esther Newton's classic text on female impersonations, Butler also explores the construct of gender as a performative parody and imitation with no basis in a real or true identity.[8] To a lesser degree, Butler also explores the interpellation of race as a form of regulatory and social control.[9] Several scholars, such as José Esteban Muñoz, have brought the two categories closer together. In his work, Muñoz pointed to "disidentifications," or the mapping of identities queerly outside of mainstream assumptions of whiteness and heterosexuality, as sites of exploration and contestation.[10]

This chapter turns to how these gendered and racialized formations played out, so to speak, on the stages of Miami's modern theater as well as the staged urban landscape that gained currency as fairyland. Urban boosters staged a fairyland they believed would attract white well-to-do tourists or visitors-turned-residents. Through the importation of flamingos from the Caribbean or the trimming of its majestic palms, city powerbrokers designed a metaphorical fairyland defined as much by Miami's tropical milieu as its emphasis on excess, the exotic, and enchantment. In other words, they staged the fairyland they believed "desirable" outsiders yearned for. As one man noted, "The Magic City provided illusion, along with grandeur."[11]

The staging of Miami as fairyland—through "illusion" and "grandeur"— not only permitted but also mandated gender, sexual, and racial forms of transgression. Miami's fairyland made allowances for explorations of gender and sexuality in large part because they were undergirded by ideologies of white supremacy and the subjugation of the city's black and ethnic communities. In their exploited service to the white tourist industry, black and brown bodies often served as "props" on the city stage, making the landscape more desirable to a moneyed white clientele.

These themes are explored in several ways. This chapter first traces the spectacle of the fairyland's marketing campaign. In addition to noting some of the powerful metaphors used to market the city's transgressive identity, it emphasizes the "exotic" features that turned the city into a spectacle ready for tourist consumption. Race and empire played a key role in this project, particularly as Miami boosters measured their city's success against developments in the Caribbean. Pérez has similarly argued how Cuba and Florida, including Miami, have historically developed their identities vis-à-vis each other, at times mirroring each other, at times as polar opposites.[12] After exploring the staging of the city as fairyland, the chapter turns to the literal stage. Miami's minstrel stage became a significant site for defining normative representations of gender, sexuality, and race in the city. Similarly, portrayals of Miami's fairyland in film and the stage outside of Miami proved critical to advertising the city as a site for white leisure and recreation. Underpinned as it was by racist and colonial practices and ideologies, the idea of Miami as a site for pushing the boundaries of gender and sexuality entered the U.S. imagination.

## Metaphor and the Making of Miami

While efforts to market Miami as fairyland preceded World War I, E. G. Sewell made a more concerted and "organized effort ... to capitalize [on] the strategic advantages of the city as a winter resort" by the mid-1910s. Sewell, who was John Sewell's brother, became president of Miami's Chamber of Commerce in 1915 and later served as mayor. He was, one contemporary noted, the "genius who ... 'sold' Miami to the world," and, "like any good advertiser," he saw to it that "Miami delivered the exact goods that were sold."[13] Although Sewell and the city's Chamber of Commerce sold the city primarily through newspaper and magazine advertisements, they also were able to get the city written about in articles. According to one man, Sewell's "indefatigable efforts to make Miami the most-talked-of city in the country resulted in inestimable free publicity in the leading newspapers and magazines of the nation."[14] Sewell secured from the city council a sizeable advertising budget for the Chamber of Commerce, mostly funded by the city's wealthy residents. He also produced multipage booklets promoting the area that were mailed to prospective visitors, and he arranged for the plastering of "artistic posters in rich colors ... in the ticket offices and resort bureaus all over the north."[15]

Much like the monikers used to describe "instant cities"—such as "magic city," "miracle city," "fantastic city," or "wonder city"—"fairyland" referenced Miami's seemingly overnight growth.[16] While newspapers proved an effective marketing tool, writers also promoted this image through books and other published works, with such titles as *What about Florida?*, *Seeing the Sunny South*, and *The Town That Climate Built*.[17] To many, Miami's swift expansion seemed to have sprung from the wave of a fairy's magic wand. This added to Miami's appeal.

One of Miami's greatest champions, particularly successful in marketing the area to tourists and investors, was Carl Fisher. The entrepreneur from Indiana made millions on his ventures, including the 1913 debut of the Lincoln Highway, the first automobile road traversing the continental United States. Like other entrepreneurs from the Midwest and Northeast, he took his ambitions and capital farther south to Miami Beach. He was the mastermind behind the Dixie Highway, the first completed interstate highway system that partially opened in late 1915 and would come to stretch from the southern peninsula of Michigan to Miami.[18] By the following year, most of Florida boasted the improved "passability and comfort for tourists."[19]

Much like Henry Flagler, who connected Florida's resorts with the railroad, Fisher understood that inaccessibility was one of the greatest impediments to making Miami a lucrative enterprise and destination. In 1915, one contemporary noted that the Dixie Highway was "more than a road on which motorist may travel from Chicago to Miami through one of the most scenic, historic and romantic sections of our country. It is an inspiration, a bond of friendship and good will between north and south."[20] Fisher promoted the area with spectacle and pizzazz, even leading a car caravan in 1915 that traversed the entirety of the Dixie Highway to demonstrate how much easier it was to reach southern Florida.[21]

These powerful marketing men, who helped redefine consumer culture by the 1920s and 1930s, also saw themselves as harbingers of modernity. They sold consumer culture through extravagant visualization. This early marketing style of U.S. consumer culture specifically targeted and advertised products to affluent and upper-class citizens. This helped create "social tableaux" by which advertisers reified contemporary images—such as that of the "modern woman"—through marketing strategies that more closely resembled a social and class-based fantasy than a mirror of society. In Miami, one manifestation of this was that of the "Miami mermaid," an elite and respectable woman who took claim of her body and sexuality by purchasing and wearing the latest bathing suits and taking pleasure in the leisure and recreation time modernity afforded her.[22]

With all this in place, figurative language molded Miami as a white elite fairyland. One of the more popular manifestations of this was Miami as the "fountain of youth," recalling Spanish explorer Juan Ponce de León's sixteenth-century visit to the area.[23] In Miami, promoters maintained, the old could be rejuvenated. Good health, warmth, and free spirits awaited travelers. Even more so, Miami was the nation's "playground" and "winter play city."[24] Such metaphors recalled the sunny recreation and leisure the city offered outsiders, such as swimming, sunbathing, golf, and fishing. It also heavily suggested Miami's after-dark offerings. This language crafted Miami as a whore made available to tourists. As one journalist stated, Miami "is the harlot of American cities, and, like many harlots, it is unusually favored by nature."[25] It is no coincidence that these metaphors mirrored those used to represent Cuba during this period: the two competed for tourist dollars and pesos.[26]

The promotion of Miami as a play site built distinctly for white recreation boosted beliefs that one could transgress gender and sexual norms there.

One promotional brochure represented Miami Beach as a "city built for the *specific* purpose of providing mankind with health and play while most of the nation is in the grip of ice and snow."[27] This was similarly conveyed through the metaphor of Miami as a nightclub or theatrical revue. "Think of our nights—our wonderful, tropical, night-club nights," noted one source.[28] Yet another observed that in Miami Beach, "flash and excitement hold the spotlight, and when things are in full swing the island city more closely resembles a spangled revue than a wealthy resort."[29] It's not just that the city hosted nightclubs and revues. It *was* one. It specifically tailored for visitors' leisure and recreational whims. "Everything here," noted one newspaper, "is calculated to appeal to one's sense of the beautiful."[30]

Miami became a metaphorical stage where theatrical representations of the self could be performed. "Miami is a vast theatre of entertainment," maintained one brochure.[31] Fisher's wife, Jane, matter-of-factly claimed, "Miami Beach was theater—but it held the charm of music and tropical languor."[32] As actors wore costumes, visitors dressed in swimwear "costumes," as they were commonly referred to then, for the unique occasion. "By day, beach costumes compete with the spectrum and by night jewels shatter it."[33] Despite its natural beauty—which played such a significant role in defining the fairyland—the city's modernity had been physically built as a sort of theater for outside entertainment. The built environment complemented "the paraded kaleidoscopic animation of the ocean front."[34] A poet called Miami a "hodge podge town" and an "unreal, movie city." She continued, "Even 'on location' / Her stage set— / But never ready."[35] In this way, the city's staging was still a work in progress, subject to further embellishment and theatricality. Another woman wrote how "flying over Miami is a one-act drama, if you fly no farther than Biscayne Bay. To appreciate city planning you must get a bird's-eye view of it, and no city was ever more beautifully planned than Miami." In this way, the "regularity of [its] streets," the "symmetry of [its] parks," and its "gleaming bridges [that] connect palm-fringed cays with the marts of busy trade" were all part of some theatrical design. Watercrafts on Miami shores were likened to "toy boats," as if props setting the mood.[36] The constant reference to the "moon over Miami," so popular in literature and song, utilized the moon as a natural spotlight on the city stage.[37]

Like stage sets, advertisers used beautifully colored and highly stylized billboards and posters to sell a fairyland culture to recruit visitors. It was not uncommon for tourists and residents alike to find massive sets—not unlike the backdrop for a staged play—near downtown Miami that re-created the pleasures available in Miami Beach, such as bathing beauties and sports (fig. 4.1). One advertising firm pitched a colorful advertising campaign to

FIGURE 4.1. Large and highly stylized sign in Miami advertising Miami Beach as "America's Winter Playground" just "across the causeway" connecting both cities. 1921. Photograph by William A. Fishbaugh, image no. RC03718, courtesy of the State Archives of Florida.

Mayor Sewell. The firm believed such publicity "create[d] a desire" and one could only "tell that story just when the prospect is in the mood."[38] Like all good advertisers, Miami boosters became storytellers. They sold sunshine to those inundated with snow, a conquerable wilderness to those in the concrete jungle, and transgression to those bound by strict social and legal enforcement.

Not all promotional sets were placed in the city. On major highways, "from Detroit and Chicago, throughout New England and along . . . the Middle Atlantic states," drivers found "metal posters in vivid colors showing a royal palm tree and the bathing beach" branded with a Miami slogan: "The land of Palms and Sunshine." One of the more theatrical market schemes was deployed at the 1920 Rotary Convention in Atlantic City, a resort competitor. The City of Miami sent "a car load of palms, tropical fruits and coconuts," to stage at the Boardwalk there. With this, "a miniature Miami was set up where the Rotarians answered questions and distributed literature." Later that year, a similar spectacle was created in Chicago, except "bathing girls" joined the promotional display.[39]

In promoting the city's land boom, contemporaries used language that anticipated the sexual liaisons possible in Miami. "Pioneers" courted Miami by "'taking a fling'" with the city "on the side," ultimately seeing the "old boom spirit reborn in them." While investors built a "tropical empire" that recalled the "old spirit of adventure which built the West," the *New York Times* believed that "new Floridians outboost the proverbial Californians."[40] In this way, one observer noted, "The growth of Miami is one of the real romances of American business."[41] A fiscal analyst observed that the boom appeared to be "an orgy of real estate speculation." It made headlines throughout the country. Newspapers sold "cocoanut palms on moonlight nights" and tropical "islands and peninsulas which had been pumped out of the sea by enterprising promoters."[42] One man likened the city to a sexually vigorous youth: "The city is still in the adolescent stage, still growing and still reaching out for greater things, a lusty youngster, whose destiny none may yet foresee."[43]

The metaphor of a lusty, feminine city ready to be ravaged by outsiders was particularly potent after the city's mid-1920s economic downturn caused by the local market collapse and a hurricane. To recover, boosters turned to the theatrics of hosting popular dog and horse races, which "assured the north that Miami was not a mass of ruins."[44] Things got even more serious after the 1929 crash. If Miami did not amp up its offerings, one booster suggested, it should update its playground slogan to read: "For Sale—Excellently located, highly developed pleasure resort. Reason for selling, business not sufficient to justify size."[45] Despite the economic depression, Miami Beach's city council not only sustained its marketing scheme, it *increased* it. City employees, however, dealt with decreased wages.[46] More than ever, Miami became "a lusty youngster" awaiting the penetration of outside capital and investment.[47] This youngster city was so fertile and full of stamina, maintained one source, that she birthed several adjoining suburbs and municipalities, the "lusty brood of communities spawned by the 'Magic City.'"[48] Visitors, tourists, and investors were paying customers, seduced by the lustful opportunities. "Folk desiring complete satisfaction should come hither," seduced another source. "Miami has the goods; all she craves now is customers who prefer sunshine to chilblains; coconuts to cough drops."[49]

The promotion of this fairyland to a white and wealthy clientele heavily depended on harkening a colonial past and present. Early investors sought to turn Miami into an "American Riviera." Vizcaya's Venetian influence was not the exception. It was the rule. This Mediterranean inspiration—even as Italy and Spain were often confused or conflated—was a promotional attempt to bring a little piece of the "old world" to the urban frontier, once again straddling the lines between the old and the new. There was a particular emphasis on Andalusian architecture and culture. This is evident in the street names of Coral Gables: Granada, Galiano, Ovideo, and Ponce de Leon.[50] Another form of colonial fetishization regularly played out when white tourists flocked to the Seminole Indian Village in Miami, where they watched indigenous peoples wrestle "huge, man-killing alligators." So popular was this "spectacle tourism" that Seminoles took the show on the road, attracting visitors across the country.[51] The spectacle of seeing both the Seminoles and alligators colonized proved most profitable. Similarly, Fisher stressed that Miami Beach advertisements, particularly moving pictures and photographs, had to be "staged right" for outsiders. In staging the area's "unusual" offerings, he proposed capturing on film his "little elephant ... that can do some very funny stunts," a reference to his real-life elephant, or prop, kept in Miami Beach. "It is easy to stage things at Miami Beach that have never been seen on the screen and it would be immensely interesting to ... people who have never seen such things," Fisher believed.[52] In fact, "Rosie the Elephant" became such a spectacle that Fisher allowed visitors to use her trunk as a golfing tee.[53] Through such spectacle, Fisher manipulated the advertising business by rebranding it as feature or entertainment "news." He stressed the necessity of making promotional pictures of the elephant "the key-note." He maintained that, "otherwise, it would be clearly classed as an advertisement by any newspaper and thrown in the waste basket."[54] Miami was a modern, colonial spectacle-city.

*Enter the Caribbean, or Miami's Second Act*

Much of Miami's fairyland and colonial lure depended on its ability to associate with the Caribbean. A 1905 poem noted that "charmed Miami is the pivot sweet / which Cuba and Bahamas over ocean greet.... / Like sail bird rounding past her magic southern shore / this fairy land exclaims a welcome to her door."[55] Another source noted how the east coast "hotel system" Flagler started was the "most elegant and best appointed ... in America." After all, it extended "along the line from Atlantic Beach on the north end to Miami; also a steamship line and hotel system reaching from Miami to Key West, Nassau, and Cuba, as well as many points in the Bahama Islands where the most fastidious tourist can ... regret not having found this fairyland before."[56] Similarly, in listing Cuba's many enchantments to outsiders, the U.S.-produced song "Cuban Moon" declared, "How I love you, Fairy land's silv'ry sands."[57]

Many who visited Miami for leisure, recreation, or health often coordinated that trip as part of a longer excursion through the Caribbean, including stops in Cuba. In March 1914, a party of 100 well-to-do visitors from the

Carolinas and Virginia stopped in Miami as part of their trip to Cuba.[58] By the 1920s, this was standard practice among the nation's wealthy. William G. Stuber, vice president of Eastman Kodak, and his wife spent time in Havana in 1924 before visiting Miami for several weeks.[59] That same season, David Ressler, a New York resident and president of the Yonkers Fur Company, honeymooned with his wife in Havana and extended their vacation with a sojourn in Miami Beach.[60]

Meanwhile, U.S. imperialist policies—which Miami boosters capitalized on—facilitated the rule of U.S.-backed, corrupt Cuban governments that particularly established the island as a site for U.S. American sexual indulgence and experimentation. A few months after the United States intervened in Cuba's war of independence against Spain in 1898, travelers from across the country recommenced their travel to Cuba, via Miami or Tampa.[61] One traveler noted that men dominated the gambling joints in Havana. After all, "the Cuban women are kept for their beauty, not as companions."[62] While this suggests men generally frequented spaces of vice unaccompanied, it also reveals that Cuban women were subjugated by men—both native and foreign. This too was colonially suggestive. Tour guidebooks available in Miami insisted that visitors be knowledgeable so they could "conquer Havana in brave style."[63]

Travel to places like Havana was also a transnational form of slumming, whereby wealthy white visitors explored parts of the Caribbean they deemed exotic and whose people they determined were sexually available. For U.S. Americans, travel to Cuba proved risky enough for a dangerous and titillating experience beyond the confines of their traditional social and cultural barriers. Despite new restrictions and public health campaigns the United States imposed in Cuba after 1898, the colonial vestige of regulated prostitution on the island remained intact. As Tiffany A. Sippial has argued, "The official sanction of prostitution in Cuba seems jarringly out of synch with the island's new modern status, especially considering that U.S.-based antiprostitution activity," or Progressive-era reform, "reached its apogee at precisely the same moment that the United States exercised its most direct influence in Cuba."[64]

In 1911 the *Cleveland Press*, the hometown newspaper of many of Miami's early settlers, published an "investigation" into "the shocking and alarming state of public and private morality" in Cuba. A U.S. observer stated, "Cubans are prototyped in the Egyptian fellaheen—the remnant—the whittlings of a race. Sex and cigaret cover all." He maintained, "The fault is racial. Cuba, the criminal dumping ground of Spain ... yields a hard, indocile mixed blood that riots in depravity and gives foundation for monumental political misdemeanor." In addition to introducing the United States to the sexual permissiveness available in Cuba, this paternalism helped justify U.S. occupation and intervention. In Cuba, U.S. travelers could attend the "fiestas diabolos" where women and men exhibited "the finality of depravity." These were deemed "proper, legal, and protected" by the Cuban government. Prostitution ran rampant. On Cuba's streets, the writer purported, one could find "courtesans sitting in the doorway loudly 'soliciting' the passing public." This threatened the "moral" United States, as "hundreds of American young men are en route to Cuba on business or pleasure bent"—likely by way of Florida. Cuba afforded U.S. travelers a locale with "the most daring in displayed vice" and lax or no legal restrictions.[65] Miami proved key to this sexual paradise.

Many travelers also stopped in Miami on their way to or from the Bahamas. Although the British colony was not yet fully prepared for an onslaught of U.S. tourists, this industry grew with every passing season. Oftentimes, this was the work of U.S. investors, who capitalized on making this economic relationship work. Such investments only made travel to Miami more desirable, as the city was either a stepping-stone for or an extension of a Caribbean destination. The Bahamas was not yet a vacation spot for middle-class tourists; it remained prohibitively expensive for most and served as a tropical playground for wealthy sportsmen and an elite, international crowd. Indeed, "by the early twentieth century these islands began to be transformed into a playground for itinerant Caucasians in search of health and enjoyment." Such Caribbean destinations, "once tropical plantations, purportedly unfit for white residence," were now being "touted as veritable gardens of Eden."[66] This proved particularly potent during World War I. Unlike those of cities in war-torn Europe, Nassau's main street had "only to do with the feeding and decorating and entertaining of tourists." There was so much demand in the capital that tourists complained that boats sailing back to the United States were too infrequent to keep up.[67] Interestingly, one man, who first visited Miami, preferred "the loneliness and wildness" of Nassau over the "advertisement and vulgarity of Miami."[68] For some, the Bahamas seemed primitive while Miami appeared ultramodern and vulgar in its spectacle. Indeed, one identity depended on the other.

Like in Cuba, tourists found gambling dens and other sites of vice in the Bahamas, which created new anxieties on the islands.[69] As early as 1917, the Bahamian colonial government proposed an act to regulate sex work, particularly in the capital. It passed the Music and Dancing Licenses Act in 1919. It noted that "dance halls are principally places of assignation and centres for the dissemination of venereal disease. They appear to be Meccas for the worst type of prostitute and the happy hunting ground for characters of ill repute." The act mandated that each operation first receive a license from the head of the police, and it gave local law enforcement plenary powers to shut down sites deemed "unseemly or vulgar." In addition, much like Miami officers had done during these years, local Bahamian police were tasked with removing or arresting those they believed were guilty of "disorderly conduct" or any person they believed was "guilty of improper conduct." Official reports implied that U.S. visitors and passersby exacerbated these problems. At these dance halls and entertainment venues, which often catered to outsiders, "women go ... for the purpose of soliciting and the men for the purpose of 'picking up a woman.'" The success of Miami as a fairyland contributed greatly to formalizing Nassau's sexual economy.[70] Illicit trade from the Bahamas similarly helped carve out sexual demimondes in both Nassau and Miami. A report connected to the 1919 act noted that Bahamian colonial officials observed illegal activity and trade in "these dance halls ... or in the immediate vicinity."[71] Alcohol was, after all, legally available there with proper licenses.

Conversely, Dade County went "dry" in 1913, seven years before the Eighteenth Amendment to the U.S. Constitution prohibited the national manufacture and transportation of liquor. Despite that, a 1923 report described Miami as "a city where, if you feel the need of a drink and don't happen to have your own flask with you, all you need to do is wait in the shade of a palm tree until a resident comes along, ask him where you can find a bootlegger, and if he is not one himself, he will tell you where to go.... You can buy all the whiskey you want in Miami at $5 a quart."[72] The passage of Prohibition did not equate to strict enforcement in Miami. In fact, the laxity authorities applied to this illicit business helped solidify the city's turn-a-blind-eye attitude toward many nonnormative gender and sexual forms of entertainment.

Miami's proximity and regular liquor supply from the Caribbean proved critical to its marketing and tourist appeal and transformed both places. Miami owed much of its "wetness" to the illicit trade of alcohol from nearby Bahamian islands. This trade and the traffic connected to it particularly altered Bimini, the Bahamian island nearest to Miami. By 1930, the island, which had a population of roughly 300, had become a site for vice, with five salons and one licensed club.[73] Meanwhile, travel to Miami grew in popularity in large part because of a visible market of available vice and sex. Indeed, in Miami, "bootlegging was as much a natural tourist attraction as palm trees and sparkling Atlantic beaches."[74]

Miami often staged this subversion. In the midst of Prohibition, wealthy white tourists who visited Hardie's Casino in Miami Beach could pose in a photo booth that displayed them "buying" booze from an attractive and modern female bartender (fig. 4.2). Right across from that set, the casino staged another scene: a near-identical drink stand in Havana (fig.4. 3). White tourists posed in front of countless bottles of liquor—taunting the law and the prudishness associated with it. In acting out these scenes, visitors not only partook in the fairyland culture—one premised on colonialism, permissiveness, and hedonism—but they also helped market that image when they brought the souvenir photo of their staged transgression back north.

Meanwhile, like the Bahamians asked to wear necklaces of live crustaceans to entertain Miami's white guests, Cubans added to the city's colonial lure and exoticism. Cuban athletes were imported from the island to play jai alai for spectators. "Between games, music for dancing" was "furnished by a Spanish or Cuban orchestra."[75] One nightspot manager "brag[ged] about his acquisition of some full-fledged Cuban-American bartenders to cater to folks with Havana appetites." These laborers constituted part of Miami's exotic appeal, particularly in light of the city's growing ambitions to compete with Cuban tourism.[76] When Paul Chalfin and Louis Koons went on their "pleasure trip to Cuba," they "bought . . . rare articles of furnishing for the Deering mansion."[77] When Chalfin or James Deering required relics from the old world to embellish Vizcaya, "roof tiles of mellow Venetian red" were "imported from old Cuba."[78] This represented a growing trend in Miami, where developers purchased "weathered" tiles stripped off the roofs of entire Cuban villages. Over 2 million tiles were imported from the U.S.-controlled island from 1925 to 1926 alone.[79] At the expense of Cuba's heritage, such acts helped shape fairyland's image. Boosters also sought to replicate the Caribbean's natural beauty with colonial props. South of the Miami River on Brickell Avenue, for instance, urban designers planted black olive trees imported from Jamaica.[80] In the early 1930s, boosters staged the new Hialeah racetrack as a tropical oasis by importing flamingos from Cuba and the Bahamas to beautify the infield. The track's embellishments created "the background for fashions of the wealthy."[81]

For their part, Cuban urban planners similarly embraced the image—albeit often cautiously—of an island made available to Miami and U.S. tourists. The newspaper *Diario de la Marina* observed that tourists often preferred to visit the island and stay on a modern ship because it secured them access to certain "luxuries" and "amenities" they could not necessarily expect in Cuba: "cold and hot water, a comfortable and very clean bed, their towels changed several times a day, electric service bells, a fan or air conditioning . . . all a few steps away from the bar." This allowed them to "leave 'civilization' anchored at the port" when they explored Cuba's offerings. This too was a form of slumming. Tourist demands transformed Cuba's landscape, par-

FIGURE 4.2. Man posing at a tourist photo booth of a drink stand at Hardie's Casino in Miami Beach during Prohibition. Note the stuffed alligator prop by his feet, creating the illusion of Miami as an untamed and uninhibited wilderness prime for conquer. 1925. Image no. RC12518, courtesy of the State Archives of Florida.

FIGURE 4.3. This staged photo booth for tourists moves the drinking and gaiety to Havana, an essential stopping point for Miami tourists. Miami capitalized on Havana's wide-open reputation to lure more tourists its way. 1925. Image no. Pr24550, courtesy of the State Archives of Florida.

ticularly in Havana. Buildings got modern facelifts, renovations, and amenities to compete with the "floating hotels," or ships, and other resort cities, like Miami Beach. Cuban boosters straddled the line between emphasizing Cuba's colonial past and appearing modern, an effective strategy to compete with Miami. If Miami boosters were quick to call Cuba unsafe for U.S. travel, Cuba's promoters rebutted that Miami lacked history and appeared artificial and "congested" with overeager visitors.[82]

Cuban boosters similarly relied on known metaphors to shape the island's image, which, in turn, helped attract visitors to Miami. One Cuban promoter argued that a tourist city is like a big "department store," where new merchandise and advertising became necessary for success.[83] By the 1930s, Cuban promoters called modern tourism a sign of "social progress" and a "democratic display," since it was no longer limited to the wealthy.[84] As this suggests, Cuba was in the midst of major social and political upheaval. Rising nationalism and anti-imperialist fervor led to revolution, phenomena further explored in subsequent chapters. Miami boosters often derided Cuba's circumstances through powerful metaphors of theater and spectacle. "The Cuban situation has pretty nearly entered the stages of comic opera," noted one Miami entertainment newspaper. "It would be funny if it weren't so serious."[85] The following week, the same paper joked, "Why doesn't the Cuban Tourist commission take advantage of the daily revolutions and invite tourists to view some at first hand?"[86] Both Miami and Cuban boosters knew each tourism industry depended on the success of the other.[87]

## Performing Race and Gender in Miami

While Miami and its intimate ties with the Caribbean were marketed as fairyland for a white, moneyed, and modern clientele, most of the Miami area's black, ethnic, and working-class people lived on the outskirts of a city where they disproportionately endured violence, poverty, and discrimination.[88] The *Chicago Defender*, one of the country's most prominent black newspapers, claimed Miami was "the fairest of playgrounds for *white* people in the South," while blacks experienced Miami as "the city of the damned." Blacks in Miami, according to the newspaper, were "not regarded as highly as ... a black dog." This too had significant sexual connotations. The writer observed that in Miami "a black man is shot down for speaking to a black woman if a white man happens to desire her." The historical record certainly reveals the prevalence of these desires. The conditions that criminalized, violently oppressed, and subjugated Miami's black residents most often made the city for them "the modern Sodom and Gomorrah."[89]

In this vein, Miami's law enforcement acted out on the white urban control's belief in a black hypersexuality in maintaining social order. It was not uncommon for local police to use makeshift shock devices to secure a black suspect's "confession" to a crime. Similarly, some black women were at least partially stripped, physically exposed, and forced to sit in an electric chair. Other reports indicate that electrical devices were applied directly to a black suspect's genitalia to get her or him to speak.[90] For these people, the fairyland so heavily promoted by urban boosters seemed distant, foreign, unfamiliar, and no more real than the mystical land of the fairies. Fairyland needed the city's sordid Sodom, however, to fully deliver on its wide-open reputation. In this way, fairyland and Sodom did not stand apart so much as they coexisted as opposite sides of the same coin. They were divided more by race, ethnicity, and class than by their mutual transgression of gender and sexuality.

A fairly small but powerful group of black leaders established successful businesses in Miami, albeit with more limits than their white counterparts, that sometimes also contributed to the making of that so-called Sodom. Like many middle- and upper-class white landlords and investors, some black businesspeople exploited poorer blacks with predatory rental and real estate practices in their pursuit of capital, property, and greater social mobility. As early as 1900, black businessmen in Miami established the Colored Board of Trade (CBT) to help grow black commerce and represent the interests of the city's black professional class. As N. D. B. Connolly has argued, for many of these black women and men, "the question . . . was not *whether* to endorse white supremacy, but rather *which* white supremacy seemed most likely to provide the desired benefits."[91] In their pursuit of upward social mobility—particularly defined by the attainment of property—these black entrepreneurs frequently abandoned the needs of blacks of lesser means as well as grandiose ideas of black solidarity. Many of these property owners capitalized on and "directly abetted" the vice and sex trades that ran rampant in black neighborhoods.[92]

In their pursuit of respectability in the face of Jim Crow, several of Miami's black businesspeople joined white investors in criminalizing the black, working-class neighborhoods where women and men transgressed gender and sexual norms—often across racial and class lines. From Miami's earliest years, a working-class black entertainment culture thrived in Miami's Colored Town, despite constant criminalization and police harassment. This was an extension of the queer frontier's vice and sexual culture detailed in previous chapters. Early on, the CBT maintained that the "best and respectable colored people" had to commit themselves to "assist[ing] the authorities in making it decidedly unpleasant for the low and criminal elements of all races." This would make "the community better, the atmosphere purer and the relation of the races more satisfactory."[93] The CBT's conciliatory alliance with white, antiblack interests was evident in the case against a black Bahamian named Herbert Brooks. He had been accused of sexually assaulting a white woman, even though the evidence against him was, at best, flimsy and circumstantial. In conceding that it was in the group's best interest to cooperate with police, the CBT canvassed Colored Town to find the man white police suspected of the crime. The CBT, along with a black veterans organization, handed Brooks over to the white police upon being promised he would receive a fair trial. He never did. White "mob formations" gathered "in the downtown district" with "threats to lynch Brooks."[94] Police put him on a train, from which white witnesses claimed Brooks jumped to his death before he arrived in northern Florida for trial. Miami's Bahamian community did not believe this version of the story, suspecting that mob violence caught up with Brooks instead.[95]

Most blacks and many mixed-race people were excluded from making any significant gains in Miami's real estate boom and from enjoying the fairyland. De facto segregation rendered nonwhites without a proper beach to enjoy, for instance, which was central to the marketing of fairyland to white outsiders. While no local law mandated such segregation on the beach, it was socially enforced. At best, blacks might have been able to access remote and undeveloped beachfronts with dangerous riptides and swarms of insects. It was not until 1945 that the "Colored Only" Virginia Beach, located on a key three miles away from the mainland, opened and became a popular site for blacks from around the country.[96]

Instead, blacks provided the bulk of the labor that made the city's boom and white leisure culture possible and, in many cases, appeared to be mere props in the marketing of fairyland. They provided towels or drinks, worked as chauffeurs, and delivered entertainment. When Fisher placed his elephant at the center of his marketing campaign, he also suggested bringing "in a few ... native negroes" to do "stunts" and "a couple of real good looking diving girls" for spectacle.[97] While the latter fetishized white women—a significant marketing strategy tied to the development of heterosexuality—the former operated on the premise of black subservience. An editorial cartoon the *Miami Daily News* published in 1934 captured this sentiment (fig. 4.4). It depicted a man in blackface—as if on a stage—gleefully serving a lounging white man, Miami Beach mayor Frank Katzentine, a mint julep by the beach. This caricature depicted one of the central images of Miami as fairy-

"A MINT JULEP, KUNNEL, SUH?"

FIGURE 4.4.
Man in blackface
serves as a prop
in Miami's staged
fairyland that was
partially defined by
the marketability of
black subservience
and inferiority. *Miami
Daily News*, January
18, 1934, 10.

land: an imagined white superiority. Black workers catered to white clients and their racialized fantasies of black exoticism, subservience, and servitude.

Miami offers us a distinct purview to explore blackface as a product of multiple contested colonial forces. As a handful of scholars have suggested, there are limitations to interpreting blackface exclusively through a myopic U.S. lens that may be at least partially reconciled by treating the subject as a transnational phenomenon curdled less by nationalism than by colonial processes more broadly. As figure 4.4 suggests, blackface performances in Miami during this period took shape alongside discourses from the U.S. South and North *as well as* numerous Caribbean tropes, particularly from the Bahamas and Cuba. This allows us, as one scholar has noted, the possibility to factor Caribbean-mediated blackface performances as "a mask behind the mask behind the mask," or, put another way, as Afro-Caribbean-descended representations of blackness—as well as the heavy colonial burdens attached to them—among portrayals that may otherwise be read as singularly U.S. African American.[98] After all, Caribbean-descended blackface performances have also historically helped forge nationalist unity and proved critical to articulating anticolonial struggles.[99] This permits us to interpret stage actors in Miami, particularly those of African descent, as agents who shaped local understandings of race, ethnicity, gender, sexuality, nationalism, and power relations more generally.

The very essence of marketing Miami as a white fairyland depended on this notion of black inferiority, which often played out through racist entertainment and derision. Blackface minstrel shows proved a popular form of entertainment from Miami's first days as a city. Following campaigns to purge the vice cultures found in Miami's black ghettos, white investors capitalized on many of the black stereotypes they sought to criminalize in places like Colored Town by hiring performers to act them out on the minstrel and vaudeville stage. Beginning in the nineteenth century, this racially charged form of "comedy" helped consolidate whiteness by creating a space for even newly arrived immigrants and working-class laborers to parody, humiliate, and distance themselves from blackness.[100] By the turn of the century, minstrel shows gave way to vaudeville, or variety-show antics that featured a wider range of performances. These included animal tricks, slapstick, acrobatics, dancing, as well as ethnic and blackface performances.[101] Miami stood apart, however, with its distinct source of ethnoracial comedic inspiration: Bahamians. "Native dances," songs like "Nassau Boy," and improvised performances by "Nassau Negro natives" provided amusement in the city as well as on vessels transporting visitors to nearby Caribbean destinations.[102]

This form of entertainment appealed to whites of all classes and ranged from professional Broadway-esque revues to low-budget performances throughout the city. Very little was off limits. The *Miami Metropolis* praised a 1913 minstrel performance by local Boy Scouts, who were accompanied and coached by blackface adult women and men.[103] In 1929, "prominent men in Miami's public life," including a lawmaker and state's attorney, performed a minstrel show to raise city funds. A local firefighter also pleased the audience with his "negro impersonat[ion]."[104] Whether a youth or elected official staged the act, this platform allowed white entertainers to perform contemporary beliefs about blackness, including laziness, buffoonery, drunkenness, immorality, and subservience. The format helped dictate and mold a common white fantasy surrounding blackness in the city. It became an outlet to air community racist assumptions and anxieties over "Miami's Negro problem."[105]

For as much as blackface minstrelsy and vaudeville accomplished in articulating racial anxieties, these performances also greatly compounded local understandings of gender. Many of these performances included male and female impersonations. Throughout 1922, the newly opened Fairfax Theater on East Flagler Street, advertised as the "coolest spot in town," featured amateur vaudeville performances. On one night, a local clerk did his female impersonation alongside an acrobat, jazz, "Hula," and other "character" dancers, as well as a white woman playing the "Little Black Mammy of the South"—a blackface performance of a minstrel archetype.[106]

The minstrel stage became a forum for locals to publicly express contemporary racial and gender anxieties. In 1922, the fraternal order of the Miami Elks Club "gamboled, sang, danced and cracked jokes" during an amateur minstrel show. It included prominent men lampooning blacks, including one man who "made the funniest coon." It also featured a comedy sketch that took place in then-distant year 2000. In the midst of gender anxiety and fears of masculine regression in the wake of woman's suffrage, one man "appeared as a woman lawyer" and another man played the "effeminate son" of a political boss. Through these performances, local residents shared their concerns about the future—wherein they believed women acted like men and men acted like women—with a laugh. Another sketch that evening featured "one of the best female impersonators on the Miami stage."[107]

Not all stage female impersonators were amateurs. One of Miami's most popular professional female impersonators was Karl Russell Denton, an Ohio native who frequently performed in the city with traveling shows. Born in 1892, Denton enlisted in the army during World War I when he was twenty-five. He served in a machine gun battalion of the Eighty-Fourth Division that was sent to France but never saw battle.[108] He later sustained significant injuries and was honorably discharged.[109] Within a few weeks, a few years shy of thirty, he found his way to the stage. His career in the minstrel business took off quickly and he became a popular female impersonator by the early 1920s. Denton must have been quite the sight, standing at five feet ten with a fit build, a ruddy complexion, and piercing gray eyes (fig. 4.5).[110] Audiences were enamored of his high, feminine voice, which fit his early bill: "minstrelsy's premier soprano."[111] He gained this reputation throughout Florida and parts of the U.S. South. One critic referred to him as the "prima donna of minstrelsy," which also referenced a minstrel archetype.[112] By 1923, promoters claimed they intended to add Havana to the traveling show's "extended itinerary."[113] While it is unclear whether they ever made it there, it is certain that entertainers—including female impersonators and minstrel performers—understood Havana as a key market directly connected to the success they experienced in Miami.

Denton was a big success. By 1924, Denton had joined the popular Lasses White All Star Minstrel. The show's leader, Le Roy "Lasses" White, was a Texan and blackface pioneer who recorded a song titled "Nigger Blues" in 1913, further demonstrating how central racist tropes were to the formation

FIGURE 4.5. Karl Denton as "prima donna" female impersonator with suitor, an actor in blackface, c. 1920s. Box 13: Dwight Wilson, Denton Scrapbook, Denton Family Collection, 1920–1991, University of North Texas Special Collections, Denton, TX.

of these gender-bending performances.[114] During one of their minstrel sets, White re-created the "humor" of life on a "Dixie plantation." Denton did most of his female impersonations solo, however.[115] Onstage, he portrayed the desirable "prima donna," sometimes referred to as the "wench."[116] He embodied the female lead through his feminine performance and voice. Critics praised him for complementing the deep male voices on the stage with his "soprano."[117] One reviewer observed how Denton "made a fascinating dame, and his singing voice was one of the best imitations of a lady's that ever came from an Adam's apple."[118]

It is important that we not take for granted the power of the audience in assessing and shaping what was permissible and desirable. Locals often admired the minstrel and vaudeville actors who passed through Miami, emulating them onstage in amateur acts. Audiences also had a great deal of influence in selecting the material the actors performed. With deafening interjections, boos, and cheers, audiences frequently dictated when a performer's act was done. They similarly demanded encore performances and persuaded the show to allocate a particular act more stage time.[119]

Miami audiences overwhelmingly praised Denton's gender-bending act. He always received "a good hand from a Miami audience." One local critic celebrated the return of Denton's "girlish figure."[120] Another Miami observer praised Denton's female impersonations as "clever" and showing great "versatility."[121] Yet another Miami critic called Denton's performance "about the cleverest in that line ever seen here."[122] What exactly made his performances clever or versatile is unclear, although reports suggest his ability to pass as a woman was at the center of his success. "Denton is an artist at make-up," observed one Florida review. "He looks and acts like a woman."[123] By all accounts, audiences appreciated and seemed fixated by Denton's convincing performance as a woman. Everyone "wondered how . . . he came by those good-looking hands and neck and shoulders."[124] The realistic attributes associated with his staged impersonation allowed men to "safely" appreciate his feminine beauty and women to admire his fashion and style.

At the height of his popularity in the city, in the 1920s, no major reviewer even hinted at any sign of local contempt or disgust for Denton's female impersonations. Rather, as one Florida critic reported, Denton's "every portrayal bears the mark of class."[125] He also put on an elaborate show. "Mr. Denton spent last summer in Paris and while there arranged for this season's cotume [sic], which are said to be the costliest ever used by a minstrel." Audiences loved his costumes. In fact, if his troupe's engagement in a city was long enough, Denton's wardrobe was "displayed in the windows of one of the leading stores" for all to enjoy.[126] Local communities not only found his gender-bending performances fascinating or tolerable, but they also celebrated them as decent and a form of studied art. Like those of other prima donnas before him, Denton's performance provided Miami women a preview of the latest and lavish fashions. This drew in an increasing female audience who wanted to imitate his style and demeanor.[127]

Certain factors facilitated Denton's warm reception in Miami and beyond. The aggressive marketing of Miami as fairyland encouraged challenges to established gender norms. Denton's female impersonations appeared tame to some of the less "convincing" gender-transgressive images visible in the fairyland. In part, this was because Denton easily passed as a woman and he performed on a respectable stage. In one of Denton's earlier performances, a Florida critic suggested the audience did not want to see the actor ever appear onstage as a man. In one performance, Denton performed with the troupe dressed as a man prior to appearing in his solo act as a woman. This, the critic believed, rendered his female impersonation "less effective" because it lost shock value or tainted their experience.[128] His audiences might be swayed into seeing Denton as an impersonator rather than feeling duped by his convincing female persona. In his performance of the prima donna, he could also become the object of desire for the audience. For members in the audience to read him as a man dressed in women's clothes—rather than as a feminine seductress—might evoke perversion.

Although anxieties of the mannish woman and the effeminate man may have signaled some concern over sexual deviancy in some circles, particularly medical communities, these performances most often registered as a sign of changing social and gender norms. Medical experts and pseudo-experts had identified the "gender invert" whose sexual deviancy was understood as a product of gender transgression. Those in Miami did not yet consider acts like Denton's to be an affront to moral behavior and social decency, even though the homosexual as distinct individual—one who may or may not subvert gender norms—was increasingly entering public consciousness. Up until the late 1920s, such minstrel and vaudeville performances, particularly in their employment of blackface, proved both popular and representative of the area's shared values and morals. In lampooning undesirable characters—such as feminists, queers, immigrants, or blacks—the community defined who they were as a people and the characteristics that made them so. They became "normal" by making clear, through their performances, who they were *not*.[129]

Perhaps nothing facilitated the warm praise of Denton's gender transgression more than the racialized environment in which he appeared onstage. Although it seems that Denton generally did not perform his female impersonations in blackface, he certainly appeared alongside many others who did. He performed alongside another male actor who staged "the natural acting of Mammy," which provided "the local color necessary to get the act over."[130] It appears audiences responded most to the sexualized impersonations of the light-skinned "mulatta," who simultaneously represented the perceived respectability of white femininity and the hypersexuality of black women.[131] This would have particularly resonated with white audiences in Miami, where Caribbean migrants and immigrants challenged racial binaries and a thriving sexual economy saw countless white men pursue sex with women of color. It is possible that Denton emulated or recalled the *mulata* onstage. A contemporary called Denton the "Helen Morgan of the minstrels."[132] This was a reference to the mysterious white celebrity and "torch singer" who offered a "*white* female counterpoint to black female blues and jazz performers." Morgan managed "to give expression to a body and soul tortured by unrequited love for a good-for-nothing man."[133] This comparison reiterates two significant points about Denton: that he performed his female impersonations as either a white or light-skinned black woman on the minstrel stage and that male audiences sympathized and read his stage character as a woman wronged. It was entirely possible for men in the audience to lust after or comfort Denton's staged woman without necessarily interpreting that desire as perverse.

Indeed, we must place Denton's female impersonations in the context of the staged minstrel that lampooned and disgraced Miami's black communities. These spaces and performances weaved a powerful narrative of black buffoonery and deviancy. Denton's female impersonations took place in stages where blackface provided white women and men a temporary cover or shield against being read as deviant. White actors like Denton who performed in these minstrel circuits—where "Negro impersonations" proved central to the core entertainment value—could present gender-bending performances to audiences without risking being read as indecent or immoral *because* blackness was already understood as such. Blackface provided a figurative mask for white male performers who might otherwise have to contend with how female impersonations might pose a challenge to their white masculinity.

We get another glimpse of this in a local 1925 advertisement for the performance of "Leary and Lee—Eccentric Dandies."[134] It seems this performance was held in an outdoor pavilion over either Biscayne Bay or the Atlantic Ocean. While the identities of these performers, presumed male, has been lost, they were packaged as the "best eccentric dancers ever in Miami." The category of the "eccentric dancer" generally referred to either an exotic performance such as the "Hula" or "native" Bahamian dances, for instance, or something of the acrobatic variety. Although the descriptor "eccentric dandies" may suggest that they were highly stylized, effeminate aesthetes and performers—as the dandy figure proved central to articulating modern gay subjectivity—it is much more likely a reference to their blackface portrayal of that minstrel archetype. In that context, the dandy was a similarly stylized, ostentatious faux-bourgeois, whose class and masculinity was undermined by his blackness.[135]

Meanwhile, despite invoking fantasies of the past—with references to plantation life or a greater nostalgia for antebellum Dixie, where slavery mandated black subservience—these performances often took place in modern theaters such as the Fairfax. Opened in January 1922, the Fairfax was marketed as a harbinger of modernity in Miami's tropical oasis. As a theater investor noted, "I am confident that it will be run on a strictly high-class scale and will be something of which Miami may well be proud."[136] The fact that the Fairfax so frequently staged minstrel performances featuring female impersonators reveals a local ambivalence toward the arrival of modernity in the city.[137] Miami appeared modern—with the arrival of lavish theaters such as the Fairfax, for instance—but staged anxieties about race and gender "problems" that signaled a desire to return to the "good old days" when white masculinity was not challenged by blacks, immigrants and migrants, women, or queers.

Black performers in Miami did not allow white actors to fully control the image of black buffoonery, laziness, and immorality crafted on the stage. Many black performers appeared on the minstrel and vaudeville stage before black and white audiences alike. Many black women and men performed in blackface. In some ways, this was the by-product of the black professional class's civic boosterism. Like many white investors, members of the CBT and other economically privileged black businesspeople adopted civic boosterism to help fill Miami's coffers and their own pockets. While white civic boosters marketed Miami as a white fairyland defined by its exotic and subservient black population, black boosters promoted a message of racial and economic uplift by trying to recruit wealthy black investors to the area. In light of the circumstances of most blacks in Jim Crow Miami, their message was traditionally conservative and restrictive. These boosters largely sought to disassociate themselves from the Bahamians, for instance, and adopted an approach in which their pursuit of black capital, investment, and respectability would—much like that of the white investors—exploit and oppress the majority of the city's black population.[138] Similarly, much like white investors had done, some black businesspeople co-opted, appropriated, and capitalized on the city's working-class queer and subversive culture. They did so by offering more sanitized versions of Colored Town's subculture or racialized expressions of gender and sexuality made more palatable for both respectable black and white audiences.

One such black civic booster was Georgia native Geder Walker, who opened the Lyric Theater in 1913. The CBT commended Walker as one of the "most substantial citizens of the county." Despite having received little or no education, he was a "marvelous example of what mother-wit can do in the business world." After all, a CBT representative maintained, "the progressive negroes who are citizens of Miami must be considered as a potent factor in the upbuilding of the city." The Lyric was, one newspaper claimed, "possibly the most beautiful and costly playhouse owned by colored people in all the

Southland."[139] Constructed on the thriving Second Avenue area of Colored Town, it attracted black investors and visitors from throughout the United States. Right next to the Lyric, Walker also operated an ice cream parlor and café for the city's black patrons and visitors. Miami's white slummers often joined them in these spaces. The Lyric was equipped with "everything ... needed for modern theatrical performances."[140] In its first few weeks of operation alone, "the colored population of Miami simply went wild" for the vaudeville acts, including blacks in blackface and gender-bending performers who caricatured black culture through humor.[141] This included black women impersonating men on the stage.[142]

Although black minstrels often perpetuated black stereotypes through the performance of racist archetypes, these venues also provided a space for them to challenge such images. This line of work could become quite lucrative or, at the very least, offer a more desirable alternative to agricultural labor.[143] Perhaps the best example of the success of black minstrel performers remains Bert Williams (né Egbert Austin Williams), a Bahamian-born man whose family migrated to the United States by way of Florida. He became one of the most successful and popular black performers by the turn of the century, even as he was a black immigrant performing in blackface. These black performers often challenged and took ownership of their acts by providing nuanced—albeit sometimes subtle—critiques of racial discrimination and oppression.[144]

These black minstrel performances, like those at the Lyric, stood in stark contrast to those staged in Miami's white theaters. While they sometimes also wore blackface and staged gender-bending acts, black performers often parodied racist assumptions of minstrel stereotypes. In contrast to the prima donna portrayed by white actors like Denton who strived to pass as a "true" woman, female impersonators in black minstrelsy "brought the performance of color and gender of minstrelsy into a realm of being 'screamingly funny' for the audiences, which included both U.S. African American women and men."[145] These performances were both *about* blacks and *by* blacks. They launched many careers, too. One of the Lyric's earliest performers was Georgia-born Trixie Smith.[146] She became a national sensation over the next two decades, recording several gender- and sexually transgressive jazz songs such as "He May Be Your Man (But He Comes to See Me Sometime)" and "No Good Man." The latter, recorded in 1939, found Smith swooning: "I'm one woman, who can't use a no-good man because a man like him is only good for a one-night stand."[147] While such messages further cemented the idea of black promiscuity and hypersexuality, they also gave black women and men a public stage on which they could reclaim their own bodies.

*Performing the Sexual Anxieties of Fairyland*

As all this suggests, racialized representations of nonnormative gender created space for sexually transgressive people and expressions. While the medical profession proved integral in establishing the homo-heterosexual binary, George Chauncey has shown the critical role *culture* played in creating this sexual axis, which organizes our carnal desires to this day. He has shown how a middle-class repudiation of effeminate and working-class fairies helped usher in new sexual identities defined by their same-sex attractions rather than by their gender transgression.[148] As Daniel Hurewitz has argued, however, for the first three decades of the twentieth century, "multiple paradigms prevailed."[149] While some publics believed that the objects of one's sexual appetites were immutable, others perceived them as potentially fluid. Similarly, while some understood homosexual intimacy as a product or expression of one's gender identity, some believed it represented a distinct sexuality: a *homo*sexuality, as the binary crystallized and became hegemonic. Miami's fairyland image, which heavily relied on black subservience and degradation to articulate its transgression, took shape alongside these textured and multiple paradigms. The fairyland's sexual meanings and anxieties entered the U.S. imagination through contemporary films and performances staged throughout the country.

While not set in Miami, the 1914 silent film *A Florida Enchantment* introduced northerners to the gender and sexual transgression possible in Florida resort towns and cities. The film's title, to say nothing of its plot, was reminiscent of the "enchantment" of fairyland. Based on an 1891 novel of the same title, the film featured a wealthy New York woman named Lillian Travers who visits a resort hotel in St. Augustine. While there, she comes across special seeds sown from a "tree of sexual change" in Africa.[150] Lillian kisses, flirts, courts, and dances with women upon ingesting the seed. She also shaves her growing facial hair, dresses in men's clothes, and eventually assumes the identity "Lawrence."[151] One scene finds her dancing with a female love interest, reminiscent of the era's queer dances and drag balls in places such as New York and Los Angeles.[152]

Lillian's queerness surpassed gender transgression and gestured toward the *sexually* deviant. The fact that Lillian was an heiress from New York is of great importance. She assumes her male persona as Lawrence by shedding her feminine clothing and mannerisms only after her midfilm visit to New York. This seems to nod at the popular queer subculture available there, one that many wealthy travelers to Florida were familiar with and, at times, tried to re-create in the "enchanted" fairyland.[153] Meanwhile, no one seems to show any contempt, disdain, or even suspicion for Lillian's desires for women before—or after—she assumes the Lawrence identity. In large part, this reception and attitude can be attributed to her resemblance to the era's new and modern woman—later, a "flapper"—who reclaimed her body and sexuality by stepping out into the public sphere in unprecedented ways, smoking cigarettes and dancing intimately.[154]

Conversely, her fiancé Fred's queer behavior was met with great suspicion and even violence. By the end of the film, he too ingests the seed. Fred assumes an effeminate persona that is, at first, met with laughs and derision. Fred's male peers soon turn violent and implore law enforcement to contain him. In fact, his sexual deviance is read as suspicious even *prior* to ingesting the seed. At one point, Fred grows frustrated with Lillian's dancing with women. He resigns himself to dancing with another man but is quickly policed by a male observer at the ball. Unlike Lillian, Fred is read as an abnormal invert or homosexual who needs to be policed and contained.[155]

The film departed from its general acceptance of queer expressions between women, however, in its portrayal of Jane, Lillian's black maid. The film's release date coincided with an era of greater sexual anxiety surrounding gender-bending women. Corresponding debates increasingly viewed mannish women as *sexually* suspect, especially those who operated outside the confines of white respectability. Unlike Lillian's, Jane's same-sex desires are met with great resistance. The film tapped into contemporary beliefs of sexual and racial difference—certainly present in Miami—in depicting such deviances as both cause and effect of "savage" and "uncivilized" black culture. This was heavily suggested in the film's locating of the seed's origins in Africa. The film prominently featured actors, including Jane's character, in blackface. Lillian coerced Jane to ingest the seed and constantly disciplined her. Upon swallowing the seed and her subsequent transformation, Jane reacts violently against the film's white characters. Lillian is forced to subdue her and explains away her violent outburst as the product of alcoholism. Jane soon harbors sexual designs for another black maid and physically attacks a black male valet who expresses interest in her, all of whom are white actors in blackface. So while Lillian is generally read as normal, Jane's same-sex sexual desires and passions are distinctly defined by her violence, rage, jealousy, and drunkenness.[156] Jane, by way of her blackness, was the film's *real* deviant. In no small way, cultural understandings of race framed what expressions of gender and sexuality were deemed presentable and acceptable.[157]

A very different narrative of heterosexual love and lust, however, prevailed in popularity and appeared to quickly overshadow these queer images. Three years *before* the release of the film, a vaudeville show also titled *A Florida*

*Enchantment* toured the United States. That two distinct and popular productions were made with the same name less than five years apart reveals
how ubiquitous the idea of an "enchanted" Florida was in the U.S. American
imagination. Although penned by different writers, it was no coincidence
that both productions sought to capitalize on the idea that one could push
the boundaries of gender and sexuality in Florida. Unlike the film, the earlier
staged performance less ambiguously emphasized heterosexual romance.
It told the story "of two wealthy men who" sought "recreation in a Florida
health resort" and became "acquainted with two pretty young girls."[158] This
production also highlighted the supernatural, or what in Miami was marketed through the image of fairyland. Rather than African seeds, one character possessed "a magic tube that enables the holder" to seduce the love of
a woman.[159] In Florida, and resort towns like Miami, a woman could fall
under a tropical-induced trance—if not coercion—that ended with a happy
heterosexual coupling. Indeed, both productions ended with the normative conclusion of heterosexual love. The veneer of heterosexuality, however
dominant, did not altogether eradicate queer representations or spaces, as
both productions left open the possibility of transgression in the enchanted
fairyland.

While some films had already used Miami as their enchanting background, the 1924 release of *Miami*, starring the "ultra-modern" actress Betty
Compson, particularly captured the U.S. imagination.[160] Like others, it told
the story of wealthy, white socialites exploring fairyland's offerings. A film
exhibitors' publication noted that Compson provided "real star value," which
was only amplified by "the title of 'Miami,' a name made famous and allur-
ing through the society and news columns ... throughout the entire civilized
world." The Miami backdrop, then, added "a magic touch of exploitation
... that makes the picture a 'Wow.'"[161] Miami proved to be a main character that effectively advertised the film. As the "winter paradise of the ultra-
fashionable," film studios knew it was "the exclusive resort that every woman
longs to see." Both the plot and female protagonist transgressed norms. In
the midst of Prohibition, Compson's modern woman drinks alcohol, flirts
with a married man, and strips down to her skin-tight, one-piece bathing
suit.[162] While the modern woman's unleashed sexuality helped sell tickets,
it also marketed Miami as a modern, white fairyland. Promoters suggested
consumer "tie-ins" for the film's release. One suggestion: have communities
around the country re-create the Miami stage with local bathing beauties
competing for titles such as "Prettiest Bathing Girl."[163]

Several staged shows similarly articulated Miami's fairyland as the site
of gender transgression that may have also signaled sexual deviancy, includ-

ing the 1929 live production of *Miami Nights*. Initially a short feature in another musical, the Miami theme grew in popularity and spawned a stand-alone production on Broadway. It then moved to the ultramodern Valencia Theater in Jamaica, Queens, and to several other venues across the United States. It depicted winter in Miami as the "modernistic winter," since it was in vogue for well-to-do northerners to spend the colder months in the resort city.[164] It featured music, dance, acrobatics, and humor. A twenty-one-year-old woman named Evelyn Wilson stole the show as "a clever male impersonator who got a big hand."[165] Her gender-bending performance found her wearing "a full dress suit." She apparently "stopped the show with her good characterization of a drunk singing."[166] Not only did she nod to the liquor available in Prohibition-era Miami, one critic observed that her act appeared "both novel and dangerous."[167] Like the others, her staged performances of gender transgression were ubiquitously associated with the fairyland, often relying on racialized humor and sexual innuendo to attract modern audiences.

Meanwhile, some stage performers like Wilson later sought to separate themselves from images of gender transgression, perhaps fearful that this might link them to sexual deviancy. Mannish women and effeminate men became staples in contemporary staged performances in New York City, particularly in Broadway and Harlem. By the early 1930s, New York politicians and law enforcement launched attacks against the city's visible queer culture.[168] A few months after her well-received New York performances in *Miami Nights*, Wilson distanced herself from male impersonations. One report noted that "in the early days of her career she dressed as a boy but today [she dresses] in lovely costumes with elaborate backgrounds she displays her virtuosity in character songs."[169]

The course of Denton's career on the minstrel stage similarly suggests that his gender-bending act, once revered, increasingly provoked sexual anxieties. Minstrel shows waned in popularity by the late 1920s. In addition to competing with films, in some instances they saw black jazz and blues artists simply replace blackface performers.[170] As Nan Alamilla Boyd has shown, this coincided with "the increased slippage between transgender behavior and sexual deviancy (and the stigmatization of same-sex sexuality)" that resulted in the "heightened scrutiny [of female impersonators] from audiences, booking agents, reviewers, and each other."[171] Although the stage permitted such transgression in the name of spectacle and theater, many gender-bending performers and others could be seen offstage traversing city streets.

Throughout Florida, Denton was widely referred to as "the Eltinge of Minstrelsy," an homage to Julian Eltinge, an internationally successful vaude-villian actor and female impersonator who also had sexual relations with men.[172] One Miami critic believed "Denton's costuming and impersonation of the female voice would have won praise from Julian Eltinge himself."[173] By 1925, another Florida writer maintained that "the laurels that years ago were won by great Julian Eltinge as a delineator of female character in min-strels have by general opinion ben [sic] bestowed on Mr. Denton."[174] The comparison was not insignificant. While Eltinge convincingly portrayed a woman onstage, he overcompensated for that performance offstage by pre-senting himself as hypermasculine. He often claimed that he only dressed as a woman to make a living and reiterated how he would happily give the gig up.[175] Contemporary reports make no similar assertions about Denton. In-stead, his masculinity was represented as incidental or obscured. Denton's onstage success depended on his audiences' ability "to suspend disbelief and accept him as a woman, an impossibility if their immediate and lasting asso-ciations with him were as a man."[176]

While the historical record does not yield any definitive answers as to Denton's own sexual proclivities, several anomalies suggest he had to shield himself from accusations of homosexuality and offstage femininity. Denton billed his performances in late 1926 as his final appearance in minstrels, as he had "signed a contract to appear in one of the Revues in New York."[177] While it is unclear what he did in New York—or if he ever made it to the re-vue—audiences there would have likely received him as part of the thriving queer culture that prominently featured female impersonators and pansies. It does not seem Denton experienced any long-term success there. There is no indication he ever played in Miami again, either. Instead, he moved back to his native Ohio, where he partnered with John Lester Haberkorn, whom he had performed with since at least 1926, as the act "Habb and Denton."[178] They were perfectly matched. While Denton had a feminine soprano, Haber-korn sang with a deep "baritone of Grand Opera fame."[179] They reinvented themselves as a "black and tan" act, referencing the colloquialism for inter-racial resorts and establishments. As Chad Heap has demonstrated, many "slummers" wanted a peek into the black and tan world where "Negro men and white girls and white men and negro wenches" got together.[180] The duo performed as the former relationship, wherein Denton appeared as a white woman and Haberkorn smeared burnt cork on his face to create the illu-sion of a black man. As the black and tan couple toured select parts of the country, advertisements for their show no longer explicitly made reference to Denton's female impersonations. While Denton's gender-bending perfor-mances had been celebrated in Miami years before, the duo's act was now described in nondescript and relatively innocuous ways. They became "society entertainers" or the performers in a "comedy skit" called a "Study in Black and Tan."[181] A 1942 review simply called Denton's feminine act "artistic work," which brought "a roar of approval from the audience." If Denton's onstage performances of wooing men ever extended to any aspect of his personal life, this was discreetly veiled through the theatricality of the stage, or his ability to conjure "memories of the good old minstrel days."[182] While there is no evidence that the men's coupling translated offstage, neither Denton nor Haberkorn ever married, and they lived decidedly "bachelor" lives that challenged traditional societal norms.[183]

Meanwhile, gender- and sexually transgressive entertainment continued to thrive in Miami's black neighborhoods in vogue through the patronage of middle-class slummers. By the 1930s, black and white entrepreneurs developed Colored Town into a national destination for black culture and arts. This earned it the reputation of being the "Harlem of the South." Not only did entrepreneurs often sanitize and appropriate its queer culture—which similarly included female and male impersonators—as distinctly modern to more popular audiences, they made a pretty penny doing so.[184] One of the most active members of the CBT was a black man named Kelsey Leroy Pharr, who opened up a successful funeral home and had significant real estate holdings. His son, Kelsey Pharr Jr., who was called "Miami's pride and joy" by the black press, joined the popular Delta Rhythm Boys by the early 1940s.[185] Several sources have noted that the famed singer was "openly homosexual."[186] That the younger Pharr continued to succeed in Miami and elsewhere suggests that queer expressions and acts remained a visible and identifiable cultural feature in the city's black spaces.

FOR WHITE MONEYED OUTSIDERS, Miami had long been a stage. City boosters lured travelers to the area with theater and spectacle. From the very first advertisement or recruitment brochure they saw, would-be tourists and settlers were drawn to Miami's fairyland image. Promoters ensured that the area's booster gimmicks relayed the image of Miami as a lusty city ready to be devoured and penetrated by outsiders, tourists, investments, and capital. This powerful imagery crafted the city as a site where anything was possible. Boosters had staged the city specifically to give that illusion. The theatrical stage and budding film industry similarly helped market Miami as a fairyland for white pleasure. It advertised the city through oozing sensuality, Caribbean exoticism, and black subservience. Theatrical performances helped women and men—residents and visitors alike—navigate the edges of their fantasies and imagine Miami as a site of exploration and conquest.

Through these modern, theatrical performances, white women and men negotiated the acceptable boundaries of modernity. This included learning how to dress, speak, dance, flirt, and use countless other means to express and make sense of their sexualities. It also taught them how to position their desires and behaviors vis-à-vis ideas of white superiority, a critical element of the fairyland fantasy.

With the growing public presence of gender and sexual nonconformers in Miami, it became much more difficult for male audience members to imagine men like Denton as a woman, since he so clearly resembled and became associated with the legible and identifiable urban invert or homosexual. Miami's onstage female impersonations came under heightened scrutiny. Even then, however, a gender-bending performance that took place on the stage was more likely interpreted as theatrical, while the street equivalent could be perceived as deviant and subsequently criminalized. This meant the theatrical stage created a viable space for gender and sexually nonconforming women and men to express themselves.[187]

Gender- and sexually transgressive acts and expressions often spilled onto Miami streets, piers, beaches, and untamed lands. Although the city remained segregated by race, ethnicity, and class, elite spaces often proved porous enough to allow for intimate connections—albeit often temporary and with particular emphasis on differing social status—to the strapping masculinity culturally attributed to immigrant, working-class, and black male communities and spaces. It is to these spaces that we now turn our attention.

# PASSING THROUGH MIAMI'S QUEER WORLD

If Miami can rightfully be classed with a Sodom or Gomorrah, it is
because the large majority of Miami people like the excitement and
the joys of a Sodom or a Gomorrah.
—NEWSPAPER EDITORIAL, 1922

In addition to being a versatile bisexual Peter might be classified
as a delinquent, vagrant, hoodlum, prostitute, or criminal.
—MEDICAL DESCRIPTION OF MAN WHO VISITED MIAMI
IN THE 1920S AND 1930S

A medical study of a man identified only as "Peter R." described him as tall, young, blond, and good-looking.[1] He had even worked
as a professional model. Peter easily found a willing homosexual partner in
Miami. Like many others, he either cruised men or found that interested
men cruised him during his visits to the city in the 1920s and 1930s. Peter
engaged in the coy street and public game some men played in search of a
sexual partner. This could have been a "gender invert" thought to possess a
male body and female soul or, more likely, another working-class man who
was older than Peter. "In the know" men like Peter shared signs, winks, or
made themselves known and sexually available to other men through cultural markers such as their dress or style.[2]

Peter was a transient typical of Miami's many working-class gender and
sexual subversives. Unbeknownst to his immigrant parents, he dropped out
of school, and although he secured a temporary job, he had little interest in
staying in one place. He made his way throughout the United States "as a
vagrant," with brief stints in the navy and jail. A psychiatrist studying him
years later, an exercise Peter seems to have voluntarily submitted to, believed
his modeling gigs were typical of the type of work that appealed to homosexuals—particularly because it fed his vanity and placed him in closer contact to wealthy men.[3] Modeling provided Peter a fleeting existence, one in
which he could make his way from place to place and resist putting down
roots. At sixteen, Peter hitchhiked to Miami in the midst of the city's "land
boom," or before the 1926 real estate crash. Constantly on the move, Peter
often found himself returning to Miami. He took several odd jobs, including

as a dishwasher and longshoreman. He also had sex with men for money or other benefits.[4]

One time, when Peter had no place to stay in Miami—the city advertisements heralded as fairyland—he met another transient man who sexually propositioned him, a typical occurrence that provides a window into how he spent his time in the city. Peter claimed the man who picked him up asked him to penetrate him anally, which he "did a few times." It was through that sexual arrangement that he secured "a place to sleep and eat." Typical of the criminalization of drifters more generally, Florida police arrested him for hitching a ride on a freight train. He paid for this offense with thirty days of chain gang labor. Peter's punishment placed him in yet another intimate space with other men, who often performed their labor before the sun set. One day, while Peter was working on the chain gang, a "wolf applied" for him.[5] A wolf was a masculine and "predatory" man-about-town who sought out trysts with men he could sexually dominate (or claim to have sexually dominated), by preying on younger or effeminate men. Peter seemed like a perfect match. In maintaining the assertive and masculine role, these wolves maintained their normalcy, demonstrating that the homo-heterosexual regime we understand today had not yet fully developed.[6] Peter regularly experienced such encounters and was no stranger to jails or retributive labor.

While Peter's experiences reveal the greater sexual fluidity that existed prior to the emergence of the modern homo-heterosexual binary—denoted by the fact that the psychiatric study employed the term "variance" to describe the sexual histories of its case studies—a shift was on the horizon.[7] As a teenager, during one of his Florida escapades—quite possibly in Miami— Peter met a "chap" who invited him out to a dancing pavilion, much like the ones opening throughout Miami Beach at the time. The man gave Peter a brief course on homosexuality, a concept previously discussed almost exclusively by medical professionals—like those who documented Peter's experiences—but one that had increasingly held currency in more general parlance. "He started to talk to me about homosexuality," Peter recalled. "I didn't think much about it but he started playing with me and then went down on me." As he continued to have homosexual sex, he also got further acclimated into this gay culture. He came to believe that his "homosexual relations" were not "abnormal." Instead, he saw "them as a matter of course." No longer ignorant of the rules governing same-sex intimate and erotic encounters in the growing city, or even engaging in homosexual trysts simply to make cash or find shelter, he eventually claimed he had "drifted into that stage."[8] While this and other signs suggest that Peter had started to develop a heightened sense of self that was at least partially linked to his sexual behavior and appetite for same-sex intimacy, the weight of the evidence more heavily reveals a greater fluidity and ambiguity in sexual expressions and subjectivities through at least the late 1930s.

While urban boosters crafted Miami's fairyland for a white and moneyed clientele to find recreation and leisure, the city's working-class transient gender and sexual renegades similarly asserted their own spaces in the developing landscape. While queers were frequently visible as performers or staff in the city's nightclubs and bars, gender transgression and homosexual sex could similarly be found in the area's streets, beaches, wharves, and temporary residences. Miami's urban frontierism similarly ensured that outlying areas, gullies, and marshlands also became sites for homosexual activity. The very image of fairyland required the ability for such experiences to occur and become visible. Transients and vagrants, for example, could easily be confused with tourists and visitors, populations deemed necessary to fairyland's success. In tracing available arrest, medical, and commitment records, along with other contemporary sources—such as newspapers, state and local laws, and judicial testimonies and hearings—it becomes clear that gender and sexual transgression had become increasingly visible in the city's public and semipublic spaces independent of the theater. These transgressive acts were also a key ingredient in developing the image of a fleeting fairyland.

In addition to tracing the physical spaces where those listed in the historical record as men found sexual release with other men, this chapter reveals the numerous ways local law enforcement policed and surveilled gender and sexual transgression more broadly in the fairyland. While the available evidence was largely concerned with the gender-transgressive and homosexual experiences of "men," queer archetypes often challenged the very categories that differentiated "women" from "men." Similarly, by no means were women absent from these records. As this chapter shows, several institutions surveilled and regulated the bodies of women whose sexual appetites they read as "unnatural," particularly among the city's black, immigrant or migrant, and working-class communities.

As the case of Peter reveals, Miami police rarely and only selectively enforced the state's sodomy or crime against nature felony. The difficulty of prosecuting the felony charge, coupled with the increasing public visibility and awareness of gender-transgressive expressions and homosexual activity, led Florida legislators to pass a new and broadly defined misdemeanor in 1917 that criminalized "unnatural and lascivious" acts. With that, two distinct Florida laws could criminalize the act of sodomy, among other "unnatural" acts. Similarly, after World War I, state law expanded the purview of crime against nature to include oral sex, which had grown in popularity.[9]

Despite all these developments, local ordinances and lesser charges proved most effective in policing and prosecuting gender transgression, homosexuality, and other forms of nonreproductive and extramarital sexual behavior, with concepts of class, race, ethnicity, age, and (dis)ability proving critical to the legal and judicial regulation of such acts. Vagrancy and public indecency laws, for instance, served as a catch-all regulation that policed queer expressions and behaviors. In some instances, certain laws more precisely targeted street cross-dressing and gender nonconformity than sexual deviancy. The evidence reveals that Miami's law enforcement officers were more likely to charge and surveil black, immigrant, and working-class communities for these offenses. Just the same, emerging concepts of age and disability came to frame the construction of deviancy more generally, which increasingly helped reconfigure same-sex sexual acts and expressions as distinct manifestations that were measured against what became "normal" heterosexuality.

*Finding Sex and Locating Queer Spaces*

Gender, class, race, ethnicity, and age played critical roles in shaping understandings of sexual deviance. By the turn of the century, medical writers had explained homosexuality as a marker of degeneration and generally a manifestation of gender inversion. Prior to World War II, most men who engaged in homosexual acts did not view themselves as gay or their homosexual behavior as constitutive of a sexual identity. For instance, as George Chauncey and others have shown, the presence of working-class, effeminate men known as "fairies" in major metropolitan areas seemed to confirm medical assertions of a third sex, an "inverted" individual who possessed a male body but a female soul. Their sexual desires, then, were believed to have been similarly inverted. Working-class men known as "wolves" and "trade" could have sexual relations with these "inverted" men and maintain their masculinity so long as they played (or purported to play) the active or inserter role.[10] As Peter Boag has shown, however, gender transgression was not the only contributing factor that permitted "wolves" and other "normal" men to engage in homosexual behavior without threatening their masculinity. These men, especially those who lived transitory lives outside the urban center, might also seek sex from a male "punk" or "lamb" whose younger *age*—rather than gender presentation—preserved the "wolf's" masculinity.[11] Evidence of same-sex sexual relations between men in Miami suggests that although these were distinct archetypes, gender and age presentation frequently collided and overlapped. For example, not all punks were masculine in presentation, and some fairies were youths. By the 1920s, the middle class increasingly sought to emphasize the concept of an innate sexuality. Middle-class queers sought to disassociate themselves from the gender and age transgression of the working class, while "normal" middle-class men sought to part ways with these working-class cultures that facilitated sexual fluidity and instead honed new sexual identities defined by exclusive physical interest in women.[12] This development took formation in opposition to the visibility of working-class sexual pairings. Indeed, these and other working-class figures traversed Miami's fairyland seeking sex with other men before sexual appetites were generally understood as either distinctly "homosexual" or "heterosexual."

This gender- and sexually transgressive world and the medical writings about those who traversed it, such as the writings about Peter, reflected a very specific backlash against modern life and urbanization that also emphasized the so-called dangers of social mixture and race, ethnic, and class tensions. This included a contemporary assumption that "primitive lust" was confined to black, immigrant, and working-class communities.[13] Viennese psychoanalyst Sigmund Freud challenged many of these ideas in the early twentieth century. He argued that homosexuality was "neither advantage, crime, illness, nor disgrace." Freud's psychoanalytic interpretation of homosexuality maintained that, rather than constitute a form of inversion or distinct personhood, anyone proved capable of "'making a homosexual object choice' and that all had 'in fact made one in the unconscious.'"[14] Neither advantage or illness, Freud believed homosexuality was a sign of arrested psychosexual development or regression.

Rather than explain homosexuality simply as degeneration, Freud suggested it could be a by-product of *advanced* civilization, a concept that played out uniquely in Miami's urban frontier. In his view, homosexuality could be a reflection of the heightened pressures produced by a modern society that would greatly benefit from the dismantling of its Victorian sexual repression.[15] Over time it became clear that homosexuality was not confined to lower echelons of society, even as many psychoanalysts in the United States came to misinterpret Freud's theories on homosexuality.[16] As we have seen with the white gaze of Miami's black Bahamian migrants, a crucial component of Miami's sexual landscape was its dependence on the homoerotic pleasures migrant and working-class men provided. In Miami, the configuration of the black Bahamian man's availability, abundance, and punishable body constructed a distinctly gendered erotic among white moneyed men that was used to make sense of sexual appetites and proclivities more generally, in essence helping define what constituted normal and abnormal. It too was part of what made Miami fairyland.

It appears some of Miami's working-class men, possibly fairies or hus-

FIGURE 5.1. John Singer Sargent, *Basin with Sailor, Villa Vizcaya, Miami, Florida,*
1917, watercolor on paper, 13¾ × 20½ inches. Collection of the Orlando Museum of
Art. Purchased with funds provided by the Acquisition Trust. Courtesy of the Orlando
Museum of Art, Orlando, FL.

tlers, discovered fairyland's ferries as a site of pleasure. In late 1918, police
charged a man named Ely Kruger with committing a crime against nature
"involving a sailor." The "alleged crime occurred on a ferry boat at Miami
Beach one night" in June.[17] This further locates the centrality of queer erotic
desire to working-class and transient men. During his brief visit to Vizcaya,
painter John Singer Sargent drew several of these homoerotic expressions,
particularly the Bahamian workers. He also, however, paid notice to the
working-class sailors who frequented the area during the war. During his
stay in Miami, Sargent captured a harbor scene of a sailor sitting on Vizcaya's
deck.[18] In his watercolor, a sailor posed for the artist (fig. 5.1). As with his
gaze on the Bahamian body, Sargent was fascinated by the virility and strapping masculinity attributed to working-class men.

This image—especially in light of Kruger's criminal case—introduces
Vizcaya's harbor as an expansion of the men's bachelor culture by further
connecting them to sailors, fishermen, and other transient and unaccompanied working-class men. Just a few months after the United States entered

World War I, the federal government started building the U.S. Naval Aero Station in Coconut Grove, an area in southeast Miami overlooking Biscayne Bay. Workers filled in swampland to connect a small island known as Dinner Key. It housed thirty-nine new buildings, including barracks, machine shops, and hangers for the naval air station.[19] The U.S. government allocated over 1 million dollars for its development. In addition to stimulating Miami's economy, the new installations meant that at any given time several hundred men could be found in or near the city connected to the marine flying field or naval air station.[20] At least in part in rejection of the working-class bachelor society the station facilitated, Coconut Grove residents successfully petitioned the U.S. Navy to move the station from their neighborhood and relocate it farther south to the outlying South Dade's Chapman Field in late 1919. As a Miami newspaper noted, "It is supposed that the strenuous opposition to the station being made permanent, which was put up before the naval authorities by wealthy winter residents" had "much to do with the decision to abandon the site"—despite the fact that the swampland was filled at the government's expense.[21] Despite the relocation, the armed forces expanded throughout southern Florida. This found many unaccompanied men stationed throughout the county, near the urban center and in outlying areas, searching for leisure and entertainment.[22] In some cases, sailors may have found comfort with the relief fairies or hustlers provided, not unlike what Kruger probably had done. Like female prostitutes, they may have also offered their sexual services in Miami for a price.[23]

By the early 1920s, numerous naval scandals received public attention and the military came to identify a particular sexually deviant individual, or archetype, and sought to disassociate itself from the growing stigma that labeled it a queer institution.[24] No scandal was more notorious than the 1919 investigation of the Newport Naval Training Station, in which several enlisted men were instructed to act as decoys and had sex with local "perverts."[25] The U.S. military came to identify a queer archetype just as the navy expanded its presence in Miami. A white man who lived in Miami named James Ray Harwell, for instance, first enlisted in the navy in 1913. He re-enlisted when the United States entered the war in 1917, spending time in the naval station in Key West, Florida.[26] In 1921, the navy convicted him of sodomy and "scandalous conduct tending to the destruction of good morals," or oral sex.[27] His crime also included "mailing obscene material," presumably a love letter his commanding officer used as evidence that Harwell had committed the acts with another sailor at a YMCA room in Honolulu. The navy sentenced him to hard labor at Portsmouth Naval Prison in New Hampshire for fifteen years, although it appears he only served two of those years.[28] The navy maintained the penalty for his crime was necessary to achieve the "eradication of this evil" from its institution.[29]

By the early 1930s, locals associated the arrival of transient sailors in Miami with transgressive and illicit sex. A humorous poem suggested this phenomenon in the city. It included lines such as: "Miami is a charming spot to sun bathe in the nude / And it is good for whoopee, or to get discreetly stewed [drunk]." The poem stressed how being single proved a more desirable option for men, in part because sailors and other transients might successfully enamor a man's girlfriend. It added: "Miami has attractions, but tell it to the boys / If they want to have a girl friend, move to Wheaton, Illinois."[30] The poem left open the possibility for men to abandon women altogether and seek company in the arms of other men. Similarly, an alternative Miami periodical reported, "Some reformers here are denouncing the kind of entertainment the sailors off the warships take when in Miami." It playfully swapped "fleet's in" with the sexually suggestive motto: "The fleet's sin."[31]

As seen with "Peter R." jails and prisons represented another city space where gender- and sexually transgressive expressions and acts were shaped, explored, and surveilled. As early as 1908, Criminal Court of Record Judge William I. Metcalf and several wealthy Progressive attorneys expressed their anxieties over the need to "separate the sexes and improve the sanitary conditions of the jail" in Miami. The county grand jury had previously observed this "barbarism." It criticized the "fearful conditions" under which "men and women huddled together like so many animals . . . in close iron cells." They were particularly concerned with "the safe keeping of the women incarcerated," urging "complete isolation from the male prisoners." Since the 1870s, reformers throughout the nation fought for separate women's institutions to combat rape, harassment, prostitution, and trafficking. Reformers gradually secured sex-segregated jails and prisons throughout the country. This facilitated same-sex intimacy between prisoners. Even though sexual experiences in prisons were fluid and varied, thereby challenging the very idea of sexual object choice as constitutive of a particular sexual identity, prison reformers ultimately helped reify the notion of distinct sexual identities.[32] In Miami, as elsewhere, reformers expressed great anxiety over the prisoners' lack of privacy and the intimacy of their confined sex-segregated spaces. In short, they remained concerned about homosexuality. Miami's reformers, for instance, drew attention to how the prison "bathroom and toilet permits no privacy" among inmates. The conditions of Miami's jails, they maintained, were "an outrage on decency and morals."[33]

In addition to Miami's jails, harbors, ports, and schooners, other working-class spaces—such as the Young Men's Christian Association (YMCA)—created countless opportunities for men to engage in homosexual activity. The founding of Miami's YMCA, or the Y, coincided with the greater public visibility of queers in the city. The YMCA was initially founded in London as a space and movement in which to further develop young men's bodies, minds, and Christian principles. Its influence spread throughout the world. Miami's urban designers and powerbrokers met in 1916 to discuss opening the city's first YMCA and, within a few months, raised enough money to purchase a permanent home. They listed several reasons for building a Y in the city. This included the fact that at least "3,000 young men and boys in Miami ... need the safeguarding and developing influences of such an association," that the "failure to provide a place of clean resort and intellectual opportunity for these boys during their leisure hours has been characterized as criminal negligence," and that its opening would further mark Miami as "a progressive, growing city."[34] On May 16, 1918, hundreds of residents celebrated the opening of the new building, located at the center of Miami near Biscayne Bay. The new building hosted countless events for young white men and boys—both locals and passersby.[35] While many of the wealthy funders attended activities at the Y, the city's transient and working-class populations transformed the space in the coming years.

The YMCA's leadership, like local powerbrokers in Miami, came to identify the so-called dangers of same-sex intimacies during these years. As John Donald Gustav-Wrathall has noted, since its founding, the Y offered men an alternative to traditional family models that would soon be categorized and understood as heterosexual. As part of this Christian commitment to "healthy" masculinities and sexualities, the Y's leadership pushed a rigid sex education program that promoted heterosexuality. In early 1938, upon a six-day investigation of Miami's programs, members of the Y's national leadership recommended the city host more "mixed social events for young men and women" as a means of teaching the young men about "courtship and marriage."[36] It implemented programs in service to a heterosexual ideal, while simultaneously offering physical education, recreation, and other homoerotic spaces and activities for men. Same-sex intimacy was not only possible there, it was guaranteed.[37]

Located in a city in large part defined by its transience, Miami's YMCA became a popular site for homosexual activity. So strong was the association of the YMCA with homosexuality that it became the source of a national gay folklore. As one source recalled, the YMCA more correctly "stood for 'Why I'm So Gay.'"[38] Peter R., for instance, remembered how another transient, working-class man cruised him at the Miami YMCA, a gesture that led to multiple sexual sessions between the men.[39] Experiences like that led the Y's national leadership to observe that "Miami presents certain problems of climate and shifting population." Indeed, both these factors made regulating men's behaviors—including sexual intimacy—increasingly difficult. Miami's first YMCA was a four-story structure that offered a number of spaces and activities that facilitated intimacy among men, including public baths, swimming, massages, and a gymnasium.[40] The building also offered cheaper residence for transients and visitors. The dormitories and hotel rooms represented not only a much more affordable option than the pricey hotels near the Miami River and across the bay in Miami Beach (which were often overbooked), but they were also spaces of comradeship and fraternity.[41] By the early 1940s, Miami's Y provided low-cost housing for roughly 32,500 men a year.[42] Further adding to its reputation as a site for cruising, less than a decade after Miami's first Y was built, city designers unveiled Bayfront Park across the street. In the coming years, and into at least the 1980s, the park served as popular cruising sites for men looking for sex. This included homosexual encounters, both commercial and otherwise.[43] As an alternative newspaper joked in 1933, "Any Miami policeman will tell you pigeons are not the only birds that pick up crumbs in Bayfront park!"[44]

Although records for this period do not always specifically indicate where all arrests for same-sex sexual acts occurred, the evidence allows us to make some deductions. Those interested in finding a sexual partner—and, it seems, the law enforcement that selectively surveilled those deemed suspicious—likely associated certain public or semipublic spaces, such as the YMCA and Bayfront Park, as sites where same-sex sexual acts could take place or be initiated. Data presented in past chapters similarly demonstrates that the homosocial spaces migrant and working-class men often found themselves in—such as farms, shacks, or other intimate living and sleeping quarters—often facilitated homosexual encounters. Indeed, sexual encounters often took place in isolated or outlying parts of the city, which made policing them difficult and prosecution less frequent. The case of Ely Kruger demonstrates that such encounters often occurred in public or semipublic spaces throughout the city. This included streets, parks, and beaches. A 1918 Dade County Grand Jury report maintained that illicit sex and forms of sexual "misconduct" were "not carried on in houses" but rather "in remote places in the woods and parks in and adjacent to Miami."[45]

Similarly, as the advent of the Dixie Highway suggests, the car became a site for sexual exploration. As Tim Retzloff has shown, the automobile helps explain how transgressive sex occurred so frequently in the "hinterland," including Miami's urban frontier.[46] While cars were used for relatively mild "petting," or fondling, among the modern, middle-class set, others used the car as a literal vehicle for penetrative sexual encounters.[47] "Automobiles are hired" to take prostitutes and their clients to remote places, maintained Dade County's grand jury report. "Chauffeurs," who were often men of color, "reap a harvest for the use of their machines during the night time." With this, the citizens who made up the body blamed the area's black population for being complicit in—and capitalizing on—their white daughters' violated chastity. These sexual encounters did not just victimize the prostitutes, they claimed. "Young girls of the city are being debauched by this condition of affairs because they do not exercise sufficient care as to the character of the men with whom they associate." The grand jury sought, then, to put an end to the "promiscuous joy riding by young girls" in Miami.[48]

Meanwhile, certain archetypes, including the loafer, hobo, and vagrant, regularly loitered Miami's streets, parks, and beaches and became an integral part of fairyland's landscape. Like other archetypes associated with metropolitan areas—such as the lesbian, dandy, and flaneur—these transient figures represented "the view from the margins characteristic of modern urban life."[49] Several Miami boosters heralded loafers as the engines that fueled the city. One maintained, "Imagine Miami without her loafing element—imagine the gray dullness of her summer afternoons without the interchange of the loafers' thoughts—imagine her moonlight nights without the spice of toothsome gossip whispered by these loafers on shaded verandas!" The source noted that not all loafers were "seedy individuals" but that they also included "the fellow who always has time for a few hours' gossip at the club—the fellow, who builds his popularity by the number of scandals he can retail in an evening," making clear that they also functioned as part of a broader illicit economy. Miami housed "both the masculine and feminine variety of loafer." With that assertion, the man pondered, "What would the city social life be if they existed not?"[50] As scholars such as Kwame Holmes have urged, it is important that we make room for this gossip to "function as an archive of experience even as it resists recognition and institutionalization."[51] While Miami's loafer relayed information through gossip and spectacle, often at a price, she or he also kept a watchful eye on the streets and served as a roadmap for where residents and visitors alike could find particular establishments and types of people—queer or otherwise. They too made fairyland work.

Gender-transgressive transients, including queers and pansies, also traversed city streets and could easily blend in with and represent a crucial part of the fairyland's scenery. After all, fairyland encouraged visitors to explore their own desires and even strip down to enjoy the weather. So-called vagrants and beachcombers were, at times, mistaken for well-to-do beach bathers dressed in trunks and, possibly, a light shirt; that is, by the late 1930s, men were increasingly bathing and sunbathing shirtless in public.[52] One visitor spotted "many men sprawled on the grass soaking up sunshine and two of them were stripped to the waist" in Bayfront Park. "Many of them looked like they were jobless and broke," noted the observer. "The men without shirts had on trousers, not bathing suits." The visitor seemed troubled by the fact that in Miami, sunbathing tourists looked a lot like vagrants ripe for arrest.[53]

The fairyland's tropical climate similarly provided plentiful opportunities for physical and sexual exhibitionism. In the early 1930s, an observer poked fun at visitors dressed in unusual attire that made them appear less presentable than the status their class afforded them. Since most of Miami's street archetypes could easily be confused, the source joked: "Say, mister, is there a good waxworks museum in Miami where all the people have got signs on 'em and a lecturer to tell you who they are?" In fairyland, the writer suggested, distinguishing the reputable from the disreputable—as well as the normative and deviant—seemed a tricky affair.[54]

The pansy and other gender-transgressive men were among Miami's discernible street tropes. One city writer clearly identified the pansy traversing Miami's streets: "Yessir, some funny people in this town. Say, mister, lookit what's comin' down the street. If that ain't a typical pansy? Now ain't he just too cute."[55] Not only was the pansy a discernible figure in Miami's streets, but sometimes he also appeared to be a welcome addition to Miami's fairyland landscape. A Miami gossip column regularly featured comical tidbits on girlish "boys" around the city (and, in at least one instance, a masculine "Terry" who was "really a girl").[56] Gender transgression was not only made possible but also encouraged in Miami. One "plumb, fair-haired" Miami resident, referred to as a man in the historical record, reportedly grew tired of being told "his voice sounded so feminine" over the telephone and "masquerade[d] as a woman" for thirteen years in Miami and beyond. According to the report, "he decided to change his 'way of living'" and was only identified by authorities as a man to fulfill conscription notice during World War II. In Miami, such a "masquerade" could more easily go unnoticed and blend into the fairyland.[57]

By the late 1930s, some male entertainers—stage pansies and female impersonators—shared apartment spaces and lived near one another just northwest of downtown Miami and near the southern border of Colored Town. Entertainers' greater visibility and promotion meant their experiences were more likely to appear in the historical record. While the focus of this chapter is not onstage performers, such evidence yields significant insight into queer lives in Miami. This includes housing patterns, procurement of private space, and perhaps the formation of queer networks. Police arrested over a dozen women and men, mostly the latter, following raids on two queer nightspots in 1939. In one nightclub raid, three men characterized as "dancers"—two in their early twenties and the other in his late thirties—told police they lived together. All but one of the other dancers arrested during that raid lived within walking distance, or less than a mile away from them. In the other raided club, police arrested queer male entertainers who told crude jokes onstage. Two of those men similarly told police they lived together in a place within walking distance of their workplace. The other arrested men lived farther east, but similarly near one another.[58]

These living patterns suggest several things. In addition to working together, some performers shared intimate spaces in rental apartments or hotel rooms. They may have split costs, fought isolation, or found recreation and pleasure outside of their time onstage, all of which may suggest the forging of queer networks, which also proved critical to fighting against habitual violence. It seems very likely, too, that nightclub operators found these entertainers, who also included female burlesque dancers and wait staff, a place to stay during peak tourist season. Evidence reveals managers assisted employees in fighting legal battles following such arrests, even providing them private counsel.[59] It was in the club's financial interest to keep its performers reasonably safe and out of the jail. It is important to note that none of the women who were arrested resided with the others taken in by police. Perhaps they lived alone, with someone not connected to queer nightlife, or with someone at the club who simply avoided arrest. Altogether, however, the evidence most heavily suggests that these were temporary housing conditions for temporary residents. One female dancer, for instance, reported a hotel as her address to police. Many stage performers generally spent a few weeks or months in Miami during the height of tourist season in places likely secured—and possibly subsidized or fully paid for—by club operators. Entertainers then packed their bags to live or perform in another city. Although it seems they often had greater financial security and status than many of the other folk arrested for gender or sexual transgression in Miami, these queer performers were similarly transient and on the move.[60]

*Policing Deviance*

Miami law enforcement regulated these and other forms of gender and sexual transgression in numerous ways. The Florida legislature passed a new state law in 1917 that, like the sodomy and crime against nature charge, also criminalized "unnatural" sex. New lesser charges and existing local laws proved most effective in policing deviant gender and sexual acts and expressions, however.

Although most people did not read medical or pseudo-medical reports about homosexuality, such discourses and prevailing cultural and social tensions influenced how gender and sexual nonconformists were surveilled within Miami and its borders. Indeed, many of Freud's ideas had become popular in the United States by the mid-1910s, even though, as Henry Abelove has argued, they were frequently misinterpreted or misrepresented.[61] This is evident in medical discourses concerning the so-called arrested physical and sexual development of immigrants deemed undesirable in Miami and elsewhere. In addition, existing race, ethnic, and class anxieties helped determine not just who was deemed a desirable entrant or weeded out, but also who was more likely to be policed more generally.[62]

Sexual anxieties collided with concerns over public health and disease in Miami during the Great War, which sparked significant changes in the visibility and policing of transgressive sex and other queer expressions. In addition to prompting immigration restrictions, the war also helped shift reformers' attention to questions of sexuality. Moral reformers' concerns over "social hygiene"—including anxieties over the spread of vice and venereal disease (VD)—manifested in new laws throughout the nation during the World War I era. In 1917 alone, legislatures around the country introduced nearly 300 bills pertaining to social hygiene. Of these, 160 became law. In Florida, this included criminalizing—or recriminalizing—the publication and distribution of obscene literature, pictures, or prints; indecent exposure; and the "injunction and abatement" of vice and places of ill fame.[63]

In the midst of the war, the U.S. Army enacted several measures in Miami to combat another "Triple Alliance" it believed plagued its men: alcohol, prostitution, and venereal disease. This included educating soldiers and civilians on VD, providing medical care and prophylactics, and other "social measures to diminish sexual temptation." The latter included working with the antiprostitution and antivice arm of the War Department, the Commission on Training Camp Activities, and the YMCA, among other agencies, to offer "proper social surroundings and recreation for the men both in the camps and the towns near the camps." The U.S. Army maintained it needed to offer "wholesome amusements" in the city to keep the men from "seeking vicious resorts." "This is largely a matter for civilian enterprise," it noted. The city was tasked with keeping the men in line and minimizing their sexual "temptations."[64] In late 1918, the City of Miami contributed $1,500 to support the U.S. Army's anti–venereal disease campaigns in the area.[65] The army could not afford to have these men "waste health and strength in the red-light district." After all, syphilis and gonorrhea threatened the men's "future wives and children"—making clear that a return to the traditional family model was not only expected but also necessary in the postwar period.[66] The War Department applied new pressure on Miami to regulate its vice districts and sexual economy.

While these campaigns affected the lives of queer working-class women and men in Miami, the Florida legislature's enactment of Chapter 7361 on May 28, 1917, perhaps made an ever bigger impact. The law dictated: "Whoever commits any unnatural and lascivious act with another person shall be punished by fine not exceeding five hundred dollars, or by imprisonment not exceeding six months, or by both."[67] This broad designation could be interpreted in numerous ways and could overlap with the state's sodomy or crime against nature felony. This misdemeanor added *another* provision against "unnatural" sexual acts, including homosexuality. It seems likely legislators primarily sought to target oral sex, which had grown in popularity during this era.

A review of contemporary court decisions also suggests lawmakers may have believed it was necessary to pass a new statute that would prove more effective in policing same-sex sexual acts more generally. Court rulings on other offenses, such as carnal knowledge and rape, that targeted coercive and nonconsensual sex and sexual assault—which was how crime against nature charges were still generally interpreted in Florida—increasingly specified that they could only be used to punish cross-sex sexual acts.[68] While those crimes had always been understood as pertaining to cross-sex acts, judges' rulings began making these specifications during this period in ways that exposed statutory blind spots for same-sex sexual acts. Surely, the crime against nature felony existed and primarily targeted same-sex anal intercourse, but the evidentiary standard of proof for the new "unnatural" misdemeanor charge appears to have been considerably lower and would therefore prove more effective in criminalizing homosexual behavior.[69]

It is crucial to place the passage of the "unnatural and lascivious" misdemeanor alongside the other wartime-influenced laws Florida's legislature passed that session. The state also passed Chapter 7359 and Chapter 7360. The former was an amendment to an existing Florida statute to further expand the punishment for the importation, sale, exhibition, and dissemination of "obscene prints, pictures, and literature." Its reach was massive, ranging from moving pictures to ballads. The latter statute made it "unlawful for any person to expose or exhibit his or her sexual organs in any public" or semipublic place. Someone caught having sex on a public beach, or perhaps wearing too revealing clothing, could be arrested for indecent exposure. Trading homoerotic or sexually explicit prints or literature with friends might also cost you jail time or a fine. Altogether, these wartime laws sought to quash a growing, visible sexual culture.[70]

It is also during this period that judges ruled oral sex was punishable under Florida's existing law. Fellatio became a more common practice in the United States in the early twentieth century, partly due to improved personal hygiene and the proliferation of new urban sites such as public parks and restrooms.[71] In addition, the zipper was introduced in 1893 and became widely available to the public by 1912, making receiving or performing oral sex a quick zip away.[72] Some people also believed that engaging in oral sex made them less likely to be infected with a venereal disease, which, as we saw with the military's wartime VD campaign in Miami, was a source of great anxiety.[73] Some queers and fairies, much like many female prostitutes, were frequently willing to perform oral sex, a practice many working- and middle-class women "rejected as unbecoming to a woman."[74] While no state in the union criminalized fellatio before 1878, most had laws banning the act on the books by 1921. During this period, Florida courts made clear that existing state law, the crime against nature felony, covered fellatio, too. The new unnatural and lascivious act misdemeanor was broad enough to cover both fellatio and cunnilingus, although police seemed oblivious to the latter. In fact, the Florida Supreme Court only decided cunnilingus constituted a crime against nature felony in 1943, over twenty years after it ruled fellatio fell under the law's purview.[75] As this suggests, judges expressed great reticence in discussing what they interpreted as an unnatural and despicable crime, further complicating judicial and legal interpretation of the statute's vagueness. The court referred to homosexuality as the "unmentionable crime," while another of its rulings argued that a "discussion of the loathsome, revolting crime would be of no edification to the people, nor interest to the members of the bar."[76]

Indeed, Florida's laws against oral sex were vague and ambiguous. When the Florida legislature passed the unnatural and lascivious act law in 1917, it clarified it "shall not be so construed as to repeal" the common law crime against nature charge, a felony.[77] In addition to being a charge distinct from the crime against nature, this also suggests that the 1917 law was meant as an addendum to criminalizing "unnatural" acts. The evidence heavily suggests that the legislature, at least in part, passed the misdemeanor to target oral sex and secure more convictions. The Supreme Court of Florida, however, thought differently. In 1921, it reviewed a case involving three men in north-central Florida. Jim Ephraim and Martello Metz were convicted of committing a crime against nature, a felony charge. Testimony revealed that another man, Son Gary, performed oral sex on both of them. The highest court in the state decided the "abominable and detestable crime against nature" included "the act of copulation between two human beings per os," or oral sex. Ephraim and Metz were each sentenced to five years in the state prison. So while it appeared the recently passed misdemeanor punishing "unnatural and lascivious" acts sought to criminalize oral sex, among other forms of sexual transgression, the Florida Supreme Court noted it did "not apply to" cases such as the one involving Ephraim and Metz. It believed oral sex was more appropriately punishable under the crime against nature felony instead.[78]

Meanwhile, Miami's criminal records reveal an increase in sodomy and crime against nature charges, although in very low numbers considering the area's exponential population increase. While the county criminal General Index reveals only six arrests for either sodomy or crimes against nature before 1917—when the state amended its laws to include the new misdemeanor—law enforcement made considerably more arrests in the 1920s. This was particularly true from 1925 to 1927, a period of significant economic decline and limited jobs for the working class in Miami. Considering how often these offenses were paid sexual arrangements, it is possible this slight increase was a product of Miami's economic downturn. While the numbers seem to suggest a significant increase in policing during this period, this is misleading. These charges do not correspond to the drastic increase in the city's population. Miami proper's population, for instance, increased a whopping 274 percent from 1920 to 1930. The numbers are even more extraordinary for Miami Beach, where the population jumped 980 percent during that decade.[79]

In fact, residents and neighbors often grew frustrated by lax enforcement of sex offenses, such as bigamy, which was also often prosecuted following community surveillance. One angry Miami resident asked the governor in 1935 why a "citizen and property owner cannot get the cooperation of . . . public officials . . . being paid to enforce the law." He reported a bigamy case to Dade's assistant county solicitor to no avail. Bigamists, he believed, were among the "criminals" who were "let . . . off so easy."[80]

Police arrests for crimes against nature throughout the county were negligible. From 1896 to 1929, the Dade County General Index for criminal cases listed only thirty-three distinct crime against nature charges, including "sodomy," "attempted sodomy," and "buggery." While it is possible that other charges were dropped, reduced, or modified, these recorded statistics appear to have captured all *original* charges that made it to the main county tribunals, which reveal the limited effect the crime against nature felony had in policing predominantly same-sex sodomy in Miami. After 1921, the statute's purview was expanded to include oral sex. While the statute was primarily used to criminalize same-sex sexual acts, cross-sex anal and oral sex, as well as bestiality, were occasionally targeted under this felony. It is similarly important to note that although thirty-three charges for this offense appear in this index through 1929, even those charges were made against no more than twenty-three—perhaps even fewer—individuals. That is, several of the men the police arrested were repeat offenders.[81]

The evidence heavily suggests that, in the rare circumstance in which local law enforcement officers filed crime against nature charges, they targeted particular individuals. For instance, Miami police charged a man named John Holmes with sodomy in 1913. Four years later, in 1917, they arrested Holmes again for committing a crime against nature. While this rarely occurred during the World War I years, it occurred with greater frequency in the following decade. A white man named C. J. Huddleston was arrested *three* times in 1925—in what appears to be at least several days apart—on buggery charges.[82] The evidence suggests that police began targeting particular men, perhaps those whose mannerisms or expressions did not conform to masculine ideals and were perhaps understood as gender inverts, or those thought to be preying on young "punks." The evidence similarly suggests that in addition to gender, particular assumptions based on class, race, ethnicity, and (dis)ability led to increased surveillance and policing.

Several other significant changes occurred in the policing of queer men during this period. It is in the 1920s that Miami police officers started charging suspects with *two* counts of committing a homosexual act. Police arrested Charles Montgomery in 1927 and charged him with two counts of committing a crime against nature. That same year, police arrested W. T. Jones and charged him with two counts of committing sodomy. It is possible he was the same "Tom Jones" listed in the county's criminal General Index for a crime against nature charge eleven years earlier, in 1916.[83]

This reveals several things. First, it too suggests law enforcement had coded certain individuals as perpetrators of homosexual acts and policed them accordingly. This could have included surveilling certain individuals, groups, and hangouts. The fact that men were charged with two consecutive counts of the same crime also suggests that arresting officers paid notice to the changes in the Florida statute. That is, they likely filed two felony charges against particular men for engaging in anal *and* oral sex. After all, Florida's Supreme Court decided, despite the lesser misdemeanor charge available to them, that the crime against nature law also criminalized oral sex. Put another way, while officers could have arrested these men with a crime against nature felony for committing anal sex and perhaps a separate unnatural and lascivious act misdemeanor for oral sex, police sidestepped the lesser charge and instead filed two consecutive felony counts. It is also possible that these double counts meant that, much like the two men charged in north-central Florida, some men were caught in a triad or with more than one partner. As such, police could have arrested them on separate counts of committing a crime against nature. It is also clear that local prosecutors kept abreast of developments in the state's regulation of homosexuality.

It is also during this period that local law enforcement first charged men for *attempted* sodomy. While attempted sodomy had been a criminal offense in Florida since at least 1868, it made its first appearance in the Dade County criminal General Index in 1920, when law enforcement arrested a man named Roy Lewis.[84] After that, attempted sodomy charges appeared twice in 1926, when police brought in A. E. White and a bricklayer named Harry Riley.[85] This may also suggest police made certain assumptions—based on a man's class, race, age, (dis)ability, form of dress, mannerisms, and speech, for instance—about his intentions when around other men or youths, perhaps especially when found in a certain location. It may also suggest that police targeted men they deemed sexually suspect, perhaps informed by their associations with any of the above influences, when congregating in public or semipublic places but could not provide ample evidence to pursue the full felony charge.

The strongest suggestion, however, is that many, if not most, of these criminal charges likely resulted from an accusation rather than from someone's being caught in the act by police. In some instances, the accusation was made by an "accomplice," that is, someone who *consensually* participated in the act. This testimony had to be "corroborated" by another source. Prosecution was made even more difficult by judicial interpretations of whether adolescents could be complicit in the offense or constitute an "accomplice," a significant factor considering so many of Florida's crime against nature cases during these years involved intergenerational sexual encounters. Just the same, the courts factored age considerably in determining whether boys could offer consent, and therefore be an accomplice, in the first place, particularly after the 1920s, when new concepts of childhood, adolescence, and homosexuality came to inform judicial interpretations.[86]

An attempted sodomy charge became a more effective way to prosecute because the state often lacked sufficient evidence or an admissible corroboration to successfully prosecute. Florida law criminalized "attempts to commit an offence prohibited by law," although they carried shorter prison terms and punishments than for defendants who actually followed through.[87] It was not unlikely for someone who consented to anal or oral sex to later become an "accomplice" in an attempted sodomy criminal trial that accused another party of the crime. An "accomplice" may have accused and testified against the other party to disassociate himself from homosexuality and the social shame and stigma that could jeopardize family relationships, employment, and social standing.[88]

One "sex variant" accused police of harassing queer men in other ways: demanding sex from them. Peter R., the transient man who spent considerable time in Miami, recalled, "Detectives have picked me up time and time again and wanted to have an affair with me for their own pleasure." Considering he spent some time in jail in Miami under suspicion of stealing jewelry—a common transient heist during the city's economic downturn—it seems likely he was specifically referring to an experience he had in southern Florida. He maintained, "In certain cities, most of the police are queer."[89] While there is little evidence to either corroborate or debunk his claims, it is revealing that Peter presented a narrative in which he could be arrested for vagrancy, for instance, if he did not favorably respond to a policeman's sexual advances. It also suggests that he understood, at the very least, that police in cities like Miami used their own judgment to selectively enforce laws targeting homosexual acts.

Other evidence suggests the possibility that those who committed homosexual acts had increasingly been understood as a personage, or an archetype legible in the city landscape. The 1921 Florida Supreme Court decision that ruled oral sex was a crime against nature felony referred to homosexuals as a distinct, albeit repulsive, trope. It ruled, "The *creatures* who are guilty are entitled to a consideration because they are called human beings and are entitled to the protection of the laws." Despite its offensive tone, the ruling suggested those who engaged in same-sex acts be understood as distinct "creatures" who, while seemingly despicable to the court, were "human beings" with a particular sexual predilection. They were, according to the court, "creatures whose low moral and intellectual standard entitles them to a kind of pity," to say nothing of constitutional protections.[90]

While there appears to be limited evidence that some who engaged in same-sex sexual acts (or desired to) in Miami had increasingly registered their own sexual proclivities with distinct sexual identities by the 1920s, sources from the following decade reveal that authoritative forces—such as judges, legislators, and police—had started to view them as a *class* of people that constituted part of a growing sexual community. For instance, a 1932 crime against nature case in Miami found law enforcement prejudicially questioning members of the community as to the suspect's reputation to better assess the suspect's likely association to sexual perversity. The defendant's attorney argued, "The act charged … is certainly revolting to the sensibilities of any decent person." He continued, "There is no doubt people who, from general depravity or diseased minds, indulge in this unmentionable practice, but such record as we have of this class of characters, commonly called degenerates, shows that those who do practice this vice are unnatural and abnormal, criminally inclined and deficient persons."[91] Some evidence suggests that articulations of identities or proto-identities gained currency in some Miami spaces by the late 1930s, when queer performances thrived in the city's tourist-driven nightlife culture. These seem to have been more discernible through their transgressions of gender presentation than through their sexual behaviors, however.[92]

Indeed, while some evidence suggests the legibility of a sexually deviant trope by the 1930s, new *local* legislation and subsequent enforcement more heavily suggests the visibility of gender-transgressive people in Miami who may or may not have been linked to sexual deviance. Since 1896, local police selectively enforced Florida laws such as the crime against nature. Urban legislators, however, soon passed their own ordinances that targeted—and therefore also acknowledged—*gender* transgression in Miami's public and semipublic areas. In 1917, in the midst of the area's changing landscape caused by the wartime influx of new transients, Miami's city council tasked City Attorney F. W. Cason with arranging, codifying, and supplementing local ordinances. The city council adopted the compiled ordinances, both existing and new, on September 20, 1917. With this, the Code of the City of Miami became the local law.[93]

Municipal laws policed and attacked gender and sexual transgression in several ways. Chapter 19 of the City Code legislated "peace, good order and morals." Those who transgressed gender norms could be arrested under Section 684 and charged with "indecent behavior," much like the Florida statute indicated a few months prior. In fact, it appears the City Code drew greatly from the Florida statutes passed a few months earlier. It is revealing, however, that unlike Florida's indecent exposure law, Miami's "indecent behavior" law added a clause distinctly targeting gender nonconformity. The local law criminalized those who, "in any public place" were "found in a state of nudity, or in a dress not becoming to his or her sex, or in an indecent exposure of his or her person." In this way, local legislators may have sought to tailor the state's own criminal definitions to local circumstances, including the presence of gender transgression in the urban setting. Indeed, the local law specifically sought to suppress cross-dressing, gender deviance, and overt expressions of sexuality. The law was so broad it also included anyone "guilty of any indecent or lewd behavior" or someone who tried to "exhibit, sell or offer to sell any indecent or lewd book, picture or other thing," similarly reflecting the Florida statute. It similarly criminalized performances deemed "indecent, immoral or lewd." Considering police did not target them until the 1930s, it seems Miami's popular, gender-bending minstrel and vaudeville shows were not yet interpreted as indecent or lewd. It was only when they became more directly associated with homosexuality, rather than a form of derision or entertainment, that such acts were selectively criminalized or subject to police harassment. According to the City Code, those found guilty of indecent behavior faced a fine of up to fifty dollars or a sentence to hard labor for up to twenty days.[94] Vagrancy charges remained similarly effective in policing queer communities during this and later periods and also mandated hard labor as retribution.[95]

Some evidence also suggests local law enforcement more forcefully policed the effeminate "invert," or the person who played the passive role in the sexual encounter—not necessarily the gender-conforming "normal" man or "trade." Perhaps the arrested Kruger had performed oral sex on the sailor or allowed the sailor to penetrate him—or perhaps both. It is also possible that the sailor simply purported this to be the arrangement. Criminal records make clear that the sailor was *not* charged with committing a crime against nature. This is likely because, in claiming the assertive role, he maintained his masculinity and gender-conforming identity.[96]

The policing of Miami's gender-transgressive men, or at least those recorded as "men" in the historical record, who had sex with a man—perhaps a fairy or hustler—often collided with the city's surveillance of its ethnic, racial, and working-class communities—many of whom were made up of transients. This is heavily suggested by the fact that neither Paul Chalfin nor Louis Koons appeared in the county's General Index for criminal cases, despite their living openly as male lovers and despite Chalfin's being described as a gender-bending "pansy." Local police seemed particularly keen on policing working-class gender-transgressive and homosexual behavior, when they did so at all. Miami police arrested at least one Florida-born black lodger, as well as a white married man who worked as a carpenter, on sodomy charges.[97] Many of those arrested for engaging in sodomy were black or otherwise racialized by their ethnic origins. These men frequently found themselves living or working in tight, homosocial spaces because of their labor, industry, and social standing.

Surviving records also suggest that at least one of these ethnic men also exhibited prototypical fairy behavior. Miami police arrested Irving Finn in 1919 for committing a crime against nature. Born in Massachusetts to a mother from the same state and an Irish immigrant father, Finn reported working as an "actor." While it is not known, it is possible he worked on-stage in a gender-bending act, for example as a female impersonator. Prison records reveal the forty-year-old was convicted of this crime and sentenced to a year at the Florida State Farm, or prison, in Raiford. There he was housed in the Women's Ward and Hospital Building, a place deemed suitable for a sick invert. In this case, it appears his homosexual behavior and gender—as an effeminate actor, pansy, or fairy—led doctors to believe he suffered from inversion.[98]

As Finn's Irish heritage suggests, Miami's law enforcement was more likely to police immigrants' perceived "suspect" sexualities, as was also the case with the city's relatively small and transient Greek population. The 1920 census lists only 69 Greek-born residents in Miami. This number is dwarfed by that of the city's West Indians who, at 5,304, easily represented Miami's largest foreign-born population during that period.[99] The low number of Greek inhabitants in Miami may be misleading, however. Like Bahamians, many uncounted Greeks or Greek-descended people often passed through Miami for days or weeks at a time.

As early as 1910, an estimated one to two thousand Greeks resided in Tarpon Springs—a coastal town about thirty miles north of Tampa and a relatively short boat ride to Miami—lured by the lucrative sponges available in Florida's seabeds.[100] This number only increased over the next decade, and many others were likely never counted, as borderland Greeks remained under Turkish or Italian rule during this period and were not categorized as Greek. While some fled political turmoil and oppression in the region, others took the long journey to Florida in search of wealth they hoped to amass by fishing the relatively untapped sponges in the Gulf of Mexico and Atlantic. After all, much of the sponges their descendants had recovered in the Mediterranean Sea had since been stripped, and ruling Turkish forces often limited Greek extraction of the product. Florida businessmen actively recruited spongers from the world's most experienced location connected to that trade: the Dodecanese in the southeastern Aegean, particularly Kalymnos.[101]

This early wave of Greek migrants was 80–90 percent male, creating bachelor societies that easily found sexual release in the hands of female prostitutes and gender- or sexually nonconforming men. Like many of the Bahamians, the Greek men who went to Florida left their families behind for months or years at a time, with the expectation of returning to their homeland with pockets full of money. While many Greek men returned home to participate in the Balkan Wars of 1912–13 and later in the Great War, the turmoil prompted even more of their wives and children to join them in Florida.[102] Even those who were reunited with their families still often found themselves isolated from them in Florida—and accompanied only by other men—for months at a time in the sponge industry. These men worked on floating schooners and did everything imaginable in these tight spaces with only other able-bodied men as companions. Several contemporaries maintained that these bachelor societies, prompted by their pursuit of capital, led to homosexuality. In terms of "sexual immorality," one U.S. man observed, "it appears that the effect of American life upon the [Greek] immigrants is injurious, rather than the reverse." He continued, "This is in part due, no doubt, to the fact that the Greek colonies are largely composed of young men, freed from the restraints of family ties and the surroundings of home, where the close watch kept upon the women prevents active immorality to a large extent."[103] These seamen often made stops in places like Miami to eat and rest or were otherwise driven to land to dodge an incoming storm.[104] In other instances, businessmen specifically orchestrated "exhibition" trips to showcase sponging in cities like Miami to survey new seabeds. In 1928 several Miami residents protested a proposal for one such exhibition that would bring Greek fishermen to the city.[105]

Evidence suggests these Greek transient fishermen-migrants contributed to Miami's early queer landscape, finding other men for sexual trysts during their short stays. One contemporary described Florida's Greek fishermen as "an exuberant, cheerful lot, well-built and handsome, brown of skin, black-haired, blue-eyed and sturdy." In addition, she noted, "they walked with a swagger, swaying from the hips."[106] It appears some men also took notice of their striking presence and comportment. Sometime in the 1920s or 1930s, one man—also a transient and the son of immigrants from Russia and Austria—claimed "a Greek picked" him up at the Miami YMCA. The "Greek" wanted the young man to "brown him," or penetrate him anally.[107] In this context, it appears the man was referring to a Greek-descended person. It is also possible, however, that he used "Greek" as a noun for a man who pursued sex—particularly anal sex—with another man. So prevalent was this ethnic association with homosexuality in the United States that it became a slang word by the 1930s.[108] In 1934, a Miami gossip columnist, cognizant of the homosexual associations with Greeks and the YMCA, cheekily asked readers to find scandal in why a "Greek" man "went to the YMCA . . . the other day."[109]

The link between Greeks and homosexuality was similarly strong among immigration officials across the United States, a phenomenon that seems to have extended to Miami's borders and ports of entry. Some may have referenced the ancient Greek practice of pederasty and male love.[110] Peter Boag has shown how a "Greek scandal" concerning homosexuality among ethnic, working-class men and youths that took shape in 1913 in Portland, Oregon, helped forge this association.[111] It is also important to note the reverse: that this ethnic association helped influence the unfolding of the "Greek scandal." Indeed, this link was further fueled by anti-immigrant fervor which especially targeted "undesirables" from southern and eastern Europe. One social reformer observed the "disproportions between the sexes" among incoming immigrants from southern and eastern Europe that render them with "no opportunity whatsoever for female companionship." Considering that, he posed, "Must we not expect perverted leisure and recreation ... in most serious forms?" The Greeks, he noted, "may carry on a dance without the presence of a single woman," allowing them to then "drift into immorality."[112] Another man noted that Greeks who came from rural districts in the Mediterranean often did not have "elevated" moralities. Rather, "their passions find frequent expression in such vices as sodomy."[113]

It is no surprise that the discourse that associated Greek men with sexual deviancy and femininity collided with the era's anti-immigrant and restrictionist movements. This was particularly evident as many laborers viewed these migrants as stealing jobs from "native" residents. To help combat this, one doctor wrote in 1911 about the need to perform medical inspections of immigrants. He maintained that such a policy "not only offers the opportunity to weed out the *individually* unfit, but likewise presents a rich field for the investigation of the broad problems of *racial* unfitness."[114] In this way, undesirable populations could be ferreted out through gross renderings of their "racial unfitness." Because U.S. immigration officials had not yet fully conceived of a concrete homosexual category through which to exclude foreigners from entering the country, they often screened those they believed had a "degenerate" body as potentially indicative of sexual perversity.[115] One restrictionist argued that, "if the Englishman evinced the same signs of emotion which the Greek shows on a slight provocation, his sanity would at once be in question." This was part of the distinction between "racial characteristics" and "pathological conditions of mind or body." It was no coincidence that his example juxtaposed the "desirable" Englishman with the "undesirable" Greek, viewed as an "inferior stock."[116] Another doctor observed that "the flabby muscles, apathetic countenances, and arrested physical and sexual development so common among Greek immigrants is probably due to the chronic malaria with which that nation is afflicted."[117]

This discourse, which reflected another form of eugenics, stands in stark contrast to the queer erotic constructed in Miami and the Caribbean-U.S. border that depicted black Bahamians as hypersexual, robust, and unequivocally masculine. Although still read as perverse, the Greek man's physical body and sexual proclivities were described as weak, susceptible, and averse to manliness. This juxtaposition further illuminates the critical role sexuality played in reconfiguring race in the United States, and in the Jim Crow South in particular. As several scholars have shown, Greeks constituted an "inbetween" racial status. The white portion of their "inbetween" standing became more pronounced and gradually erased the vestiges of their non-whiteness beginning in the 1920s through processes—such as the disassociation of blackness and assimilation into whiteness—in which black Bahamians were unable to participate.[118]

These ethnoracial associations to sexual deviancy were at least partially responsible for the policing of Greeks in Miami and its shores. A contemporary novel based in Miami tapped into this image of Greeks in the city with its character "Mr. Gallipolis." The author depicted him as "svelte, almost feminine." His clothes similarly revealed his effeminacy. "He wore a pink polo shirt open at the neck, khaki pants, and very clean white tennis shoes." In addition to having "hands ... as slender as a girl's," Mr. Gallipolis, suggested the author, may have been homosexual.[119] These associations appear to have seeped into Miami's criminal records, too. At least one of Dade County's relatively few crime against nature charges was linked to a Greek migrant. Miami police arrested a man in his early thirties named Sam Mouchachos in 1927.[120] Others were likely arrested for lesser crimes with a broader range, such as vagrancy and disorderly conduct. Similarly, the biases of those who kept the county's records have further complicated tracing police targets. Local courts often had difficulty or seemed uninterested in documenting Greek surnames correctly, even with the assistance of a language interpreter. In 1933 a Clearwater court reported it arrested one "Theodore Milton." That entry, however, represented the court's "Anglicized version of an unpronounceable name of a Tarpon Springs Greek."[121] The available evidence heavily suggests that these migrants, like the Bahamians, were more targeted by police and civilians than others. Reports reveal that nativist fervor fueled several forms of violence and discrimination, from both the state and civilian communities, leveled at Greek-descended people throughout Florida.[122]

This heightened surveillance does not necessarily mean that Greeks in Florida or elsewhere engaged in sodomy with greater frequency than other ethnic groups. Rather, as with the Bahamians, it seems likely that law enforcement policed them with the impression that they were prone to sexual depravity, marked by the Greek men's perceived "femininity." This nativist fervor led to much tighter U.S. border control by the early 1920s. In 1924, the United States passed the Johnson-Reed Act, which included numerical restrictions or quotas that sought to keep out Asians and southern and eastern Europeans—including Greeks. The policy permitted only 100 quota-bound Greeks to enter the United States that year. That ceiling was raised to a pitiful 307 in 1929, and it would mostly stay there for three decades.[123]

Although it appears that "undesirable" immigrants were policed more heavily, it is important to also note the transnational and cultural factors that dictated these Greek migrants' lives and facilitated what appears to be a greater frequency in homosexual behavior. In the seafaring island of Kalymnos, whole families often shared one bed in small abodes. This led to the "development of a genre of humor regarding sexual privacy (or lack of it)."[124] Some Mediterranean cultures, including the Kalymnian, permitted greater physical contact and intimacy among men. In the Greek Orthodox tradition, sex more generally appears to have been less stigmatized than in other cultures. Homosexual relations were problematic insofar as they hindered the end result of marriage and the creation of a family. Arranged marriages were also the norm, and great social pressure was applied on single people to find an appropriate partner. This was further compounded by the local tradition of female primogeniture, wherein the first daughter received the lion's share of the family's inheritance or dowry. As a means to help secure these financial resources, Greek families often discouraged sons from marrying before any and all daughters had done so. In addition, the nature of the Kalymnian seafarer's work created homosocial spaces at sea for the men and back at home for the women. This male absenteeism afforded women greater social and political power on the islands. So while these women may have often appeared more assertive in some realms, men maintained their masculinity in other ways. This included taking risks in their dangerous trade, such as forgoing diving equipment and exemplifying "their precious manhood by showing their contempt for death." Those who were overly cautious appeared "effeminate, scorned and ridiculed by their fellows."[125] Similarly, homosexual relations among these men seemed permissible, especially when a man did not tarnish his masculinity by playing the "passive" sexual role.[126] Altogether, these factors contributed to what appears to be—on the surface—a higher frequency of homosexuality among Greek migrants in places like Miami.[127]

While these immigrants and migrants may have been labeled sexually suspect and believed to embody dubious masculinity, the relatively small number of crime against nature felony charges—even among the Greeks and Bahamians—heavily suggests that local ordinances proved more effective in criminalizing homosexual acts in Miami. Crime against nature charges were costlier to pursue and convictions more difficult to obtain. Local ordinances served as a sort of regulatory catch-all that streamlined the policing of gender- and sexually transgressive behaviors and expressions. These laws proved so effective *because* their vagueness rendered them legally dubious and criminalized what courts found too challenging or repulsive to articulate. After all, who defined what clothes were "not becoming to his or her sex?" What exactly constituted "indecent or lewd behavior?" At times, local police complained they were overburdened with cases charging individuals with lewd and lascivious conduct, as the West Palm Beach Police Department did in early 1923.[128] Indeed, local police had great leeway in defining who was a criminal or an outlier in civil society.

Vagrancy and disorderly conduct charges frequently policed queer women and men, particularly transients and the city's black and ethnic communities. By 1935, the chairman of the Dade County Commission wrote the Florida governor about the area's "situation" concerning "insane persons," which proved "very expensive." The commission asked the Florida State Hospital, located in Chattahoochee in northern Florida, to "relieve" the city of "insane persons as rapidly as they are thrown upon us." In some instances, these "insane persons" were held "in private institutions" at the county's expense, particularly a place called the Miami Retreat. Much more frequently, lack of funds and resources led to the inmates being kept "in the County Jail."[129]

Commitment and medical records reveal that several of these "insane persons" were deemed such because of their transience, unemployment, drunkenness, and gender and sexual difference. By the turn of the century, the Florida State Hospital had earned a reputation "as a dumping ground for unwanted people regardless of their actual mental state."[130] In fact, while the Florida State Hospital largely served as a mental institute and the Florida Farm Colony operated as a facility for epileptic and feeble-minded youths, their services were often blurred. Feeble-minded black patients, in particular, often found themselves in the Florida State Hospital since the Florida Farm Colony followed strict Jim Crow laws prohibiting the admission of "colored patients."[131] Also, by 1931, state law eased the commitment process and patient transfers from the Florida Farm Colony, the state's only public institution for the "feeble-minded" during this period.[132]

While many patients at the Florida State Hospital were quite ill—both mentally and physically—these records help us re-create the circumstances that landed them there. The justifications for commitment were various. An older white man in Miami, for instance, became mentally unstable when he lost his financial investments following the city's real estate collapse and the hurricane.[133] In other instances, a family member or neighbor reported erratic behavior to officials. Such behaviors were as diverse as senility, alcoholism, anemia, epilepsy, homosexuality, and signs of gender transgression.

The evidence reveals that in Miami, one of the more common paths to commitment was being arrested and having police vouch before a county judge that the subject in question was indigent, incapable of self-support, and likely to become a public charge or burden to the state.[134] With broad local laws on the books that criminalized so-called vagrants, particularly in the midst of economic depression, the Florida State Hospital became a vicious and violent form of state welfare. Reports reveal hospital attendants sometimes abused and neglected inmates.[135] Only in the rarest of circumstances did someone voluntarily enter this space.

As several historians have observed, this institutionalization was part of a larger project to regulate populations and curb the reproduction of the "unfit"—defined as such through perceptions of race, ethnicity, class, (dis)ability, gender, and sexuality—that had many parallels and was connected to the eugenicist discourse that sought to regulate U.S. borders by weeding out those deemed physically and mentally "undesirable" and "unfit." In 1913, for instance, a prominent Florida women's organization pleaded, "In order to decrease the number of feeble-minded, insane and blind, defectives of these classes must be prevented from reproducing their kind."[136] These eugenicist policies particularly targeted the state's "unfit" women. As feeblemindedness and degeneracy were linked to "moral delinquency," Florida officials expressed the desire to enforce sterilization on such women. This reflected a larger eugenics movement that took off during the Progressive period throughout the country wherein "the growing use of state power" was put into effect "to intercede in previously private affairs for an assumed public benefit."[137] So-called delinquent young women and girls in Florida, defined as such largely on the basis of their race, ethnicity, and class, were recommended for sterilization because they were known "habitual sex delinquent[s]" or thought to live lives of "immorality and prostitution."[138] Unlike other states, Florida failed to pass a sterilization law; institutional administrators, however, would continue to segregate and contain these women in the name of advancing civilization.[139]

In Miami, committed patients were often single or unattached, or their families were similarly destitute and incapable of assisting them. Miami officials sent a twenty-one-year-old black laborer named E. S. Strong to the hospital in 1929. He died a month later from syphilis and pellagra. His family and background information was unknown, so news of his death only reached Miami police.[140] Miami law enforcement sent another young black man there that year. Walter General listed his guardian as the pastor at his local Baptist church. He told medical inspectors that he had been sequestered in the Miami jail and that "he has always been of afraid of white folks."[141] William Birdsong, a middle-aged black cook living in Miami, was brought to the state hospital in 1930. The disoriented and widowed man "had been drinking moonshine whiskey" and "was taken out and beat unconscious by four men." When he "came to [his] senses," he found himself inside a Fort Pierce jail. He was then taken to Chattahoochee.[142] Black and single men became prime targets for state institutionalization.

Much as in Miami's arrest records for sodomy and crime against nature charges, it seems black Bahamians—both women and men—were regularly if not disproportionately committed. This included Israel Saunders, who was taken to Chattahoochee in 1929 from southern Florida and died less than eight months later from the effects of syphilis.[143] Meanwhile, George Simmonet's case shines light on the criminalization of habitual drunks and vagrants. The thirty-two-year-old Bahamian man, who had "never been married," often drank "plenty of moon-shine" and "raised Hell." Although Simmonet spent many nights in jail for drunkenness, he "pa[id] his fine and c[ame] right out," usually "in time to go to work."[144] Such processes tore families apart. Bimini native and war veteran Fred Anthom was taken to Florida State Hospital in 1933. He had been "gassed in [the] World War" and sustained head injuries.[145] His wife, Pearl, a black woman originally from Georgia, had been committed two years prior.[146] Bahamian women were also taken to Chattahoochee. A twenty-year-old Bahamian maid named Vienna Joseph spent several months there in 1929, even though she was "not acutely ill." Officials discharged her once she received anti-syphilis treatment.[147] This high inmate representation of blacks, both native- and foreign-born, suggests the heightened policing of these communities in Miami as well as the violent substitute for social welfare in the city.[148]

Once committed, black women appear to have been subjected to particularly invasive medical examinations and reports reveal physicians operated under certain assumptions about the patients' sexual proclivities. Some doctors believed female genitals "offered clues for detecting a woman's proclivity toward lesbianism, masturbation, frigidity, and promiscuity."[149] Florida physicians observed that one Miami black woman's vagina "readily admit[ted] two extending fingers." While such pelvic exams were customary, the ad hoc description—which insinuated she was a "loose" woman—stood in stark contrast to the commentary most commonly given for committed married white women: "marital." Indeed, Mamie Baxton was denied this consideration, even though she was, in fact, also married.[150] Many black women resisted these invasive examinations that also operated under racialized assumptions about their bodies and sex lives. Examiners described Mamie Coleman, another black woman living in Miami, as "very resistant to [vaginal and rectal] examination." No such exam was therefore given.[151] Similarly, Tislane Russell, a Bahamian woman living in Miami who also proved "uncooperative" in permitting the exam, told examiners she had "never been seen by any man but her husband."[152] While much of this was procedure—including noting the size of the cervix and whether there was any tenderness—additional commentary suggests physicians were informed by preconceived notions about black and immigrant women, particularly that they were hypersexual, nonmonogamous, and sexually deviant.

As the prejudicial commitment of single or unattached women and men suggests, several of the inmates sent from Dade County during these years were deemed ill because of "sex perversion." A twenty-six-year-old white man living in Miami named Lacy Curtis Atkinson was hospitalized in 1926. He suffered from hallucinations of "a sex nature."[153] Similarly, Miami police arrested a black man named Irving Young who suffered from "psychosis with psychopathic personality." Chattahoochee became his grave. Although this working-class man was institutionalized in 1951, his file reveals his trouble with local police began in the 1930s. Medical examiners described him as a "sexual pervert" who regularly masturbated and "practiced fellatio on numerous occasions and submitted to it many times." He had also "submitted to pederasty hundreds of times." Officials similarly observed how he was "very effeminate in speech, manner and movements." In this way, his "sex perversion" justified his commitment.[154]

Evidence reveals Miami officials also attempted to send young men thought to be suffering from "sexual perversion" to the Florida Farm Colony for the "feeble-minded." In 1929, that institution's superintendent complained to a Miami probation officer about the facility's overcrowded conditions caused "by the large number of truant, delinquent, and incorrigible children the courts" had sent there. Four years later, another Miami officer petitioned the colony to take in an eighteen-year-old man believed to have a penchant for "petty crimes, perversion, and self-abuse." The superintendent declined his request, claiming feeble-minded children at the institution "might be mislead [sic] by such a good boy." As Steve Noll has argued, institutional overseers frequently tried to keep patients believed to have mental disabilities apart from those with a criminal record, even as the conditions of deficiency and criminality were sometimes understood as interconnected.[155] Considering that Miami law enforcement played an instrumental role in patient institutionalization, thereby thrusting criminality into a patient's file, it appears cases in which perceived mental deficiency converged with lawbreaking more likely led to the Florida State Hospital than to the Florida Farm Colony.

While the archives yield less information on women in this regard, evidence suggests immigrant women were also institutionalized in Miami and suspected of lesbianism. Take Adele Galy, a Catholic dressmaker born in Damascus, Syria, and living in Miami with her mother—a noted concern for medical examiners, who believed it was indicative of her antisocial behavior. She was taken to the Florida State Hospital in 1938 for chronic insanity, which doctors believed was brought on by the onset of menopause. Galy's husband separated from her because they could not have sex. Her pelvic exam observed that the "perforation of the hymen will not admit one finger and bleeds when an attempt is made." They seemed particularly interested in exploring her sexual history. The "patient denies ever masturbating," noted her file. Her inability to have sex with men, or her lack of interest in this, at least partially connected to the likelihood that she was syphilitic, led examiners to specify that there was "no sexual perversion" in her history.[156] Nativist sentiments informed the belief that the immigrant woman's failure to submit to a man might be a product of sexual perversion.[157]

*Prosecuting Deviance*

In addition to race, ethnicity, class, and gender, the policing and prosecuting of same-sex sexual acts also took form in relation to questions of normalcy and deviancy that were defined by concepts of age and (dis)ability. While the evidence suggests most gender-transgressive behavior and homosexual acts, when prosecuted at all, were more effectively regulated by local ordinances, the much more detailed and surviving cases for sodomy and crimes against nature that reached the Florida Supreme Court reveal the biases and systemic logic local police, legislators, public officials, and judges employed in their surveillance and interpretation of such acts. After all, the court took up the state's crime against nature felony *five* times before 1940, likely a product of the statute's vagueness. The court's rulings had major ramifications for decades. The court affirmed its 1921 *Ephraim* ruling that oral sex constituted a crime against nature the following year in *Jackson v. State*.[158] In 1929's *Drawdy v. State*, the court took up a case of a man accused of bestiality with a mare. As with rape cases, Florida ruled that emission was *not* necessary for one to be found guilty of a crime against nature.[159]

The court's last two cases on the matter before World War II occurred in Dade County's urban frontier. In 1932, Florida's Supreme Court heard

*Blameuser v. State*, which charged a sixty-year-old man with committing a crime against nature on a nine-year-old boy in Miami. In December 1930, the boy told his uncle that a year prior Benjamin Blameuser had taken him to a vacant garage in northwest Miami, a less populated residential area just north of Flagler Street, and performed oral sex on him. By the time the Dade County solicitor filed charges against the man, fourteen months had passed since the incident allegedly took place. Miami jurors found Blameuser guilty and sentenced him to ten years of hard labor at the state penitentiary.[160] In 1935, three years after the *Blameuser* decision, the Florida Supreme Court heard *English v. Florida*. Dade County jurors found John English, a man in his mid-twenties, guilty of a crime against nature. In this case, the court prosecuted English for performing oral sex on two boys, aged eleven and seven, in a gully also in the northwest section of the city. Like Blameuser, English was sentenced to ten years of hard labor at the state penitentiary.[161]

The two Miami cases reveal several significant changes in the state's understanding of same-sex sexual behavior. The small number of Miami charges suggests local police's hesitance to file felony charges for sodomy. It appears not only that police rarely enforced the state's sodomy or crime against nature law but also that they most often sought lesser charges to prosecute offenders. Sodomy cases, for instance, were more frequently prosecuted only after a neighbor, relative, or "accomplice" reported it. Police did not often catch alleged offenders in the act.

It is also significant that both these cases received notoriety because they involved young boys and an older man accused of preying on them, which further centers age and intergenerational intercourse as informing local- and state-level conceptions of homosexuality. In his work on homosexuality in the Pacific Northwest, Peter Boag argued that age difference, rather than gender difference, constituted the prevailing dynamic in working-class homosexual relations. This was, in large part, a product of the transience associated with day and seasonal adult laborers—known as "jockers"—out on the road and in outlying areas of the frontier who found sexual release with young hustlers, or "punks," also on the move. The evidence suggests that "jockers" and "punks" were among the distinct archetypes made legible in particular cities and rural areas throughout the United States, depending on a number of circumstances, including class relations, prevailing economic systems, geography, and modes of homosociability. Miami's urban frontier seems to have made space for the legibility of many gender- and sexually transgressive characters that at least resembled the jocker, punk, fairy, pansy, or trade.[162] These urban tropes, however, appear to have been less prominent or discernible in Miami's historical record, perhaps because of the marketing scheme that promoted gender and sexual transgression more broadly or the absence of a great public scandal concerning homosexuality during this period.

In both legal cases, age also proved central to implications that the crime against nature felony more accurately targeted what we would interpret as sexual assault or rape. As Stephen Robertson has argued, prior to the 1920s courts generally focused on gender rather than age in prosecuting sexual offenses. By the 1930s, with "the emergence of new ideas about childhood [that] centered on physiological and psychological development," age difference more discernibly came to inform sexual violence against both girls and boys—who were increasingly understood, before the law, as collective "children" rather than by distinct gender constructions.[163] We get glimpses of this gendered impulse, for instance, in the changes made by Florida's legislature in 1901. That year, state lawmakers increased the age of consent for carnal intercourse with an unmarried woman to eighteen, effectively widening the state's purview for criminalizing statutory rape—which the law interpreted as something that could only occur to females. That same session, however, Florida's legislature amended common law practice in passing an act that charged juries with deciphering whether "a boy under fourteen" could commit rape. Prior to that, the state operated under the assumption that boys younger than fourteen were incapable of committing such an offense.[164] So while the law created new measures to protect the "innocence" and potential "ruin" of young and adolescent girls from sexual engagement, new judicial assessments based on the potential masculine traits among young boys— particularly their capability of being "eager and impulsive, aggressive to an almost brutish extent"—expanded the state's purview of rape to be more mindful of gender than by a universal concept of age.[165]

Similarly, after the 1930s, the court's new understanding of age collided with emerging notions of homosexuality. This meant that, before the law, young and adolescent boys involved in sodomy cases were increasingly regarded the way the courts had long viewed young and adolescent girls in sexual violence cases: "as objects in narratives in which only the defendant acted, and in which, at most, only passing mention was made of force."[166] Whether a young boy or adolescent resisted such sexual advances became less central to the defense than, as had been the case with young girls and adolescents for decades, the victim's age-presumed lack of understanding of such acts. Just the same, as these two Florida Supreme Court cases reveal, judges heavily focused on the lack of sexual knowledge and overall victimization of the young "accomplice" to sodomy rather than whether he demonstrated resistance or lack of consent. In this way, independent of the distinct circumstances of an individual case, it appears courts continued to interpret the crime against nature felony primarily through the lens of same-sex rape and came to prosecute such acts as forms of coercive sex.

Several of the sodomy cases that reached the Florida Supreme Court presented evidence that the offense was a sexual assault *and* a monetary exchange that went awry. English, for instance, reportedly promised the boys fifty cents. The boys often protested they never received payment.[167] The two defendants in 1921's *Ephraim et al. v. State*, Ephraim and Metz, took turns receiving oral sex from Gary. A witness who claimed he saw the whole encounter through a slightly open window testified that Metz told Gary "that if he bit him" while performing fellatio, "he would knock his brains out." Testimony also depicted Ephraim's role as coercive: "Jim Ephraim kept telling him [Gary] to get his mouth open a little more." It is also possible, however, to interpret that Gary, the "accomplice," sought to disassociate himself from homosexuality during the trial. Other testimony, which was not read as contradictory to sexual assault, stressed how, upon completing the act, Gary told the other men: "Now pay me my money. You owe me two dollars." To that, the witness testified, Metz told Gary: "I will pay you nothing, but I will give you a drink of [moon]shine to wash your mouth out with." While it appears that courts generally interpreted Florida's crime against nature felony as homosexual assault, the evidence suggests "accomplices" may have also stressed that claim as a means to disassociate themselves from stigma. Gary was not prosecuted for "go[ing] down on" the men, even as other courts throughout the country may have viewed him as a young street hustler equally at fault.[168]

The 1921 *Ephraim* ruling that sought to resolve whether oral sex constituted a crime against nature felony—despite the fact that the legislature had passed a statute in 1917 that seemed to criminalize the act as a misdemeanor—remained ambiguous and was challenged for decades. Subsequent cases before the Florida Supreme Court expressed confusion over the existence of the two distinct statutes, which had the potential to target the same offense. The "abominable and detestable crime against nature" offense was a felony, while the "unnatural and lascivious" offense was a misdemeanor. Four years after the latter statute was passed, the *Ephraim* decision decided oral sex *also* constituted a crime against nature felony. Both Miami cases took issue with how this decision licensed police to selectively prosecute anal and oral sex as either a felony or misdemeanor. Blameuser's attorneys argued that the two "sections charge separate and distinct crimes but of the same character."[169] Three years later, in English's arrest of judgment, lawyers observed that the "information is duplicitous and fails to inform this defendant whether he is charged" with "a crime against nature, or a lewd and lascivious act."[170] The ambiguity and vagueness of these laws was partially resolved in a Florida Supreme Court case forty years later, 1971's *Franklin v. State*. It ruled the state's felony statute against sodomy and bestiality, or "the abominable and detestable crime against nature," was "unconstitutional for vagueness and uncertainly in its language, violating constitutional due process to the defendants." The court, instead, gestured toward the employment of the separate "unnatural and lascivious" offense misdemeanor. "Society will continue to be protected from [this] sort of reprehensible act," noted the court in 1971, through that misdemeanor charge.[171] In other words, after 1971, consensual anal and oral sex—largely construed by police as same-sex sexual encounters—remained illegal in Florida, but as a lesser crime.

The *Ephraim* case influenced the prosecution of same-sex behaviors at the local level, as was made clear in the 1935 *English* case in Miami. When the county solicitor filed an information against English for the offense, he followed the statute for the crime against nature felony except he added "per os," Latin for "by mouth." English's lawyers protested: "Evidently the County Solicitor felt it was necessary for him to go some further than the language of the statute and allege in what manner and on what part of the anatomy of the boy the assault was made." His attorneys noted that every indictment should be intelligible and in the English language.[172] The state, for its part, cited the *Ephraim* case, which used the phrase, and noted that Latin terms such as "per annum" and "per capita" are generally understood in English.[173] The Florida Supreme Court agreed and upheld the conviction.[174] The Dade County solicitor's decision to add "per os" suggests that he was keenly aware of the *Ephraim* ruling and that the felony crime against nature targeted oral sex, even as it seems that less severe charges remained preferable in less notorious cases.

The two Miami cases that reached the Florida Supreme Court during this period reveal how factors such as class and (dis)ability also informed the policing of same-sex sexual acts in the city. We only know about these cases because they reached the state's high court through the work of private attorneys. The well-established Miami-based firm Kehoe & Kehoe represented both plaintiffs.[175] The legal team uncluded J. Walter Kehoe, a former congressman with great influence in Tallahassee.[176] In the *English* case, the court initially assigned a public attorney who did not object to hearsay evidence or question the ambiguous nature of the charge. English's family hired the private attorney, who argued "substantial injury had been done to the defendant because his rights were not properly protected by the assigned counsel." Although the court did not reverse English's conviction, he only had a fighting chance because his family could afford a private attorney, something beyond the reach of most defendants.[177]

It appears English had a physical disability that marked him as suspicious and unreliable before the law, and perhaps as more likely to be suffering from what was understood as a mental illness that gave way to sexual perversion. In this period, "whether a disability originated in the body or mind could be almost impossible to distinguish," and those with disabilities were readily associated with the dangerous notion of "perverted deviance" or infantilized by being characterized as demonstrating "angelic innocence."[178] It appears English's neighbors associated him with the former. When the boys reported the incident, they noted the man was "bow-legged." The case also relied on witness testimony from "two negroes" that placed English in the vicinity of the reported crime. In his testimony, one of the black witnesses claimed English ran "like he was sort of crippled." This information heavily informed the incriminating evidence that followed. Paul Martens, a Dade County probation officer, learned from a charity worker that "two boys had been abused" and initiated a "house to house canvass through the entire neighborhood." One neighbor told Martens, "I know who you are looking for; you are looking for Crazy John." Later testimony altered this to "Goofy John." The common laborer with a physical disability had apparently acquired a questionable reputation in the community. Martens claimed he also "investigated his reputation as to his conduct with little boys," which proved to be "very bad." Such testimony became admissible in the court, despite the fact that community interpretations of his behavior and comportment seemed influenced by the common laborer's class, low education (he could barely read or write), and physical disability.[179]

The issue of community reputation, status, and class in prosecuting same-sex sexual acts in Miami was even clearer in Blameuser's case. Originally from Illinois, Blameuser, like so many others, moved to Miami and purchased real estate. He owned several bungalows and residences off of Flagler Street in northwest Miami. Just before the accusation was made, Blameuser received a visit from the accuser's mother "to see about renting a house from him to live in." The mother admitted the two parties did not reach an agreement on a rental. A few weeks later, the boy accused the sixty-year-old man of having performed oral sex on him more than a year earlier. N. D. B. Connolly has shown the centrality of real estate in provoking class and racial tensions in Miami, as both white and black landlords exploited renters and perpetuated violence, poverty, and discrimination onto marginalized communities.[180] Whether or not the rental discussion sparked the young boy to make his accusation, Blameuser's lawyers certainly understood that the court might register that possibility. Unlike in the *English* case, Blameuser's respectable status in the community—particularly as the owner of multiple properties—led eight witnesses to testify to his good character. They characterized Blameuser as a decent, moral, church-going, sober, hard-working, and Christian man, neighbor, and husband with an outstanding reputation.[181] Unlike all the other crime against nature charges that reached the Florida Supreme Court before World War II, the judges overturned Blameuser's conviction. He became a free man.[182]

MIAMI BOOSTERS' PROMOTION of fairyland coincided with the formation of queer expressions, desires, and behaviors in the city. As we have seen in previous chapters, the early city's labor needs and racial and class segregation produced bachelor societies that made possible homosexual acts, particularly among Miami's working-class men. These sex-segregated spaces included shacks, apartments, wharves, ferryboats, beaches, jails, and military training camps.

The transience associated with Miami life—with its brief tourist seasons, entertainment circuits, seasonal labor, service-industry jobs, and status as a hub for air and sea traffic to the Caribbean and Latin America—proved critical to creating a new sexual regime in the coming years. The evidence reveals authorities and leaders at the local and state level—including the police, lawmakers, newspapers, and judges—increasingly identified a particular personhood as having a penchant for gender transgression and, later, as fostering unnatural sexual desires for members of the same sex. To fully understand these shifts, we must now explore how Miami boosters commodified a particular white heterosexual identity to counteract the queer, and often racialized, acts and expressions made visible in the fairyland. As the next chapter shows, the heterosexual identity that today enjoys a privileged status as the desirable "norm" had very queer origins.

# WOMEN AND THE MAKING OF
# MIAMI'S HETEROSEXUAL CULTURE

No less lovely is the Miami of today, but it costs more to give
a girl a taste of all its glories.
— REPORT ON COURTSHIP, 1924

Under the swingin' drug store sign
The Miami flapper waits;
The flap, a clever kid is she,
Who never lacks for dates.
Laughing, smiling, petting—
All "set" for another bloke;
Each evening sees a man picked up.
Each morning finds him broke!
— PUBLISHED IN A MIAMI NEWSPAPER, 1924

"Florida today offers the newest frontier of happiness for
woman," claimed Dorothy Frooks, a "woman lawyer of New York" in the
mid-1920s. While boosters balanced marketing Miami as both a frontier *and*
modern city, middle- and upper-class white women and men sought out
their individual visions for the fairyland. Women like Frooks reimagined
Florida at large as a space not yet tainted by the era's gender- and sexually
transgressive "flapper," or other manifestations of modernity. Frooks based
her "sanguine hopes of a rosy future for this state" on "the reward Florida
offer[ed] to the women who c[a]me to help in her upbuilding." After all, "no
girl should work who can afford not to." She maintained women too often
"live on a plane that scares the man away from marriage, or, if they do in-
veigle him to marriage, they soon lose him because of expensive tastes and
independence built up by their own efforts." Frooks believed "every woman's
object and innate ambition in life is to have a home and children." Frooks,
who was unmarried, "professe[d] to be a young woman of the order of
women, not flappers."[1]

As Frooks's perspective suggests, this chapter turns to the queerness of
mannish, modern, and heterosexual women. It explores the textured ways
white women's articulation of gender and sexuality interplayed through his-

torically fraught and evolving notions of deviance and normativity. After all, in Frooks's view, the modern woman was not a woman at all; she was *something* else. Even though Frooks was a lawyer—a profession still then largely read as masculine and the source of great gender anxiety, as we saw with contemporary stage performances in Miami, including a man who "appeared as a woman lawyer" to laugh off existing tensions—she "preserve[d] her appearance as a woman."[2] Frooks claimed, "I'm against the derby and the mannish frock. I'm for the womanly garments and the corsage. I'm against the flapper, and I think she is against herself." She hoped to chip away at Florida's growing reputation as a modern oasis—one largely built by Miami—and instead promote the state as a space for women to return to a mythologized Victorian femininity and propriety. In her view, its frontier status served as a corrective to women's entrance into the wage-earning workforce and the "desexing" effects of labor that largely began with industrialization in the North. This vision simultaneously licensed men to view Miami as a site of exploration where single women were made readily available to them, both romantically and sexually.[3]

This view also sought to challenge Miami promoters' marketing of a fairyland as embodying both the pinnacle of American modernity and the local charm of a permissive frontierland. The growing visibility of queerness in Miami created a public knowledge concerning the interplay of gender difference and sexual deviance. This followed a very dangerous revelation in the city: cross-gender expressions and homosexual inclinations were not limited to black, immigrant, and working-class communities. Rather, these so-called perversions could also be found or were perhaps innate among white middle- and upper-class women and men.

This revelation ignited a new identity and commodity to complement—or, rather, counteract—the gender and sexual deviant's presence in Miami: *hetero*sexuality. Miami promoters consolidated the pervasive and competing images of the city as both modern and jungle by reimagining the area as a site for heterosexual pleasure and leisure. Urban promoters began aggressively marketing a fairyland that touted the arrival of a new modern woman. She was simultaneously white, moneyed, attractive, and available. Unlike before, and in many ways a rebuttal to the city's mannish woman, she was also viewed as inherently sexual—heterosexual, at that. A white middle- and upper-class constituency in the city made sense of and refashioned the urban and frontier deviancy Miami boosters had carefully crafted—including the gender transgression of the modern woman—by promoting the image of a sexualized woman made available to men in Miami; these were processes she too was keenly involved in shaping. Through her image, locals and travelers became acquainted with the beautiful, modern, and fashionable "Miami mermaid" or "bathing beauty." Her arrival in the city, and her subsequent promotion, was tied to a growing consumer culture in Miami, the United States, and the Caribbean that sold not only her image but also her style, dress, and demeanor. Her association with a growing consumer culture situated this heterosexual woman within the middle class, a class of people fairyland's boosters increasingly targeted.

The "Miami mermaid" became a commodity and consumable identity in the fairyland by the late 1920s, made readily available in the marketing of Miami's leisure and recreational culture that ultimately sought to satiate men's sexual desires. Urban designers aggressively marketed the city as a site for men to explore their "natural" and "masculine" sexual desires for this newly sexualized woman. A male heterosexual identity soon emerged that was, in large part, defined by the pursuit of this available and liberated woman. As city boosters more succinctly marketed Miami as modern, they increasingly abandoned the image of a frontier wilderness ripe for white conquest. Instead, *women* became the object of the "normal" man's conquest. In many ways rejecting the femininity of the queer and reasserting the masculinity believed to have been robbed by the mannish woman, middle-class men in the city and throughout the nation increasingly came to understand their carnal desires for sexually available women as constitutive of their being by redefining and consolidating understandings of masculinity. Not only did these processes give birth to distinct and commodified heterosexual identities in the city, they also firmly entrenched the dominance of these identities in this urban space, even as the emphasis on tourism continued to allow spaces for gender and sexually nonconforming people and networks.

It is important to remember that although most of these modern women became normative, largely through complex processes that emphasized their ultimate submission to a man and their collective whiteness, they defied the era's traditional confines of femininity. They laid claim to their own bodies and sexualities in significant and extraordinarily queer ways that abandoned the feminine propriety of the past. Indeed, they challenged, negotiated, and redefined what feminine norms looked like. One must resist a one-dimensional interpretation of viewing them as victims of a heterosexual and patriarchal system, and instead understand them as active agents who also upended social, cultural, economic, and political norms.

### The Modern Woman and Threats to Masculinity

Miami's 1896 municipal incorporation and its earliest years coincided with massive changes in women's social, political, and economic lives; modernity challenged gender relations in significant ways. The nascent city had long permitted or facilitated several forms of gender transgression. Miami's distinct statuses as an urban frontier and fairyland, in particular, allowed white women—residents and travelers alike—greater opportunity to explore their bodies and desires and to participate in public life outside of the home. These processes helped redefine white femininity and, in turn, the parameters of white male masculinity.

Before the early twentieth century, respectable white women in the United States were often described or believed to be inherently asexual and passionless. This did not mean, of course, that respectable women did not have sexual feelings. In fact, sex and physical pleasure were frequently articulated as part of the concept of "true love" that defined Victorian romanticism.[4] Instead, society emphasized women's moral and spiritual faculties. Even as the idea of a marriage of equal love and companionship took off among middle- and upper-class women in the early and mid-nineteenth century, the rigidity of gender roles facilitated "separate spheres" that promoted patriarchal marriages and romantic arrangements. Or, put another way, women's real-life limitations in political, social, and economic matters often rendered them dependent on men and undermined the very idea of a companionate ideal.[5] By the late nineteenth century, a growing number of white middle-class women throughout the country sought alternatives to these social divisions and increasingly sought women-dominated spaces, such as women's colleges, where they cultivated intense bonds with their peers. Not only were "romantic friendships" between women common, but they were often encouraged and sometimes understood as practical "rehearsals" for a future heterosexual marriage, even as many women defied these social expectations and remained committed to other women.[6]

No women's colleges were established in the Miami area prior to the 1940s; however, the city's status as an urban frontier had weakened the "separate spheres" ideology by the late nineteenth century.[7] Pioneer women took on multiple roles beyond the domestic realm and created intimate bonds with other women in numerous ways. Travelers and residents similarly took notice of Miami's "mannish" woman, whose economic, social, and political independence defied feminine mores, particularly that of domesticity.

In the United States, this first generation of New Women, born in the 1850s and 1860s, predominantly transgressed *gender* norms by rejecting domesticity and seeking out male privilege. These women, identified primarily by their masculine behavior and dress, came to represent this new archetype. They increasingly entered professions previously restricted to them, received advanced educations, engaged in politics, entered the public sphere, and sought economic independence from men. Most bourgeois women who partook in such gender-transgressive behavior were not socially or culturally understood as *sexually* suspect until at least the late nineteenth or early twentieth centuries. By then, however, feminist activism helped shift gender norms again and redefined the confines of respectable white femininity.[8]

The separate spheres paradigm did not reflect the lives of the working class and women of color, whose statuses and circumstances broke from the confines of domestic spaces—and therefore, the "feminine purity"— culturally ascribed to bourgeois, white women.[9] This is evident in the criminal records pertaining to working-class, black, and immigrant women explored in past chapters. For these Miami women, their social lives in the farm, fields, saloons, houses of ill fame, and at the borders removed them from the confines of traditional domesticity while also stripping them of respectability. In most instances, sexual deviance was thus associated with the perceived impurity of the lower classes and people of color.

This is clear in Constance Fenimore Woolson's 1876 Florida-based short story "Felipa." The title character is a young immigrant girl who can pass as a boy and becomes romantically infatuated with a white bourgeois woman. While the author suggests the title character suffers from some form of sexual perversion, it is never distinctly expressed. Instead, Woolson emphasizes Felipa's *gender* deviancy.[10] In 1880, a review of the story described Felipa as the "semi-savage little mongrel ... who wears boy's trousers" and makes remarks "apropos of these same trousers." The reviewer, who found the plot "incredulous," seemed to struggle with the "complexity of thought which is out of keeping with Felipa's primitive nature." The reviewer maintained, "In the case of Felipa, however (who is a charming creature, or, we rather suspect, a charmingly elaborated sketch from some living original), this is the only lapse from psychological realism." The reviewer made sense of Felipa's deviancy entirely in terms of her "savagery": "The passionate attachment of the yellow little savage to the beautiful, fair-skinned Northern lady, her hunger for praise and her resolute despair at being repulsed, are in themselves very pathetic."[11]

The turn of the century ushered in significant changes to understandings of gender. As elsewhere, the prominence of white women's organizations in Miami proved critical to creating more stringent and defined gender categories for both women and men in later years. As women started to occupy roles and spaces once reserved for men in greater numbers, they questioned the permanence and dominance of white middle-class masculinity. Local women's groups fought for the vote, endorsed prison reform, and urged the prohibition of alcohol.[12] In reference to the latter, for example, women played a key role in the October 30, 1913, vote that made Dade County dry. Residents in all county precincts—except for Miami proper, Perrine, and North Miami, where saloons proliferated and business owners stood to lose their investments—voted in favor of Prohibition.[13] All saloons were required to shut down by the evening of November 3. Selling liquor became illegal.[14]

Indeed, Miami became a central site for white feminist reform. By the early 1910s, Miami had the largest and most active women's suffrage organizations in all of Florida.[15] On March 15 and 16, 1917, Miami's Equal Suffrage League hosted suffragette Anna Howard Shaw for the Florida Equal Suffrage Convention.[16] Later that year, the Miami league read and approved statements from Vance Thompson's text *Woman*.[17] The group specifically agreed that "woman's first rebellion must be against the indecency of wearing specialized sex-garments in public." A woman's skirt was a "sex-badge" that "shroud[s] the Woman." In this regard, the mannish "Dr. Mary Walker was right."[18] While women got the vote at the national level on August 18, 1920, with the ratification of the Nineteenth Amendment, a handful of female property owners in Miami voted in their first municipal election a year prior. On August 16, 1919, twenty-six women voted in a special city bond election. In a sexist rendering of that historic moment, a Miami newspaper poked fun of one woman who "absentmindedly" placed her ballot "in her pocketbook" rather than the box.[19] In addition to redefining a woman's role in both private and public spaces, such efforts to dismantle markers of gender also caused a reflexive middle-class articulation of masculinity that later found release in the sharpened linking of sexual desires to the "true" self.

Women's political organizing also occurred among some of the Bahamian migrants introduced in previous chapters. The transnational effects of their migration found some Bahamian women transgressing gender roles on the islands by moving into the male-dominated realm of politics. Bahamians were instrumental to the founding of Miami's chapter of the Universal Negro Improvement Association (UNIA) in 1920.[20] Following their experiences with the UNIA's Ladies Auxiliary in Miami, two Bahamian women named "Mother" Frances Butler and Lettie Tinker returned to Nassau and helped found the "Mothers' Club" in 1929. In addition to raising funds and distributing clothes and food to the needy, this organization was later involved in the trade union movement.[21] This anticipated the Bahamian suffrage movement, even though women did not get the vote on the islands until 1962.[22]

Although Miami saw both Bahamian and U.S. women organize through social and political means, the latter often invoked a form of imperial feminism that diminished the former's efforts to claim their place in Miami's public sphere.[23] As a borderland territory wedged between the Caribbean and the U.S. South, Miami saw early feminism play out very differently between black and white, foreign and native. Miami's white middle- and upper-class feminists asserted their space in urban politics and the public sphere more generally through causes such as prohibition of alcohol and promotion of the arts. Miami's white feminists were also vocal in the city's anti-Bahamian nativism of the 1910s and 1920s. In the summer of 1912, the Woman's Club asked the Miami City Council to "refuse residence in Miami to any Nassau negro unless he or she declares his or her intention to become an American citizen." They recommended that the council create a board "of reputable men and women" to investigate whether those asking for citizenship would "make a desirable citizen." They had grown anxious over the "transient 'Nassaus,'" who they believed were "inferior servants" who drove away the better "African element," or the "American negroes." While these women acknowledged the difficulty of enforcing such an ordinance—which would require arriving foreigners in Miami to "foreswear their native lands" and effectively see local policy trump federal law—they stressed this "protest" came "from the 'very souls' of the women of the city ... contending with the servant problem."[24] These women asserted themselves in political debates at the expense of the Bahamian women and men who applied to work for them.

The Woman's Club entered this transnational, urban debate by proposing that white middle- and upper-class women serve as the moral guardians for the city's labor shortage and so-called idle class. It proposed a "Housekeepers' Union" to oversee housing for "respectable, thrifty negro families from Virginia and the Carolinas." The white women's union proposed prescreening these black families to ensure their cheap workers were laborious, subservient, and respectable. The U.S. African American women would provide domestic work for white families, while their husbands labored in the fields or tracks. The Woman's Club maintained this would "solve the question of the worthless, idle negro class," largely understood as foreign-born Bahamians.[25]

Meanwhile, this white feminist momentum also led to the establishment of Miami's Young Women's Christian Association (YWCA), a key homosocial space for women. On June 16, 1919, dozens of white women were recruited to establish a YWCA in Miami. Even though "women adrift" had entered the wage-earning workforce in unprecedented numbers over the past few decades, Miami's seasonally defined economy frequently rendered many working-class and transient white women unemployed or underpaid.[26] This proved especially challenging at times, as the proposal of the Housekeepers' Unions shows, because the city was home to so many cheap, black, often migrant workers prime for labor exploitation in the city's domestic and service industries.[27] The YWCA took over a hotel and offered women room and board for $8.75 a week. Within a few months, local investors helped fund the purchasing of a permanent structure for the YWCA, the Fort Dallas Hotel located at the center of downtown Miami. This institution provided countless working-class and transient women a place to stay and oftentimes coordinated with businesses to find them work, even as reports demonstrate recruiters often exploited their situation with low wages.[28] Miami's YWCA regularly hosted the Daughters of the British Empire, which organized fundraisers in Nassau that attracted "socially prominent visitors" from Miami and Havana. It also offered Spanish lessons, observing increased trade and travel with the Spanish-speaking Caribbean and Latin America as well as diasporic communities in Miami.[29]

Much like Miami's YMCA had done for men, the YWCA provided women intimate spaces with other women and made possible alternatives to heterosexual marriage, romance, and sociability. The *Miami Herald* called Miami's early manifestation of the YWCA an "Adamless Eden." There, "girls and women ... manage[d] their own affairs at the camp." Similarly, influential Miami resident William Jennings Bryan, a three-time presidential candidate and impassioned orator, called the YWCA a "first aid to the newcomer, friend to the stranger within our gates, home to the girls residing in the city, guardian of the welfare of the women of Miami."[30] The area saw a spike in population in the mid-1920s prior to the real estate bust that found hundreds of young women flocking to the city with few jobs to sustain them.[31] The old hotel had been filled to capacity, even as cots were placed throughout the building to accommodate more women. In 1925 Miami's YWCA bought another hotel to counter the room shortage. Each room accommodated at least two women, although it is likely that even more shared rooms and beds when space was particularly limited.[32] The opportunities for romantic and sexual relationships were bountiful.

While no available evidence directly links Miami's free-thinking artist Dewing Woodward to lesbianism, her life encapsulated aspects of the era's independent and mannish woman who rejected heterosexual traditions in favor of intimate bonds with other women. One contemporary observed that the "YWCA is intimately concerned with women's physical freedom, women's new economic independence, and women's spiritual liberation."[33] Woodward sought out all of these. The 1920 census listed Woodward as a lodger at the YWCA. Louise Johnson, who initially moved to Miami with Woodward, similarly stayed there.[34] They were likely strapped for cash, as they were often underpaid or went uncompensated for their work in a male-driven industry. They were also, however, drifter-transients who documented their lives as such in Woodward's semiautobiographical book *Some Adventures of Two Vagabonds*.[35] Other contemporary works suggested that wandering women—read as particularly masculine and deviant—were frequently inducted or exposed to the "hobo" life in the United States. This potentially included lesbianism, prostitution, and dressing or passing as men.[36] At the very least, as gender-transgressive drifters, Woodward and Johnson sought alternatives to the confines of white middle-class femininity and heterosexual marriage.

Miami writer, feminist, and activist Marjory Stoneman Douglas personified many of the gender-transgressive features of the New Woman. Douglas, who was born in Minnesota and raised in Massachusetts, was influenced by a generation of suffragettes. She attended Wellesley College in 1912, choosing female-dominated environments during her transformative years.[37] Upon graduation, she shucked middle-class conveniences and rented an apartment with two other women. These women pursued independent lives and employment, training as department store salesgirls. In her own words, Douglas was "filled with the spirit of the new age, eager for womanly independence, and economic freedom."[38] She met a male journalist in 1914 who wrote about vice in Newark for the city's *Evening News*. They married and she briefly "discovered sex."[39] It turned out to be a toxic and short-lived marriage that further cemented her feminist perspective. "In my marriage I was completely dominated," she wrote. "Since then I've never wanted to give myself over to the control or even the slightest possible domination of anybody, particularly a man."[40] She soon joined her father, cofounder of the *Miami Herald*, in Miami and took a position as the newspaper's society editor. The newspaper asked her to cover the first woman in Florida to enlist in World War I. She *became* the story by volunteering to serve in the navy. She was discharged in 1918 and joined the American Red Cross, serving overseas.[41] In these and several other ways, Douglas transgressed traditional feminine conventions. Some have consequently speculated that she was a lesbian.[42] While no evidence suggests she had physical relationships or romantic feelings for other women (outside of her intimate bonds with peers and flatmates), she certainly represented the era's renegotiation of feminine and masculine norms that increasingly associated gender deviancy with sexual difference.

Perhaps a product of her own transgressive persona, Douglas wrote sympathetically of queer men in Miami. She was the reporter who covered the costume charity ball Paul Chalfin and Louis Koons attended as a couple.[43] In the 1920s, she found work writing short stories for the *Saturday Evening*

*Post.* Set in Florida, these stories provided a window into the resort area many had only dreamed about visiting. They also gave shape to outsiders' perspective on life in southern Florida.[44] Published in 1927, her short story "He-Man" centered on a nineteen-year-old man named Ronny described as weak, cowardly, unathletic, awkward, and not a "real man," in stark contrast to his burly father. The story blamed his bourgeois upbringing. Ronny had had "too much schooling" and "too many women nurses as a small boy."[45] In the interwar years, some psychologists labeled private or home-school instruction as "negative" and indicative of a poor "family history" or even effeminacy and homosexuality.[46] In this vein, Ronny dreaded visiting his father in Miami for the summer, which coincided with his twentieth birthday. The young man worried that should he be "found out"—that is, should his father and his friends learn of his unmanliness—his father "would disown him." "I'll make a man of you yet," his father assured him.[47] His disdain was only made worse by Ronny's discomfort with the bold and "handsome" modern woman, or flapper, also prominent in this story. Her masculine presence in Miami, as women like Frooks would have understood it, robbed men like Ronny some of their manliness and were therefore at fault. Indeed, Ronny disappointed his father, for whom "assured gallantry to women was … the fundamental of red-blooded masculinity."[48]

Douglas heavily suggests that Ronny is homosexual, describing him as the prototypical queer. She even references the medical model that labeled such men inverts: "Perhaps it was not only that he was utterly unlike his father but that he was different from all *normal* men. Perhaps within his very brain crawled the maggots of unbalance." All the while, Ronny acknowledged, "a he man would never have been troubled by fancies as sick as that."[49] At the very least, Ronny grew anxious over the possibility that what he perceived as his gender inversion, or feminine traits, might give way to sexual perversions.

Douglas pushed this queer anxiety further with the introduction of another character: an aviator named Bill. Like so many wealthy Miami travelers of the day, Ronny's father planned a trip to Bimini. Ronny and his father boarded a small plane with several of the latter's moneyed friends. Although Ronny was initially nauseated by his fear of flying, he overcame this and proved his manly worth when the plane crashed at sea. Ronny and Bill immediately bonded. After the plane went down, they tried to save the others from drowning. Douglas described their immediate connection: "As they stared at each other for a long moment, Ronny felt a sudden warmth of understanding and comradeship leap between them."[50] Despite their best efforts, Ronny and Bill were the only survivors.

It is critical that we understand their intimate bond in the context of Douglas's description of Bill. When Bill took off his helmet following the crash, the reader learns that he had "bleached hair" and that his "eyelashes were bleached."[51] During this period, bleached hair was a common marker for so-called inverts and fairies, signaling their availability to male sexual partners; it seems likely Douglas knew this as well.[52] It is not just that Douglas introduced these two nonnormative and gender-transgressive characters to readers as legible characters in Miami and the Caribbean. Since they were sole survivors who proved more than capable in such dire circumstances, she also seems to have celebrated their existence.

Indeed, part of Miami's early appeal to outsiders was that it was a fairyland where one could shuck traditional gender conventions. One 1929 source maintained, "Miami doesn't care for set styles and in this respect is most unconventional." Bending gender in the city appeared as natural as Miami's humidity. "There are men with hair long enough to bob and women with hair cut short." The women, in particular, drew a lot of attention. One could spot "scores of pretty girls, many of whom may be grandmothers but one can never guess. Rouge? Yes. Smoke? Why of course."[53] In addition to being a veritable fountain of youth, many women who visited or settled in Miami came to understand the city as a space where they could violate and thereby redefine respectable norms of femininity. These were the changes that caused people like Frooks so much anxiety. Discussions of a woman's gender-transgressive behavior and style turned to questions of sexuality more generally as such deviance came to be more closely associated with lesbianism in the 1910s and 1920s. Lest we forget, Chapter 19 of Miami's 1917 City Code also criminalized women in a "state of nudity, or in a dress not becoming to ... her sex, or in an indecent exposure of ... her person."[54]

This shift proved to be a complex and gradual development. As they had done with the third sex or male invert, nineteenth-century sexologists birthed a mannish female invert who possessed a male soul trapped in a woman's body. Meanwhile, a second generation of New Women born in the 1870s and 1880s flourished in the early twentieth century. Building on the advancements of the first generation, these New Women further departed from Victorian mores and asserted their modernity by reclaiming their sexualities from the realm of the private, the pathological, and male authority.[55]

In the first decades of the twentieth century women perceived as "deviant" were more broadly defined by their sexual desire for women and not just by their gender transgression. As Carroll Smith-Rosenberg has argued, a powerful male discourse defensively responded to the early feminists' demands by redefining the woman's fight for political and economic rights in *sexual* terms. As such, the "mannish lesbian" was made nearly impotent by the changing sexual mores that more aptly pitted her against the "liberated" heterosexual woman, rather than the New Man of the modern era. The "mannish lesbian," then, served as a foil through which to define and regulate the modern heterosexual woman, whose subordination to a man became a requisite to be understood as "normal."[56] In this context, despite the "birth" of the lesbian at the turn of the century, she did not have a distinct and widely understood social identity in the United States until at least the 1930s.[57]

In fact, all overt, public expressions of white female sexuality appeared taboo in Miami's early days. On the afternoon of July 14, 1913, Miami police chief Charles R. Ferguson visited the popular Smith's Bookstore downtown with some alarming news. "You can't have a picture like that on public display in Miami," he told the bookstore owner. "She hasn't any clothes on at all!" The Georgia-born chief referred to a reproduction of a 1911 painting titled *September Morn* by a French artist named Paul Chabas. The painting depicts a nude young woman standing in the shallows of a lake. The image had grown in popularity in the United States, even as it proved controversial within some conservative circles (which only served to fuel its popularity among U.S. masses). In fact, Victorian antivice crusader Anthony Comstock had filed a complaint about the image, which was similarly featured in a New York shop, a month before it went up in Miami.[58] Instead of taking the owner to jail, Ferguson permitted him to take the picture down.[59]

This local affair, which was informed by national scandal surrounding the image, reveals growing tensions concerning the display of female sexuality and its place in the beachfront setting Miami so heavily promoted. For his part, Chief Ferguson claimed he did not find the image offensive. "I wouldn't care [if the image was on display]," he stated. While opinions espoused by crusaders like Comstock resonated with some Miami residents, the "majority hardly cared which way the fight turned out."[60] Ferguson stated he took action in the name of the several residents who *did* find it offensive and "inimical of the moral welfare of the town."[61]

It is important to note that the public display of white women's bodies had not yet become normative. As an ideology, heterosexuality did not hold the desirable and dominant currency it enjoys today. Into the first decades of the early twentieth century, both "heterosexuality" and "homosexuality" were obscure medical terms most people would have been unfamiliar with. The hegemonic mapping of an individual's sexual appetites onto an identity-based binary that defined heterosexuality as normative in opposition to the sexual deviancy—or even psychosexual arrested development, as Sigmund

Freud argued—of homosexuality had not yet developed. As a defensive concept created in the face of gender and sexual inversion, the term "heterosexuality" only appeared in print in the United States in 1892. In fact, into the early twentieth century, the term often correlated with acts of nonprocreative, cross-sex eroticism and thus could be read as another form of "perversion."[62]

Some reactions to Miami's *September Morn* scandal support this pre-binary understanding of cross-sex eroticism, as several residents expressed concerns that displaying the image of a young, nude white woman might provoke perverse sexual desires among otherwise "normal" men and youths. One Miami physician named A. G. Holmes shared information he read in national medical journals with city residents in his editorial to a local newspaper. He lamented how "the great majority of men and almost all boys under twenty" could not control their innate lust when "art ... is dressed up in undress." Holmes recalled an earlier instance in Miami where a man "accosted a lady ... in a manner not very complimentary to her," likely a catcall. She protested. To that, the accoster told the woman: "I could see no difference in your dress and manner and some other women who advertise 'their goods' upon our public streets." In other words, he claimed he could not distinguish her from Miami's prostitutes. Holmes also concurred with a Northwestern University professor who believed that women who dress—or mothers who allow their daughters to dress—"like a chorus girl or doll" were to blame. He maintained that sexually titillating visuals could "cause various disturbances" in men. Again citing the medical expert, Holmes believed women's "tight skirts, showy slippers or shoes and fancy silk hosiery simply fan flames of licentiousness."[63] Although most people would not have read medical literature, clinical interpretations often reached the masses through popular explanations such as this.

Indicative of Miami's fairyland promotion, it seems the majority of city residents did not support this conservatism. One Miami man criticized Holmes's position. He mocked him "as one of the many self-appointed censors of the morals of Miami" who rushed "to the rescue of the gilded youth and men further advanced in years already steeped in naughty wishes and unholy desires." "If the absurd claims he sets up were true," the man argued, "he would have us believe all things are vile; that the young boys of Miami are embryo roués and the older ones seasoned veterans."[64] Several newspaper columns similarly condemned this prudishness. After all, Miami had promoted its tropical climate alongside the ability for travelers to explore pleasure and perhaps even unleash their sexual prowess. How could those in Miami, of all places, find this image offensive? This conservative attitude, they suggested, represented the *real* inimicality to the city's welfare.[65] The Miami public's rejection of this conservatism was made clear by the election results of the following week. Ferguson, up for reelection as chief of police, finished fifth out of seven candidates. The winner had defended the right to display the image.[66]

It was hard to ignore that the representation of a nude woman ankle-deep in water might soon become the norm in a resort city like Miami. One resident the *Miami Daily Metropolis* called a "hot-headed reformer" chimed, "You wouldn't let a woman go down the street like that, and how much better is a picture of a woman than a real woman?"[67] The resident expressed concern over the likelihood that a woman might one day traverse Miami in a degree of undress. Holmes made the association clearest. He blamed the mental harm he believed men were susceptible to on the "'living pictures' parading before" their "eyes which ... do not fill their minds with Sunday school thoughts."[68] The subject of *September Morn* had a real-life equivalent walking down Miami's streets. In fact, despite such concerns, she became ubiquitous by the following decade.

The arrival of the modern woman by the 1920s made much of that lingering conservatism appear more out of place in Miami than ever. By World War I, Freud's influence helped spark more popular discussions of sexuality that helped dismantle any vestiges of white, respectable women as asexual beings and end the mainstream silence on most sexual matters among the middle class. This gained potency in the coming decades. Similarly, the work of Margaret Sanger and others in promoting contraceptives and birth control gradually helped decouple sex from the confines of reproduction. Although Comstock Law prohibitions on birth control remained in place until 1936 and many legal and social barriers remained in place for years to come, these efforts increasingly allowed more women to see sex as recreational.[69] All the while, women secured the vote by 1920. All of these developments helped convert the mannish woman—save the lesbian—as fittingly modern and sexual.

As a marker of this modernity, new theatrical depictions of a woman's gender-transgressive behavior became standard in Miami by the late 1920s as a representation of her newfound sexual prowess. Beginning in the late 1910s, Miami boosters sought to capitalize on the area's tropical climate and growing fairyland reputation and recruited movie studios and investors to jump-start a local film industry. Many of the motion pictures filmed in Miami seeped of boosterism and were screened to excited audiences in new and modern local theaters, thereby establishing an avid audience for film and a culture of sociability in these spaces.[70] The popularity of the modern and gender-transgressive woman is made clear in Miami's showplace offerings for the week of January 7, 1927. Films included *The Clinging Vine*, featuring "a young woman secretary, mannish in dress and an accomplished business woman"; a woman who lets "her cigarette droop" and who "chew[s] gums" in *The Little Irish Girl*; and a storyline exploring "a woman's rights in the business world and her ability" in *The Waning Sex*.[71] That April, the city also screened *The Adventurous Sex*, starring Clara Bow. As this and several of the other picture titles suggest, that film depicted a liberated woman who defied traditional conventions. In its brief description, the newspaper quoted one of the lines of Bow's character: "Parents ... stick their heads in the sands of old fashioned ideas and as a result never see that the world is skipping along past them at 60 miles an hour. How can they expect their daughters to travel at a horse and buggy gait when the whole world is speeding in fast motor cars and airplanes?"[72] Such representations were a by-product of the arrival of modernity and of the modern woman, who now wielded greater public power. This articulation also signaled new sexual anxieties of what that gender transgression might *mean*. These motion pictures, for instance, were also a reflection of Hollywood's queer heyday, when homosexual relationships were commonplace and often celebrated.[73]

For many in Miami, the mannish woman, and suggestions of her sexual deviancy in the city, inspired both fascination and anxiety. In its blurb on the 1927 silent film *Special Delivery*, which played at a Miami theater, a local newspaper observed, "All men and women look alike in the dressing rooms of a theater to Eddie Cantor when he tries to deliver a 'Special Delivery' letter to a female impersonator, and thereby starts all the action in his latest picture."[74] The newspaper's focus on the confusion of gender—a complete misreading of the film's plot—suggests its fascination with changing meanings of both the feminine and masculine. Later that year, the *Miami News* reported that a university professor predicted that in less than two decades "men will be using rouge, will carry vanity cases and will sport sweetly-scented handkerchiefs." This perceived femininity found in men was partially due to a similar prediction that women "will be wearing their trousers tucked in their boots, will grow whiskers, carry revolvers, smoke a pipe, swear and tell dirty stories." It was "ordained by nature," the newspaper claimed, "that there be at all times a distinctly masculine sex." Since men had "desert[ed] the job," women had to "naturally take up the fallen flag."[75] In this view, masculine women were both cause and effect of the city's growing queer culture. Similarly, in 1932, a Miami newspaper updated its readers on Radclyffe Hall, the queer English writer who popularized understandings of the female invert and lesbian with her 1928 novel *Well of Loneliness*.

It informed Miami readers that Hall "dresses mannishly, wears a monocle and is known as 'John' to friends."[76] In signaling the legibility of urban mannish women, these occurrences also revealed the growing fascination and anxiety surrounding what such transgression might *mean* for Miami's modern counterpart.

Indeed, in many ways a reflexive defense against the increasingly legible image of the sexually deviant lesbian, a white woman's mannish behavior was soon understood alongside new overt displays of female sexuality. The modern and gender-transgressive woman more aggressively claimed her body and sexuality, particularly vis-à-vis an emerging heterosexual identity that sharpened by the late 1920s and 1930s. In particular, a social fear of lesbianism—which represented an obstacle to mixed-sex romance—helped develop heterosexuality as the hegemonic norm in U.S. culture.[77]

### Heterosexuality and Marketing Women's Bodies in Miami

The shift from homosocial to mixed-sex environments signaled a departure from Victorian mores and the arrival of modernity that enabled women to express their sexualities more publicly.[78] By the mid-1910s, even the YWCA and YMCA—which had historically been spaces for same-sex sociability—opened their programs and facilities and promoted more mixed-sex settings and affection.[79] Clearly, the separate spheres model that limited white middle-class women's access to the public arena was crumbling and the myth of white middle-class women's "passionless-ness" seemed archaic.

With these changes in place, a distinctly heterosexual "companionate marriage" that stressed the happiness and sexual fulfillment of both partners—while also decentering procreation—more forcefully entered the white middle-class vernacular. First coined by social scientists in 1924, a "companionate marriage" made room for both women and men to have a sex life and career without compromising their respectability. This modern arrangement hinged on the fact that contraceptives were more readily available. They also functioned under the pretense that, if a couple's companionate marriage failed, either party would have easy access to a divorce. These ideas reached wider audiences—including those in Miami—through Judge Ben B. Lindsey, who published his book *Companionate Marriage* in 1927. Several Miami reports reveal a growing interest for these more egalitarian relationships, even as they noted "there was no such thing as a 'companionate marriage' license."[80] Conservative critics of these modern arrangements associated their liberal attitude with atheism, anarchy, the destruction of social order, and "Bolshevism." Conversely, a religiously sanctioned heterosexual and monogamous matrimony upheld traditional U.S. values, particularly democracy and capitalism.[81]

Modern courtship and leisure became entrenched in Miami's expanding consumer culture.[82] White middle-class dates in Miami became more modern and expensive. "A girl expects to be taken out to dinner and be presented with huge boxes of candy and flowers, all costing many a dollar," noted one Miami resident. As Miami roads improved, often through chain-gang labor, bike rides were replaced with joyrides on modern automobiles. A couple might plan a date at one of the beachfront casinos. They often attended a movie at one of the city's modern facilities. Before home air conditioning became available and affordable, these theaters were one of the few spaces where one could escape Miami's heat and humidity. After catching a flick or taking a dip, a couple often grabbed a bite at a soda fountain, ice cream parlor, or restaurant. All this cost a pretty penny, even in relation to the economic prosperity that helped fuel the "roaring twenties," which had ended abruptly for most people in Miami with the real estate burst and hurricane of 1926. One Miami man lamented, "The kind of date a girl thinks she ought to have costs all kind of money." In what appears to be a slightly exaggerated claim, he noted one date could cost as much as $25 in the early 1920s. That figure correlates to just over $355 in 2017.[83]

Young women and men also increasingly expected physical intimacy during their courtship. As Paula Fass has shown, young people adopted new sexual habits that shucked the moral standards their parents imposed. Instead, they were influenced by trends set forth by their peers. Middle-class couples generally set their own gradual sexual restrictions and expectations. While sex increasingly became a premarital phenomenon, it often built up from kissing, necking, and "petting." The latter was an ambiguous term that might range from intimate kissing to fondling.[84] Vilona Cutler, general secretary of Miami's YWCA, made several observations about the young women living on her premises. She lamented that these women—who often had no adult supervision other than Cutler—did "not have [a] living room to entertain their boy friends." Their courtship required the man pick her up in his car, or "his dad's" car, and make the most of the growing metropolis. "The boy without an available car has no chance with a girl in Miami these days," Cutler asserted. The modern city of Miami provided couples numerous opportunities to explore their sexual and romantic desires. One young man grew excited over how "girls . . . like to park down by the bay front or the ocean, and watch the beautiful moon."[85] This romantic, moonlit backdrop and mood-setter proved an ideal space for sexual exploration. In the absence

FIGURE 6.1. *El Paso Herald* cartoon featuring women in Miami Beach wearing revealing bathing suits. Its caption read: "Bathing suits wore [*sic*] by the gals at Miami Beach make the Palm Beach gals look like eskimos." *El Paso Herald*, March 3, 1923, 26.

of private spaces, automobiles provided a perfect balance of seclusion and visibility.[86] Under peer pressure, couples frequently wanted their romances known among friends.

Miami's fairyland proved an ideal site to express and exhibit one's sexual prowess, especially as women of means traveled there to explore their bodies and desires. Miami's beaches, in particular, provided women many opportunities for sexual exhibitionism. A local newspaper noted that it was "nothing unusual to see men and women in bathing suits" throughout the city. In this way, the fears of moralists during the local *September Morn* scandal had become reality. Skin exposure proved a hallmark of the cityscape. In Miami, "one ... wears as much or as little as one pleases," noted one commentator.[87] In 1923, famed journalist Ring Lardner similarly wrote about the much talked about "Miami mermaids," or elite and upper-middle-class female bathers who frequented the beach resorts. He joked that the skimpiness of their bathing suits made "the Palm Beach gals look like eskimos [*sic*]" in comparison (fig. 6.1).[88] Miami marketers took credit for creating a space for these "mermaids" to explore their sensuality and bodies.

Ironically, although urban designers in the 1920s had previously promoted Miami Beach as an exclusive space for wealthy and, increasingly, middle-class white travelers, they advanced that image by contrasting it to Palm Beach—which they now described as both old-fashioned and elitist. Roughly seventy-five miles north of Miami Beach, Palm Beach was one of Henry Flagler's most popular resort towns for the wealthy. It predated Miami Beach as a resort area by two decades. To stand apart, city promoters constructed an image of Miami Beach as distinctly modern. This was why sunbathing women in Palm Beach appeared like "eskimos" compared to women in Miami Beach. One advertisement juxtaposed Miami's youth and "overnight" development with Palm Beach's catering to "America's oldest and most aristocratic families."[89] As this suggests, Miami boosters also increased marketing to middle-class tourists. One commentator noted that "Palm Beach still insists upon being rather 'prissy' about its bathing" because women there had to "wear skirts and stockings." Women in Miami Beach were increasingly not wearing stockings at all. The observer also lamented that in Palm Beach, "that land of the wealthy," fashionable "nudes [sheer stockings]" would be "frowned upon." Pitting it against yet another resort area, the commentator argued that "Palm Beach is as bad or a little worse than Atlantic City about its beach censors."[90] This further situates the association of heterosexuality and its burgeoning consumer culture as "bourgeois productions."[91]

This language was a strategic attempt by urban designers to market Miami Beach as a fairyland where sexuality—and, more specifically, a sharpening consumer-driven heterosexuality—would be celebrated, not "frowned upon." So while urban promoters depicted Palm Beach as "prissy," the commentator argued that "Miami Beach is younger and more virile." After all, the "elderly dowagers of aristocratic Palm Beach" wanted to "impose their own restrictions upon the younger set."[92] Under this logic, young, white, fit, and well-to-do women could plot their escape—and liberate their own bodies and sexualities—in Miami Beach. By constructing Miami Beach as the antithesis of the prudish forces that sought to censor young white women's bodies, city promoters marketed the area as both sexual and modern. As the *Saturday Evening Post* notified its readers in 1922, "The prudish element hasn't been able to make its influence felt at Miami Beach to any noticeable extent."[93]

The "Miami mermaid" signaled the arrival, promotion, and dominance of white women's *hetero*sexuality in the resort city, in spite of—or as a response to—some aspects of their persona that were previously read as "mannishly" modern. A Miami newspaper welcomed two white, young, and moneyed "mermaids" from New York City in 1925. It noted that they were "causing many heart palpitations at Miami Beach" with their "bobbed hair," "slender" physiques, and "pretty" features. "These sun bronzed maidens are among the most attractive invaders of beachdom this season," it maintained.[94] Similarly, Katherine Rawls, an Olympic diver, was widely revered for her impressive skills in the water. Reports frequently highlighted her "boyish" or "mannish" appearance. One Florida report introduced her as the "Miami Beach girl, with the close-clipped hair of a boy."[95]

Perhaps no one represented this modern and distinctly heterosexual woman better than Jane Fisher, Carl Fisher's wife. Nearly twenty years his junior, she too came from Indiana. She believed Miami Beach's bathing beauties proved central to her husband's promotion schemes and attracted visitors and settlers to the area. "Northerners plodding through streets of frozen slush were maddened," she remembered, "by posters of beautiful girls ocean-bathing in January." Jane became synonymous with Miami Beach's distinct brand of youth and modernity. One day, likely in the late 1910s, she practiced her swimming strokes wearing "a shockingly short skirt that came only to" her "knees, and, most daring of all, anklets instead of the modest long black stockings."[96] This places her, and Miami, comfortably ahead of the cutting edge of national bathing standards.[97] According to Jane, this was "the first form-fitting bathing suit" to make a splash, so to speak, in the area. A few weeks later, she claimed, "not a black cotton stocking was to be seen on the Beach." Whether she pioneered the more risqué look in Miami or not, one thing was clear: a new trend had caught on and there was no turning back.[98]

Male boosters like Carl Fisher packaged this new modern image of youthful female sexuality to recruit new visitors, settlers, and investments to his prized city. He told his young wife, "By God, Jane, you've started something!" He had been "trying for months to think up an idea for advertising the Beach nationally," and her provocative beach attire gave him an idea. "We'll get the prettiest girls we can find and put them in the goddamnedest tightest and shortest bathing suits and no stockings or swim shoes either."[99] He revamped whatever was left of Miami's frontier image by selling women and men across the nation—and beyond—a modern site for romance and sex. The latter was often still articulated subtly and generally hinted at through implications of the former. What was really being sold was a growing heterosexual culture. For a price, Miami's modern beaches, dance pavilions, shops, theaters, and sea- and airports catered to this new consumer: the heterosexual.

Carl Fisher hired a publicist named Steve Hannagan to spearhead an ambitious marketing campaign to associate Miami Beach with available "cheesecake," or scantily clad bathing beauties.[100] Also a Hoosier, Hannagan "sold Miami to the world on a basis of semi-naked women surrounded by citrus."[101] Hannagan began promoting Miami Beach in 1924, working in the city's News Bureau, which worked on behalf of the municipality and private property owners. The city promoted the bureau as the first municipality-based office of its kind in which publicists sent material and photographs—masked as "news"—to every newspaper, magazine, and news agency possible.[102] Hannagan was tasked with keeping "Miami Beach . . . constantly before snowbound Northerners who may then be lured to Florida." Hannagan accomplished this by flooding the press with "pictures of pretty girls in bathing suits."[103] These young white women became a commodity insofar as they promoted tourism and advanced boosters' strategy to market Miami Beach as a tropical playground where such feminine "cheesecake" could be devoured. The marketing presented these women in ways that urged other women to emulate them, and men to want to have them.

While challenges to Victorian sexual mores occurred throughout the country, southern Florida's distinctive tropical climate and fairyland image marked it as a harbinger of change and sexual liberation. Census records reveal that 1930 marked the first time in Dade County's history that the area housed more women than men, even if just slightly.[104] By the mid-1930s, boosters succeeded in selling Miami Beach as the site for the most modern fashions for white women. One newsreel that flaunted Miami Beach's latest bathing suits and the beauties modeling them found the male announcer interjecting, "Lady, lady, how this would have shocked your great-grandmother!"[105] This recalled the message behind famed composer Cole Porter's popular 1934 Broadway musical *Anything Goes*. "In olden days, a glimpse of stocking was looked on as something shocking," rhymed the song, "but now, God knows, anything goes."[106] Porter, a gay man married to a wealthy lesbian several years his senior, made light of the era's radical shift in sexual mores.[107] His lyrics left open the possibility that modern society's "anything goes" attitude might include gender bending and homosexuality. More directly, however, he referenced the popular embrace of sexuality more generally. Among puritans, this new world would incite nothing short of scandal. It represented, as Freud and others hoped, a form of sexuality broken free from Victorian repression and the confines of procreation.

Writers in Miami and throughout the country flooded the U.S. Copyright Office with applications to register songs, lyrics, and melodies that promoted the image of Miami as a tropical paradise for heterosexual love and lust. Titles such as "Miami, You Wonderful City of Dreams" (1931), "Miami Calls to Me" (1932), and "The Magic of Miami" (1932) alluded to the lure of fairyland. Other compositions more specifically suggested that the city might serve as a space for heterosexual physical intimacy—both marital and extramarital. This included "When My Wife Goes to Miami Monami Comes to Me" (1931), "Miami Gon'na Tampa on My Honeymoon" (1933), "I Met

My Amy in Miami, Down on the Sea Shore" (1935), and "I Never Leave My Amie in Miami" (1936). These works of boosterism playfully suggested that Miami might tempt men to stray from their marriage or partnership. The rhythmic references to "Monami" and "My Amy" recall the French term of endearment *mon ami* (or more likely, *mon amie*, to signal a heterosexual coupling, although this also leaves open the possibility for homosexual companionship). Similarly, while it may appear that the mention of Tampa in one composition referenced a protracted Florida vacation, it is also likely a phonetic entendre signaling how Miami might "tamper" with the protagonist's honeymoon. While these musical compositions were registered in the United States, many were written or stylized by Latinos—oftentimes based in Miami.[108]

*Countering and Capitalizing on the Romance of the Caribbean*

The marketing of Miami as a site for heterosexual romance and tourism also depended on the city's proximity to the Caribbean, particularly Cuba. In the midst of Prohibition, Cuba represented a tropical sanctuary for those who wanted to let loose. As elsewhere, Miami boosters had made much of the city's tropical setting by way of the romantic moon that lit lovers' glances. Similarly, U.S.-crafted compositions that promoted travel to Cuba, such as the 1926 "Dreamy Havana Moon Song," reveled in the romance made available there.[109] One 1921 U.S. song titled "I'm Going Down to Old Havana Town" set the Cuban capital as a place where "lovers are spooning." The sheet cover prominently featured two elite couples sipping alcohol at an outdoor restaurant. A woman and man stare intensely into each other's eyes, gently holding hands over the table. In the distance, an unaccompanied modern woman looks longingly at the shore, waiting for a suitor. Havana appeared untouched by the prudishness associated with Prohibition, an exotic place untouched by the moral police. In Havana one could enjoy "the good times that used to be." The song's male protagonist believed "it would go against my nature" to pass on the chance to visit Cuba, suggesting that his "natural" masculine and heterosexual urges included booze and women.[110] Miami proved critical to this backdrop. As early as 1920, just as national Prohibition took effect, the Havana-American Steamship Corporation began direct service from Miami to the Cuban capital.[111]

While Miami's modernity was initially linked to female mannishness, the tropical climate and carefree ambiance helped change women's fashion in more permanent ways by ushering in an era when exposing more of one's skin proved both possible and desirable, redefining the confines of respectable femininity. In Miami, this became clearest in women's bathing suits.

"The one-piece bathing suit is heavily displayed by engaging young women" in Miami Beach, noted one source in 1922. There were "also large numbers of bathing suits which appear to be one-half-piece or even two-fifths-piece." The latter suit, which was not worn with stockings, exposed roughly two-fifths of the woman's body.[112]

Women's sexualities got entangled with an expanding heterosexual consumer culture that increasingly turned to "feminine" tastes and pleasures for the dictates of the market. As Kathy Peiss and others have shown, working women with access to disposable income and leisure time asserted their autonomy and claimed their modernity by occupying social spaces outside the home and participating in leisure activities that permitted the exploration of sexual and romantic interests.[113] This also took shape as a middle- and upper-class assertion of respectability that sought to distinguish itself from—even as it often appropriated and mimicked—working women's cultures. These women helped propel modern consumerism while also exploring their "sensory gratification, fulfillment of personal taste, and release from self-restraint."[114] By the 1930s, in response to the economic conditions of the Great Depression, women proved critical to the formation of a national consumer ideal. The marketplace became a space in which women could assert their power by strengthening the capitalist polity and the nation's well-being.[115]

Consumers throughout the United States and abroad increasingly looked to Miami Beach for the "very latest and smartest styles in resort wear."[116] As early as 1924, the *New York Times* placed Miami alongside Palm Beach as an "ultra-fashionable" resort.[117] By the following year, Miami Beach hosted fashion shows to better promote its status as the harbinger of modernity and women's styles.[118] This included brighter colors and shorter-length bathing suits. Local boosters crafted this message by running ads in fashionable magazines, such as *Vanity Fair*, *Vogue*, and *Harper's Bazaar*.[119] Although Miami became a fashion trendsetter by the mid-1920s, it did not establish a sizable garment industry for another two decades.[120] As tourism flourished, city fashion designers and stylists capitalized on Miami's association with the Caribbean. They created, for example, "Bahama blue" as one of the new vibrant colors for women's leisurewear.[121]

As early as the mid-1910s, travel to the Caribbean via southern Florida contributed to these changes, as tourism to the Bahamas often challenged the gender comportment and sexual modalities of those visiting the British colony. In Nassau, described by one U.S. visitor as a "Mecca of freedom," one could find "young girls and women visitors at the hotels smok[ing] cirgarets [*sic*] when entering or leaving [a] public dining room, or out on the verandas."[122] Such acts were often read as distinctly modern and gained greater acceptance once associated with the upper and middle classes. Similarly, fashion, as a marker or expression of gender, changed in the Bahamas as a product of the Great War. By 1916, Nassau's *Tribune* reported that one of "the unexpected effects" of the war was "a revolution in the dress of women." It noted "a very general revolt" among working girls, who shucked "graceful" skirts for pants. While this report pertained to Great Britain, the colony seems to have shared at least some of this anxiety.[123]

Even more so, tourism to Cuba—by way of Miami—proved instrumental to creating this modern style and romantic setting. By the mid-1920s, Miami-based travel companies coordinated leisure trips from Miami to Havana. U.S. travelers could board a cruise, a steamship, or, later, an airplane to Cuba. One company opened an office in the Cuban capital and hired local guides, drivers, and translators to conduct its business. Further building the image of a heterosexual tropical paradise, Havana invited visitors to "listen to the voice of romance as you stroll beside the sea."[124] "To Latin people love and courtship are a romantic affair," remarked another Miami-based tour company. Promoters stressed that Cuban women were objects of lust and sources of deceit. The tour company warned: "Girls try to break men's hearts but not their own." Guidebooks implied the availability of Cuban women to U.S. American men. They assured men that chaperons were increasingly becoming "extinct," removing a significant hurdle to intimacy. One guidebook provided roughly two dozen Spanish phrases a traveler "might like to know." It included how to communicate "give me a kiss" and "you are very charming."[125] U.S. travel to Cuba, with the possibilities of sexual tourism, sparked new entrepreneurial ventures. Cuban lawyers and doctors, for instance, offered U.S. visitors advice on local marriage laws and treating venereal disease, such as syphilis.[126] Although these neocolonial efforts clearly defined the Caribbean as a site for U.S. American sexual pleasure, they similarly sought to safeguard the reproductive imperatives of white visitors and future generations. Lest we forget, birth control and reproductive politics sought to regulate racialized populations, such as Cuban women interpreted as genetically unfit and inferior.[127]

For their part, Cuban boosters similarly emphasized the island's availability of fashionable and available modern women. The trendy Cuban magazine *Carteles* promoted the image of a modern island, particularly through artist Andrés García Benítez's cover illustrations. He stylized modern silhouettes of young, modern, and fashionable women, often depicted in revealing dress, if not nude or seminude.[128] U.S. American influence contributed to the radical transformation of the Cuban woman's dress, as she wore "fewer undergarments, shorter hem lines, lower necklines, sleeveless tops, and form-revealing silhouettes."[129] While women appeared to be dressed in climate-appropriate beachwear, their style also suggested the extent to which this modern woman also invited sexual advances from Cubans and visitors. These modern women were often coupled with a man, enhancing the illusion of Cuba as a site of heterosexual romance and lust.[130]

The dominant U.S. influence over the island helped alter gender norms and beauty standards. Popular Cuban author Alfonso Hernández Catá published *El placer de sufrir* (The pleasure of suffering) in 1920. The novel reveals how Cuban women looked to representations of the modern U.S. woman as a symbol of freedom and liberation. The story finds a Cuban woman who, upon seeing a movie from the United States, grew inspired by the "images from other countries where women could, without harm to their social reputation, earn a living through wage labor." Cuban women felt damned, however, as they were "born in a backward country with such crummy traditions."[131] The narrator also maintained that, for Cuban women, life "rested in choosing a man, luring him, and doing away with his selfish fears of marriage." This was, regrettably, a "common sign of poor, backward countries."[132]

Race and sexuality played critical roles in this narrative. The novel's narrator also suggested that a Cuban woman's sensuality depended heavily on her complexion and the social status it assigned to her. She implied that *morenas*, brunettes who were also often dark-skinned, appeared naturally sensual as a product of their "inevitable stigma, as if a sign of original sin." Conversely, the sexual prowess of blonde women appeared to be a "disgusting perversion against nature," as it went against the "angelic nature of their sky-blue eyes and radiant blonde hair."[133] In this way, the Cuban *mulata* was made sexually available to men, while white women's response to a heavily U.S.-crafted vision of modernity—including public expressions and claims to their own bodies and sexualities—appeared unnatural and unbecoming of femininity. This too had to change, lest Cuba remain "backward."

The growing trend of looking toward Miami for these trends particularly resonated in Cuba, where the climate, among many other things, mirrored that of southern Florida. As Louis Pérez Jr. has argued, Florida and cities like Miami "developed as a parallel universe of Cuba, something of a Cuban counterpart, as a standard by which to take measure of the Cuban condition."[134] Miami further touted its "Latin" status in the 1920s. As with the Bahamians, Cuban laborers, particularly those in the service and entertainment sectors, fueled the city's eroticism and exoticism. Conversely, many Cuban boosters turned to Miami for claims to modernity and cosmopolitanism. It is important to note, however, that Cuban designers' embrace of "modernity" in architecture and art after 1898—beginning with art nouveau and later art deco—predated Miami's own push for these styles. While some have attributed this to Cuba's rejection of colonial aesthetics, new waves of Catalan immigrants on the island and a post–World War I economic boom played critical roles in this shift.[135] Perceptions of "modernity," or lack thereof, were heavily defined by concepts of race and empire. Even as Miami promoted its own image as an exotic fairyland, as a U.S. city, it became associated with modernity and progress. Cuban boosters often had a more difficult time employing a similar marketing scheme to promote Havana to U.S. tourists. While promotional language for Cuban tourism touted the island as providing the "thrill of being in a foreign land, without being too far away from 'home base,'" Miami could offer both such thrills and the comfort and the perceived safety of remaining in national borders.[136]

Just as Miami's urban designers fine-tuned their promotion of the fairyland as a modern and conquerable space in the 1920s—with the former largely eclipsing the latter—many Cubans desperately sought to appear distinctly modern. Descriptions of Havana during this period often stressed that it had all the charm of a Spanish colony and the modernity of the new Cuban Republic. As one ad claimed, "If you go in for freedom and happiness in a large, personal way, then Cuba is *your* playground." Cuba was "infinitely varied," "piquant and brilliant in its modern life," while also "provocative of dreams in its century-worn court yards, streets and villages ... where ghosts from a glorious age of Old Spain still swagger."[137]

Promotional materials often depicted Cuba as a metaphorical woman who was refined, modern, and congenial to U.S. tourism and commerce.[138] In one travel guide, a female embodiment of the United States holds hands— a gesture of affection, solidarity, and mutual cooperation—with her Cuban counterpart (fig. 6.2). The gendered metaphor for the United States is attractive, young, and modern. While she is identified as "Miss U.S.A.," the context is distinctly Floridian. As the guidebook demonstrates, the sun is beaming and it spotlights, as if by providence, the glories waiting for tourists in Florida and the Caribbean. A noticeably darker-skinned "Miss Cuba" is equally attractive and available to outsiders. While also modern, she is stylized with a traditional Spanish sensibility—with the flower in her hair and the floral fan, or *abanico*, in her hand.[139]

In its efforts to appear modern and consolidate its national identity, the Cuban state afforded its women greater social and political advances. This was a sign of progress, too, as Cuba transitioned from Spanish colony to republic. Although some acts sought to emulate the modernity attributed to the United States, others, such as the 1913 abolishment of the island's regu-

FIGURE 6.2.
In this U.S.-produced guidebook, two modern women, "Miss U.S.A." and "Miss Cuba," hold hands in a sign of mutual friendship just as tourism to Cuba by way of Florida increased. Guidebook, *The Miami— Palm Beach—Havana Gimlet, Season of 1929–30*, 1929. New York: John Ashe Scott. 9½ × 5⅛ inches. Photo by Lynton Gardiner. XC2002.11.4.218, Vicki Gold Levi Collection. The Wolfsonian—Florida International University, Miami Beach, FL.

lated prostitution system, which the United States had kept intact during its occupation, were a manifestation of a new republicanism that sought to distinguish itself from imperial forces and influences. That decree, for instance, reframed prostitution as a general public health issue that affected *all* citizens, while simultaneously acknowledging that the regulated prostitution of the past had done nothing to benefit Cubans.[140] Another critical change was the feminist push for no-fault divorce by 1914. Moving away from traditional Catholic thought, the 1918 legalization of divorce in Cuba could liberate a woman from an unhappy or oppressive marriage. Many reformers particularly looked to the U.S. law, cited as "rational and progressive," as a source of influence.[141] Suffrage for Cuban women was achieved in 1934, fourteen years after women got the vote in the United States. As K. Lynn Stoner has documented, some influential U.S. feminists argued in the 1920s against supporting Cuban women's suffrage. They believed "Latin American women had not fought long enough to appreciate the responsibilities of an electoral public," a position that diminished by the early 1930s.[142] Through a largely U.S.-informed image of modernity, changes in Cuban women's employment, education, political involvement, fashion, consumption, and expressive sexualities allowed them to restructure their everyday lives and sensibilities.[143]

Miami boosters implemented two major strategies in response to Cuba's status as an exotic, sensual, and modern tourist destination for U.S. tourists. U.S. investors capitalized on Cuban tourism by including Miami as either a starting point or port of call in the itinerary. They also responded by maintaining a loose moral code that at least matched, but did not necessarily compete, with that found in Cuba.

In addition to promoting Miami as distinctly modern, marketing campaigns stressed that the city was a site of leisure and physical exploration for outsiders who could afford to visit, or perhaps even make their stay permanent. In 1924 a Scranton, Pennsylvania, newspaper celebrated Miami Beach's "'wide open' ocean," a nod to its being a wide-open city with lax moral codes. The article observed that Miami Beach "authorities ... seem agreed that the American girl needs no censoring. She is her own best censor." It argued that while women of a particular age, shape, and color would know to flaunt it, those who had "passed beyond the aphrodite [sic] stage" or otherwise did not fit the desired image were "more conservative in their dress."[144]

The urban designers' marketing strategy to promote Miami Beach as a fairyland helped demarcate the area as a popular site for upper- and middle-class, white, young, slender women to strip down and take in the sun and, simultaneously, signal their availability to men. This informal "Miami code" created a standard of female beauty that came to define the city's overt sexuality. If a woman "be good to look upon, she will clothe or unclothe herself accordingly," maintained one newspaper. "If she be fair of face and form, she will do nothing to hide either. If her limbs are a glistening white, why dim their luster with dowdy stockings? If her waist be slender and her hips rounded and firm, why do more than encase them in the closest of clinging Jersey?"[145] As this reveals, in the 1920s renegotiated gender roles created new slim expectations for women, in particular through new forms of diets, social stigma, shame, and guilt. As Peter N. Stearns has shown, overweight women became sexually undesirable and in direct opposition to the new slim beauty standard.[146] Just the same, a woman's whiteness remained key to her marketability and desirability.

Miami Beach also provided this young woman the illusion of temporarily suspending her whiteness in favor of a darker complexion through sunbathing. The Miami mermaid, one report noted, "is a sun worshiper. Her arms and legs are almost the color of copper."[147] Although white women had long sought to preserve their pale, fair skins as a sign of pious femininity, several factors led many of them to embrace tanning in earnest by the 1920s. This included the growing popularity of beach resorts like Miami Beach, paid vacations, publicized health benefits of phototherapy and vitamin D, beauty standards shaped by the fashion and cosmetics industries, and the influence of celebrity culture.[148]

The modernity of sunbathing was imbued with deep racial, class, gender, and sexual implications. White women who opted to tan in Miami were given the opportunity to temporarily look more like the travel guide's rendering of "Miss Cuba" than "Miss U.S.A." In addition to viewing sunbathing as a natural tonic that offered strength and vitality, white women and men interpreted this "civilized" recreation as a means of attaining a "primitive" empowerment underpinned by a notion of white supremacy in the face of blackness. Just as white men turned to "primitive masculinity" to make sense of their civilized status, many white women embraced new relationships with the natural world to articulate "powerful womanhood."[149] As Catherine Cocks has argued, "turning brown gave whites privileged access to traits otherwise lost to civilization's triumph—and yet, crucially, it was transient, the underlying whiteness always liable to reappear."[150] The ability to peel away darkness after a tan was just one of the ways white women and men believed they could exercise their civilized restraint and overcome the dangers associated with blackness.

For white women in Miami Beach, sunbathing represented a modern, liberatory, and status-conscious act. If a Miami mermaid happened to be a temporary visitor, her tanned skinned revealed she could afford vacations or recreational and leisure time. It also marked her as distinctly fashionable and able to appear "ethnic" or "exotic," as the cosmetics industry had more forcefully started selling beauty culture. As Kathy Peiss has shown, it was in the late 1920s that "sunburn" tints and powders became readily available for purchase in the United States. A white woman's sun-kissed skin, or the use of cosmetics that feigned that look, marked her as an upper- or middle-class woman directly linked to the consumer culture associated with resort cities like Miami Beach.[151]

As all this suggests, sunbathing was also implicitly and explicitly a sexualized act. It required women to strip down and bare much of their skin. Some suntan lotions made clear references to sex by advertising that women who use the product "let the sun go just as far as they please—and not a bit farther."[152] Also, by the early 1920s, reports noted that "nude" stockings had become the most popular set in Miami Beach. The Miami mermaid's tanned body advanced the sexual illusion of her public nudity because it made the "nude" stockings appear less "palpable" than the black or gray variety worn elsewhere.[153]

Meanwhile, Miami promoters advertised the city as a fairyland for well-to-do white men to take notice of and consume women's bodies so prominently displayed and made available to them. One visitor noted that men become "so accustomed" to seeing women in their revealing bathing suits in Miami Beach that one "feels disappointed if he doesn't see them."[154] One man joked that the only "casualty" attached to seeing women in varying degrees of undress was that northern men "constantly are losing their breath." Miami Beach proved to be the "land of glorification and exaltation supreme of the feminine form."[155] By 1937, this had become so entrenched that men were literally fishing for women in the area. One recreational activity found "pretty mermaids" swimming in a Miami Beach pool with "lines attached to them." Male "anglers" fished them out with their rods, a phallic gesture that could hardly go unnoticed.[156] Similarly, two men visiting Miami together sent a postcard to their "pal" in Paducah, Kentucky, featuring several waving white women in skimpy bathing suits posing alongside a massive and phallic thermometer that read 81 degrees. In this way, they assured their friend that their libidos ran high in Miami and that he was missing out.[157]

Indeed, by the late 1920s, Miami promoters succeeded in branding fairyland as a distinctly heterosexual space that mirrored the romantic opportunities made available in the nearby Caribbean, even as the city's focus on tourism and sexuality still carved out spaces for gender and sexual renegades. In Miami, heterosexuality had become a middle-class commodity to be consumed. While the fairyland offered white women a space to claim their own pleasure, it more aggressively put them on display for men's enjoyment. In this way, the fairyland promoted an image of a resort that harbored sexual, yet respectable, women made available to moneyed, white male consumers.[158]

Men visiting Miami responded to women's sexual liberation with a reflexive heterosexual masculinity that also sought to disassociate them from any sign of effeminacy. In contrast to the women, whose colorful and skimpy fashion trends made them modern, men at the resorts opted to accentuate their masculinity by taking notice of the women—rather than their fashion, which became a marker of effeminacy. "No pink for them, no stockings, no fads that change with every ocean breeze," noted one source about Miami's men. In fact, some sources expressed their frustration that men more frequently wore faded bathing suits they rented directly from the casinos. "No woman would do that, you bet."[159] While women became mermaids and showed less skin in Miami Beach, many men continued to cover up. Even by the mid-1930s, some of the bathing suits men wore at the resort city were "strictly two piece variety." The latest fashion craze did not include shirtless "trunks."[160] Even then, however, it is important to note that, for men, sunbathing "promised continued mastery over white women and nonwhites, precisely by endowing the masculine sunbather with some of the youthful potency associated with the latter."[161]

In response to the modern developments that saw Miami women making new demands—economic, political, cultural, and even sexual—on their romantic interests, middle-class men reflexively responded with a recharged hetero-masculine sense of self. When taken on a date, young women in Miami who had paying jobs might "go half way on expenses, such as insisting on paying for her own share." This was more likely to occur if her male companion did not have money, or was less "flush."[162] While such acts could have challenged a man's masculinity, several factors defused these anxieties.

A middle-class articulation of white superiority played a significant role in undergirding a man's masculinity in the face of female liberation.[163] Dating in Miami for white middle-class couples operated in the same way the promotion of fairyland advertised: blacks providing service to white clientele. To diversify their dating options, some young white men in Miami would rent a store space to host a dance with their friends and romantic interests. They corralled their money to hire a "negro to play the piano and another to play the French harp [harmonica]."[164] As white couples danced away, black subjects functioned as props in the service of white heterosexual courtship and romance.

The reinforcement of black subjugation and male dominance made the white women's sexual liberation possible and respectable. The eugenicist policies that sought to control sex and reproduction in both the Caribbean and Miami's black, ethnic, and working-class neighborhoods allowed white women to express their sexuality as a healthy service to advance "the race." With "unfit" women living and regulated in the Caribbean or segregated in state institutions, the Miami mermaid and other sexually liberated white women were not regarded as "part of the perceived widespread decline in female sexual morality." As Wendy Kline has argued, this occurred "because that morality had been an exclusively white female privilege to begin with."[165] Similarly, as Christina Simmons has argued, the "ideal woman was ... neither moralistic and sexually withholding nor mature and sexually assertive; rather, she was inexperienced and/or accepting of male initiative." The desirability and prospect of motherhood and reproduction served as a foil to the anxieties of her sexual liberation.[166] In this way, the Miami mermaid's public expression of her sexuality appeared less threatening to a man, who was expected to tame and subdue her sexuality through his own sexual prowess and masculine vigor.

Mimicking the "primitive" sexuality ascribed to the city's working class and the nearby Caribbean, middle-class white men also abandoned the prudish gentlemanliness and repression of the Victorian era. These men increasingly came to expect sexual favors and payment from the women they courted. As modern women entered the public sphere, modern men responded by embracing their "natural" urges, the very ones that Victorian mores once asked them to suppress, just as it kept the white, pious woman isolated to protect her from those urges' unleashing. According to Kevin White, "By driving courtship into the male world, the dating system accelerated and accentuated male power."[167] As men grew anxious over the sexual demands women made in marriage, many increasingly rejected such commitments and arranged their relationships with women on terms that suited them. Miami men joked that courting women could prove a "risky proceeding." One man observed how dating could "likely ... result in an engagement." Miami's romantic landscape, he maintained, could lead to him being "booked for life" (married). His description—which jokingly equated marriage with imprisonment—suggested that he could easily fall into a trap in which his sexual options and urges came to an abrupt end.[168] Anxieties concerning homosexuality played a significant role in this heterosexual revolution, as men accentuated their masculinity by juxtaposing it to effeminate queers found onstage or in the streets.[169] Just the same, the free love ideology espoused by the likes of Emma Goldman and Alden Freeman soon dissipated with the newly entrenched binary that defined "normal" heterosexuality by its juxtaposition to homosexual deviance.

Miami boosters responded to these changes, as well as to the competition of the Caribbean's offerings, by making it clear that laws would not interfere with the expressive heterosexual cultures modern women and men sought to consume in the fairyland. Most of the area's politicians and law enforcement officers were complicit in promoting what they called the "Miami code." By 1928, Miami Beach politicians passed an ordinance that prohibited men and women from changing their "clothes in ... Miami Beach ... for the purpose of donning a bathing suit, or for any other purpose" in public spaces, excluding the beach, swimming pool, and some parks. This generally constituted "indecent exposure."[170] Charles Chase Sr., who served as secretary of the Miami Beach Chamber of Commerce, assuaged conservative residents by noting the necessity of enforcing city laws. He also acknowledged that "fashion decrees what people shall wear on land and in sea" and that it was "impossible for us to break universal customs." Chase clarified, "We have not and never shall have any desire to regulate what bathers shall or shall not wear, so long as they keep within the bounds of decency."[171] As we have seen, class, race, ethnicity, and age helped define the confines of that decency.

The urban designers who marketed Miami as a distinctly heterosexual fairyland largely got their way, as police rarely enforced the prudish laws on white women and men, who increasingly flaunted their bodies and sexualities in public. One newspaper observed that the "Miami motto" was "wear just enough in winter to keep warm, and just enough in summer to keep from being arrested." Miami's marketing team wanted it this way and refused to "station any cops at the beach[,] . . . only life-savers."[172] In 1928, a *Miami Daily News* editorial promoted "freedom for bathers." The newspaper maintained that what the "winter visitor finds so charming" about the area is the ability to be "clad only in bathing suits." It cited "modern tendencies" and even medical literature that "agreed it is conducive to better health" to wear "less clothing" and sunbathe. Even more important was the notion that a liberal attitude was "one of Greater Miami's selling points. . . . The Miami area is a place where thousands of persons come for rest and relaxation. Why cramp their relaxation with more regulations?"[173]

While the articulation of male heterosexuality operated under a rubric in which white men tamed women's bodies and desires through processes such as courtship and marriage—and reified their masculinity by expressing dominance over black and immigrant communities—it is critical to reiterate that women were active agents in this change. Their self-expression and comportment challenged the confines of normative femininity. These women regularly defied and resisted attempts to legislate decency through standards that sought to suppress their sexualities, as in the case of the Miami Beach law many of them mocked (fig. 6.3). Indeed, in taking greater claim of their bodies and sexualities, these white women renegotiated the confines of decency and white femininity.

BY THE EARLY 1930S, a distinct heterosexual consumer culture dominated Miami's landscape. Urban boosters began distinctly marketing fairyland as a space for young, attractive white women to explore their bodies and sexu-

FIGURE 6.3. Four white women publicly defy a signpost warning that the law mandates they wear full bathing suits. Not only did these women wear more revealing two-piece suits, they could also be seen, as the caption reads, "giving [the] rules the razz." Photo dated July 4, 1934. Gleason Waite Romer Photograph Collection, control no. 259195, Miami-Dade Public Library, Miami, FL.

alities, made available to a particular class of white men. These women rewrote the strict gender scripts that had long confined them. They were, indeed, harbingers of change. Our modern eyes may insist that we interpret this as entirely normative, but something far more complex was taking place. As Jane Fisher recalled, "Miami Beach was compared to Sodom and Gomorrah, and I to a female biblical character I prefer not to name," presumably the prostitute Mary Magdalene.[174] A Miami newspaper that sought to offer some humor suspected the closing of the 1934–35 tourist season would see several women tourists, or "Ladies of the Incandescent," leaving the city "posing as virgins en route."[175] It suggested Miami had forever corrupted them. Indeed, the Miami mermaid took risks in expressing her sexuality, including associations with "undesirable" women. While Fisher referenced prostitutes, the stigma in Miami was more directly linked to black, immigrant, and working-class cultures. To combat that, white women and men articulated their love and romance through processes that buttressed concepts of white dominance.

That fairyland had been redefined as a heterosexual and white commodity for modern women and men does not suggest that it eradicated other deviant expressions of gender and sexuality in the city. This shift *consolidated* the sexual lives of women and men in ways that became legible for residents and tourists alike. As heterosexuals played in fairyland, they still relied on a visible and thriving queer visibility—critically connected to the city's tourist trade—to make sense of their own sexual lives, desires, and burgeoning identities.

# QUEERS DURING AND AFTER PROHIBITION

Sodom, Gomorrah and Monte Carlo all rolled into one—that is
Miami.
—MIAMI NEWSPAPER, CIRCA 1929

We had great crowds in Miami this winter ... and we had a town
running wide open in defiance of all law and of decency.
—FLORIDA ANTIVICE ACTIVIST, CIRCA 1930

Why should this abnormality [cross-dressing performances and
commercialized homosexual encounters] be sold at a price in Miami?
We aren't naïve or juvenile, here in the winter playground of the
world.... Several off color clubs have functioned during the winter
season.
—MIAMI JOURNALIST, 1939

Patrons of Miami's popular La Paloma club paid for a night of
sexual thrills and entertainment. When national Prohibition ended in 1933,
liquor flowed even more freely than before in dry-in-name-only Miami.
Fears of prosecution for selling alcohol, particularly among small-time illicit
traders who constituted the bulk of those harassed by authorities, dissipated.
Bootlegging, however, did not. Prohibition taught Miami businesses that
operating outside the law remained most profitable. Such was the case with
La Paloma. There, women wearing G-strings and brassieres danced and
stripped onstage. Other "immoral perform[ers]" included female impersonators and queers who treated audiences to "indecent jokes and songs." La
Paloma was, among other things, a queer establishment that was increasingly understood to be "gay."[1]

So long as tourists and others sought titillating entertainment, Miami
businessmen like Al Youst, operator of La Paloma, were happy to oblige.
On the evening of November 15, 1937, as music blared, backlights dimmed,
dancers gyrated, and glasses clinked, dozens of women and men forced their
way into the club. Even though it was a Monday night, attendance and sales
were strong. It was, after all, the beginning of tourist season. The intruders,
dressed from head to toe in long, white, hooded robes, meant to strike fear

in the hearts of the club's customers and staff. The club orchestra kept playing, believing it was all part of an act. They soon learned, however, that La Paloma had been raided.[2]

This raid had been conducted not by local law enforcement but by nearly 200 members of the local Ku Klux Klan (KKK). The mob burned "a fiery cross" in front of the establishment, located in an unincorporated section of northwest Miami. Reports claimed they stormed into the club, "smashed tables and chairs," and "ordered all patrons and employes [sic] ... be searched for weapons." They then "compelled patrons to leave" and threatened to burn the place down if they did not comply. KKK members reportedly roughed up some of La Paloma's workers, including "chok[ing] three girl entertainers" and "manhandl[ing] a waiter." The terrorists believed everyone connected to the establishment was guilty of immorality and threatened the city's moral fabric.[3]

With mounting pressure from such conservative forces, local law enforcement tacitly approved of the Klan's actions that night, but to little effect. Dade County sheriff David C. Coleman agreed that La Paloma was a "menace" to the city. "I am going to do everything in my power within the law to keep the club closed," the Georgia native claimed. Youst had reportedly been arrested six times before, on charges varying from intercourse with a minor, to selling liquor without a proper license, to assault and battery. Coleman even hired "several citizens to go into the club to obtain evidence" of illegal activity.[4] Many residents, including those wearing the hoods, had grown frustrated, however, because no charge ever seemed to stick.[5] Following the raid, Coleman ordered that La Paloma remain closed and temporarily "clamped the lid on nightspots ... where intoxicating beverages" were sold and "where revelry" had "been rampant."[6] Less than two weeks later, Coleman and his men conducted their own raid on the establishment. It's possible these raids were connected and that some of the hooded intruders were connected to city powerbrokers, including law enforcement officials. La Paloma, however, soon reopened. Coleman's closing order was in effect a mere two days before he reversed it. Miami's tourist economy depended on it.[7]

Miami underwent massive urban transformation in the 1920s and 1930s. In some ways, the city opened up and became far more egalitarian. The city's mid-1920s economic crises compounded after the global Great Depression. Under these circumstances, Miami's white urban boosters and investors came to embrace new middle-class tourists. New working-class visitors also made their way to the city, often as transients searching for work in the midst of economic uncertainty. These people hitched a ride on trains, in automobiles, and even in mobile trailers to partake in the fairyland culture once only available to them through literature, film, and the stage. By the 1930s, the area's tourist season that previously catered to northern snowbirds expanded to begin in late October and end by mid-March. Economic necessity pushed urban boosters to turn Miami into a year-round resort city for the bourgeoisie. They began aggressively marketing the area to tourists during summertime, assuring them that "Florida is really 'air-conditioned' by nature."[8]

While Miami's "opening up" and liberal policy may appear to be a far more egalitarian form of urban control, the city was mired in numerous restrictions and contradictions.[9] Even as Miami was happy to accept money from communities deemed less desirable—whether transients, immigrants, or trailer park tourists, for instance—by no means did this mean such visitors were warmly met by residents. One of the best-documented accounts of this phenomenon concerns the city's Jewish community. Miami's Jewish population grew from 50 in the mid-1910s to almost 8,000 in 1940. The economic downturn forced anti-Semitic forces to embrace Jewish investors in the area. We should not confuse the acceptance of Jewish capital with diminishing prejudice, as discrimination abounded.[10] In part, it was this "opening up" that the KKK fought against.

Meanwhile, the rise of the aviation industry further promoted Miami's fairyland as a tourist destination and hub for many playgrounds in the Caribbean and Latin America. Miami boosters competed with Caribbean markets in the tourist trade. U.S. imperialism ensured that Cuba, in particular, became a site of racialized sex tourism deeply connected to Miami's own markets. With regular flights to Havana, however, the once-requisite stop in Miami seemed less critical to tourists. One Cuban critic called Miami and Havana "rivals and even enemies" fighting for the upper hand in the tourist trade.[11]

Miami boosters responded by rebranding the city as a much more modern version of the tropical exoticism places like Havana offered. One such manifestation of this was the Florida legislature's legalization of pari-mutuel gambling in 1931, which brought to light what had long been underground in Miami. Other forms of illicit gambling continued to thrive, too, and remained underground. Before Prohibition ended in the United States, alcoholic contraband from the Caribbean, particularly the Bahamas, provided a steady supply to southern Florida. Similarly, travel to the Caribbean, especially Cuba, provided a recreational outlet for U.S. visitors escaping "dry" laws. In order to compete, Miami officials implemented a tacit policy of lax enforcement. All the while, Miami boosters capitalized on the political turmoil in Cuba that greatly diminished the island's own tourism.

Miami's entrenched relationship to the Caribbean provides a necessary transnational view of Prohibition-era politics and the uneasy urban battles that ensued upon repeal—two key phenomena to the development of queer cultures and networks. In his study of New York, George Chauncey argued that the repeal of Prohibition in 1933 ultimately brought to light the gender- and sexually transgressive culture that thrived in the shadows of illicit and underground economies. This significantly curtailed New York's visible and vibrant gay culture, even if it did not eradicate it.[12] Something similar occurred in Chicago, where local law enforcement generally permitted the "pansy and lesbian craze" to go undisturbed as a means to reap greater profits from visitors to the World's Fair there. As Chad Heap has argued, however, once Prohibition had been repealed in New York—and, in Chicago, when repeal coupled with the fair's closing the following year—this queer culture did not exactly disappear. Rather, it successfully relocated to the city's black entertainment districts.[13] While this temporarily extended the public visibility of New York's and Chicago's queer nightlives, Miami's liberal policy that catered to its king industry, tourism, gave the city an even longer shelf life. Miami's own trajectory more closely resembled San Francisco's, where, as Nan Alamilla Boyd has uncovered, an *increase* in queer entertainment and culture followed repeal. This occurred, in large part, due to California's need to fill its coffers—not necessarily curbing vice.[14] Miami's queer past, however, demonstrates the need to treat historical moments and processes such as Prohibition as transnational and global phenomena. Sexual and pleasure-seeking economies, along with illicit trade connected to the Caribbean, critically informed Miami's Prohibition and post-Prohibition cultural politics; urban powerbrokers responded to these transnational forces by rebranding the city as a more modern, affordable, and safer version of the exoticized playground places like Havana offered.

Indeed, several local, national, and transnational factors nudged Miami further toward becoming a "wide-open" urban space, a status that allowed gender and sexual transgressives and some emerging queer networks to carve out distinct spaces in the city, particularly during the height of tourist season. Queers exploited Miami's urban shifts and the competing visions for the city that pitted urban boosters who wanted a liberal policy against conservative residents who wanted to uphold Miami as a "model city." Exploring the social and cultural dynamics of queer labor in Miami reveals that, as economic pressures led the liberal policy to prevail until the late 1940s, queers became critical actors in keeping Miami profitable. Like Miami's "exotic" connections to the Caribbean, queers made fairyland work.

## A Transnational Tourist Paradise

In the 1920s and early 1930s, one of the more significant enterprises that helped Miami combat the Great Depression was the smuggling and transport of prohibited alcohol, largely for tourists. Residents voted to make Miami "dry" in 1913, seven years before the Eighteenth Amendment to the U.S. Constitution prohibited the national manufacture and transportation of liquor. One visitor recalled "the ease with which liquor can be purchased" in Miami. He maintained that purchasing liquor in Miami did not occur in seedy or underground operations or establishments. Rather, "your Miami bootlegger is a businessman, and meets you in a business-like way."[15] This near-formal economy thrived in Miami, which had long been promoted as a space to sow one's oats. By 1928, New York congressman and soon-to-be mayor of New York City Fiorello LaGuardia stood before the House of Representatives to defend his state, particularly its major city, which maintained the notorious reputation of being among the "wettest" in the country. "There are more prohibition lawbreakers in Florida than in my state," LaGuardia argued. Florida representative Robert A. Green countered that Florida was as "dry as the Sahara Desert!" No one in the chambers could keep a straight face. Instead, Green "found his words drowned out by laughter" and was forced to sit down.[16] Prohibition helped forge the image of Miami as a transgressive fairyland. Despite official law, local police corruption, bribes, and lax enforcement ensured that liquor flowed in Miami.

The majority of this contraband entered Florida by way of the Caribbean.[17] A July 1923 article reported that "rum running along the south Atlantic seaboard has assumed such tremendous proportions that the inhabitants of poverty stricken little islands have become rich almost over night and ... [their islands have] become known as 'bootleggers paradise.'"[18] The Bahamas, with so many hidden bays and inlets, was especially central to this business. One publication noted that "every outlaw, every thief, every criminal who can get the price and can give the password of bootleggery ... has acquired a voting residence in Nassau."[19] In Bimini, vessels built in southern Florida "almost under the noses of government enforcement agents" transported cases of alcohol to Miami. In fact, Florida-based bootleggers often owned the "Bimini boats" used to bring in the contraband to Miami—just forty-five miles east of the small island—after dark.[20] Bimini became so notorious for supplying illicit liquor that Senator James A. Reed, a Democrat from Missouri, channeled the imperial ethos in recommending that the United States purchase the island from Great Britain, in part to curb the problem.[21] Meanwhile, further demonstrating the transnational nature of

UNCLE'S ROSEATE NOSE.
—McGill in the Atlanta *Georgian*.

FIGURE 7.1.
In this 1922 cartoon, the United States is anthropomorphized as Uncle Sam who appears to be sick with a "roseate nose." A Prohibition investigator serves as his doctor and notes: "No sir! That isn't sunburn—that's moonshine!" In this view, Florida's vice culture had made the United States morally weak. Reprinted in *Literary Digest*, Dec. 30, 1922, 32.

Prohibition in Miami, the U.S. Coast Guard proved just as significant as municipal police, county law enforcement, and state authorities in regulating liquor flow in the area, albeit not stringently. In fact, these multiple levels of government added to the bureaucratic ineffectiveness of liquor control.[22]

Those who transgressed gender and sexual norms and often thrived in the underground culture Prohibition created in Miami were "drawn together by their common bond of lawlessness." "A man is either 'right' or 'queer,'" maintained U.S. Prohibition investigator Frank K. Dolan in discussing the bootlegging business that had entered Miami and elsewhere from the Bahamas. In the early 1920s, the *New York Daily News* sent Dolan to the Bahamas "to study the rum-runners' methods." On the islands, he believed, "bootleggers and whiskey smugglers . . . laugh at Uncle Sam" (fig. 7.1). He explained that those in the British colony who were "suspected of being 'queer'" were "'curtly told to leave town, and in some instances blackjacked and beaten.'" In this context, a "queer" was "a revenue officer, a detective, or some one likely to interfere with the rum-smugglers' operations." Their word choice poses a revealing parallel to those read as "normal"—or "right"—in and near Miami. After all, these "queers" were those who *got in the way* of this illicit economy and not those who partook in it. It was the law enforcement and the reformers who sought to eliminate this vice who were in danger of being beaten. In fact, "when the news penetrated the American underworld that Nassau ... had been transformed with one stroke of the magic wand ... to a bustling smugglers' nest, the call of easy money was heard and heeded by hundreds." This description mimics that of Miami as fairyland, a logical sequence considering Miami's critical role in this illicit enterprise.[23]

So while both the Bahamas and Cuba benefited from the liquor-smuggling business during Prohibition, U.S. empire ensured that Cuba would be particularly primed to compete with Miami in the tourism trade. Rosalie Schwartz has argued that "Havana was a logical geographic extension to the progression of resort cities that marched southward along Florida's coastlines from the 1880s to the 1920s, promoted by capitalists no less ambitious than their Cuban counterparts." New York hotelier John McEntee Bowman opened the Hotel Sevilla-Biltmore in Havana in 1920 just as the antiliquor laws were implemented in the United States. He later purchased land in Miami during the boom and built the Biltmore Hotel in Coral Gables in 1926. While both hotels welcomed consumers who sought both titillation and an escape from "dry" environments, Cuba provided the full security of having no such laws on its books (fig. 7.2). Men like Bowman looked to Cuba as a "city that was short of hotel rooms and long on liquor—a perfect combination for a man with wealthy, thirsty friends who could no longer drink openly at his stateside hotels."[24]

Composer Irving Berlin's 1920 song "I'll See You in C-U-B-A" captured the appeal of the exotic, sexual tourism made available to U.S. Americans during Prohibition. In noting, "Not very far from here, / there's a very lively atmosphere," the song stressed Cuba's proximity to the United States, particularly Miami. This became increasingly important to U.S. travelers who looked for alternative "exotic" vacation spots outside of war-torn Europe. "Ever since the U.S.A. went dry, / ev'rybody's going there ... / I'm on my way to Cuba /... / where wine is flowing," went Berlin's song. As a nod to the "gay" culture of excess, it noted, "Cuba, where all is happy / Cuba, where all is gay." The sexual subtext was again suggested when the singer rhymed how Cuban women, or "dark-eyed Stellas," would "light their fellers' Panatelas," or their phallic cigars.[25]

Berlin's song was by no means anomalous; other musical works depicted booze as a lubricant for sexual exploration. That same year U.S. artists re-

FIGURE 7.2.
A Bacardi postcard depicting an inebriated Uncle Sam gaily traveling to Cuba, where liquor flows freely. Note the juxtaposition to southern Florida, where a decree that reads "dry law" is depicted as severely limiting vice culture. Postcard, *Flying from the Desert*, c. 1930. Bacardi, publisher. Compañia Litográfica de La Habana, printer. 5½ × 3½ inches. Photo by David Almeida. XC2002.11.4.118, Vicki Gold Levi Collection, The Wolfsonian— Florida International University, Miami Beach, FL.

leased another song aptly titled "It Will Never Be Dry in Havana (No Matter What Happens 'Round Here)." In it, the singer states, "I'm as thirsty as can be / prohibition ruined me." The cover art featured a U.S. American man, suitcases in tow, fantasizing about a Cuban woman by the beach. The song also found a man telling his friend about the wonders of visiting Cuba: "This old town has gone all wrong / I want women, wine and song." In promoting tourism to the island where "señoritas sway," the song further demarcated Cuba as site for sex and vice for U.S. Americans. Travel to Miami proved critical to this formulation.[26]

One popular U.S. film, *The Pagan Lady*, similarly depicted this Cuba-Miami wide-open reputation, as both sites united for tourist consumption. The 1931 film was based on a stage play of the same name that reached Broadway audiences the previous year.[27] The film opens with a young, attractive U.S. woman nicknamed Dot living in Havana during Prohibition and working as a foul-mouthed bartender. The Cuban bar catered to an unsavory crowd, including mafiosi. A U.S.-based bootlegger named Dingo catches her eye, sweeps her away, and drops her off in North Carolina so he can tend to his bootlegging affairs in Miami. The film made several references to sexual transgression. Dot reclaims her sexuality and proudly holds up her social disrepute. At one point, a woman questions Dingo's manhood by suggesting that he cut his brandy with some club soda. He responds: "Use your head, woman! What do you think I am, a buttercup?"[28]

Cuban politics, economics, and social unrest played a central role in shaping Miami during this period. As Miami continued to suffer the consequences of its economic downturn after 1926, Havana, "where recreational activities were abundantly available," boomed.[29] Cuban journalist, artist, scholar, and urban critic Armando Maribona revealed the island's competition with Miami for tourist dollars and pesos. Working for the island's national tourism office, Maribona noted that "many people see the matter as a sort of boxing match, 'Miami versus Cuba,' with no shortage, unfortunately, of Cubans placing their bets on Miami in hopes of seeing their own country's tourism fail in order to hurt a person or entity they dislike," likely a leftist-nationalist leader or organization.[30] In the age of rising *cubanidad*, many Cuban venture capitalists invested in Miami's success to the detriment, Cuban nationalists maintained, of their land and people.

Cuban nationalists as well as local and foreign investors employed versions of Maribona's ideas to further advance the island's tourism industry prior to the 1959 Communist revolution. Reinaldo López Lima, another Cuban tourism official, built on Maribona's arguments in saying tourism had the potential to become "Cuba's second harvest" and help with the monoculture. Incidentally, the island's tourism season—which overlapped with Miami's—coincided with the *zafra*, or sugar cane harvest, limiting tourism's potential impact in dismantling the monoculture or sustaining a viable year-round workforce in either industry. Maribona studied the success of Miami tourism and concluded that the city reaped roughly the same gains as Cuba's sugar industry *during the island's best years*.[31] Maribona was a staunch nationalist who emphasized Cuba's natural beauty, including Varadero, the famous resort town some eighty-seven miles east of Havana. He also sought to take advantage, albeit cautiously, of Cuba's intimate ties with the United States—particularly Miami.[32] As the title of his study, *Tourism and Citizenship*, suggests, Maribona believed it was every Cuban's civic duty to embrace tourism. He believed tourism would make the island modern by improving its people's education, health, cleanliness, and urban planning.[33] He supported opening Cuba as a means of bringing capital to the nation—

not individuals—while also resisting the idea that "Cuba should be ready to get used."[34]

Some Cuban boosters, however, believed it necessary to further develop the island's sexual markets to remain competitive with places like Miami. One Cuban periodical called Cuba's "refined 'gigolo'" a "necessary auxiliary of tourism." Both female and male escorts who would "dance, converse, entertain, and drink with" unaccompanied foreigners were deemed instrumental to building the island's tourism. Some women visiting the island might seek a Cuban gigolo's companionship because their husbands were too "tired, overweight" or "inept dancers." Maribona distinguished this "refined" service from the perverse, but popular, trade that thrived in Havana. Indeed, sources suggest Cuban escorts offered a number of other nighttime services.[35]

Sexual tourism was sometimes seen as necessary for Cuba's economic diversification. "In Cuba we lack refined showgirls and 'escorts,'" argued Maribona. "Instead, there exists a gross system that disgraces our country." On the island, tourists were offered the "entertainment of '*cuadros plásticos*'"— defined in this source as the "lowest form of immoral theater" and suggestive of a show that was sexual and exhibitionist in nature—which were "open to the public with the authorization of the government, and other bad or worse things that have given Barcelona and Marseilles such bad reputations."[36] Maribona found blame in the United States and Cuba, as U.S. promoters advertised the island as a metaphorical whore and Cuban capitalists obliged such fantasies by exploiting their own people for personal gain.[37] He condemned U.S. travel literature that "induce[d] tourists to visit Cuba only through controlled excursions wherein, with the pernicious assistance of some Cuban tour guides, travelers get to know the worst Havana has to offer, including pornographic entertainment especially made for this double racket."[38]

These concerns were tied to changes in Cuban politics. Maribona emphasized the frustration of the Cuban Republic's first president, Tomás Estrada Palma: "This is a Republic without citizens." He believed not only that the state worked against the nation but also that self-interest and greed prevailed among corrupt leaders and well-to-do Cubans. "Since the fall of Estrada Palma," Maribona argued, "government officials and their cronies have had at their fingertips the means by which to satisfy their personal ambitions. In this way, the republican period in Cuba has not impeded the extortion characteristic of past political regimes." He even lamented that "should communism ever be installed in Cuba, the favors, corrupt patronage [*las botellas*], and the enrichment of a regime's backers would continue," so long as "self-proclaimed decent people keep trying to indulge in luxuries and physical pleasures, vices, and aristocratic trappings."[39] He added, "If Cuba is not the 'Tourist Paradise' we advertise, it is also a far stretch from being the Eden Republic that the selfless heroes of our independence dreamed of."[40]

This reflected the political climate that led to the ousting of Cuban dictator Gerardo Machado in 1933. Elected Cuba's president in 1925, Machado initially received widespread support despite his abuses of power, including extending his term as president. When the global economy collapsed in 1929, so too did Cuba's sugar exports. Cubans had had enough. Diverse factions made up of student protestors, merchants, and labor defenders helped topple Machado's government and ushered in a short-lived revolution. The U.S. abrogation of the Platt Amendment in 1934 and the progressive constitution of 1940 were among Cuba's nationalist gains. The former, however, actually solidified the U.S. naval base in Guantánamo Bay. Sergeant Fulgencio Batista, who helped depose Machado, ultimately undercut the latter reform. Batista usurped the Cuban government and ruled as a dictator-caudillo—at times as president himself and at times through puppet presidents—until the 1959 revolution.[41]

Cuba's social and political turmoil helped market Miami as a sinful paradise that could simultaneously guarantee its tourists' stability and safety. After all, Machado's expulsion coincided with the repeal of Prohibition in the United States. Throughout Miami, rumors abounded that Cuba's troubles had drastically curtailed its tourism by the late 1920s.[42] Cuba's loss was Miami's gain. Novelist and elite Miami resident Elizabeth Goodnow Cooper flew to Havana in the midst of these changes and described the Cuban capital as "a city of departed glory." Demonstrating the imperial ethos espoused by Miami investors who benefited from U.S. involvement in Cuba, she speculated: "Perhaps it was American business that had pulled out, perhaps it was the repeal or prohibition that had, with the revolution, kept the tourists away, or the low price of sugar—anyway, neither the town nor the people looked happy."[43] Similarly, many Cubans blamed "Miami hoteliers," including some who had built hotels in Cuba to the chagrin of nationalists who sought to purge foreign investments from the island. Cuban sources claimed influential Miami boosters had exaggerated conditions on the island in the press to deter visitors from Havana and into Miami, Havana's similarly tropical, but younger and more modern, sister city. While Miami boosters often touted southern Florida's tropical and Caribbean connection, they also emphasized the safety and patriotism they attributed to visiting a city officially part of the United States.[44] During the 1933–34 season, some travel companies even responded to Cuba's turmoil by removing the island from their itineraries.[45]

Even prior to the repeal of Prohibition, this competition for tourist dollars and pesos nudged Miami in the direction of becoming a wide-open city, often by mimicking the exoticism linked to Cuba. Selective and lax enforcement of laws became necessary for Miami to compete with Cuba as the most accommodating fairyland.[46] A British traveler believed Florida "was the wettest country" that did not even espouse "an 'attitude' towards prohibition—people had simply forgotten about it altogether."[47] During a 1930 U.S. congressional hearing over the effectiveness of the antiliquor law, the House Committee on the Judiciary heard testimony from Bonnie Melbourne Busch of Miami, the vice chair of Florida's chapter of the National Women's Democratic Law Enforcement League. The committee asked her to explain the "general increase in arrests for drunkenness in the State of Florida" during Prohibition. She told the congressmen that Florida "natives" did not violate the law, suggesting instead that it was tourists and transients. She elaborated, "I think it is a tourists' country entirely now, and they are on the way to and from Cuba and other places." The congressmen pushed further: "Would you say aside from the very ideal climate and other native attractions, that the proximity of Florida to the Bahama Islands and the Republic of Cuba was also part of the attractions?" To that, Busch simply replied, "I do not know. The climate takes me there."[48] While Busch's testimony reveals the popular belief that cities like Miami rarely enforced the law, it also connects Miami's identity to the Caribbean and its racialized "attractions."

It became clear that if law enforcement cracked down on Miami's vice culture, tourists "would go to Cuba" and indulge in her fairyland instead.[49] One journalist noted that "pleasures that do not come within the pale are so readily obtainable" in Miami in large part because Havana "is only three hours away by plane, and offers to do as you please." In this way, "Havana has become the *bête noir* [*sic*] of Miami." He believed that if "Miami retains the best features of the sin-cursed Cuban capital, the dollars that might fly across the Straits will stay where they will do the most good," that is, in Miami.[50] Similarly, during Prohibition playwright and journalist Basil Woon joked that he would "pop over to Florida and tell" tourists there "about Havana." "I will tell them that we have a perfect climate, and horse racing, and plenty of drinks, and open gambling, and a wonderful beach, and good roads." He then realized that Miami offered the very same. "It seems to me that about the only chance Havana stands ... is to organize a slush fund and elect another reform governor of Florida." He correctly added, "And what a slim chance that would be."[51]

## Queers and Shifting Urban Power

The corruption, graft, and vice that plagued Cuba, especially in Havana, shared striking similarities with Miami's own urban politics. Many U.S. American mobsters "located in Havana" had direct connections to Miami and its underground economies. Many had also established residence in Miami.[52] This changing power structure did not go unnoticed by Miami elites, small-time merchants, middle-class residents, religious organizations, or terrorist groups like the KKK. This tension was palpable in a broadcast that observed: "Residents and businessmen of Miami Beach seem finally to have reached the point where they must choose between the wealthy conservative element, which has played so large a part in building up their community, and the flashy fly-by-night followers of Lady Luck, who are literally here today and gone tomorrow."[53] By the 1930s, a battle for urban power—one in which new city standards, morals, and identities would take shape—ensued unlike Miami had ever seen.

Miami's conservative elites and growing middle class particularly mobilized following the arrival of northern and midwestern syndicates, especially in the person of notorious gangster Alphonse (Al or "Scarface") Capone. Although Capone earned his notoriety in Chicago, where the mob controlled much of the city's sexual demimonde, he too eventually took advantage of Florida's land boom.[54] In 1928, he bought a luxurious home on Miami Beach's Palm Island, where he escaped Chicago's law enforcement. Capone was not alone. Mafiosi Jake Guzik, Frank Erickson, Meyer Lansky, and Frank Costello also put down roots in southern Florida.[55]

The city's ruling class challenged Miami's changing urban power structure, which had been supplanted by new residents and underground economies. Twelve wealthy and politically influential men met in 1926 after the local economic crises to "combat the effects of the disaster" and formed a new group with a particular vision for the city that did not include its perceived "low-life" element. They formed the Committee of One Hundred to help build Miami Beach in the vision of their elite members.[56] The committee's newsletter most often reflected the opinions of its editor and first president, Clayton Sedgwick Cooper, also publisher of the *Miami Tribune.*[57] Other prominent members of the committee included real estate pioneer Carl G. Fisher, Firestone Tires founder Harvey S. Firestone, and millionaire-inventor Joseph H. Adams. A separate women's group was also formed.[58]

The Committee of One Hundred sought to carve "a new civilization" in Miami Beach that catered to white and moneyed tastes. In this fairyland, successful white women and men could "bring their families to enjoy the right kind of government and civic advantages and safe guards." It was the committee's "desire and intention" to protect its "membership as far as possible in their property rights." Committee members envisioned Miami Beach *not* as "simply a resort city" but rather as a place with "good schools and churches and first class social organizations with regard for high standards and self respect." Members worked to protect "decency, good order and administration" in the city they controlled. They were "opposed to making Miami Beach a home of gangsters and thievery and grafting politicians."[59]

Miami's well-to-do residents who believed Capone and connected illegal ventures threatened this vision for the city exerted their influence to change law enforcement policies. Following Capone's arrival, the Miami Beach City Council held a special meeting with Mayor Val Cleary, the city attorney, and several Committee of One Hundred members. Committee members expressed their concern over "the influx of undesirable gamblers, gangsters and racketeers here for the purpose of preying on the wealthy." They insisted that "the lid be put on" and "that all laws be rigidly enforced." The mayor and city council said they would oblige.[60] In the early 1930s, committee members paid experts to train local police on the strategies employed by law enforcement in cities such as New York, Los Angeles, Detroit, Chicago, Baltimore, and Washington. Members also helped privatize streets "along the ocean front" by closing them off to traffic and converting them into parkways and made sure slot machines were never installed in Miami Beach. They also pushed for legislation requiring that all "hotel employees, including bellboys [and] chefs ... be registered" and fingerprinted. This policy weeded out dozens of people "with criminal records" who were "immediately sent out of the State of Florida."[61]

These actions were also influenced by and further fueled xenophobic, racist, and class-based warfare in the urban center. A representative of the Miami Bank and Trust Company charged, "Inadequate punishment is a great hindrance to law enforcement.... If the court would only stop licensing the bootlegger by the punishment of only a fine" and instead require hard labor for the city as retribution, "prohibition officers would ... have very little to do."[62] Well-to-do residents also blamed out-of-towners for the cesspool of "petty vice ... gaining a foothold" in Miami and prompted Police Chief L. O. Scarboro to lead a new drive in May 1929 to purge underground economies. Police raided bootlegging and gambling establishments, arresting ninety-two people. Charges included driving while intoxicated, drunkenness, and gambling. This was part of a "determined effort ... to stop an increasing number of petty criminals," which included at least nine "negroes," from "coming to Miami."[63]

New urban anxieties also surfaced in response to changing class demographics among Miami's tourists. Although Miami had long catered to a wealthy clientele from the U.S. North and Midwest, several changes—particularly the real estate bust, natural disaster, and the global Great Depression—forced urban boosters to reach out to tourists of more modest means. One such manifestation of this change came with the growing trend of mobile tourists. The Tin Can Tourists of the World (TCT) officially organized in January 1920. New and improved roads and more affordable automobiles transformed tourism in the United States.[64] They also created a new industry of trailer living and camping. The TCT formed in the nascent "auto touring" years to build a community among mostly middle-class tourists. Some brought tents along with them, hitched a makeshift home to their Model Ts, or converted their pickup trucks into boxlike campers. Those with greater means bought a proper mobile trailer. When the Depression hit, many unemployed transients joined them on the road, traveling from place to place in search of work.[65] Miami politicians and boosters realized there was money to be made in this new market and welcomed these "tin can tourists" to the city. So successful was the broadening of Miami's tourist market that Cuban tourism officials kept track of Miami's transient camps and the number of vehicles that passed through the area to learn from their competitor.[66] While these new tourists stimulated the local economy, the city's wealthiest sector and, especially, its growing middle-class residents labeled them an "undesirable" presence that threatened property investments.

By the following decade, Miami housed several trailer parks and camps near downtown that became a steady source of municipal revenue. Miami's Tamiami Tourist Court, near where US1 and Route 41 meet, offered 36 cottages for rent at $1 a day and could house 150 trailers at either 50 cents a day or $2.50 a week. The city also "assessed a fee of $1 for each trailer."[67] This replenished city coffers and introduced a much more affordable way to experience the tropical fairyland. State numbers reveal that by 1934, 24.3 percent of the motor tourists who entered the state—over 1.3 million—spent their time in *southern* Florida. This represented the highest regional percentage in the state. Most of these tourists drove in from Georgia and Alabama and spent an average of twenty-nine days in the state.[68]

Class tensions helped define these new visitors as undesirable and a threat to community morals. After all, they were nothing like the wealthy vacationers and settlers who first transformed this fairyland into the nation's playground. In noting these changes, the *New York Herald Tribune* carried a cartoon series titled "Trailer Tintypes" poking fun at Florida's growing mobile culture. It fixated on class. In one cartoon, a woman scolds her son:

"I will not have you playing with those children in that homemade trailer! You must remember that we live in a super de luxe."[69] These visitors often left their trash behind, did not put out their fires, damaged property, and stole resources such as food and water. As one "tin can" tourist recalled, they "soon became looked upon as a band of Gypsies, unwanted, undesirable and something to keep out of the neighborhood."[70]

Several residents suggested these spaces facilitated sexual depravity because they attracted undesirable transients of weak moral character. One Miami newspaper referred to these camps as "hobo jungles."[71] A former St. Petersburg mayor asked the Miami Realty Board, "What is the use of fussing with the class of 'undesirables'" when the "good ones" were lining up to visit and "willing to pay any price"?[72] Headlines advanced this view for years, even after the repeal of Prohibition. For instance, police arrested Wilbur Shipman *four* separate times in the span of a week on child molestation charges. Shipman was a transient living in a tourist camp. He escaped from the police three times, including one time when police allowed him to "return to the tourist camp to get his baggage and lock up his cabin." Perhaps police preferred he just leave town, despite charges "of the man's unnatural attentions." This suggests the lax and selective enforcement of sodomy laws in Miami during this period. After all, it appears police encouraged him to leave rather than pursue a lengthy and costly legal process at the time. As we have seen, sodomy and crimes against nature felonies were primarily utilized to criminalize intergenerational sex—especially if the suspected offender was black, immigrant or migrant, or working class—that may or may not have been consensual. Although the accusations against Shipman also fell into this category, police struggled to keep him in custody. Although it appears Shipman was later convicted, reports like this fueled moralists' fears that these transient spaces, populated by an undesirable class of people, would inevitably give way to unnatural sex and that law enforcement simply proved incapable or disinterested in upholding the law.[73]

In 1930, to combat these changing demographics, Miami's property owners used their influence to tailor a new law against the city's so-called vagrants. Officials from Miami, Miami Beach, and the Dade County solicitor's office formed a united front to oppose Capone and the "undesirables" he attracted to the area.[74] In particular, on May 23, 1930, Miami passed an anti-vagrancy ordinance "as a weapon . . . to drive Capone and other racketeers and gangsters from the community." The City Commission voted 3-to-1 in favor of the ordinance. To no avail, organized labor joined Capone's attorney in protesting the law. The sole commissioner to vote against the law believed it "violated his legal training." A commissioner who favored the law defended his position by arguing, "We must continue to bring high class people here." He stressed the "imperative for Miami to have a good reputation as a resort center as visitors from the north will come here, build homes and become winter residents."[75]

As before, this law was representative of the white urban authority's legal tactics to regulate, monitor, and purge a wide range of "undesirables." While it was primarily crafted to target mafiosi, the area's changing racial, ethnic, and class composition further motivated property owners to seek increased law enforcement more generally. The initial law criminalized "any person or persons having visible means of support acquired by unlawful or illegal means or methods, or any person who is dangerous to the peace or safety of the city of Miami, or any person or persons known or reputed to be crooks, gangsters, or hijackers."[76] The unnamed representatives of organized labor who attacked this law correctly pointed out that the law criminalized a wide spectrum of people and communities. In particular, this law policed the city's blacks, immigrants, and working class. This included numerous "negro vagrant drive[s]" conducted by both city and county law enforcement.[77]

Attempts by Miami's moralist elite and middle class to persuade police to tighten enforcement and lawmakers to craft new ordinances to purge un- desirables was temporarily effective. Law enforcement cracked down on Capone's illicit Miami businesses, including bootlegging, speakeasies, gam- bling, and sex work. Within a few months, state beverage agents raided his estate and found illicit liquor. With that, a court petition was filed against Capone as a "public nuisance" in the hopes of evicting him from the area.[78] Several Committee of One Hundred members were instrumental to this process. Fisher testified before a county judge that Capone's mere presence made Miami Beach residents—particularly women—fearful and "nervous" and devalued property investments.[79] Capone left southern Florida for Illi- nois in 1930. By 1932, the federal government succeeded in placing him be- hind bars for tax evasion and other charges.[80] Capone was gone from Miami, but the vice culture he came to represent remained.

This moral impetus found local conservatives attacking Miami's vice culture that catered to tourists, with reformists believing urban designers had forced them to pick a side: "Capone or Civilization?" By 1929, a Florida clergyman named Frank Nelson launched *Sky Talk*, a publication "devoted to the moral and spiritual welfare of the State." It focused on the "evils" of bootlegging and gambling and lamented Miami's perceived decay. Un- savory characters "flocked to the state," Nelson claimed, "attracted by wide- open Miami . . . where the law had been trodden underfoot with impunity." "Florida needs boosting," he concurred, but one "never can boost a thing unless you have something solid to stand on." He believed dependence on tourism created moral chaos and put out a welcome mat for "undesirables." Miami could not house "beer kings, hold-up men, prostitutes, and professional gamblers, and also have doctors, lawyers, merchants, and other varieties of law-abiding citizens."[81]

Miami's wide-open, tourist-driven policy mobilized several moralist forces, including many middle-class residents and religious organizations. They looked to the Ministerial Association of Greater Miami for guidance, as it claimed to represent all Protestant churches in the area and had a membership of more than 30,000.[82] Adding to its sphere of influence, the group was buttressed by the nationally influential, DC-based Board of Temperance, Prohibition, and Public Morals of the Methodist Episcopal Church.[83] Local ministers implored their congregations to dismantle the argument that a wide-open policy was necessary to maintain and grow Miami's economy. "Miami does not need the dollar so much as she needs the ideal. Of the two—financial or moral bankruptcy—may she never choose or experience the latter."[84] Members of the Miami Christian Council even petitioned to have the group's members appointed as county deputy sheriffs to assist in purging vice.[85]

Transgressive expressions of gender and sexuality were key targets of this moral crusade. Nelson placed women's "lack of clothes" alongside the pervasion of the speakeasy, gambling, "the arts of the underworld," red-light districts, and polygamy. A Miami pastor claimed that "disreputable characters" attracted to the city's vice culture were breaking into his church "to sleep and for worse purposes."[86] Similarly, "like flies at an open syrup spigot," "women of the street" waited for those with "their night's winnings" in their pockets.[87] One man wanted a return to the time when he could "walk on Miami Avenue," downtown's thoroughfare, "without being molested by" the "ladies of the evening."[88]

Many of the city's merchant-class residents took this position. Lilburn Railey, a prominent lawyer and Virginia native who moved to Miami in the early 1900s, was another major shaker in the city's crusade against vice. He shared local merchants' concerns that gambling "saps the life" of a community and drains people of the money they could otherwise "spend in the stores."[89] Florida-born James Carson, another attorney with a private practice, blamed local newspapers for being mouthpieces for Miami's tourist-driven wide-open policy. In this vein, moral people had "been handicapped by organized propaganda," such as that promoted by many boosters, hoteliers, "nightclubs and the class of people who patronize all such institutions, not to mention the organized underworld."[90] In this urban war, conservative forces believed those of "the prophetic persuasion" were losing out to vice and sin boosterism.[91]

The KKK, which reemerged during this period, joined this crusade against the city's "undesirables." Despite the KKK's revival across the country by the end of the Great War, it only made its presence officially known in Miami in 1921. Klansmen and kamelias (female auxiliary) employed violence and scare tactics—mob action, lynchings, bombings, parades, abductions, and lashings—to enforce the urban ideology of white power.[92] Much of this was sexual. Klansmen, for instance, kidnapped a black minister whom they suspected of preaching racial equality and miscegenation.[93] This "reactionary populism," as Nancy MacLean has called it, only grew in intensity with Prohibition. The Klan revitalized its image during this period by shoring up support with middle-class whites who shared a commitment to "correct evils" in their communities—"particularly vices tending to the destruction of the home, family, childhood, and womanhood."[94]

This reenergized moral crusade, the scale of which Miami had not seen in two decades, also saw the return, and almost immediate suspension, of Dade County's elected sheriff and reformer Dan Hardie, who had "cleaned up" Miami's saloons and pushed the city's vice and crime into black neighborhoods, particularly the eponymous "Hardieville." Hardie had withdrawn from politics in 1916 to invest in Miami Beach real estate, but he ran for sheriff again in 1932. The elite and middle-class residents who wanted to "clean up" the city again resoundingly elected him. Even Hardie, however, acknowledged that Miami had drastically changed since his previous tenure. He ran on a campaign that he was "*not* a 'reformer.'" He assured voters that he was "liberal in his views regarding the conduct of resort cities."[95] That was, after all, what was required of a tourist-dependent fairyland. He took office January 3, 1933, but Governor David Sholtz relieved him of his duties less than a year later, on October 17, following charges that Hardie lacked "sound judgment" and "mental stability." In Hardie's dismissal hearing, the state cited several instances of "malfeasance and misfeasance."[96]

The evidence heavily suggests, as so many Miami residents suspected and complained about, that the maintenance of a liberal policy for the tourist-dependent area in the midst of an international economic depression played a central role in Hardie's removal. Many believed that Hardie failed to live up to his campaign promise that he would not play the role of moralist reformer at the expense of the city's tourist economy. Hardie's supporters believed, and ample evidence corroborates their suspicions, that many law enforcement officials were bribed by gangsters or simply not inclined to enforce the laws if this might discourage tourists from coming to the city.[97] Several organizations—including the Miami Woman's Christian Temperance Union, Dade County's League of Democratic Women Voters, and the Committee of One Hundred—condemned the governor's decision.[98] For them, Hardie represented Miami's "new deal," much like the one President Franklin D. Roosevelt had promised the nation. One man argued, "We need him [Hardie], and the nation needs such officers in this time of striving for a new deal."[99] Another resident defined *Hardie* as Miami's new deal, a man whose efforts would "mean for this community more solid and enduring prosperity than any contrary policy could possibly promote."[100]

Although Hardie's supporters believed Governor Sholtz had "been won over to the cause of the gamblers, racketeers and prostitutes," many others supported his decision and believed prosperity came in the form of a liberal policy in which law enforcement permitted its tourists to take pleasure in Miami's fairyland.[101] For them, a new deal came through the enforcement of a liberal policy—*not* the strict enforcement of the law. A Democrat born in Brooklyn to Russian immigrant parents, Sholtz became governor in 1933 riding the wave of change that landed Roosevelt in the White House. He touted himself an outsider who ultimately became a "New Deal governor" by accepting federal funds and programs and expanding state spending, including protecting tourism.[102]

Sholtz proved particularly attentive to Miami Beach business owners, who sent him countless letters commending him for removing Hardie and promoting a more lax approach to law enforcement. A delegate personally delivered a petition signed by hundreds of Miami Beach entrepreneurs asking the governor to uphold "a liberal policy of government" in Dade County during the peak of the tourist season.[103] One man wrote, "All institutions are suffering from the unscrupulous crusade of disgruntled minority interests," referring to Hardie's supporters. The letter noted, "I urge you to immediately observe a more liberal policy so that our citizenry may yet salvage something from an already ruined [tourist] season."[104] The Labor Citizenship Committee agreed. It asserted "the undisputed fact that Dade County is wholly a winter resort" that only operates on "the whims and desires of our tourist visitors." As such, the labor group noted, "all effort should be made to cater to the wishes of our visitors."[105] Others argued that police were too rigid and that most infractions were "criminal trivialities." "Tourists expect a certain number of gambling clubs to operate in Dade County." The quest to shut them down had also closed down "nightclubs that ... imported leading American attractions."[106] This included queer performers and entertainment.

While some of these business owners were also members of the middle class, several factors separated them from the middle-class reformers who implored local government to quash vice. In addition to catering to a more moneyed clientele that also helped separate them from the "petit-bourgeois," these Miami Beach entrepreneurs were mostly individual merchants and hotel or rental managers largely at the service of tourists.[107] By 1934, 40 percent of the area's unemployed were connected to the construction industry, such as bricklayers and carpenters, who suffered during the building freezes that followed economic crises.[108] The evidence heavily suggests that they were more likely to be among the moralist reformers who, as the La Paloma raid suggests, grew frustrated by Miami's tourist-driven economy. Even among the Miami Beach merchants who pleaded with the governor that illegal gambling be permitted, they too restricted it to "'high class' night clubs" that served a wealthy clientele.[109]

Sholtz's liberal policy stance was perhaps clearest in his decision to at least tacitly support Fred Pine in his campaign for Dade County solicitor. Pine had previously served as county solicitor in the early 1930s, but he had been charged with corruption and working with mobsters to permit illicit gambling and prostitution. Pine was acquitted of the charges and voters returned him to the position.[110] In a revealing turn of events, by 1937, he found himself working on the other side of the law, when Youst hired him to represent La Paloma against Miami law enforcement.[111]

While the effectiveness of the reformers' moral crusade was quickly diminishing, other forces led Miami police to temporarily tighten up law enforcement in the early 1930s. The city found itself under the microscope after major events exposed its lax code to the entire nation. Safety in the city was called into question on February 15, 1933, when a man named Giuseppe Zangara attempted to assassinate President-elect Roosevelt following a speech in Miami's Bayfront Park. Like so many others, Roosevelt arrived in Miami after a vacation to the Bahamas. Although Zangara killed Chicago mayor Anton Cermak, Roosevelt was not physically harmed. In addition, in March 1933 police finally caught the notorious jewel thief Harry Sitamore. In the several years he resided in Miami, Sitamore stole several hundred thousand dollars' worth of gems from wealthy travelers. Sitamore was not alone. In fact, resort heisting became more commonplace, as urban law enforcement was notoriously inefficient and lax.[112] The early vision of Miami Beach as a privileged space for the rich and powerful espoused by the Committee of One Hundred members and others ultimately attracted a network of underground "undesirables" who preyed on the socialites' wealth.[113] In this context, the city's liberal policy had the potential to *hurt* tourism. After all, it fostered an impression of the city as too dangerous, much as Miami boosters described Cuba.

Miami endured another extraordinary urban transformation with the ousting of Cuba's president-dictator Machado in August 1933, which sent a flood of exiles to the city. Cubans became another source of anxiety for urban powerbrokers and consumed much of the law enforcement's time and energy during this period. The Cuban exiles were diverse. Prior to the overthrow, they were largely revolutionaries fighting Machado's regime. Once their rebellion succeeded, it was Machado's allies and supporters who fled to Miami. In 1932, the Dade County sheriff expressed difficulty investigating "the Cuban refugee situation in Miami," as the Cubans "are extremely cautious and suspicious." In November of that year, law enforcement believed Cubans broke into a Miami hardware store and stole "several revolvers and shotguns," likely to smuggle into Cuba. Officials, both local and federal, similarly kept an eye on the several "camps" located throughout Miami that housed dozens of Cuban men forced to flee the island.[114] Machado's government reminded the U.S. government of its neutrality agreement and described the Cubans in Miami as subversive, criminal, and communist.[115] By the late 1930s, at least 6,000 Cubans called Miami home.[116] This too fueled the city's moralist and nativist furnace.

These conservative forces further mobilized when Florida legalized parimutuel gambling in 1931. Instead of shining a light on the underground spaces in the city, pari-mutuel legalization increased and reinforced vice cultures in establishments queers had long frequented. Illegal gambling had been commonplace for years. The Miami Jockey Club, later renamed the Hialeah Race Course, opened in the midst of the area's boom. Lax law enforcement defined the atmosphere at the tracks, where spectators wagered on horses and dogs. This enterprise attracted many tourists. In response to the Great Depression, Florida's legislature—overturning Governor Doyle Carlton's veto—opted to capitalize on the financial successes Miami found with this illegal venture by passing the "Turf Bill," which mandated that Florida's sixty-seven counties share the profits equally. The state received 2 percent of every legal wager and 15 percent of all admissions as a tax. In 1933, the counties split $308,531.56 from Hialeah's earnings alone. This number was quite small compared to the $8 million that circulated the racetrack during that forty-five-day season.[117] While other budding Florida cities reaped a small percentage of the profits, many could not afford to finance their own operations. This made southern Florida the epicenter of the state's new venture.[118]

Despite recent and fleeting crackdowns, queers remained visible in the vice cultures that further developed through Miami's new attempts to respond to economic necessity by attracting more tourists. In 1931, wealthy New York mobster-bootlegger William "Big Bill" Vincent Dwyer opened the new Tropical Park racetrack in south Miami. It had its first proper season two years later. Despite Dwyer's bootlegger reputation, many locals supported his bid to expand horseracing season. Many even saw him as a heroic figure helping the area overcome the Depression.[119] His supporters overlooked Dwyer's underground activities and lifestyle. This aggravated the county sheriff, who claimed Dwyer made threatening phone calls to the police to allow him to operate his businesses without harassment.[120] Journalist Barbara Walters recalled Dwyer during her childhood in Miami where, in a strange turn of events, she lived with the notorious gangster. Walters claimed Dwyer shared his bedroom with his "chauffeur/bodyguard" and that in retrospect "it seems somewhat logical" that he was "gay."[121]

Similarly, queers were connected to or somehow incriminated in some of the era's crime rings, particularly those surrounding jewel theft. "Sex pervert" Irving Young had been arrested "many times for robbery," as well as for "breaking [and entering] and stealing."[122] "Peter R.," the "sex variant" who spent considerable time in Miami, was similarly arrested in the city when "some diamond rings were stolen." He claimed police fingerprinted him and kept him in jail for three days before releasing him.[123] In popular fiction, Miami's female impersonators were regularly depicted as a jewel thieves.[124] In later years, sexually deviant women and lesbians were similarly depicted as transient thieves connected to the city.[125]

Queers were also among the so-called undesirables, unsavory characters, vagrants, and "colorful crowds" who fueled and staffed Miami's tourist economy.[126] In an anonymous letter to Miami moral crusader Lilburn Railey, the writer argued that "the lice that follow the stables [at the legal racetracks] are unworthy of mixing with decent people." These "lice" included "coke fiends, crooks, pickpockets and parasites of every description."[127] Queers were a major presence in clubs, cabarets, speakeasies, and revues in several parts of the city, even as repeal seemed certain. A cartoon in the alternative newspaper *Friday Night* depicted a limp-wristed club bouncer throwing out a patron, who asks him, "Why do you expel me so gently?" (fig. 7.3). Stressing his effeminacy, the queer jokes that his establishment is not allowed to put a "kick in 3.2 beer," a reference to the alcohol content permitted to be sold under the 1933 Cullen-Harrison Act, which started the repeal of Prohibition.[128]

"But, bouncer, why do you expel me so gently?"
"Listen, bo, don't you know we ain't allowed to put no kick in 3.2 beer?"

## Miami after Prohibition

While Havana had the upper hand over Miami during U.S. Prohibition, repeal and the "dangers" and "anti-Americanism" associated with Cuba's 1933 revolution quickly leveled the playing field.[129] Miami had been in economic recovery for nearly a decade. Miami's 1933–34 tourist season saw the area's best returns in five years. Its tourist industry was bouncing back. Although Cuba's turmoil diverted more tourists to Miami, much of this recovery was also a product of a strategic combination of state- and privately funded projects that made Miami more desirable in the mid-1930s. Private enterprise, for instance, contributed to a construction boom in Miami Beach. The proliferation of modern "Art Deco" seasonal apartment buildings and mini-hotels was complemented by numerous New Deal public works projects. Indeed, improved and new roads, schools, public housing, and civic and community spaces flourished. Although many hoped these projects would make Miami more attractive for "natives," or local residents, and "desirable" new settlers, the construction boom ultimately strengthened the area's dependence on tourists who used these new facilities. As federal monies dried up by 1937, the new built environment made Miami more attractive and accessible to middle-class and even some working-class tourists.[130]

This helps explain the reenergized efforts of frustrated Miami moralists who sought greater economic relief independent of tourist-driven industry. They believed that the New Deal in southern Florida made the local economy even more reliant on the whims of tourists. To them, this seemed like Miami's formal transformation from fairyland to Sodom. "Wide-open gambling ... would inevitably lead to the fatal reputation of [Florida] being a vice state," noted one source.[131] The city faced major changes in the post-Prohibition era as social, economic, and political forces collided and reinforced Miami's liberal policy. Queers benefited from these changes, which ultimately gave them work and spaces to express themselves.

The national repeal of Prohibition—prompted by public opposition, economic turmoil, and legal inefficiency—was a major catalyst for urban change in Miami. The nation's "Noble Experiment" ended on December 5, 1933, with the passage of the Twenty-First Amendment. Months before, on April 6, the U.S. Congress passed the "beer bill" that redefined "intoxicating" to mean more than 3.2 percent alcohol, thereby legalizing anything below that. The renewal of legal flow of alcohol took longer in Florida. The state passed its own "bone dry" law in 1918 that took effect on January 1, 1919. Federal, state, and local laws stood in the way of legalizing liquor. A representative from Dade County spearheaded an initiative to legalize "nonintoxicating" alcohol in the state and, a month after U.S. Congress passed its "beer bill," Florida's governor signed bills to accomplish the same. Shortly thereafter, the passage of the Twenty-First Amendment helped strip power away from federal courts by returning jurisdiction to state and local courts. Finally, on November 6, 1934, Floridians voted two-to-one to suspend the state's "bone dry" law, allowing counties to decide whether they would be wet or dry. Dade opted for the former.[132]

Queers played a significant role in the nightlife culture that took shape after Prohibition. Advocates of tourism and a liberal policy hoped the repeal of Prohibition would "cause a large number of nightspots to open soon." After all, "several beer gardens that folded quietly after the novelty of 3.2 wore off will be opened by hopefuls." Queer performers, particularly female impersonators, remained critical to this enterprise. "One thing about a lid that is lifted a little," one source maintained, is that "it provides the coconuts to pay high priced entertainers." Representatives of these "hopefuls" noted that "an open season on those queer wheels and dotted ivories," that is, turning a blind eye on illicit gambling joints, "will put a crimp in the Hollywood layouts." These were the high-profile and expensive clubs that, at times, featured gender-transgressive performers. "The boys and girls go up there when there's no place else to go," noted one source.[133] The more popular and high-end clubs charged customers exorbitant prices. In part this meant customers expected to see big names on the stage. Many of the top billers were imported straight from Broadway during the winter months, when they undertook tours that brought them to places like Miami and Havana.[134]

One such high-end and glitzy site was Mother Kelly's, a nightclub on Dade Boulevard in Miami Beach. New York native Robert A. Kelly, or "Mother Kelly," ran the club and offered entertainment that made light of rigid gender and sexual norms.[135] The establishment opened in 1932 and underwent several changes throughout the years.[136] It played with the fact that "Mother isn't a woman. She's a him!" In fact, Mother Kelly was "a good-natured, plump in the middle, Irishman, who does a Tex Guinan [an impression of actress Texas Guinan], always in a white sport shirt."[137] Mother Kelly's female impersonation was a source of comedy for heterosexual and queer tourists and residents alike. By 1941, *Time* magazine noted that "fat, male Mother Kelly dishes up steaks, drinks and hermaphroditic comedy."[138] While Mother Kelly's sexual proclivities are unknown, his persona certainly referenced homosexuality. Patrons could purchase a penny bank in Mother Kelly's likeness wherein the coin slot was coyly placed in between his buttocks, suggestive of their penetrability (fig. 7.4). These souvenirs proved quite popular. Mother Kelly advertised that he would be happy to autograph them.[139]

Many of these costly, stylized spots in Miami and Miami Beach capitalized on the exoticism tourists associated with the Caribbean, particularly Cuba. Mother Kelly's advertised itself as Miami Beach's version of Havana's notorious club Sans Souci. Its specialty drink was a rum cocktail made "West Indies Style."[140] The thousands of Cuban immigrants and exiles who made Miami home during this period contributed significantly to this tropical fairyland image. Many Cubans worked in Miami's service industry, including as musicians and entertainers. Queers were among them.[141] While this helped market Miami as a fairyland, some residents responded to their presence with nativist fervor. One Miami woman described Cubans in the midst of a heated discussion: "As I watched them, I thought it a shame to waste so much energy. Why not put belts on the Cubans and generate something; make ice or electricity, or better still hook a lot of them together and have

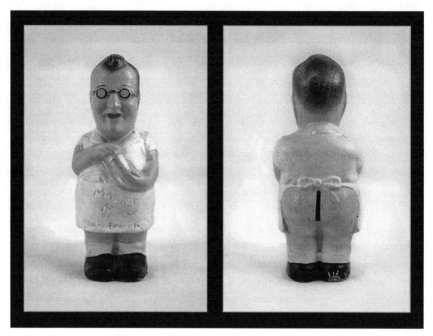

FIGURE 7.4. Piggy bank of likeness of Mother Kelly, the bartender-owner of the eponymous nightspot who was a big hit on Miami Beach. In addition to impersonating Hollywood actresses, he made not-so-subtle references to anal penetration and homosexuality. Photography by Annie Sollinger. Piggy Bank, c. 1940. Author's collection.

perpetual motion."[142] One religious reformer condemned the popular belief that immigrants who had to "work off their energy" were the cause of lawlessness.[143] This popular rhetoric of "energetic" Cubans was simultaneously used to describe their perceived hypersexuality, criminality, and undesirability.

One "energetic" Cuban exile who added flair to Miami's nightlife during this period was Desiderio Alberto Arnaz y de Acha, better known as Desi Arnaz of *I Love Lucy* fame. He came from a wealthy, influential family from Santiago de Cuba in the southeast part of the island. Arnaz's father had been elected to the Cuban Congress in 1932 and, because of the family's association with Machado's government, feared retaliation by revolutionaries. In 1934 the family fled to Miami where Desi Arnaz befriended Al Capone Jr. Two years later, he landed a job playing guitar at the Roney Plaza in Miami Beach. Bandleader and rumba king Xavier Cugat then took him under his wing in New York City. When Arnaz returned to Miami the following year, he improvised the rhythms of Afro-Cuban music and popularized conga music and dance in Miami and around the nation. A young Arnaz negotiated that breakout gig with Mother Kelly and his son, Bobby, who was looking for performers for his "Latin motif" revue.[144] Arnaz popularized the conga line in Miami working with Mother Kelly, whose gender and sexual playfulness matched what tourists had come to expect from fairyland.

While queers and other fairyland "props" may have provided entertainment or staffed the clubs, many were priced out as patrons at swankier nightspots at the center of Miami and Miami Beach. A rawer version of Miami after dark could be found in the less "plush establishments" on the city's outskirts. As one contemporary recalled, "Some club-owners slit their gullets with ridiculous prices, or check-padding." Others, however, "found temporary sanctuary from bankruptcy by canceling standard acts and substituting strip-teasers" and queer performers who offered crude jokes onstage and perhaps other services on the side. *These* acts could "be lured at waitresses' pay" and were therefore a safe investment for club owners who tapped into the fairyland market priced out of the elaborate, Broadway-esque entertainment found in central Miami and Miami Beach. Several of these clubs and bars "made a play for the homosexual trade." The evidence heavily suggests that these spaces were more policed than the "expensive night-club" that offered female impersonators, such as Mother Kelly's, even as local law enforcement also largely turned a blind eye to the smaller joints during the winter months.[145]

Indeed, despite Prohibition's repeal, years of profits and experience working around the law ensured that subversive investors and businesspeople would expand their bootlegging and underground enterprises. Before the Twenty-First Amendment went into effect, a Committee of One Hundred member maintained that "Florida will certainly vote for the repeal of prohibition." Such a vote, he believed, would not be to "bring back alcohol." After all, "there is no lack of that" in southern Florida. Rather, repeal would help "get rid of crime."[146] His latter point proved naïve. During Prohibition, officers in Florida targeted "suspects based on a high probability of securing a conviction." This meant that those convicted in the state were "small-time moonshiners who lived marginal lives, lacked strong community ties, and/or possessed limited knowledge of due process."[147] As Lisa McGirr has argued, Prohibition expanded the state in most significant ways and constituted its first major narcotics war.[148] Florida's legislature passed a far-reaching bill in 1933 regulating—among other things—the sale, possession, control, and growth of narcotic drugs. In many ways, it substituted the illegality of alcohol under Prohibition with that of a wide range of narcotics. The law also designated spaces frequented by narcotic users as a public nuisance.[149] In

1934, Florida narcotic agents uncovered the sale "of marijuana cigarettes in a marathon dance hall in Miami," which they believed "deprive[d] the addict of all reason and" induced him or her to commit "revolting crimes."[150] Organized crime and business had long since been formalized in Miami. After Prohibition, bootlegging persisted and expanded to include new illicit forms of trade, racketeering, gambling, extortion, narcotics, and sex trafficking.[151]

While this certainly demonstrates state efforts to regulate the confines of respectability, it more pressingly reflects governmental frustrations over the continued loss of tax and license revenue. Still in recovery mode, state and local governments knew they had long missed out on the opportunity to tax alcohol, which had flowed both freely and illegally under Prohibition. In 1933, the Florida legislature passed a law regulating the manufacture, transport, and sale of permitted liquor. It excluded those "convicted of any offense involving moral turpitude," which could include homosexuality or other transgressive sex acts, from legally selling alcohol. Perhaps more important, the law created high tax rates for such sales. The state of Florida charged vendors an annual fee for the license. It also authorized state counties *and* incorporated cities or towns to assess an additional license tax not in excess of 50 percent of the state's fee.[152] Miami's City Commission passed an "emergency measure" to begin issuing license fees in late 1934, and Miami Beach's city council did the same the following year. In addition to nearly doubling Miami Beach's revenue, this act brought to light the many illicit operations in the area. The municipality would once again seek stricter regulation, enforcement, and control, if only because it needed the income.[153] Testimonies reveal some of the harassing tactics law enforcement threatened to use against nightclub owners suspected of operating illegally: violent and destructive raids, increases or changes to license fees, and a greater police presence. The latter included threatening to follow exiting patrons to "charge them with driving while under the influence of liquor," which would hurt business.[154] Municipal and county law enforcement appeared responsive to complaints—particularly pertaining to extortion—when they came from tourists. In 1935 a tourist complained that the staff at the Frolic's Club, which was notorious for its burlesque shows, overcharged and extorted patrons once they started to leave the establishment. Even worse, the tourist noted, "police would not protect" them.[155] As this suggests, the loss of revenue remained the major motivating factor for local law enforcement, especially during the off-season.

To avoid selective harassment and municipal fees, several queer nightspots—speakeasies, bars, clubs, and revues—set up shop in Hialeah in the northwest section of the county.[156] Incorporated as an autonomous city in

1925, Hialeah grew in large part due to its famed racetrack. The races helped earn Hialeah a reputation for illicit business and lax law enforcement, before and after the state legalized pari-mutuel betting in 1931. By the mid-1930s, Hialeah's police department could not keep up with complaints—in both the "white" and "colored" sections of the city—and relied on county deputies, who were also limited in number, to assist them.[157] The county sheriff noted that Hialeah residents complained about Smith's Grill, which purportedly sold liquor without a license, housed illegal gambling, and kept "immoral women."[158] One resident reported that the owner's daughter, roughly twelve years old, "sings ... dances and does acrobatic dances" at the establishment. She also occasionally "serve[d] the drinks."[159] Fears that nightspots were corrupting youth abounded, fueled by the rape and murder of a teenage girl from Miami who aspired to enter the entertainment business. It prompted Dade County officials to launch an investigation into young people's employment in nightclubs, bars, gambling joints, and brothels (fig. 7.5).[160] By the late 1930s, Hialeah's city council raised its nightclub license fee to $2,000 a year, more than double its assessment from the year prior. It did so to discourage Kelly's Torch club, a nightspot with a queer clientele, from staying in the area.[161]

Other Prohibition-era nightspots that employed and served queers reacted to the changes caused by repeal by relocating to the city outskirts or to unincorporated parts of the county.[162] Bootleggers who had dodged such fees for years under Prohibition did not welcome the loss of profits. A Miami newspaper observed, "Under the present system ... legitimate liquor will cost about twice as much as the smuggled variety, and this because of taxes and license fees." It concluded, "All branches of the government will lose."[163] Indeed, many nightspots simply abandoned city limits. Vacationers discovered that "'jook joints' were the Florida equivalent of Northern roadhouses: dives located outside the city limits, hence beyond the reach of the metropolitan police."[164] Unincorporated Dade County offered more loosely defined zoning regulations and no mandated taxes and license fees, as well as less law enforcement jurisdiction for entrepreneurs to deal with.[165] A "dance hall" called Polly's Cage, which seems to have also catered to a queer clientele, opened in the mid-1930s in the northwest corner of the county. It sold "intoxicating drinks as usual," even though its license had been revoked. With fewer eyes on the ground than municipal police, county law enforcement relied on residents' complaints of illegality.[166] Much like San Francisco during this period, Miami's queer nightspots constituted a significant part of the city's urban economy and sex tourism. Miami, however, was even more dependent on tourism—which was, unlike San Francisco's, distinctly sea-

# WARNING!

## FROM JUVENILE COURT OF DADE COUNTY, FLORIDA

### PROTECT THE MORALS OF CHILDREN!

**YOU ARE WARNED** against contributing to juvenile delinquency or employing child performers in night clubs, theatres, or similar places, or allowing them to entertain or beg therein.

**YOU ARE WARNED** against selling intoxicating beer, wines, or liquors, to minors or employing minors in any place where such intoxicating drinks are sold!

**YOU ARE WARNED** against allowing minors to play coin "slot machines" for money, or play other gambling devices!

Section 7981 of the Compiled General Laws of Florida, 1927, provides a criminal penalty for adults encouraging or contributing to the dependency or delinquency of any minor child.

Section 5943 of the Compiled General Laws of Florida 1927 makes it a criminal offense for children under fourteen years of age to engage in theatrical performances or similar performances, or be employed in such occupations, in Florida.

Likewise Section 3684, Compiled General Laws of Florida, 1927, provides that any child under seventeen years of age found in any public place for the purpose of begging or receiving alms, or giving any public entertainment for money or other thing of value, or who accepts money therein, or is used in aid of such enterprise, is likewise a dependent child and subject to the jurisdiction of the Juvenile Court.

Likewise the same section provides that any child under seventeen years of age who frequents, visits, or is found in any disorderly house, bawdy house, or house of ill fame, or in any place where liquors, wines, intoxicants or malt liquors are sold at retail, exchanged or given away, or who patronizes, frequents, or visits, or is found in any gambling house, or is found in any place where a gambling house is operated, is a delinquent child and subject to the jurisdiction of the Juvenile Court. Also the state slot machine law, the labor law and liquor laws protect minors.

Section 5950 of the Compiled General Laws of Florida, 1927, prohibits the employment of any person under twenty-one in a place where intoxicating liquors are manufactured or sold.

Section 7696 Compiled General Laws of Florida, 1927, makes it unlawful to sell or give away any cigarettes or cigarette papers to a minor or person under 21 years of age.

Florida school laws require all children to attend school until they are 16 years of age or complete the 8th grade.

All persons, firms, and corporations are earnestly invited and requested to fully cooperate with the Juvenile Court and other law enforcement agencies in carrying out both the spirit and purpose of these wise provisions which are for the protection of minor children, in order that all children may have a fair chance to grow up under proper conditions and environment. The above laws will be strictly enforced and any and all violations will be vigorously prosecuted.

Approved:
W. H. Beckham,
Judge of the Juvenile Court,
In and For Dade County.

By PAUL M. MARTENS, Probation Officer,
Juvenile Court In and For Dade County.

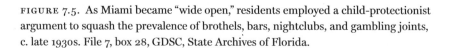

FIGURE 7.5. As Miami became "wide open," residents employed a child-protectionist argument to squash the prevalence of brothels, bars, nightclubs, and gambling joints, c. late 1930s. File 7, box 28, GDSC, State Archives of Florida.

sonal because of southern Florida's tropical climate—and had to counter-balance a healthy promotion and separation from the racialized sex tourism the Caribbean offered U.S. visitors.[167]

La Paloma was among the gay nightspots located in unincorporated Dade County. The KKK had long threatened to take action against the club in the name of the "clean thinking citizens of Dade County" because law enforcement failed to do so.[168] A few months before the Klan's raid, Miami's city commission received a letter from the local chapter of the KKK demanding an immediate solution to "the disorganization and disruption of police department personnel as evidenced by petty crime waves" and "the extraordinary amount of gambling during the … tourist season." If action was not immediately taken, the Klan maintained, "We owe this community to take over the situation ourselves and provide our own protection."[169] The raid should not have come as a surprise to law enforcement.

In addition to being a gambling den, La Paloma was a queer bar staffed and patronized by gender and sexual nonconformists. Described as "dimly lit," its atmosphere catered to those willing to push the boundaries of their gender and sexual expressions. One man recalled that La Paloma's "low-ceilinged main room presented shows filthy beyond words." There, you could find "homosexuals in evening gowns, trousered lesbians, and prostitutes." They were not just the performers, however. They were also the clientele. Queer performers "solicited customers for normal or abnormal sex practices."[170]

Unlike the ritzier joints that featured gender-bending performances near the centers of Miami and Miami Beach, outlying gay nightspots like La Paloma, staffed and frequented by working-class queers, were often open during the off-season and, possibly, year-round.[171] These seemed to be more affordable establishments. A queer club in Hialeah called Kelly's Torch Club advertised that it had no cover charge for admission and no minimum purchase. "Spend What You Like," one of its advertisements promised potential patrons. While such promises could easily be broken, they seemed successful in attracting more working-class clientele.[172] Leslie Charteris described the patrons and ambiance at one of these Miami speakeasies in his novel *The Saint in Miami*. The club emcee was a "slim-waisted creature," or pansy, whose "blond hair was beautifully waved, and he had a smudge under one eye that looked like mascara." He spoke with "an ingratiating lisp." The spot was a site of "obvious queernesses." A character observed that "some of the groups of highly made-up girls who sat at inferior tables with an air of hoping to be invited to better ones were a trifle sinewy in the arms and neck," in other words, cross-dressing men available to the highest-paying customer. Conversely, he noted that "some of the delicate-featured young men who sat apart from them were too well-developed in the chest for the breadth of their shoulders." This Miami club and gambling joint, then, also found queer women who passed as men among its clientele. That the gender-bending women and men so clearly congregated in distinct sections of the establishment suggests they were regular patrons. One character noted that this sight was all too typical of Miami after dark: "Those eccentricities were standard in the honky-tonks of Miami."[173]

Queer folk similarly patronized and were visible at the races and gambling joints connected to them. One visitor noted that the men's "powder room" at the Tropical Park racetrack had "enough male aids to beauty to make an effeminate man happy." He warned, "If you don't watch out, you can come out of there feeling like a lady, and smelling like one too." He made another subtle reference to the effeminacy he attributed to these tourist spaces when he juxtaposed the rugged trees of California to the "swishy" and "sissy-like" pines he found in Miami.[174] Irving Young, a black Miami man committed to the state asylum and deemed a "sexual pervert," had also been flagged for his excessive use of alcohol and his habitual gambling.[175] Young was likely connected to the *bolita* racket, a transnational lottery game rooted in the Cuban lottery that had been played in Miami since at least the 1920s.[176] The games were particularly popular "among the Negro population," with numbers "sold throughout the Dade Negro areas."[177] The county sheriff called *bolita* "nigger crap games."[178]

This queer-vice nexus frequently appeared in popular culture, entangled with more violent forms of criminal activity. The plot of Walter Gibson's 1940 *Crime over Miami* (written under the pen name Maxwell Grant) centered on the city's *bolita* and jewel theft racket. One of the story's villains played the "circuit as a female impersonator."[179] As this pulp novel and *The Saint in Miami* suggest, fictional detective tales with Miami as backdrop relied on queer characters for plot twists that added to the city's lure. In a 1936 crime serial titled *Murder off Miami*, gender and sexual transgression were also central to the city's criminal and underworld reputation, one particularly tailored for tourist consumption. In that fictional work, a bishop defended himself from a "public scandal" he had the "ill-fortune" of being involved in "with the troops in 1917"—heavily suggestive of the public scandals involving fairies and other "perverts" in naval institutions.[180] Similarly, *Murder Masks Miami* (1939) was full of gay subtext: hazed sailors wore mermaid costumes at sea, the murderer is thought to be a male cross-dresser, the author details the rippling muscles of his Miami protagonists, a reference is made to a pansy playwright, and a fit man notes how "an artist from Provincetown" once persuaded him to model in the nude.[181] These works, as well as their after-dark associations, proved popular and invited visitors to view Miami as a site for such queer experiences.

One of the greatest insights we can glean from these and other sources concerns the nature of "queer work" and the general labor practices of some of Miami's nightspots. As the fictional accounts above suggest, some queer performers and clientele offered sexual services at a price in these spaces. One observer likened the acts he saw in these queer spaces to what you might expect at a "Paris bagnio," or brothel. In addition to the "vile" acts they performed onstage, queers and members of the "third sex"—a term used to refer to effeminate, male-bodied "inverts" who desired men—"would take" certain patrons "to rooms behind the so-called night club for exhibitions still more degrading."[182] Queers who worked in these clubs, particularly those located on municipal outskirts, found steady work offering patrons a number of services, including special dances, performances, companionship, and sex.

Those services seem to have been less known or legible to the clubs' heterosexual clientele, which seemed awestruck by the gender and sexual transgression and general derision queers offered through "drag" performances. As Chad Heap has argued, heterosexual men took women to view these performances in large part because they served as "the perfect counterpoint to highlight their own masculinity."[183] Their masculinity was particularly sharpened through the contrast of onstage pansies and female impersonators who offered "obscene simperings and gesturings." Queer performers were described as "twisted caricatures of humanity." They challenged gender norms by lampooning the so-called naturalness of masculinity and femininity.[184] Many of these performers—some of whom were not in drag—joined "scantily clad" women in telling "smutty" stories, jokes, and songs, some of which hinted at or referenced homosexuality.[185] They played to the audience's sexual sensibilities and, according to one spectator, "gain[ed] most of their revenue from money tossed derisively [by the audience] during the public entertainment," not unlike drag performances today. While queers certainly patronized these spaces, these performances proved incredibly popular among the heterosexual slummers who comprised the bulk of "the crowds jammed" into these clubs. One man argued the only reason such nightspots were tolerated in Miami was because "people seem willing to pay for the privilege of visiting them."[186] Evidence also suggests, however, that when a club gained particular notoriety through scathing newspaper reports and perhaps police raids as a site of sexual perversion, some heterosexual audience grew anxious about their presence in such spaces. To assuage their concerns, club management emphasized the *artistic* quality of the "feminine impersonations" that proved a "highly popular diversion that the public relishes," disassociating itself from any sexual transgression that had been reported. For one queer joint, this "diversion" meant welcoming predominantly heterosexual slummers, or "the night-life crowd," to enjoy a night at "Miami's Oddest Night Club."[187]

The club stage, as well as special backstage "exhibitions," provided gender- and sexually transgressive folk a steady income source as well as a safer place to express themselves and build community. Some of the onstage entertainers were amateurs or less-seasoned performers. In most instances, it was a performer's derision of gender and sexual norms that primarily elicited audience laughter, applause, and cash, not necessarily one's singing voice or dance moves. In "dimly lighted" spaces, women in brassieres joined "males in evening gowns" and others who spoke "in high, affected tones" night after night to perform, rehearse, and presumably share their experiences and insights. Queers were increasingly grouped together as members of the "third sex." A Miami journalist noted that medical professionals believed these "so-called 'children of the moon'"—a reference to the third sex conceptualization in classical Greece—were "afflicted by nature" and should "be pitied." The law, or "policeman's clubs," could do nothing to change their "quirk."[188] Another observer identified the "known perverts" who made up the "chorus of male dancers, impersonating females" as "unfortunate, sexually-deranged people."[189] Although this commentary suggests ideas of sexual difference among the queer staffers and performers, who were increasingly described as a group of people with a distinct "quirk," reports generally emphasized their cross- or trans*gender* expressions and personas as the markers of their variance. Meanwhile, some observers held more tolerant views than others about queers' presence in the city. One claimed to not care if "the boys want to have their own 'drags' in private," for instance.[190] The evidence heavily suggests that they did, in fact, have private shows among themselves in addition to the public performances that constituted their work. In fact, some of these working-class queers lived in the same residence or, at times, near each other and their place of employment.[191]

As several reports reveal, queers who worked in these entertainment spaces were also susceptible to casual violence and harassment.[192] In addition to selective harassment from police, violence against sex workers who solicited clients at bars and clubs and in the streets would have mostly gone unreported. As we have seen, the queer, subversive, illegal, and often violent associations that appeared in fictional works had real-life equivalences. In October 1939, a "riot" took place at Kelly's Torch Club in Hialeah. Three club employees were convicted of beating three patrons in the club. A female dancer testified that the violence ensued when her colleagues defended her against the men's attempt "to strip her of her clothing."[193] A month prior, a "brawl" erupted at La Paloma's "men's washroom."[194] While queers remained vulnerable to habitual violence from police, clients, and employers, these well-known after-dark associations further invited visitors to view Miami as a site for queer, titillating experiences tempered by the voyeuristic lure of potential danger.

Overall, the relationship between these queer entertainers and staff and club managers appears to have been chiefly one of mutual convenience and benefit. For instance, in the late 1930s, a judge fined several employees of Kelly's Torch Club for "indecent exposure" as well as several men "on charges of using obscene language." While the former referred to women striptease performers, the latter included comedians of the pansy or female impersonator variety. Days later, police raided La Paloma and arrested "four men employed … to wear feminine clothes and impersonate women in songs and dances." They all pleaded guilty and had to either pay a fine of twenty-five dollars or serve "30 days on charges of vagrancy." The report suggests club management looked out for them. None of the men appeared in court and were instead represented by the club's attorney.[195] In 1935, when a newspaper condemned the presence of queers at one nightclub, the club manager wrote a letter to the editor. The letter defended both the bar and its queer "cast" by emphasizing the artistic and theatrical qualities of its "unique floor show." The queer performers were, it disputed, "some of the best talent in amusement circles," with many of the entertainers completing "successful engagements in nationally-known organizations."[196] Club managers believed queers were instrumental to their businesses and profit margins.

The case of a female impersonator named Robert Trent corroborates other evidence, however, that queers remained vulnerable to the whims of their employers and business profit margins. It seems Trent was working at La Paloma when police raided it. Unlike other performers that night who were represented by the club's attorney, Trent defended himself before the judge.[197] It is possible club management wanted to part ways with Trent, or perhaps the reverse was true. While entrepreneurs may have been fond of their employees, they were, first and foremost, driven by the profitability of the transgressive enterprise. "I'd say such places couldn't exist unless there was a laying out of silver," insisted one man.[198] Some evidence also suggests that queer performers and staffers—whether female impersonators, stage pansies, or female burlesque dancers—were also "aged out," or let go once they reached a certain age and a perceived desirability to audiences. For instance, in a multisited raid that netted over a dozen performers and staffers, the average reported age was twenty-nine. It is important to note the possibility that those arrested may have lied to law enforcement—and their employers—about their names or age, possibly as a form of resistance or to avoid further legal troubles (i.e., if they had a criminal record or were underage). The youngest told police he was twenty-three years old, while the oldest two, also both men, said they were thirty-eight.[199]Although these subversive spaces provided queers with work and a place to congregate and express themselves, queer workers seem to have been tolerated only as long as it remained profitable for club managers to keep them around.

Similarly, queers' gender- and sexually transgressive behavior often spilled into the streets, where they became vulnerable to the select harassment of law enforcement and moral crusaders. One Miami gossip column wondered in 1935 where one man "acquired that Torch Club walk," a reference to the local queer joint and likely the sashaying of one of its popular female impersonators.[200] Queers who were not in some way connected to powerful club managers, or highly valued by them as performers, could fall victim to police harassment on the streets. Those who were already most vulnerable to harassment as a result of their race, ethnicity, class, age, and (dis)ability were especially susceptible to violence and persecution. State medical records reveal, for instance, that queer working-class women and men were apprehended by police—in ways reminiscent of the state's roundup of vagrants—and sent to jails, hospitals, or insane asylums.[201]

Although Miami's queer nightlife thrived following the repeal of Prohibition, moral reformers had not ditched efforts to squash it. Despite assertions that "Klan activity declined" in Miami during the 1930s, the evidence suggests a more complicated story.[202] The KKK shifted its attention to policing the subversive spaces that popped up as a result of significant urban change. Although it never wavered in its hostility to blacks, its vision more directly converged with attacks on the vice culture—including queer entertainment and spaces—that became so visible in this decade. The Klan's 1937 raid of La Paloma was but one manifestation of this. Similarly, while the white Greater Miami Ministerial Association denied connection to the Klan by the 1940s, the association seems to have been quiet on the matter in the 1930s.[203] This suggests that their memberships may have converged. Conservative backlash also was directed against Caribbean-descended people, particularly from the Bahamas, who complicated the city's black-white binary. In 1933, "white men and negroes from Georgia" violently harassed Bahamians they believed had not been naturalized and had taken "higher wage" work away from U.S. citizens—both white and black.[204] In these ways, racism, nativism, and antivice collided in this aggressive middle-class movement.

The KKK, however, is but one manifestation of Miami's moralist vigilantism. Residents also formed the Committee of Fair Minded Citizens, a group that tasked its mostly middle-class members with identifying "gangland's crooked operation[s]" in the city. It listed the addresses of more than a dozen establishments that members believed threatened the city with immorality. While this included the notorious Ball and Chain vice joint tucked away in the area west of the city center, most places were a short walk away from Biscayne Boulevard in downtown Miami.[205] At the very least, the Committee of Fair Minded Citizens shared some basic tenets with the KKK. Two years before the raid at La Paloma, several dozen Miami residents mobilized to shut the nightspot down. One man called it a "menace" to the community's "health," particularly because "women and liquor prevail[ed]" without a proper license.[206]

While sporadic police raids occurred in Miami, the Klan's foray into La Paloma ultimately served to *strengthen* the area's liberal policy to promote tourism. Although local police officially condoned the Klan's actions, several other influential urban forces denounced it. The *Miami Herald* wrote a scathing column in which it reiterated, "Law enforcement has not been turned over to the Ku Klux Klan in Dade County."[207] Meanwhile, newspapers around the country reported the affair, which had the potential to affect the fairyland reputation that brought tourists to Miami. The *New York Times* concluded that, as a result of the raid, "the accent" for tourists seeking adventure and leisure "will be more on bathing, fishing, golf and tennis than on strip-tease dancers, private 'clubs' where anything goes and heavy-tariff gambling emporiums." The report cited the closing or taming of several "once-famous hot spots" that were now "apparently indefinitely off the list of Miami entertainment centers." This included La Paloma and other places "familiar to Northern pleasure-seekers down for the season." While the view that "tourists need not expect the hectic after-dusk amusement of the old days" reached many would-be tourists, it was far from accurate.[208] County law enforcement failed to successfully prosecute any serious charges against Youst or his nightclub. The club reopened less than two weeks after the raid.[209] Youst stayed true to his word that La Paloma would "reopen ... with spicier entertainment than ever."[210]

Havana wasn't the only city Miami boosters measured their fairyland against during these years; New York City also frequently factored into their marketing schemes. Miami's nightspot operators informed would-be tourists that while New York City turned up the heat on its queer night-life after the repeal of Prohibition, Miami boosters had further embraced the marketability of the gender and sexual transgression available at their fairyland. Upon repeal, New York's "pansy craze" faded from Greenwich Village and Times Square and relocated to Harlem. Even then, by 1937, it had run its course there, too.[211] During that time, an increasing number of Miami nightspots more prominently featured queer entertainment. Consid-ering that so many of Miami's visitors came from New York, their audiences must have frequently overlapped.[212] One observer noted that some acts at Miami Beach's Mother Kelly's seemed to be "a throwback to the Tenderloin days," a reference to New York City's entertainment and red-light district.[213] Other reviews and advertisements also described Miami's nightlife discern-ibly using the language of New York City's gay heyday. Referring to the city's nightclubs, one critic noted, "This Miami area reeks with atmosphere. It fea-tures 'Greenwich Village' type spots such as the Jazzy Ha-Ha club and the La Paloma," two queer joints.[214] Both featured "painted men" who "danced and profaned sweet songs."[215] Advertisements for Kelly's Torch Club called the nightspot "The Greenwich Village of the South" and emphasized its "Bohe-mian Atmosphere."[216] None of this was subtle. As George Chauncey has documented, it was well known that Greenwich Village "hosted the best-known gay enclave in both the city and the nation," at least before repeal. Not incidentally, the metaphor of fairyland was connected to both the Vil-lage and Harlem. As one contemporary song noted, "Fairyland's not far from Washington Square."[217] The reviewer didn't just single out Greenwich Vil-lage. He observed that Miami and Miami Beach also featured "'Broadway' style places" and "'52nd street' type rendezvous." The review again listed sev-eral popular and ritzy queer joints. For the latter, it included Mother Kelly's and a bar that catered to both queer and heterosexual clientele called the Five O'Clock Club.[218] In this way, the gay subculture so many middle-class women and men saw publicly subdued in New York—or made less visible in that city's public spaces—had actually been relocated to the nation's play-ground: Miami.[219]

In Miami, law enforcement surveilled queer nightspots like La Paloma, but to temporary or minimal effect. In one of the county's more outrageous raids, Sheriff David Coleman disguised himself as "the gay fellow" on his spree to clamp down on "female impersonators and strip teasers." While Coleman visited Kelly's Torch Club with a "hick" disguise, one of his men posed as a "gay blade in dyed hair and an open-throated sports shirt" at La Paloma. The Sheriff's Department was responding to complaints of "ob-scenity and vulgarity at night resorts." Posing as queer clients, the undercover deputies coaxed the entertainers—three women doing stripteases and ten female impersonators—to their "ringside table." They reported that "all the men but one wore women's clothing and were heavily rouged."[220]

These arrests are revealing for several reasons. The report indicates that Coleman and his deputies visited the clubs more than once to see if objections were "justified." In voyeuristic fashion, Coleman concluded they were. He and his men had a great familiarity with queer culture. Their disguise also suggests they understood that tourists and other transients passed through the club, or that the performers would expect to regularly see new faces there. When asked how he fooled the club owners and performers with his disguise, Coleman laughed and coyly responded, "That's my secret." He and his deputies found the acts to be derisive forms of entertainment that reflected the area's suspension of reality, notwithstanding the fact that they received "'many complaints from reputable citizens.'"[221] The spectacle of these theatrically orchestrated raids—resplendent with costumes and dramatic reveals—made the raids seem like part of an act, an exhilarating performance for audiences who rarely got arrested in the process.[222] Several years later, for instance, a "heavy-set cop who ... had the hots for" a female impersonator who worked at one of the more respectable revues escorted the cross-gender entertainer to the annual policeman's ball in a patrol wagon. The officer blared the sirens en route to the event, adding further to the spectacle.[223]

Indeed, despite sporadic raids, Youst and others continued to offer queer and risqué entertainment for tourists and locals. Law enforcement occasionally raided La Paloma in response to public nuisance charges. Following a 1939 raid, a waiter, possibly an arrested queer employee, uttered, "Although the show is pretty flat at present, we expect to reopen next week as soon as the heat is off."[224] Other entertainers interpreted the raids as "business as usual."[225] These raids represented a veiled attempt to placate conservative residents, but by no means did police seek to permanently eradicate such nighttime offerings.

The evidence is clear: police upheld a laxer attitude during winter months, when most tourists visited Miami. All reported raids on queer joints in 1939 were conducted during the tourist off-season. That is why a report referred to one raid as "belated."[226] By the early 1940s, this had become national knowledge. "Normally," police raided these spaces, bookie and queer joints alike, "on an average of about once a month and after paying a fine, [the targets were allowed to] return to business at the old stand." By March, police conducted what one newspaper referred to as "Miami's seasonal 'face washing,'" wherein at least the veneer of respectability would reign for a few months before the start of the new tourist season would once again demand more transgression for tourist consumption.[227] The evidence also reveals club managers and law enforcement often played a coy game of cat and mouse, wherein nightspots under the heat tamed the shows just long enough for police attention to wane. Inevitably, they reintroduced their most risqué acts—or, as one observer called it, "commercializing the abnormal"—for tourists.[228] Law enforcement officials indulged conservative residents' complaints from time to time, but only temporarily and without any long-term results. Indeed, fully assuaging moralists had its limits, too, lest we forget Florida's ambitious plans to continue expanding the tourist season until it became a year-round affair. Acting on behalf of powerful politicians and investors who believed a wide-open policy was necessary to keep Miami profitable, police generally did not inhibit what vacationers had come to expect from fairyland.

A major consequence of this seasonal, tourist-conscious law enforcement appears to have been the mainstreaming of queer performances on the stage, particularly female and, to a much smaller extent, male impersonations. This is evident in the "Hollywood" or "high-class" productions that catered to tourists with more money to spend. Many were also white middle-class establishments like Mother Kelly's. Others were more working-class spaces that catered to queer crowds, particularly those who sought homosexual sex. One such bar, which reinvented itself many times throughout its history, was Tobacco Road in the Brickell downtown district. By the late 1930s or early 1940s, it catered to queer clientele with "obscene shows" that included "male strip tease" acts.[229] Rae Bourbon, the transgender pioneer whose female impersonations and comedic acts proved incredibly popular, opened Miami's winter season in 1941 with an eight-week gig at Tobacco Road.[230] Tamer queer performances more definitively entered Miami's mainstream and heterosexual nighttime repertoire—both in its black and white neighborhoods.

Colored Town became a black cultural and entertainment center by the 1930s that thousands of black tourists—as well as white slummers—visited.[231] Colored Town had long been seen as a site for illicit sex, vice, and the social taboo. Racist urban design helped ensure that crime-ridden slums and ghettos predominated.[232] These efforts notwithstanding, many looked to Colored Town as the Harlem of the South, or "Little Harlem," in reference to the vibrant and often queer nightlife of Manhattan's historic black neighborhood.[233] Down on northwest Second Avenue, where the Lyric Theater was located, visitors found countless shops, theaters, clubs, and people. Business thrived, even if only for the benefit of a select few. Nightspots like the Rockland Palace, the Cotton Club, and the Harlem Square Club featured risqué entertainment that often rivaled that of New York.[234] Since blacks could not enter white spaces except as workers, popular entertainers of the jazz and blues era brought massive black and white audiences to Colored Town. This included Ella Fitzgerald, Cab Calloway, Louis Armstrong, Sammy Davis Jr., and Billie Holiday. Several queer entertainers, such as Josephine Baker, also performed there. In fact, in 1936 Baker sang a haunting and modified version of "Moon over Miami" in French, "Nuits de Miami." Her version elevates Miami's romanticism and sexual possibilities. She referred to Miami as a "troublant paradis," or a thrilling paradise.[235] Indeed, sex, *bolita*, and other vices were readily available on most street corners. The evidence reveals that female impersonations were popular there as well. The oversized Calypso Club, near Twentieth Street and Third Avenue, featured a female impersonator called Princess Carlotta. "To go in there and see him in his fabulous gowns ... was really something," recalled one black resident.[236]

Nothing better represents Miami's popularization of queer culture—or, rather, queer culture made more palatable for heterosexual audiences— than the success of the Jewel Box Revue. Today, the "Femme-Mimics" revue is best remembered as a pioneering show that traveled all over the United States and even parts of Mexico and Canada. Unlike other shows, it placed female impersonation—and, to a smaller extent, male impersonation—at center stage and included performers of black, Latino, and indigenous descent. Miami's liberal policy catering to tourists and prioritizing high profits facilitated the revue's success. As with many of the city's entertainment offerings, northern transplants created the Jewel Box. New Yorkers Danny Brown and Doc Brenner were male lovers and business partners for at least four decades.[237] Unlike their massive cast of talent, they did not cross-dress for the revue. Perhaps this was to maintain a respectable façade for outsiders, considering that their audiences were primarily heterosexual. Doc, who was seven years Danny's senior, sang and participated in some acts as a man, sometimes wearing no more than revealing briefs. Danny was rugged and muscular and served as the show's emcee. His appearance and charisma made him particularly popular among women in the audience, which proved critical to the show's emphasis that it was a clean and moral (i.e., nonhomosexual) production.[238] As one critic noted, "The 'girls' are perfect gentlemen."[239]

Danny and Doc maintained that female impersonation was nothing more than "an old mannish custom," a marketing strategy used to attract mainstream, heterosexual audiences in Miami and elsewhere. They separated themselves from sexual deviancy by linking female impersonations to

Elizabethan theater. The revue, they stressed, "maintained the art in its true and original sense."[240] The *Miami Sun* agreed: "The production numbers are presented with more skill than this town has seen in a long time."[241] The revue recalled the revival of female impersonation popularized by Julian Eltinge throughout the country at the turn of the century, and by Karl Denton in Miami in the 1920s. It had been over a decade since Miami audiences were treated to high-class femme mimics, several critics believed. In part, this was because it had become more challenging to stage "clean" gender-transgressive shows that audiences wouldn't necessarily associate with the increasingly discernible homosexual.

While the Jewel Box Revue was cognizant of this and tailored most of its acts to heterosexual audience's sensibilities, queers utilized the club to express themselves, find sexual partners, build community, and make a living. Although souvenir programs for the revue note that the production did not formally exist until 1939, Danny and Doc had been connected to the city's queer nightlife for at least a few years before then.[242] A "Jewel Box" cocktail lounge operated at the Embassy Hotel, located on 30th and Collins Avenue in Miami Beach, by December 1936.[243] It started as a bar that catered to those who transgressed gender and sexual norms and who were increasingly understood as "gay."[244] Although the Jewel Box changed locations, by early 1946, Danny and Doc had opened up their own space, Club Jewel Box, on the Miami side of the Venetian Causeway.[245] By then, although queers continued to attend shows, "it was straight audiences that supported the troupe."[246]

The Jewel Box Revue remained a queer institution in Miami, however. Lesbians, gays, as well as sexually fluid and gender-ambiguous people made up the bulk of the staff. One man recalled that the "waitresses were lesbians" and that female impersonators flirted and sought out homosexual flings or relationships.[247] Miami's Jewel Box, with all of its incarnations, also became a respectable place for queers—performers, visitors, and locals alike—to congregate and socialize. In this "prepolitical" moment in which queer folk developed a cultural politics of resistance and community-building, the Jewel Box proved fiercely committed to promoting queerness across generational, gender, sexual, racial, ethnic, and class lines.[248] Take the case of Stormé DeLarverié, a U.S. African American male impersonator and butch lesbian who worked with the Jewel Box Revue in the 1950s and 1960s. She later played an instrumental role in the 1969 Stonewall rebellion that helped spark the gay liberation movement in the United States. The Jewel Box Revue mobilized people, built community, combated isolation, and provided a social and political platform for many queers.[249]

The Jewel Box Revue's success and operation strategy is also representative of fairyland's *temporary* suspension of reality, or Miami's liberal policy that generally tolerated queer entertainment during tourist season. The business replicated the successful formula urban boosters used to sell fairyland. The revue followed the city's tourist season and complied with Miami's "seasonal 'face washing'" policy. It operated out of its Miami club during the winter months, when the city welcomed thousands of tourists, and went on tour during the summer and warmer months, when tourism was slower.[250] The Jewel Box was not alone. The majority of these posh nightspots, including Mother Kelly's and the Five O'Clock Club, generally "remained 'dark'" until the first tourist tide in November.[251] Many club operators and employees left Miami once tourist season ended, as profit potential waned and law enforcement's tolerance for transgression reached its limit. Queers connected to the Jewel Box, for instance, traveled to cities and towns across the nation and beyond. The revue's tours functioned as free marketing for the city's fairyland. Nearly all advertisements for its shows touted that the show came direct from Miami, Florida. One noted that the "lively extravaganza is the Miami group that packed them in at its own Florida club last winter." In this way, the revue brought fairyland to the masses, which got a taste of the queerness Miami had to offer. The show "that was such a sensation in Miami," hyped one review, "is in full swish and sway."[252] It seems appropriate that such an important U.S. American queer institution began in Miami.

Similarly, although the Jewel Box seemed particularly progressive in hiring a diverse cast and staff and, at some venues, in hosting a racially integrated audience, it also capitalized on the cast's real or imagined cultural backgrounds. Much like Miami boosters who promoted fairyland by emphasizing the city's black and brown subservience and its "primitive" past, the revue fetishized the "exotic."[253] Its shows included acts titled "Harlem Square," "A Bit of Old Mexico," "From Spain to You," "Straight Out of the Arabian Nights," "Calypso Time," and "A Fantasy of Satan." Many of these performances recalled the exoticism of the Caribbean, including fantasies of the sensual "Latin lover" and the barbarity of Haitian vodou, which had long helped market Miami as fairyland.[254] Famed pianist and arranger Joe Harnell recalled a "brooding Cuban" named Carlos who followed him around "with love-struck, soulful, cow eyes" at the Miami club. According to Harnell, Carlos tried to convince him to be a "switch-hitter," or sexually interested in both women and men. In his recollection, Harnell clearly portrayed Carlos as an overly sexual, flirtatious, effeminate, and hot-headed gay Cuban who spoke "in a heavy Spanish accent." His very presence in the club added to its allure, a human prop among the spectacle that made the Jewel Box—and fairyland more generally—so entertaining and popular.[255]

Although the Jewel Box Revue ran into some minor trouble with the law from time to time, local police and lawmakers generally condoned and even patronized the queer nightspots marketed in the tourist-dependent fairyland. Jackie Johnson, an early Jewel Box star who had been performing in Miami since the 1920s and attended the 1948 policeman's ball as an officer's date, recalled how "many big shots" frequented the club. This included local commissioners who sometimes asked to be taken backstage to meet the "ladies."[256] Danny and Doc had minor hiccups with law enforcement in the late 1940s over liquor licenses and building permits.[257] Police raided their establishment—as well as several other city queer nightspots—on suspicion of illegal gambling, liquor violations, and immorality. These raids occurred just as Miami's winter season closed, or, as one source called it, "closing time." By mid-March, or when "the money crowd leaves," such operations had to sanitize their acts or board up until the next tourist season.[258]

WHILE SOME MIAMI LAW enforcement, much like the conservative vigilante groups and residents who fought against the city's urban upheavals, did not approve of queer entertainment, the fairyland marketed its "wide-open" and liberal attitude to further promote its main industry: tourism. This industry was defined by its suspension of conservative values and morality. It operated on the transgression of gender and sexual norms, which permitted many of the city's queer residents a space to exist and thrive, even if seasonally or fleetingly. While cities like New York tightened up on their queer culture after the repeal of Prohibition, the reverse occurred in Miami. In part to compete with the Caribbean's queer racialized offerings, made readily available through the tentacles of U.S. imperialism, Miami boosters, lawmakers, and police adopted a liberal moral code during its ever-expanding tourist season. This occurred much to the chagrin of the city's conservative and religious forces that sought to curb, but could not eradicate, Miami's growing queer visibility. Over the years, queers had become a central feature in making Miami a fairyland.

# EPILOGUE

e don't want [sexual] perverts to set up housekeeping in this county," claimed Dade County Sheriff Thomas J. Kelly in 1954. "We want them to know that they're not welcome."[1] By the 1950s, Kelly's perspective had become the norm among Miami's powerbrokers. What happened to Miami's visible queer culture in the post–World War II period? Surely, queers—especially those marked distinctly suspect because of their race, ethnicity, class, age, or (dis)ability—had been harassed by Miami law enforcement in previous decades. Their presence was often tolerated, however, and understood as a necessary feature in the promotion of the tourist-dependent fairyland. Miami's liberal policy remained in place—albeit with some post-tourist-season or arbitrary crackdowns and raids—until the late 1940s. The early Cold War era brought about massive changes that radically altered the lives and experiences of the city's gender and sexual renegades.

Uncovering the fate of several queer establishments helps explain this shifting tide, beginning with the downfall of La Paloma. Although club operator Al Youst stayed true to his word and made the entertainment there even racier after the Ku Klux Klan's 1937 raid, he soon ran into trouble with the *federal* government. By 1941, Youst had been convicted on charges pertaining to the transportation of five young women from Chattanooga to "perform" at La Paloma and for other "immoral purposes." The feds got involved because the women's travel to Florida violated white slavery laws across state lines. The prosecutor told the jury: "For a long time decency, morals and justice have taken a beating in this section of the State.... Vice, corruption and debauchery have ridden roughshod over all who tried to stop them, and have made this community the talk of the nation." Conversely, Youst's attorney argued such a position was hypocritical and really the product of local graft. "If they're going to clean up Miami why is this the only club they pick on? Is it because Al Youst wouldn't turn rat and save himself by giving false testimony against the sheriff?"[2] Youst's defense team claimed the crackdown came about when the club owner refused to testify against local police, who were purported to have accepted bribes in exchange for permitting continued operation.

At least in part, both arguments rested on the premise that local law enforcement permitted clubs like La Paloma—which served as a gay bar, site for prostitution, and gambling den—to operate relatively undisturbed in the city through a pay-to-play system. The club closed down after Youst's arrest. In addition, the following year, Fred Pine—who a few years before had served as the Dade County solicitor and, in a strange turn of events, later became Youst's attorney—was convicted on similar charges. Witnesses testified he had a financial stake in the club. One "girl performer" even claimed Pine threatened her and other performers, telling them that if they quit he would use his influence to persuade local police to "arrest them on vagrancy charges."[3]

The fates of two other queer spots similarly reveal this change in policy in the late 1940s. Miami Beach's bar and club Mother Kelly's closed in 1947, after fifteen years in business. The "hermaphroditic" man known as Mother Kelly had run the establishment all that time. As one reviewer observed, "Fifteen years is a long time to operate a bar and restaurant in a get-rich-quick, fly-by-night town where businesses change hands overnight."[4] Also in 1947, the nearby Trinity Episcopal Church and a major hotel owner sued the City of Miami to shut down the Club Jewel Box.[5] By then, lovers Danny and Doc had operated the gender-bending extravaganza in its standalone site on the Venetian Causeway for a little over a year. While these conservative forces did not immediately succeed, they netted a major win in August 1950 in "their fight to keep from having a nightclub as their permanent neighbor." In what one newspaper described as a "stormy session," Miami's planning board voted unanimously to refuse Danny and Doc's request for the zoning permits needed to keep operating the club in that location. "'The entrance to the causeway at the Miami end is dignified and attractive—with the exception of that one spot,'" argued a member of the planning board. Many local residents and businesses turned up to support denying the Jewel Box the zoning license. Some "pointed out that the nightclub advertises its 'female impersonators' and is an eyesore."[6] Without the proper zoning license, it appears the club was forced to close the following summer.[7] Although the Jewel Box lived on until 1975 through its extensive tours around North America, time gradually eclipsed its Miami origins.[8]

As this suggests, Miami's economy had begun to significantly change by the 1940s. The area usually received a flood of snowbirds in December. In 1941, however, Japan's bombing of Pearl Harbor helped alter Miami's local economy. The U.S. military leased Miami and Miami Beach hotels as a cheaper and quicker housing solution than building new basic training facilities. By late 1942, 342 hotels in the area had been converted for this purpose.[9] The war created new social and economic opportunities for women and men to transgress gender and sexual norms in the city. Miami was among the war-boom U.S. cities that housed a growing community of gender and sexual nonconformists, many of whom would increasingly be understood as lesbians and gays. Many who came to Miami for wartime efforts, both women and men, later returned and sought to settle permanently there. For example, as Allan Bérubé has argued, "Once they left the constraints of family life and watchful neighbors, many recruits were surprised to find that military service gave them opportunities to begin a 'coming-out' process."[10]

Meanwhile, a number of other contemporary factors made Miami's economy less dependent on tourism. Although the city was the least industrialized metropolitan area in the country before World War II, the following decades witnessed gradual increases in smaller-scale manufacturing. A fashion trendsetter by the mid-1920s, Miami had established a sizable garment industry by the early 1940s. As Melanie Shell-Weiss has observed, "by 1943, only New York and Los Angeles produced more apparel than Miami."[11] Miami's increased manufacturing included needle trades, food processing, and furniture and fixtures. Even then, by the late 1950s, factories in the city employed only roughly 13 percent of the labor force. These industries grew in the 1960s and 1970s as the city catered more aggressively to foreign markets. Construction work increased too, to accommodate the area's population growth.[12] The City of Miami and the largest of its surrounding municipalities—Miami Beach, Coral Gables, North Miami, and Hialeah—more than doubled in size from 1940 to 1960, standing at 214,409 in 1940, 345,805 in 1950, and 485,306 in 1960.[13] Even though many of the developing industries, including aviation and textiles, remained heavily connected to tourism, these changes helped chip away at the city's economic dependence on tourists.

With such changes in Miami's economy, the entrenched "liberal policy" seemed less necessary (fig. E.1). Conservative forces had long fought against the idea that the city's tourist-dependent economy mandated a loose moral code that permitted queer clubs to operate. A growing tension in the late 1940s and early 1950s, however, brought the city's queer culture under attack like never before. As the Jewel Box and La Paloma cases make particularly clear, local politicians, law enforcement, and even tourist-dependent entrepreneurs now joined conservative forces' campaign against Miami's thriving and visible queer culture. That the newspaper described the Miami planning board's meeting as a "stormy session" suggests no consensus had yet been reached concerning the full abandonment of the area's liberal policy. But the tide was shifting. This can largely be attributed to the growing visibility of those who increasingly understood themselves as having particular identities and were connected to communities and networks more discernibly defined by their gender expressions and sexual desires.[14] By the 1950s, Miami politi-

FIGURE E.1. By the early 1950s, tensions were again on the rise among moralist conservatives who challenged the arguments made by many small business owners, fly-by-night investors, mafiosi, and politicians that Dade County "must have a liberal policy to attract tourists." As Miami celebrated "record season[s]," reformers grew angry and frustrated by those who maintained that lax morals were necessary to attract tourists and capital to the city. *Miami Daily News*, January 28, 1951. Cartoon by Anne Briardy Mergen. 1979-216-86, HistoryMiami Museum, Miami, FL.

cians, judges, and law enforcement officials fought over who was the toughest on "sexual perverts" and their growing "colonies" throughout the city.[15]

Another case illuminates this shift. In 1952, a fifteen-year-old boy entered an older man's home in El Portal, in the northeast section of Miami, and shot him "between the eyes." The deceased was a sixty-seven-year-old man described by newspapers as a "wealthy recluse" and a "wealthy eccentric" living in an "unfinished mansion."[16] The dead man was found wearing only shorts, and the teenager had driven off in the deceased's Cadillac. According to reports, the teenager confessed to the murder and claimed the older man had asked him "to do 'jobs'" for him. While this included being asked "to steal and hold up places," the boy maintained he had also been asked to "bring boys to his [the older man's] house." The teenager alleged he had been "victimized by a sex pervert."[17] Whether or not the boy's claims were true, sex clearly framed this murder case.

While the description of the deceased parallels that of men in Miami like Paul Chalfin and Alden Freeman a few decades prior—he was wealthy, unmarried, extravagant, feminine, and artistic—something had changed by the 1950s. The newspapers were sure to mention that the older man was an art and antique collector, or even a hoarder, who displayed nude photos and art throughout his dark home.[18] This information seemed to corroborate that he was, in fact, homosexual. Records show that he had lived there since at least 1932 and that he worked in Miami real estate in the 1940s.[19] It is also certain that he lived with only his black servant, roughly ten years his junior and similarly unmarried, for several years prior to his murder.[20] While we cannot be sure what the deceased man did with men or boys in that residence in the two decades he lived there, and whether any such acts were consensual or coercive, the evidence heavily suggests that his presence in the city went unnoticed or uncontested prior to the 1950s. Indeed, a resuscitated moral panic that particularly associated homosexuality with murder, rape, and pedophilia informed the treatment of those who would, in later years, largely come to see themselves as lesbian, gay, bisexual, and transgender people.[21]

Although it seems quite possible that others knew of the older man's same-sex desires in the 1930s or 1940s, it was only in the midst of an intensely conservative movement during the early Cold War of the 1950s that city residents came to worry about him as a "sex pervert." In that decade's "lavender scare," it was not uncommon for young boys to rob and beat up, or "roll," older men and then successfully claim that their acts were necessary to repel the "sex pervert."[22] It appears that in those two decades, the older man likely went from engaging in homosexual sex in the city to being read as a "pervert" whose sexual inclinations were understood as a threat to family order, decency, and even national security.

In the midst of the Cold War attack on suspected "communists," the federal government joined state and local officials throughout the country in a campaign to purge lesbians and gays altogether but especially from positions of power and influence. As David K. Johnson has shown, communists and homosexuals were both viewed as "subversive" and therefore potential "security risks" to the United States. Much like the red-baiting used to suppress different opinions or beliefs, a new discourse emerged wherein politicians and other public officials perceived as "soft" on homosexuality were read as anti-American and not tough enough on the "threat" posed by domestic and foreign communist forces.[23]

One such example of this is the case of a Miami transplant, George Smathers, a staunch anticommunist Democrat who served as a U.S. senator from Florida for nearly twenty years. Before that, he was assistant U.S. attorney for Florida's southern district. In fact, he prosecuted Youst's federal case, which helped catapult his public career.[24] Smathers ran a heated primary campaign for the Senate seat in 1950 that smeared and red-baited his incumbent opponent, Claude Pepper, the New Dealer who became known as "Red Pepper."[25] During his campaign, several periodicals erroneously claimed Smathers delivered a speech to a "backwoods audience" in Florida that served this purpose. Although several versions were printed, *Time* magazine captured the essence of the words wrongly attributed to Smathers: "Are you aware that Claude Pepper is known all over Washington as a shameless extrovert? Not only that, but this man is reliably reported to practice nepotism with his sister-in-law, and he has a sister who was once a thespian in wicked New York. Worst of all, it is an established fact that Mr. Pepper before his marriage habitually practiced celibacy." While it appears he never uttered these words and that it was, instead, a journalistic hoax, it is significant to note how many reputable periodicals reprinted it as truth—or at least reproduced the logic behind it. The media believed a "backwoods" Florida crowd may not exactly know the meanings of suspicious-sounding words like "extrovert," "nepotism," "thespian," and "celibacy"—possibly confusing them with words such as pervert, incest, lesbian, and deviancy. What's more, they framed these words in ways that particularly invited readers to understand a narrative in which Smathers was accusing Pepper of being both sexually deviant and a communist. Pepper was also depicted as "shameless," a feminine bachelor, and connected to "wicked New York." These phrases had taken new meaning in the midst of the lavender scare.[26]

Meanwhile, as Youst's federal case anticipated, by 1950 the federal government more aggressively joined the fight to rid Miami of its corruption and graft. One man recalled how the "best night-club period Miami knew came between the end of Prohibition and the death of unrestricted play at dice and roulette."[27] The highly publicized campaign by Senator Estes Kefauver of Tennessee to expose and disband organized crime challenged Miami's reputation as the nation's vice capital. From 1950 to 1951, Senator Kefauver headed the Senate's Special Committee to Investigate Organized Crime in Interstate Commerce. The media televised much of the Kefauver hearings and thereby advertised Miami's vice culture to a consumer nation equipped with new TVs. The committee concluded that Miami's illicit gambling and bookmaking circles, particularly the S. and G. Investment Company (known as the "S&G boys"), had direct connections to notorious syndicates along the Northeast and in Chicago, including Al Capone's "mob."[28] When Capone died in 1947, his enterprise continued in the city.[29] Florida governor Fuller Warren also came under fire following accusations that he had accepted dirty contributions and coddled the Mafia. Upset that gambling laws were being enforced, he stated, "Do you think the winter customers will flock here as usual if the element of chance is missing?"[30] It became clear that corruption was widespread. The committee discovered that tourist dollars had long trumped the law in Miami. As Kefauver noted,

Miami had indeed become a "Polluted Playground."[31] The fairyland had run amok and politicians and residents alike would now call for restored order.

Several other major urban changes occurred during these years that help explain the change in policy. Despite the area's population increase, establishing a municipality in Florida required very few people. Prior to 1949, Florida law permitted areas with 25 or more freeholding, registered voters to form an autonomous municipality. Nonmunicipal areas with more than 25 and fewer than 300 people voting in favor of a charter would be designated a town. Those with more than 300 votes would be designated cities.[32] This remained a critical feature in helping populate the frontier. Several new municipalities, including Miami Beach (1915), Coral Gables (1925), Opa-Locka (1926), Miami Shores (1931), El Portal (1937), Sweetwater (1941), and Medley (1949), joined the constellation of more than two dozen distinct municipalities that made up Dade County. In 1949, however, the Florida legislature passed a law prohibiting new municipalities.[33]

Zoning laws had long been a thorn in the side of Miami's queer joints. This was clear in the queer establishment migration to unincorporated Dade County in the 1930s. Youst opened La Paloma in such a space, free from the codes and taxes of municipalities. Note too the trouble Danny and Doc had in the late 1940s, part of which originated because the city had zoned the west end of the Venetian Causeway, where Club Jewel Box was located, for hotels and apartment buildings. In order to open the club, Danny and Doc first secured what is known as a "variance permit," which functioned as an amendment or supplement to existing zoning laws. The laws concerning variance permits in Miami, which had already proven most effective in maintaining racial segregation, changed in 1941: "No variance permit shall be issued ... except in instances where practical difficulties and unnecessary hardship shall be incurred by the applicant if said permit were refused."[34] Danny and Doc regularly had to apply for an exception. By 1950, they petitioned for a "permanent variance." Under mounting pressure from residents and businesses, the planning board rejected their zoning appeal and the club soon closed.[35]

Many entrepreneurs exploited Florida's lax incorporation laws, just as pioneer-developers had long taken advantage of these codes. After all, forming a municipality permitted wealthy investors "all the powers of taxation and regulation granted by the state to municipal corporations." In this way, their business operations gained legal standing under state law. Since early cities like Miami predominantly fattened the pockets of industrial capitalists from the Northeast and Midwest, tax money entering city coffers essentially went right back to funding these developers' industries.[36] By the 1940s, these exploitative tactics converged with the city's corruption and graft. In the summer of 1948, it became clear that "'liquor interests' had sponsored the incorporation" of three new towns (scarcely populated areas with fewer than 300 votes in favor of incorporation) as a means to "open the way for new liquor licenses." Almost overnight, entrepreneurs created the towns of "Gladeview," "Westgate," and "Northwest Miami." The third housed or was near some of Miami's raunchiest queer nightspots. Florida's state beverage commission discovered that the attorney representing all three towns "had been paid $5,000 to obtain a liquor license" for a particular tavern owner. He started an illegal business of securing liquor licenses, which were increasingly difficult to get in the municipalities, to those able to pay his "fee."[37] By November 1948, the South Florida Liquor Board filed a lawsuit to crack down on a corrupt system that issued more liquor licenses than were permitted by law. The complaint also noted that several establishments with proper liquor licenses were, in reality, gambling joints featuring "lewd, lascivious and obscene shows," or queer establishments.[38] Something had to change, particularly because city coffers were not receiving their share of the profits.

Even more critical was the way so-called urban renewal programs forever changed Colored Town's thriving cultural and business epicenter. Miami's segregated black neighborhoods had historically been designed in ways that profited white investors, and they often shared spaces with the city's red-light district. This is certainly suggested by the contested incorporation of the three new towns noted above. White vice entrepreneurs increasingly encroached on black, immigrant, and working-class spaces on the fringes of Miami proper, particularly its northwest district. Several factors motivated the bulldozing of Miami's "blighted" Colored Town. Most of the community's black inhabitants lived in shacks and slums, and in the mid-1930s New Deal housing programs gave urban planners an opportunity to consolidate their plans to relocate these communities farther northwest. Predominantly white businesses and civic boosters sought to expand Miami's downtown, which proved an effective plan to redistrict the city's black communities out of Colored Town. New Deal housing agencies contributed to this process by pricing black communities out of the neighborhood and implementing "redlining" policies that denied them mortgage loans. This was more complex than targeted racism-for-profit. It was also a manifestation of "black liberalism" that found black middle-class investors inadvertently propping up Jim Crow through the cultural politics of property rights and consumerism.[39]

Entire black neighborhoods were bulldozed to make room for the new interstate highway. Shortly after the 1937 completion of a black public housing project called Liberty Square, the area that became known as Liberty City expanded and became Miami's second black ghetto. It housed many of the residents forced to leave Colored Town, or today's Overtown. This occurred quite rapidly after the federal interstate program routed Interstate 95 right through the heart of Colored Town.[40] Demolition in Miami's Central Negro District began in 1965, even though the building of new housing did not start for another four years.[41]

Miami's antislum and black dislocation campaign was frequently articulated as an effort to "clean up" the neighborhood, including its queer and transgressive cultures and economies. Into the 1950s, efforts to build black public housing—particularly in the new Liberty City projects—found even well-intentioned advocates claiming it would rid the neighborhood of immorality, crime, disease, and juvenile delinquency (fig. E.2). In the end, nightspots like the Rockland Palace, Cotton Club, and Harlem Square Club—once the centerpiece of Little Broadway—shut down. Vacant lots and parking lots stood in their place.[42]

That these construction projects are indicative of Miami's growing diversified economy, which made Miami less dependent on a tourism industry that had long encouraged the transgression of gender and sexual norms, by no means suggests that queer folks and communities disappeared. Although no longer promoted or condoned by local officials, queers became more creative and bold in their use of public and private space. Throughout the 1950s, police charged many black residents and travelers with committing lewd and lascivious acts in Colored Town. These cases were heard in the all-black Negro Municipal Court, which was established in 1950. For instance, in 1951, two young women faced charges after being found in the "nude, and having [an] unnatural relationship."[43] The following year, Essie Mae Calloway—described as "a man, in spite of the feminine name"—was arrested after being found naked in a car and "in a compromising position" with a man. A report noted Calloway was "an obvious homosexual."[44] While it may be tempting to interpret this information as a police crackdown, it also reveals queer resistance to cleanup campaigns of the era and their continued presence in the city.

Despite such forms of everyday resistance, several conservative forces in Miami, along with the city's relatively small and transient population, helped delay a more formalized and concerted *local* political movement for gender- and sexual-transgressive people in the city until the 1970s. Miami was not the major city we think of today. In 1960, when New York, Chicago, Los Angeles, Philadelphia, and Detroit were the five most populous urban cities in the United States, Miami ranked *forty-forth*—just ahead of Akron,

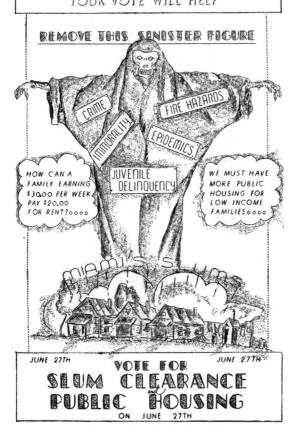

FIGURE E.2.
Ominous flyer imploring Miami residents to vote in favor of seeking federal funds to clear slums and build low-cost housing for blacks. Voters approved the measure in a referendum held on June 27, 1950. Slum clearance flyer, Elizabeth Virrick Papers, file 10, box 15, HistoryMiami Museum, Miami, FL.

Ohio. Similarly, in the South a number of cities had larger populations than Miami, including Houston (the 7th-largest U.S. city), Dallas (14th), New Orleans (15th), San Antonio (17th), Memphis (22nd), Atlanta (24th), Louisville (31st), and Birmingham (36th). While Miami's ranking increased if one included its surrounding municipalities in Dade County, its population still paled in comparison to most of these cities.[45] Homophile organizing simply did not take form in Miami the way it did in some major cities primarily, but by no means exclusively, in California and the Northeast during the 1950s and 1960s[46] In many ways, Miami's queer activism during these years generally followed that in the rest of the South in largely challenging violence and discrimination through other modes of resistance outside of traditional political organizing or less guided by an emerging sexual identity politics. While there were small and short-lived homophile organizations in Louisiana, Texas, and Mississippi, Miami particularly stood out for housing the first state-chartered homosexual organization in the South dedicated to social and political reform.[47] In 1964, a man named Richard Inman founded the Atheneum Society of America in Miami. Despite Inman's committed efforts and labor, the organization and its offshoots disbanded within five years with relatively little success in effecting change in Miami or recruiting and sustaining a membership base.[48] The transient nature of Miami's population did not help. Altogether, the area's rapid growth, fluctuating markets, seasonal tourism and entertainment economies, part-time and "snowbird" residents, international labor migration patterns, and status as a site of political refuge (often intended to be temporary), particularly from the Caribbean and Latin America, created obstacles that made it difficult for such a local movement to gain momentum.

Despite significant changes to Miami's socioeconomic and cultural landscape, tourism remained a central feature in defining the lives and experiences of people living or passing through the area. One foreign couple's honeymoon vacation to Miami seems, in many ways, reflective of the era's tourist trade, albeit for those of greater means. The couple brought quite a lot of money with them from their home country and spent nearly two weeks in one of Miami Beach's finest hotels, no doubt indulging in the area's sunny days and flashy nights. From Miami, the honeymooners later visited New York City. Miami was not only the centerpiece of their itinerary but also a hub for other destinations.[49]

We might read this as a typical vacation for a moneyed foreign couple, until we read the name of the groom: Fidel Castro. In 1948, the twenty-two-year-old brought his bride, Mirta Díaz Balart, to the area, joining the thousands of Cubans who visited southern Florida after World War II. In 1959, he led the Cuban Revolution that ousted Fulgencio Batista, who had come to power yet again in Cuba following a military coup seven years before.[50]

Cuban revolutionaries sought to put an end to the corrupt system that favored the rich and foreign investors, particularly U.S. property owners on the island, and also to purge the vice, corruption, and sexual exploitation U.S. Americans had grown to expect from the island. In fact, the U.S. government's early-1950s anticrime crusade had further pushed southern Florida's illegal gambling offshore to the Caribbean.[51] In a scathing 1952 report titled *Miami after Dark*, a writer explained that, in Miami, "no longer can you stroll into a magnificent club and gamble as openly as though you were in Havana or Ciudad Trujillo," then the name of the capital of the Dominican Republic. The writer maintained that despite the new city limitations on gambling, "legalized gambling is in operation from the beginning of November until June. For players dissatisfied with this," he explained, "there is always the opportunity to take an hour's flight to Havana, where gambling of all kinds is wide open."[52] The onset of the 1959 revolution muted many of Miami boosters' former pleas to maintain a lax moral code to compete with Havana.

The Cuban Revolution radically altered Miami's demographics, culture, and general landscape, including the area's sexual politics. Over the decades, hundreds of thousands of Cubans fled the island and settled in Miami. Like before, their gender expressions and sexual practices altered the city's understandings of what constituted normative or deviant behavior. Many of these exiles were labeled good "Cold Warriors" opposed to Castro's regime and the spread of communism.[53] In this way, the Cubans' presence in Miami added textured transnational meanings to the era's red and lavender scares. By the 1970s, Miami's Cuban communities had largely embraced the rapidly changing Republican Party and joined forces with many of the city's conservative forces—many of which had roots in the campaigns detailed in this book. With other conservatives, they often fought for prayer in schools and against busing, abortion, gun control, and what we now associate with lesbian, gay, bisexual, and transgender rights. Many Miami Cubans played a key role in the emerging "New Right" and the culture wars that—often through anticommunist rhetoric that particularly appealed to those who fled the 1959 revolution—married the Religious Right with the Republican Party.[54] This was by no means a homogenous group; many other Cubans fought against these conservative efforts. In addition, over the years, several other Latin American communities also entered Miami and challenged its white urban authority, to say nothing of its sexual politics. Social and political turmoil in places like Nicaragua, Haiti, Colombia, Venezuela, and Brazil soon led other exile communities to call Miami home and to enter these debates in critical ways.[55]

All this barely scratches the surface of how the post–World War II era transformed Miami's queer landscape. Like before, however, Miami's sexual geography and cultural politics remained connected to competing visions for the city originating in the United States and parts of the Caribbean and Latin America. This included migration, tourism, trade, and the exchange of ideas and customs. Similarly, Miami's demographic makeup—both then and today—offers a distinct and significant perspective on how queer folks experienced life in the city through the prism of race, ethnicity, nationality, class, age, and (dis)ability. Altogether, it is clear that queers featured prominently in Miami's fairyland profile. Today, very few people in Miami or elsewhere remember the promotion of that textured moniker. Odes to that once-lost history, however, flow through Miami's veins.

# Notes

ABBREVIATIONS

ANC             Ancestry.com Online Database, http://www.ancestry.com/
AV              Appendix, *Votes of the Honourable Legislative Council of the
                Bahama Islands*
CGFP            Carl G. Fisher Papers
CHC             Cuban Heritage Collection
CMB             City of Miami Beach Digital Archives, Miami Beach, Florida, City of
                Miami Beach Council Minutes, http://docmgmt.miamibeachfl.gov
                /weblink/browse.aspx?dbid=0&cr=1
CMCO            City of Miami Clerk's Office, Miami, Florida
COHN            Committee of One Hundred Newsletters, no. 2007-408
COR             Colonial Office Records
CSPP            Candida Scott Piel Papers, no. MS 1831
DCR             Dade County Records, 1867–1944
FSCCF           Florida Supreme Court Case Files, 1825–2013, no. S 49
FSHCR           Florida State Hospital Commitment Records, no. S 1062
FSHMR           Florida State Hospital Medical Records, no. S 1063
GDSC            Governor David Sholtz Correspondence, no. S 278
General Index   General Index to Criminal Cases–Defendants Dade Co., before 1929
HM              HistoryMiami Museum Archives and Research Center, Miami,
                Florida
JCPC            Joe Clein Private Collection
JMA-IV          James Maher Archive Series IV, Interviews, 1964–65
JMP             James Maher Papers
MDCCA           Miami-Dade Clerk of the Court Archives, Doral, Florida
NATB            National Archives of the Bahamas, Nassau, New Providence
RFP             Railey Family Papers, no. 1986-307
RRTS            Robert R. Taylor Scrapbooks, no. 2010-235-1
SAF             State Archives of Florida, Tallahassee
TCTWR           Tin Can Tourists of the World Records, no. M93-2
UM              University of Miami, Otto Richter Library, Coral Gables, Florida
VGLC            Vicki Gold Levi Collection
VMGA            Vizcaya Museum & Gardens Archive, Miami, Florida
WFIU            Wolfsonian-Florida International University, Miami Beach, Florida
YU              Yale University, Manuscript and Archives, Sterling Memorial
                Library, New Haven, Connecticut

INTRODUCTION

1. "Good Season."

2. Ibid.

3. Ramsey, *The Spirits and the Law*, chap. 3.

4. Grapho, "In Florida," 304. While other urban spaces were sparingly called "fairy land," Miami's association with this moniker was far more widespread and characteristic of its marketing strategy. For instance, see Cronon, *Nature's Metropolis*, 349.

5. "Among the Alumni," 344.

6. Burnham, "Down the East Coast," 8.

7. "Good Season."

8. "The Rambler," March 20, 1941, 18; my emphasis.

9. "Segregated District and Home," 8.

10. Kline, *Building a Better Race*, 33.

11. "Segregated District and Home," 8.

12. 1920 United States Federal Census, Miami, Dade, FL, Roll T625_216, 34B; 1940 United States Federal Census, River Junction, Gadsden, FL, Roll T627_587, 36A, ANC.

13. "Fred Symonette," box 45, FSHCR, SAF; "Fred Symonette," file 40, box 123, FSHMR, SAF.

14. Ibid.

15. Forbes, "Ex-Sailor Who Wouldn't Be Licked," 12.

16. Murphy, *Political Manhood*.

17. Forbes, "Ex-Sailor Who Wouldn't Be Licked," 12.

18. "Miami Sex-Town," *Miami Life*, Feb. 2, 1935, 1, JCPC.

19. Gutiérrez, *When Jesus Came*; Kennedy and Ullman, "Introduction"; Mitchell, *Coyote Nation*.

20. Wade, *The Urban Frontier*; Cronon, *Nature's Metropolis*; Boag, *Re-dressing*; Sears, *Arresting Dress*.

21. Kennedy and Davis, *Boots of Leather, Slippers of Gold*; Chauncey, *Gay New York*; Stein, *City of Sisterly and Brotherly Loves*; Boyd, *Wide-Open Town*; Johnson, *The Lavender Scare*; Hurewitz, *Bohemian Los Angeles*; Beemyn, *A Queer Capital*; Stewart-Winter, *Queer Clout*.

22. Newton, *Cherry Grove, Fire Island*; Krahulik, *Provincetown*; Thompson, *The Un-natural State*; Boag, *Same-Sex Affairs*.

23. Howard, *Carryin' On*; Howard, *Men Like That*. Also see Thompson, *The Un-natural State*.

24. W. G. DeBerry to Gov. Sholtz, Feb. 19, 1935, file 6, box 28, GDSC, SAF.

25. Some historians have gestured in this direction, including Churchill, "Transnationalism"; Canaday, "Thinking Sex"; Meyerowitz, "Transnational Sex"; Rupp, "The Persistence of Transnational Organizing"; Shah, *Stranger Intimacy*; Macías-González, "The Transnational Homophile Movement"; Belmonte et al., "Colloquy"; Hobson, *Lavender and Red*; and Stein, "U.S. Homophile Internationalism."

26. Sandoval-Strausz, "Latino Landscapes."

27. Rodgers, *Atlantic Crossings*.

28. Duany, *Blurred Borders*, 7–10.

29. Sheller, "Mobility History," 145.

30. Luibhéid, *Entry Denied*; Canaday, *The Straight State*; Shah, *Stranger Intimacy*.

31. Cowie, *Capital Moves*; Decena, *Tacit Subjects*; Putnam, *Radical Moves*.

32. Stoler, *Haunted by Empire*; Briggs, *Reproducing Empire*; Renda, *Taking Haiti*; Pérez, *Cuba in the American Imagination*.

33. Connolly, *A World More Concrete*; Rose, *The Struggle for Black Freedom*.

34. Walton, "Seaside Tourism in Europe"; Barbour, *Winnipeg Beach*; Funnell, *By the Beautiful Sea*.

35. Kofoed, *Moon over Miami*, 215.

36. Newton, *Cherry Grove, Fire Island*; Krahulik, *Provincetown*; Peiss, *Cheap Amusements*; Auer, "Queerest Little City in the World."

37. Schwartz, *Pleasure Island*; Sheller, "Natural Hedonism"; Vanderwood, *Satan's Playground*; Cocks, *Tropical Whites*; Ruiz, *Americans in the Treasure House*.

38. E. R. von Ammon, "Exposé of the County Jail," Sept. 9, 1936, file 7, box 28, GDSC, SAF.

39. Pérez, *The War of 1898*, xii.

40. Hoganson, *Fighting for American Manhood*; Bederman, *Manliness & Civilization*.

41. Tweed, "An Emerging Protestant Establishment."

42. Sewell, *John Sewell's Memoirs*, 134–35.

43. Barth, *Instant Cities*, xxii.

44. Tweed, "An Emerging Protestant Establishment," 418; Warner, *Publics and Counterpublics*.

45. Rainbolt, *The Town That Climate Built*, 62.

46. Bush, "'Playground of the USA,'" 154.

47. García, *Havana USA*; Portes and Stepick, *City on the Edge*; Stepick et al., *This Land Is Our Land*.

48. Nijman, *Miami*; Shell-Weiss, *Coming to Miami*; Connolly, *A World More Concrete*.

49. Butler, "Protestant Success in the New American City," 325.

50. Lears, *Rebirth of a Nation*, 9.

51. "Old Settlers."

52. Barth, *Instant Cities*.

53. Wade, *The Urban Frontier*; Hamer, *New Towns*, 10–12.

54. Turner, "The Significance of the Frontier," 60.

55. Mohl, *South of the South*.

56. Van Ness, "Florida, New and Old," 307.

57. Wade, *The Urban Frontier*, chap. 9.

58. U.S. Census Bureau, "Table 4—Population of Urban Places," *U.S. Census of Population: 1950*, vol. 2.

59. Mohl, "Miami: The Ethnic Cauldron," 59–60.

60. Livingston, "The Annexation."

61. Jackson, *Crabgrass Frontier*, 150–56.

62. For more on these debates, see Luibhéid, *Entry Denied*; Ngai, *Impossible Subjects*; Putnam, *Radical Moves*; and Minian, *Undocumented Lives*.

63. Chauncey, *Gay New York*; Heap, *Slumming*; Boyd, *Wide-Open Town*.

64. Sherwin, "The Other Side of Paradise," 4.

65. Wolff, *Miami*, 85.

66. Sedgwick, *Epistemology of the Closet*.

67. Johnson, *Just Queer Folks*.

68. For instance, see Chauncey, *Gay New York*; and Woolner, "'Woman Slain.'"

69. Allen, "Black/Queer/Diaspora," 222.

70. Halberstam, *In a Queer Time and Place*, 1.

71. Somerville, *Queering the Color Line*.

72. Cohen, "Punks, Bulldaggers," 440.

73. Kennedy and Davis, *Boots of Leather, Slippers of Gold*, xii, xixn4. Also see Stein, *City of Sisterly and Brotherly Loves*, 6.

74. Sedgwick, *Epistemology of the Closet*.

75. Trouillot, *Silencing the Past*.

76. Marshall, Murphy, and Tortorici, "Editors' Introduction: … Historical Unravelings"; Marshall, Murphy, and Tortorici, "Editors' Introduction … Intimate Tracings."

77. Manalansan, "The 'Stuff' of Archives."

78. George, "The Evolution," 28.

79. Ibid., 28–30; Criminal Docket, Dade County Judge's Court, n.d., MDCCA.

80. General Index, binders A–F, G–M, & N–Z, MDCCA.

81. Blair, "African American Women's Sexuality."

82. "Moral Collapse of Miami," 8.

83. "Establish a Municipal Notoriety Board," *Friday Night*, Nov. 3, 1933, file 17, box 29, GDSC, SAF.

CHAPTER ONE

1. City of Miami Council Minutes, Dec. 17, 1908, 362–63, CMCO.

2. "Have the Saloon Men Made Good?," 2.

3. City of Miami Council Minutes, July 2, 1908, 255–56, CMCO.

4. Ibid.

5. Keire, *For Business and Pleasure*, 2–3.

6. Ibid., chap. 3.

7. Barth, *Instant Cities*; Wade, *The Urban Frontier*; Tweed, "An Emerging Protestant Establishment."

8. Cocks, *Tropical Whites*.

9. Duis, *The Saloon*, 1.

10. Heap, *Slumming*.

11. Mumford, *Interzones*, chap. 2.

12. Weber, *The Spanish Frontier*.

13. Combs, *The History of American Foreign Policy*, chap. 4.

14. Landers, *Black Society in Spanish Florida*.

15. Schafer, "'A Class of People.'"

16. Acts of the Legislative Council of the Territory of Florida (1832), no. 3.

17. Baptist, *Creating an Old South*.

18. Frank, "Taking the State Out," 27.

19. Reprinted in Katz, *Gay American History*, 285–86.

20. Frank, "Taking the State Out," 11.

21. Roscoe, *Changing Ones*, 12; Landers, *Black Society in Spanish Florida*; Ford and Beach, *Patterns of Sexual Behavior*, 287; Frank, "Taking the State Out," 11.

22. Rosen, *Border Law*, chap. 4.

23. Hoffman, *Florida's Frontiers*.

24. Ford and Beach, *Patterns of Sexual Behavior*, 130. Also see Roscoe, *Changing Ones*, 228, 244.

25. Lente, *Florida as a Health-Resort*. Also see Stowe, *Palmetto Leaves*.

26. Brinton, *A Guide-Book of Florida and the South*, 128.

27. Rotundo, *American Manhood*, 185.

28. Beard, "Neurasthenia," 217.

29. Seligmann, "Sexual Inversion," 11. Also see Bleys, *The Geography of Perversion*; Somerville, *Queering the Color Line*, chap. 1.

30. Woolson, "Felipa," 713, 702.

31. Dodge, "Subtropical Florida," 361–62.

32. Shire, *The Threshold of Manifest Destiny*, chap. 3.

33. Dodge, "Subtropical Florida," 361–62.

34. Woolson, "Felipa," 703.

35. Dodge, "Subtropical Florida," 362.

36. Unrau, *White Man's Wicked Water*.

37. Bederman, *Manliness & Civilization*, 42.

38. "The Seminole Still Savage," 3.

39. Muir, *Miami, U.S.A.*, 55; Sewell, *John Sewell's Memoirs*, 46–47. See Viglucci, "Intense Mediation."

40. Dodge, "Subtropical Florida," 360.

41. Shell-Weiss, *Coming to Miami*, 22–27.

42. "Florida Not Destroyed," 4.

43. Shell-Weiss, *Coming to Miami*, 27–30.

44. "Miami Incorporated," 5.

45. Ferrer, *Insurgent Cuba*.

46. Pérez, *Cuba in the American Imagination*; Hoganson, *Fighting for American Manhood*.

47. Gleijeses, "1898."

48. Kleinberg, "History of the *Miami News*."

49. Pérez, *Cuba in the American Imagination*.

50. "Talk about War," 4.

51. Schellings, "The Advent of the Spanish-American War"; Fleischmann, "'Watch Miami.'"

52. "Two More Martyrs," 6.

53. Thomas, "'Camp Hell.'"

54. Fleischmann, "'Watch Miami'"; Thomas, "'Camp Hell'"; Schellings, "Soldiers in Miami."

55. Qtd. in Clancy, "Hell's Angel," 52.

56. "Miami Mince Meat" (1898), 4.

57. Fleischmann, "'Watch Miami,'" 39–40; "He Fought in 'Battle of Miami,'" 9A.

58. Dorn, "Reflections of Early Miami," 55.

59. Cohen, *Historical Sketches*, 36.

60. "He Fought in 'Battle of Miami,'" 9A.

61. Sippial, *Prostitution*, 131.

62. Havard, "Headquarters Department of Cuba," 4.

63. Ibid.

64. See Briggs, *Reproducing Empire*, chaps. 1–2.

65. Dunn, "Headquarters Department of Cuba"; Burrelli, "An Overview," 17.

66. Sippial, *Prostitution*, 92–94.

67. Dunn, "Headquarters Department of Cuba," 5.

68. Morgan, "Court-Martial Jurisdiction," 92–93.

69. Act Providing for the Adoption of the Common Law; Act for the Apprehension of Criminals, and the Punishment of Crimes and Misdemeanors, Acts of the Legislative Council of the Territory of Florida (1822).

70. Acts of the Legislative Council of the Territory of Florida (1832), no. 55.

71. Acts of Legislative Council of the Territory of Florida (1832), no. 3.

72. 1910 United States Federal Census, North Miami, Dade, FL, Roll T624_158, 15B, Microfilm 1374171, ANC.

73. Ibid.

74. Revised Laws of Fla. (1919), §5407.

75. Laws of Fla. (1872), chap. 48, §6.

76. General Index, binders A–F, G–M, & N–Z, MDCCA.

77. Ibid.; 1910 United States Federal Census, Miami, Dade, FL, Roll T624_158, 1B, Microfilm 1374171, ANC.

78. By 1901, women's groups had successfully pressured the legislature to raise the age of consent to eighteen. Laws of Fla. (1901), chap. 4965.

79. Compiled Laws of Fla. (1915), chap. 7, §3521.

80. 1920 United States Federal Census, Milton, Santa Rosa, FL, Roll T624_231, 11A, ANC.

81. Miami, FL, City Directory, 1923, U.S. City Directories, 1821–1989, ANC.

82. General Index, binders A–F, G–M, & N–Z, MDCCA.

83. Blair, *"I've Got to Make My Livin'"*; Harris, *Sex Workers*.

84. Revised Laws of Fla. (1919), §5413.

85. Miami, FL, City Directory, 1908, U.S. City Directories, 1821–1989, ANC.

86. General Index, binder N–Z, MDCCA.

87. Mumford, *Interzones*, 15–18.

88. Laws of Fla. (1872), chap. 48, §2.

89. *Gorey v. State*, 71 So. 328 (Fla. 1916); Also see Miller, *Crime, Sexual Violence*, 179–80.

90. Stein, *City of Sisterly and Brotherly Loves*, 86, 128–36; Luibhéid, *Entry Denied*, 79–96.

91. *Luster and Another v. State*, 2 So. 690 (Fla. 1887); my emphasis.

92. Woolner, "'Woman Slain.'"

93. Acts of the Legislative Council of the Territory of Florida (1842), no. 22.

94. Acts of the Legislative Council of the Territory of Florida (1845), no. 14, §6.

95. Laws of Fla. (1868), chap. 8, §17.

96. Foucault, *The History of Sexuality*, 36–49.

97. At least two other cases involving sodomy or crime against nature charges did reach the Judge's Court before 1910, however. The presiding judge ordered at least one of those cases to go to the Circuit Court, perhaps under a lesser charge. See Criminal Docket, Dade County Judge's Court, n.d., MDCCA.

98. General Index, binders A–F, G–M, & N–Z, MDCCA.

99. Robertson, "'Boys, of Course, Cannot Be Raped,'" 362. Also see Shah, *Stranger Intimacy*, 131–32.

100. Fla. Supp. (1974), chaps. 74–121, §2.

101. Compiled Laws of Fla. (1915), chap. 2, §3221.

102. *Williams v. State*, 43 So. 431 (Fla. 1907).

103. Boag, *Same-Sex Affairs*, chap. 2.

104. General Index, binder N–Z, MDCCA; my emphasis.

105. Eskridge, *Dishonorable Passions*, 20.

106. Report of Dade County Grand Jury, 1896, DCR, HM.

107. "On the Straight Road," 1; "Duckett Gets His Man," 8.

108. "Old Settlers."

109. Report of Dade County Grand Jury, 1896, DCR, HM.

110. J. M. Graham to Board of Dade County Commissioners, Jan. 5, 1897, Jail Conditions—Dade County, DCR, HM.

111. Doherty, *The Miami Police Worksheet*, 2.

112. George, "The Evolution," 30.

113. Petition Praying for Change of Location of the County Site, March 6, 1899, Petitions and Protests to Dade County Commission, 1888–1909, DCR, HM; Sewell, *John Sewell's Memoirs*, 140, 151, 156–59.

114. George, "The Evolution," 28–30.

115. "Fiendish Assault Attempted."

116. "Segregated District and Home," 8.

117. Shell-Weiss, *Coming to Miami*, 29.

118. *Lason v. State*, 12 So.2d 305 (Fla. 1943). Also see Eskridge, *Dishonorable Passions*, 20–21.

119. "Judge Dismisses Disorderly Case," 1, 9.

120. Ibid.; my emphasis.

121. Ibid.

122. Willis, *Southern Prohibition*, 88.

123. Laws of Fla. (1868), chap. 8, §24.

124. Report of Dade County Grand Jury, 1896, DCR, HM.

125. Tatum, "What Shall Be Done?," 2.

126. Letter to Telfair Knight, July 9, 1924, Tamiami Trail Construction Papers, 1916–24, HM. For more on convict labor in the U.S. South, see Lichtenstein, *Twice the Work of Free Labor*.

127. Flynt, "Homosexuality among Tramps," 220.

128. Laws of Fla. (1868), chap. 8, §24. For more on how prostitutes and sexual subversives were policed as vagrants, see "Segregated District and Home," 8.

129. "Police Department Again," 4.

130. George, "The Evolution," 29–32.

131. "Fifty Cases on Docket," 8.

132. "Dealing with Vagrants," 2. Also see "Billingsley Gives Way," 2.

133. "Swift Justice Meted Out to Vagrants and Prostitutes," 2.

134. Qtd. in George, "The Evolution," 36.

135. George, "A Cyclone Hits Miami," 150.

136. "Our Business Interests," 7.

137. Sewell, *John Sewell's Memoirs*, 139–40.

138. State and County License for Mary Brickell, Dealer in Tobacco, Oct. 1885, Licenses—Merchant, Gun, Liquor, Tobacco, etc. 1867–99, DCR, HM.

139. "Miami Incorporated," 5.

140. "Liquor Petitioners Warned," 3.

141. Letter to Board of Dade County Commissioners, Sept. 4, 1899, Licenses—Merchant, Gun, Liquor, Tobacco, etc. 1867–99, DCR, HM.

142. W. H. Girtman, Application to Sell Liquors, Wines, and Beer, Aug. 1899, Licenses—Merchant, Gun, Liquor, Tobacco, etc. 1867–99, DCR, HM.

143. "Selling Liquor in Miami," 4.

144. "Our Business Interests," 7.

145. Sewell, *John Sewell's Memoirs*, 141–42.

146. Ibid., 142.

147. George, "Bootleggers," 35.

148. Ibid.

149. "About North Miami," 8; "Incorporating North Miami," 4.

150. George, "A Cyclone Hits Miami," 151.

151. Dunn, *Black Miami*, 71.

152. Shell-Weiss, *Coming to Miami*, 23–25, 30.

153. "Miami to Have Liquor," 8.

154. Robinson, *Dangerous Liaisons*, xiii.

155. Gilfoyle, *City of Eros*; Mumford, *Interzones*.

156. Heap, *Slumming*, 19.

157. "From Our Northern Sister," 3.

158. Sewell, *John Sewell's Memoirs*, 140; my emphasis.

159. "About North Miami," 8.

160. Ibid.

161. "Incorporating North Miami," 4.

162. Reprinted 1908 advertisement: Dan Hardie, Candidate for Sheriff, 4C.

163. Mumford, *Interzones*, 30; my emphasis.

164. Connolly, *A World More Concrete*, 7.

165. "Whiskey Dealers Warned," 1.

166. General Index, binder N–Z, MDCCA.

167. Cohen, *Historical Sketches*, 27–28.

168. "Indian Arrested," 1.

169. Laws of Fla. (1905), chap. 5443 [no. 72]; Martin, "'The Greatest Evil.'"

170. Willis, *Southern Prohibition*, 87–88.

171. "Only Two Cases before Judge Phillips," 2.

172. Blair, *I've Got to Make My Livin'*; Harris, *Sex Workers*.

173. Sewell, *John Sewell's Memoirs*, 140–41.

174. "About North Miami," 8.

175. Cohen, *Historical Sketches*, 7–8.

176. "Mrs. Dora Suggs," 1.

177. "Duckett Gets His Man," 8.

178. "On the Straight Road," 1.

179. Lydston, *The Diseases of Society*, 396; McGuire and Lydston, "Sexual Crimes," 124.

180. Duggan, *Sapphic Slashers*.

181. Tatum, "What Shall Be Done?," 2.

182. "Mrs. Dora Suggs," 1.

183. "Miami's Gallows."

184. Signed Petition to Move Club Situated in Coloredtown, n.d., Petitions and Protests to Dade County Commission, 1888–1909, DCR, HM.

185. "Just an Incident," 4.

186. George, "A Cyclone Hits Miami," 151.

187. Kleinberg, "History of the *Miami News*," 13–15.

188. "Mrs. Nation Will Lecture Next Week," 1.

189. Tweed, "An Emerging Protestant Establishment," 435.

190. "Baptist Ladies' Aid Yesterday Afternoon," 7.

191. George, "A Cyclone Hits Miami," 155.

192. "Prohibition Given a Boost," 2.

193. "Mrs. Nation Summoned before Solicitor," 3.

194. Cohen, *Historical Sketches*, 61.

195. Reprinted 1908 advertisement: Dan Hardie, Candidate for Sheriff, 4C.

196. "A Go Ahead Suburb," 3.

197. "Dade's Bloody Period: 1895, Lemon City," Angus McGregor Papers, HM.

198. "From Our Northern Sister," 3.

199. Reprinted 1908 advertisement: Dan Hardie, Candidate for Sheriff, 4C.

200. "Gang of Negroes Try to Revive Old Conditions," 1.

201. "Police Department Again," 4.

202. "Left False Teeth," 1.

203. Livingston, "The Annexation," 33.

204. "Greater Miami Approved by Residents of Suburb," 1, 8.

205. "Nothing but Prosperity and Progress Is in Store," 2.

206. Ibid.; my emphasis.

207. Cohen, *Historical Sketches*, 8; Dunn, *Black Miami*, 69–70.

208. "Arrests for Foul Murder of Ed Kinsey," 6; "City Court Severe on Wife Beaters," 7; "Busy Police Arrested 62 in 24 Hours," 5. Also see Connolly, *A World More Concrete*, 80–81.

209. City of Miami Council Minutes, Aug. 14, 1913, 254, CMCO.

210. City of Miami Council Minutes, March 15, 1917, 588–89, CMCO.

211. City of Miami Council Minutes, Aug. 14, 1913, 256, CMCO.

212. Cohen, *Historical Sketches*, 8.

213. Kleinberg, "Dan Hardie Backed Up Tough Talk," 4C.

214. Mohl, "The Origins of Miami's Liberty City."

CHAPTER TWO

1. General Index, binder A–F, MDCCA.

2. 1910 United States Federal Census, Monroe, FL, Roll T624, 7B, Microfilm 1374178; 1920 United States Federal Census, Miami, FL, Roll T625_216, 5B, ANC.

3. Canaday, *The Straight State*, chap. 1.

4. 1920 United States Federal Census, Miami, FL, Roll T625_216, 5B, ANC. For more on personal living spaces and the development of gay culture, see Chauncey, *Gay New York*, 152–63.

5. D'Emilio, "Capitalism and Gay Identity."

6. Ting, "Bachelor Society."

7. Luibhéid, *Entry Denied*, xi.

8. Foucault, *The History of Sexuality*, 17–35.

9. Moffett, "Henry Morrison Flagler," 418.

10. "Miami Mince Meat," March 12, 1897, 1.

11. Shappee, "Flagler's Undertaking," 9–12.

12. "An Isolated Plant at Nassau," 914.

13. Report on Bimini, AV, March 23–May 23, 1922, 73, 76, NATB.

14. "Miami Mince Meat," Nov. 20, 1896, 1.

15. "May Cut Out Passports." Also see Cocks, *Tropical Whites*, 64–73.

16. "Passenger Steamer Takes Up Run," 1.

17. Poyo, *With All, and for the Good of All*; Mormino and Pozzetta, *The Immigrant World of Ybor City*.

18. Putnam, *Radical Moves*.

19. Mohl, "Black Immigrants," 280.

20. Ibid., 273–75.

21. Reid, *The Negro Immigrant*, 184.

22. Report on Eleuthera (Governor's Harbor), AV, Feb. 3–Aug. 26, 1920, 140, NATB.

23. Report on Eleuthera (Rock Sound and Tarmpum Bay), AV, Feb. 3–Aug. 26, 1920, 143–44, NATB; Report on Rum Cay, AV, Feb. 3–Aug. 26, 1920, 180, NATB; Report on San Salvador (Arthur's Town), AV, Feb. 3–Aug. 26, 1920, 186, NATB.

24. Report on Long Cay, AV, Feb. 3–Aug. 26, 1920, 165, NATB.

25. Johnson, "Bahamian Labor Migration," 84–103; Mohl, "Black Immigrants"; Shell-Weiss, "Coming North to the South," 79–99.

26. Merrick, "Pre-Flagler Influences," 5.

27. Shell-Weiss, *Coming to Miami*, 47–48; Chapman, "'Watch the Port of Miami,'" 12.

28. "The Exodus to Florida," 2.

29. Johnson, "Bahamian Labor Migration," 94.

30. Bahamas Department of Statistics, *Demographic Aspects of the Bahamian Population*, 12.

31. "West Indian Contingent Committee," 1; Advertisement: Office of Recruiting Committee, 2.

32. Baldwin, "A British Colony in War Times," 731–37.

33. Bahamas Department of Statistics, *Demographic Aspects of the Bahamian Population*, 12. Other Bahamian sources suggested census records were often inaccurate because they were conducted at the peak of harvest season, when many men were away in Miami or elsewhere in Florida but expected to return. See Report on Exuma, AV, March 23–May 23, 1922, 96, NATB.

34. "The Exodus to Florida," 2.

35. Report on Long Island (Clarence Town), AV, Nov. 18, 1912–July 7, 1913, 123, NATB.

36. Report on Watlings Island, AV, Feb. 15, 1921–Jan. 16, 1922, 275, NATB.

37. "Letter to the Editor from Twist Black."

38. Report on Out Islands, AV, Feb. 15, 1921–Jan. 16, 1922, 281–83, NATB.

39. Qtd. in Mohl, "Black Immigrants," 285.

40. Bahamas Department of Statistics, *Demographic Aspects of the Bahamian Population*, 12.

41. Roberts, "A Riviera 'Conch.'" Also see Hurston, "Dance Songs and Tales," 294–312.

42. Report on Watlings Island, AV, March 23–May 23, 1922, 166, NATB.

43. "Letter to the Editor: Out Island Development," 2.

44. Ibid.

45. Johnson, "Bahamian Labor Migration," 102.

46. Report on Andros (Mangrove Cay), AV, March 23–May 23, 1922, 63–64, NATB.

47. Report on Rum Cay, AV, Feb. 3–Aug. 26, 1920, 180, NATB.

48. AV, March 23–May 23, 1922, 30–31, NATB.

49. An Act for the Regulation of Places Ordinarily Used for Public Dancing or Music or Other Public Entertainment of the Like Kind, Oct. 4, 1919, 23/284/510–14, COR, NATB.

50. Qtd. in Mohl, "Black Immigrants," 284.

51. Report on Exuma, AV, March 23–May 23, 1922, 94, NATB.

52. Report on Eleuthera (Rock Sound and Tarmpum Bay), AV, Feb. 3–Aug. 26, 1920, 143, NATB.

53. Conklin, "More than Thousand Bahama Islanders," 1.

54. Treasury Department, *Book of Instructions for the Medical Inspection of Immigrants*, 14. Also see Kraut, *Silent Travelers*; and Shah, *Contagious Divides*.

55. U.S. Department of Labor, *Annual Report of the Commissioner General of Immigration*, 193.

56. "Florida, Impressions of a Visitor."

57. Luibhéid, *Entry Denied*, 50.

58. "Florida, Impressions of a Visitor."

59. Ibid.

60. D'Emilio and Freedman, *Intimate Matters*, 137; Gilfoyle, *City of Eros*, chap. 5.

61. Report on Andros (Nicoll's Town), AV, March 9–Aug. 23, 1909, 68, NATB.

62. Advertisement, *Tribune* (Nassau), Jan. 7, 1913.

63. Bahamian colonial officials constantly noted how integral remittances from Miami were to the archipelago's economy. See Report on Eleuthera (Governor's Harbor), AV, March 9–Aug. 23, 1909, 82–83; Governor's Speech, AV, Nov. 18, 1912–July 7, 1913, 3, NATB; and Report on Exuma, AV, March 23–May 23, 1922, 96, NATB.

64. Shell-Weiss, "Coming North to the South," 87–91.

65. Reid, *The Negro Immigrant*, 184–85.

66. Qtd. in Johnson, "Bahamian Labor Migration," 94. Also see "Letter to the Editor from Twist Black."

67. Report on Eleuthera (Rock Sound and Tarpum Bay), AV, Nov. 18, 1912–July 7, 1913, 57, NATB.

68. Report on Exuma, AV, Nov. 18, 1912–July 7, 1913, 78, NATB.

69. Reid, *The Negro Immigrant*, 194.

70. Sewell, *John Sewell's Memoirs*, 37.

71. Ibid., 138–39.

72. "A Brutal Murder," 4.

73. Shah, *Stranger Intimacy*.

74. Qtd. in Rybczynski and Olin, *Vizcaya*, 221.

75. Herdrich and Weinberg, *American Drawings*, 354–56; Capozzola, "The Man Who Illuminated the Gilded Age?," 526.

76. Rybczynski and Olin, *Vizcaya*, 219–22; Corliss, "Building the Overseas Railway," 16–17.

77. Keene, *World War I*, 93–95.

78. "Dade County Young Men Flock to Registration Booths," 1–2.

79. Rybczynski and Olin, *Vizcaya*, 221.

80. John Singer Sargent, *Bather, Florida*, 1917, acc. no. 50.130.60, Metropolitan Museum of Art, New York, www.metmuseum.org.

81. John Singer Sargent, *Man on Beach, Florida*, 1917, acc. no. 50.130.61; John Singer Sargent, *Man and Pool, Florida*, 1917, acc. no. 50.130.62, Metropolitan Museum of Art, New York, www.metmuseum.org.

82. Fairbrother, *John Singer Sargent: The Sensualist*, 123, 179.

83. Chauncey, *Gay New York*, chap. 3; Boag, *Same-Sex Affairs*, chaps. 1–2.

84. Foster, "The Sexual Abuse of Black Men"; Saillant, "The Black Body Erotic"; Richardson, *Black Masculinity*. For more on the white gaze on black bodies, also see Morgan, "'Some Could Suckle over Their Shoulder.'"

85. Rybczynski and Olin, *Vizcaya*, 222.

86. Capozzola, "The Man Who Illuminated the Gilded Age?"; History Project, *Improper Bostonians*, 90–92; Murphy, *Political Manhood*.

87. Fairbrother, *John Singer Sargent: The Sensualist*, 111–13.

88. Fairbrother, *John Singer Sargent*, 142.

89. Esten, *John Singer Sargent*, 11–19.

90. Johns, *Winslow Homer*, 151; Cooper, *Winslow Homer Watercolors*, 130–49; Summers, *The Queer Encyclopedia of the Visual Arts*, 19.

91. Child, "Shark" (1910); Child, "Shark" (1911).

92. Wilson, "Miami," 31; Child, "Shark" (1911), 45.

93. "The Life That's Lived in Books," BR4.

94. Cooper, "The Clothing of Thoughts," 444.

95. Child, "The Feminist."

96. Child, "Shark" (1911), 46, 49.

97. Cooper, "The Clothing of Thoughts," 444.

98. "Current Fiction," 112.

99. Child, "Shark" (1911), 44, 46.

100. Ibid., 46–47.

101. Ibid., 53.

102. Lears, "Reconstructing Nature," 19–23.

103. Qtd. in Castillo, "Laboring in the Magic City," 34.

104. Connolly, *A World More Concrete*, 24.

105. Qtd. in Dunn, *Black Miami*, 98.

106. Mackintosh, "Pellagra in the Bahamas," 199–200.

107. Report on Mayaguana, AV, Feb. 18–Dec. 18, 1919, 165, NATB.

108. Foucault, *The History of Sexuality*.

109. Duggan, *Sapphic Slashers*, chap. 6; Somerville, *Queering the Color Line*.

110. Freedman, *Redefining Rape*, chap. 5.

111. "Circumcision for the Correction of Sexual Crimes," 345. Also see McGuire and Lydston, "Sexual Crimes," 126; Foster, "The Sexual Abuse of Black Men."

112. "Circumcision for the Correction of Sexual Crimes."

113. Eskridge, *Dishonorable Passions*, 20, 46–52.

114. Shah, *Stranger Intimacy*, 131–44; Freedman, *Redefining Rape*, 179–89.

115. Canaday, *The Straight State*, 22, 29.

116. Qtd. in Katz, *Gay American History*, 51.

117. Luibhéid, *Entry Denied*, 1–16.

118. Canaday, *The Straight State*, chap. 1.

119. Ngai, *Impossible Subjects*.

120. Carpenter, *Immigrants and Their Children*, 95.

121. Willsie, "Migration of Peoples," 188.

122. Abrams, "Polygamy, Prostitution," 701.

123. Sears, "All That Glitters," 393–97; Ngai, *Impossible Subjects*, 112–13.

124. Meriam, "Woman's Present Position," 644.

125. Shah, *Stranger Intimacy*, 144.

126. One man, John Holmes, was arrested twice: once in 1913 and again in 1917. General Index, binders A–F, G–M, & N–Z, MDCCA.

127. General Index, binder A–F, MDCCA.

128. Arrival Date Dec. 19, 1913, Passenger Lists of Vessels Arriving at Miami, FL, Passenger Lists, 1898–1951, 2788508, Records of the Immigration and Naturalization Service, 1787–2004, 85, ANC.

129. Ibid.

130. Arrival Dates April 5, 1920, and Nov. 26, 1923, Passenger Lists of Vessels Ar-

riving at Miami, FL, Passenger Lists, 1898–1951, 2788508, Records of the Immigration and Naturalization Service, 1787–2004, 85, ANC.

131. General Index, binder N–Z, MDCCA.

132. 1920 United States Federal Census, Miami, Dade, FL, Roll T625_216, 36A, 24, ANC; Arrival Date Nov. 11, 1916; Arrival Date May 28, 1919, Passenger Lists of Vessels Arriving at Miami, FL, Passenger Lists, 1898–1951, 2788508, Records of the Immigration and Naturalization Service, 1787–2004, 85, ANC.

133. Boag, *Same-Sex Affairs*, chaps. 1–2.

134. Note George Chauncey's discussion of the distinct sexual proclivities of Italian and Jewish immigrant men in New York. Chauncey, *Gay New York*, 72–76.

135. 1920 United States Federal Census, Miami, Dade, FL, Roll T625_216, 36A, 24, ANC; Arrival Date Nov. 8, 1923, Passenger Lists of Vessels Arriving at Miami, FL, Passenger Lists, 1898–1951, 2788508, Records of the Immigration and Naturalization Service, 1787–2004, 85, ANC.

136. D'Emilio, "Capitalism and Gay Identity."

137. Katz, *Gay American History*, 36–37; Eskridge, *Dishonorable Passions*, 81–82.

138. George, "Policing Miami's Black Community," 434–50. Also see Mohl, "Black Immigrants"; and Dunn, *Black Miami*.

139. City of Miami Council Minutes, Dec. 17, 1908, 362–63, CMCO.

140. Mayer, "A Cruise to Nassau from Miami," 18.

141. Reid, *The Negro Immigrant*, 184, 189.

142. Robinson, "The Expanding World of Sidney Poitier," 110.

143. Mohl, "Black Immigrants," 287–89.

144. Ibid., 288.

145. Conklin, "More than Thousand Bahama Islanders," 1.

146. "Mystery Surrounds the Wrecked V-832," 6.

147. Corliss, "Building the Overseas Railway," 17.

148. Conklin, "More than Thousand Bahama Islanders," 1.

149. Ibid.

150. Mohl, "Black Immigrants," 284.

151. Conklin, "More than Thousand Bahama Islanders," 1. Also see "Along the Color Line"; and "National Association for the Advancement of Colored People."

152. Conklin, "More than Thousand Bahama Islanders," 1.

153. Shell-Weiss, "Coming North to the South," 89–97; Connolly, *A World More Concrete*, 60–61.

154. "Birth of Another Newspaper," 2.

155. "Small War over in Colored Town," 2.

156. Report on Out Islands, AV, Feb. 15, 1921–Jan. 16, 1922, 286–87, NATB.

157. Report on Eleuthera (Governor's Harbour), AV, March 23–May 23, 1922, 82, NATB.

158. *The Encyclopedia Britannica*, 546.

159. Conklin, "More than Thousand Bahama Islanders," 1.

160. Report on Out Islands, AV, Feb. 15, 1921–Jan. 16, 1922, 285, NATB.

161. Putnam, *Radical Moves*, 40; Craton and Saunders, *Islanders in the Stream*, 117–24.

162. Miami Beach Council Minutes, Oct. 3, 1928, no. 259; D'Emilio, *Sexual Politics, Sexual Communities*, 14.

163. Qtd. in Johnson, "Bahamian Labor Migration," 100.

164. Report on Enquiry into the Circumstances of the Death of Robert Holbert, April 13, 1908, 23/264, COR, NATB; Mohl, "Black Immigrants," 288–89.

165. Letter from Ambassador James Bryce, March 29, 1908, 23/264, COR, NATB.

166. Letter from Ambassador James Bryce, April 1, 1908, 23/264, COR, NATB; Letter from Ambassador James Bryce, March 29, 1908, 23/264, COR, NATB.

167. Report on Enquiry into Murder of J. Saunders, April 13, 1908, 23/264, COR, NATB.

168. Putnam, *Radical Moves*, 85–86.

169. Senate Committee on Immigration, *Emergency Immigration Legislation*, 42. For more on anxieties concerning unionism in Miami, see Castillo, "Miami's Hidden Labor History," 438–67; and Shell-Weiss, *Coming to Miami*.

170. Memo, "Alien Immigration into U.S.," Feb. 10, 1919, 23/284, COR, NATB.

171. Senate Committee on Immigration, *Emergency Immigration Legislation*, 42.

172. Conklin, "More than Thousand Bahama Islanders," 1.

173. "Letter to the Editor: Emigration," 2.

174. Craton and Saunders, *Islanders in the Stream*, 219; Shell-Weiss, "Coming North to the South," 83–84.

175. Shell-Weiss, *Coming to Miami*, 48; Mohl, "Black Immigrants," 284.

176. Parsons, *A Winter in Paradise*, 83–84.

177. McElory and de Albuquerque, "Migration Transition," 32.

178. Alien Immigration to U.S., Feb. 1919, 23/284, COR, NATB.

179. Report on Long Island, AV, March 23–May 23, 1922, 141, NATB.

180. Report on Exuma, AV, March 23–May 23, 1922, 96, NATB.

181. Putnam, *Radical Moves*, 82–122.

182. City of Miami Council Minutes, July 8, 1924, 159, CMCO.

183. Johnson, "Bahamian Labor Migration," 96–97.

184. Class 3, 52–54 (1868) in General Assembly of the Bahama Islands, *The Statute Law of the Bahamas*.

185. Although passed in 1924, the Penal Code was drafted several years before and modeled on the Criminal Code of Grenada. The 1924 Penal Cade codified much of the Bahamas' criminal laws, while rendering unclear the status of common laws not included in the Code. In 1929 the Penal Code was amended so that nothing in the Code would affect "the liability of a person under the common law." Despite the amendment, this was only clarified in 1973, when the Judicial Committee of the Privy Council ruled in the case of *Farquharson v. The Queen* that "where the common law and Penal Code overlapped, the latter would take precedence." I am grateful to the staff at the National Archives of the Bahamas for clarifying this. See Knowles, *Elements of Bahamian Law*, chap. 10; and Judicial Committee of the Privy Council, "Joint Responsibility for Murder (*Farquharson v. The Queen*)," 206–7.

186. General Assembly of the Bahama Islands, *Bahamas*.

187. Report on Andros (Mangrove Cay), AV, March 9–Aug. 23, 1909, 61, NATB.

188. "Topics of the Times," 14.

189. Buchanan, "Miami's Bootleg Boom: A Decade of Prohibition," 92–101.

190. Chauncey, *Gay New York*; Jacobson, *Whiteness of a Different Color*; Jacobson, *Barbarian Virtues*; Roediger, *Working toward Whiteness*.

CHAPTER THREE

1. Qtd. in *Committee of One Hundred Newsletter*, May 4, 1934, 3, box 20, COHN, HM.

2. James, *The Golden Warrior*, 261.

3. Advertisement: LaFayette, 4; my emphasis.

4. Heap, *Slumming*, 84, 320n; Johnson, "The Kids of Fairytown," 101–5; Krahulik, *Provincetown*, 71–72. James N. Green similarly showed the multiple meanings of the effeminate *fresco* in Brazil. See Green, *Beyond Carnival*, 23–31.

5. Qtd. in *Committee of One Hundred Newsletter*, May 4, 1934, 3.

6. Krahulik, *Provincetown*; Newton, *Cherry Grove, Fire Island*; Peiss, *Cheap Amusements*; Funnell, *By the Beautiful Sea*; Simon, *Boardwalk of Dreams*.

7. Newton, *Cherry Grove, Fire Island*; Krahulik, *Provincetown*; Sherry, *Gay Artists*; Hurewitz, *Bohemian Los Angeles*.

8. Sedgwick, *Epistemology of the Closet*.

9. Howard, *Men Like That*, chap. 7; Decena, *Tacit Subjects*, chap. 1.

10. Sewell, *John Sewell's Memoirs*, 175–76; Shell-Weiss, *Coming to Miami*, 65–68.

11. Kleinberg, "The Real Beginning of South Beach," 1988, 4C; Kleinberg, "Smith's Casino," 4C.

12. Lavender, *Miami Beach in 1920*, 95.

13. "Miami Beach Casino Is Popular," 5; "Many Improvements for Beach Casino"; "New Bath House"; "Three Thousand Bath Rooms," 1.

14. Morris, *The Imperial Reference Library*, 1153.

15. Perrine, "The Tropic Home," 5.

16. Perry, "Lotus Spell Cast on Visitors," 10.

17. Barth, *Instant Cities*.

18. Perrine, "The Tropic Home," 5.

19. "A Message from Miami," 30.

20. "Slogans Are Numerous," 11.

21. Chauncey, *Gay New York*, chap. 2; Boyd, *Wide-Open Town*, chap. 1; Heap, *Slumming*, 82–97.

22. Carl Fisher to Thomas Pancoast, Nov. 7, 1921, Miami Beach—Advertising (Correspondence), box 10, CGFP, HM.

23. Chauncey, *Gay New York*, 191.

24. "Many Improvements for Beach Casino."

25. McIntyre, "New York Day by Day," 6.

26. "Opening of Big Bridge," 2.

27. "Tolls Be Now Charged to Cross Bay Bridge," 1.

28. "Many Improvements for Beach Casino."

29. City of Miami Beach Council Minutes, Sept. 5, 1928, CMB.

30. Terry, *An American Obsession*, 154–58.

31. Hoffman and Chalfin, "The Mechanism of a Great Estate," 69.

32. "Villa Vizcaya, Miami, Florida," 41.

33. Chudacoff, *The Age of the Bachelor.*

34. "An Auto Trip to Florida," 4.

35. Interview with F. Burrall Hoffman, 24, JMA-IV, box 2, JMP, VMGA.

36. Bishop, "Jim Bishop: Reporter," 4.

37. Interview with Lillian Gish, Sept. 22, 1964, 1, JMA-IV, box 2, JMP, VMGA.

38. For more on how Vizcaya has historically existed in Miami's queer imaginary, see Capó, "Locating Miami's Queer History," 6–8.

39. "The Joy of Beauty," 49.

40. James Deering to Paul Chalfin, March 20, 1917, Correspondence Series, Vizcaya Estate Records, VMGA.

41. Mackay, "The Story of the House That James Deering Built," 9–10.

42. Interview with Nell Dorr, Sept. 22, 1964, 2–3, JMA-IV, box 2, JMP, VMGA.

43. "Bachelor Builds a Palace," 14.

44. Interview with F. Burrall Hoffman, 20.

45. Interview with Diego Suarez, April 20 and June 4, 1965, JMA-IV, box 2, JMP, VMGA.

46. "Some Attractive Homes," 63–64; "Death of Edith E. Hanan," 20; *Brooklyn Blue Book*, 187.

47. Advertisement: A Night in Japan, 6.

48. Douglas, "Japanese Costume Ball," 12.

49. Douglas, "Japanese Costume Dance," 3. For more on the queer fetishization of the "other," see Sueyoshi, *Queer Compulsions.*

50. Douglas, "Japanese Costume Ball," 12.

51. "Miami in Paragraph," 5.

52. Schwartz, *Pleasure Island.*

53. Buchanan, "Miami's Bootleg Boom: A Decade of Prohibition," 7.

54. Advertisement: Miami Beach Has the Ocean Front, 1.

55. Vanderblue, "The Florida Land Boom," 118.

56. "Triumphant Florida," E6.

57. "Florida Realizing Dreams of Wealth," 32.

58. Vanderblue, "The Florida Land Boom," 120.

59. Vanderblue, "The Florida Land Boom II," 269.

60. "The Red Cross Fund," 23.

61. "Miami's Unconquerable Soul," 1.

62. Sessa, "Miami in 1926," 34.

63. *Committee of One Hundred Newsletter*, May 1932, 9, COHN, box 20, HM.

64. *Committee of One Hundred Newsletter*, Sept. 20, 1931, 11, COHN, box 20, HM.

65. Warren et al., "Along Miami Shore."

66. Roberts, "A Salute to Caesar LaMonaca," 5A; LaMonaca and Conner "Miami, Playground of the U.S.A."

67. "Alden Freeman Dies," 7.

68. "Freeman, Alden, Author and Political Reformer," 44–50.

69. Durant and Durant, *A Dual Autobiography*, 37.

70. "Alden Freeman Dies," 7.

71. "Will Names Harding 'Daughter,'" 2; "'Peculiar' Alden Freeman," 6.

72. "The Sad Case of Mr. Freeman," 4.

73. Kissack, *Free Comrades*.

74. Durant and Durant, *A Dual Autobiography*, 37.

75. Goldman, *Living My Life*, 451–54.

76. "A Hint to the Lawyers," 6.

77. Jervis, "Stylish Life, Brutal Death," 1A.

78. "Ornate Palace at Miami Beach," 4F.

79. "Alden Freeman Dies," 7; Petition for Naturalization of Charles Daniel Boulton, Florida Naturalization Records, 1880–1991, Record Group 21, National Archives at Atlanta, GA, ANC.

80. Schneider, *Crossing Borders*, 219–22.

81. Last Will and Testament of Alden Freeman, Dade County, FL, filed June 10, 1938, Wills, Probate Records and Related Cases, ANC; Petition for Naturalization of Charles Daniel Boulton.

82. Last Will and Testament of Alden Freeman.

83. Fowler, "Adult Adoption," 1–42.

84. Petition for Naturalization of Charles Daniel Boulton.

85. "Ornate Palace at Miami Beach," 4F.

86. See Advertisement, *Miami Daily News*, Dec. 21, 1930, 10–11.

87. "Nan Britton's Girl to Get Trust Fund," 2; "Will Names Harding 'Daughter,'" 2; Last Will and Testament of Alden Freeman.

88. Last Will and Testament of Alden Freeman.

89. Private letter partially reprinted in *The Raab Collection, Catalog 71*, 28–29.

90. Williams, "Henry Salem Hubbell's *The Building of the House*," 419–20; Pollack, *Visual Art*, 265–67.

91. MacDowell, "Miami Music and Musicians," 8D.

92. Hurewitz, *Bohemian Los Angeles*, chap. 2; Krahulik, *Provincetown*, chap. 3.

93. Pollack, *Visual Art*, 258–64.

94. "Ornate Palace at Miami Beach," 4F.

95. "No Eskimo Story," 9.

96. "Miamian Receives Psychopathic Care," 1.

97. "Reformer Held for Observation," 1.

98. Beemyn, *A Queer Capital*, 135–38; Gambino, "Mental Health," 71; Freedman, "'Uncontrolled Desires,'" 90–91.

99. "Part of Phantom Estate Claimed by Nan Britton," 14.

100. "Noted Soprano Gives Concert Here Tonight," 7.

101. "Mary Garden Will Arrive Here Today," 12; "Alden Freeman Dies," 7.

102. "Mary Garden Craze Led Girl to Suicide," 1.

103. Wood, "Sapphonics," 40.

104. Monroe, "Pioneer Women of Dade County," 52.

105. Pollack, *Visual Art*, 256–72.

106. Krahulik, *Provincetown*. Woodward is noticeably absent from this excellent study, indicative of how the artist's life has been shrouded in mystery.

107. "School Notes," 6–7.

108. Johnson, "Letter to the Editor," 10A; Rees, "The Search for Dewing Woodward," 14–15; Sieminski, "Williamsport's Bold Vagabond Artist," E1, E3.

109. Rees, "The Search for Dewing Woodward."

110. 1910 United States Federal Census, Woodstock, Ulster, NY, Roll T624_1084, 10A; 1930 United States Federal Census, Coral Gables, FL, Roll 311, 9A, ANC.

111. Johnson, "Letter to the Editor," 10A.

112. See Love and Peters, *Carl W. Peters*, 217. This work refers to Woodward and Johnson as "obscure lesbian artists."

113. Sieminski, "Willamsport's Bold Vagabond Artist," E3.

114. York, *Some Adventures of Two Vagabonds*, 23.

115. Huneker, "Portrait Drawings by Dewing Woodward," 36.

116. Pollack, *Visual Art*, 269–70.

117. "Dewing Woodward Active in Art," 7D; "Miami Art Leader, Painter Succumbs," 11; Pollack, *Visual Art*, 269–73.

118. "Sons Oust Alden Freeman," 1.

119. Goldman, *Living My Life*, 454.

120. "Escapes the Heat," 1.

121. Kramer, "Power and Connection," 1349.

122. See Sneider, *Suffragists in an Imperial Age*; Stoler, *Haunted by Empire*; and Briggs, *Reproducing Empire*.

123. "Ship Lines Are Obliged to Increase Service," 10; "Clarke Ship Aids Anglers," 12.

124. Taylor, *To Hell with Paradise*, chap. 2.

125. Shell-Weiss, *Coming to Miami*, 112–14.

126. Twa, *Visualizing Haiti*, 202.

127. Trouillot, *Haiti, State against Nation*; Derby, *The Dictator's Seduction*.

128. Stepick, "The Refugees Nobody Wants."

129. Steele, "Miami, an Air Capital," 1.

130. "Tourist Outlook for Cuba Good," file 1, box 357, Pan American World Airways, Inc. Records, UM.

131. Reck, "Plan Air Line to Buenos Aires," 20.

132. Polyné, *From Douglass to Duvalier*.

133. Reck, "Plan Air Line to Buenos Aires," 20.

134. Steele, "Miami, an Air Capital," 1.

135. *Committee of One Hundred Newsletter*, March 31, 1932, 11, box 20, COHN, HM.

136. Shell-Weiss, *Coming to Miami*, 104.

137. Tiemeyer, *Plane Queer*, 33.

138. "Miami Physician Flies to Havana," 3.

139. "On Air Trip to Havana," 10.

140. "Ornate Palace at Miami Beach," 4F.

141. Last Will and Testament of Alden Freeman.

142. "U.S. Marine Is Ruler of Haiti Kingdom," 3.

143. Turner, "King Faustin of Haitian Isle Is Expected," 3.

144. "Flights & Flyers," 25.

145. "Washington Society Has a Gay Round," 2.

146. "Consul Rescued," 1.

147. Turner, "King Faustin of Haitian Isle Is Expected," 3.

148. Last Will and Testament of Alden Freeman; "Alden Freeman Dies," 7.

149. Schmidt, *The United States Occupation of Haiti*, 68.

150. "Anchor of Ship Columbus Sailed," 1.

151. "Manufacturers' Exhibit Given New Additions," 4.

152. "New England Group Has Haitian Night," 7.

153. Renda, *Taking Haiti*, 5.

154. "Hull to Get Report on Haitian Incident," 1B.

CHAPTER FOUR

1. "Shave Is Needed," 8.

2. Pérez, *Cuba in the American Imagination*. Also see Johnson, *Latin America in Caricature*.

3. Warner, *Publics and Counterpublics*.

4. Krolikowski and Brown, "The Structure and Form," 141.

5. Gassan, "Fear, Commercialism, Reform," 1083.

6. Barker, *Ecological Psychology*; Bagnall, "Performance and Performativity"; Haldrup and Larsen, "Material Cultures of Tourism."

7. Butler, *Gender Trouble*, 185.

8. Newton, *Mother Camp*.

9. Butler, *Bodies That Matter*.

10. Muñoz, *Disidentifications*; Somerville, *Queering the Color Line*.

11. Grant, "Crime over Miami," 58.

12. Pérez, *On Becoming Cuban*; Pérez, "Between Encounter and Experience."

13. Rainbolt, *The Town That Climate Built*, 35.

14. Cohen, *Historical Sketches*, 116.

15. Weede, "Publicity and Palm Trees," 62–64.

16. Barth, *Instant Cities*, 5, 208.

17. Cammack, *What about Florida?*; Faris, *Seeing the Sunny South*; Rainbolt, *The Town That Climate Built*.

18. Ingram, *Dixie Highway*, 1–7.

19. "Florida Counties Put Millions," 9.

20. Burton, "A Promised Road," 6.

21. Bush, "'Playground of the USA,'" 160.

22. Marchand, *Advertising the American Dream*, chap. 6.

23. *Committee of One Hundred Newsletter*, May 4, 1934, 3, box 20, COHN, HM.

24. "Miami, World's 'Winter Play City,'" 3.

25. Villard, "Florida Flamboyant," 295.

26. Pérez, *Cuba in the American Imagination*, chap. 5.

27. *Miami–Palm Beach–Havana Gimlet*, Season of 1929–30, XC2002.11.4.218, VGLC, WFIU; my emphasis.

28. "About Miami," 2.

29. Florida State Planning Board, *A Guide to Miami and Dade County*, 158.

30. Dorman, "Miami Bootlegger Is a Businessman," 11.

31. *Miami–Palm Beach–Havana Gimlet.*

32. Fisher, *Fabulous Hoosier*, 128.

33. Florida State Planning Board, *A Guide to Miami and Dade County*, 158.

34. Ibid., 159.

35. Dorothy Parmer, "Miami," *Miami Life*, Oct. 13, 1934, 3, JCPC.

36. Early, *Ports of the Sun*, 268.

37. Burke and Leslie, "Moon over Miami."

38. Norman-Fennell Corp., "Selling Miami to the Tourist," c.1935, HM.

39. Weede, "Publicity and Palm Trees," 64.

40. "Triumphant Florida," E6.

41. Kofoed, "Miami," 673.

42. Vanderblue, "The Florida Land Boom," 113.

43. Rainbolt, *The Town That Climate Built*, 56.

44. Newspaper clipping, "The Last Straw," RFP, HM.

45. Ibid.

46. Leslie, "The Great Depression in Miami Beach," 38–40.

47. "Forty Years Old," 4.

48. "Miami Observes 39th Birthday," 12.

49. "About Miami," 2.

50. Portes and Stepick, *City on the Edge*, 74–75.

51. Connolly, *A World More Concrete*, 62–70; "Seminole Indians Master Alligators," 57.

52. Carl Fisher to George Ade, Oct. 21, 1921, Miami Beach—Advertising, box 10, CGFP, HM.

53. Shell-Weiss, *Coming to Miami*, 100.

54. Carl Fisher to C. W. Chase, July 13, 1923, Miami Beach—Advertising, box 10, CGFP, HM.

55. Robinson, "Florida," 13.

56. Thompson, *Locomotive Engineers' Monthly Journal*, 818.

57. Norman Spencer (music) and Joe McKiernan (lyric), "Cuban Moon," c. 1920, XC2002.11.4.156, VGLC, WFIU.

58. "100 Carolinians Be in Miami Thursday Night," 1.

59. "Miami Beach by-the-Sea," 15.

60. "Honeymooners at the Beach," 14.

61. "Seaboard Air Line Ry. Changes," 1.

62. Parsons, *A Winter in Paradise*, 40–41.

63. *Miami–Palm Beach–Havana Gimlet.*

64. Sippial, *Prostitution*, 132.

65. Gardner, "Wickedest City in World Is Havana," 1, 12.

66. Taylor, *To Hell with Paradise*, 4. Also see Stone, "Expect Shipping Activity at Nassau Harbor"; Boyle, "The Bahamas Are Fast Becoming a Vacation Paradise," 10; and Schwartz, *Pleasure Island.*

67. Baldwin, "A British Colony in War Times," 731–32.

68. Parsons, *A Winter in Paradise*, 99.

69. Ibid., 154–56.

70. An Act for the Regulation of Places Ordinarily Used for Public Dancing or Music or Other Public Entertainment of the Like Kind, Oct. 4, 1919, 23/284/510–14, COR, NATB.

71. Ibid.

72. "Florida Gulf Coast Is Called Paradise for Bootleggers," 1.

73. Buchanan, "Miami's Bootleg Boom: A Decade of Prohibition," 32.

74. Buchanan, "Miami's Bootleg Boom," 14.

75. Florida State Planning Board, *A Guide to Miami and Dade County*, 103.

76. "Social Notes," *Miami Life*, Sept. 29, 1934, 3, JCPC.

77. "Miami in Paragraph," 5.

78. "Villa Vizcaya, Miami, Florida," 41.

79. Pérez, *On Becoming Cuban*, 431.

80. Florida State Planning Board, *A Guide to Miami and Dade County*, 14.

81. "Hialeah to Open Beautiful Racing Plant," 4A. Also see Wing, "Flamingo Chicks," 2A.

82. *Diario de la Marina*, April 21, 1940, qtd. in Maribona, *Turismo y ciudadanía*, 7, G155.C9M3, CHC, UM; my translation.

83. Maribona, *Turismo y ciudadanía*, 96.

84. Miguel de Marcos, "Prólogo," in Maribona, *Turismo y ciudadanía*; my translation.

85. "The Fate of Cuba," *Friday Night*, Nov. 3, 1933, file 17, box 29, GDSC, SAF.

86. "Questions," *Friday Night*, Nov. 10, 1933, file 17, box 29, GDSC, SAF.

87. *El Mundo*, May 30, 1936, qtd. in Maribona, *Turismo y ciudadanía*, 182–83, 311–12.

88. Wilbanks and George, "Re-evaluating the 'Good Old Days'"; George, "Colored Town."

89. "The Forbidden City"; my emphasis.

90. Dunn, *Black Miami*, 133.

91. Connolly, *A World More Concrete*, 70.

92. Ibid., 79.

93. Pharr, "Colored Town Section of the City," 46.

94. "Grand Jury Is Reconvened," 1.

95. "Guardsmen Called Out," 1; Connolly, *A World More Concrete*, 54–55.

96. Connolly, *A World More Concrete*, 121–24.

97. Carl Fisher to George Ade.

98. Cole, "American Ghetto Parties," 225. Also see Chude-Sokei, *The Last "Darky."*

99. Lane, *Blackface Cuba*.

100. Roediger, *The Wages of Whiteness*, chap. 6.

101. Boyd, *Wide-Open Town*, 29–38.

102. "Catches," 5; "Negro's 'Stage' Career Stopped," 4.

103. "Boy Scouts Minstrel Success," 5.

104. "Minstrel Show's Rehearsal Set," 9.

105. "Miami's Negro Problem," 2.

106. "Fairfax Will Offer Bill of Amateurs," 2.

107. "Amateur Minstrelsy Proved by the Elks," 4.

108. Haight, *Racine County in the World War*, 282. I also consulted with the Fairfield County Chapter of the Ohio Genealogical Society in reconstructing Denton's past.

109. Carl R. Denton, The Official Roster of Ohio Soldiers, Sailors, and Marines in the World War, 1917–18, ANC.

110. Karl Russell Denton World War II Draft Registration Card, U.S., World War II Draft Registration Cards, 1942, ANC.

111. Rialto, "Coburn's Show Pleases Many," 2.

112. "Coburn Minstrels Score Hit," 18.

113. "Coburn Is Glad to Be Back," 3.

114. White, "Nigger Blues."

115. "Famous Minstrel Show Coming to City," 7.

116. Toll, *Blacking Up*, 140–42.

117. Rialto, "Coburn's Show Pleases Many," 2.

118. "Coburn Minstrels Score Hit," 18.

119. "Amateur Minstrelsy Proved by the Elks," 4; Boyd, *Wide-Open Town*, 32–34.

120. "Lasses White Brings Great Minstrel Show," 14.

121. "Coburn's Minstrels Open Up in Miami," 3.

122. "Coburn Is Glad to Be Back," 3.

123. Rialto, "Coburn's Show Pleases Many," 2.

124. "Coburn Minstrels Score Hit," 18.

125. "Bradenton Has Lasses White Show," 8.

126. Ibid.

127. Toll, *Blacking Up*, 144; May, "Middle-Class Morality," 170–73.

128. Rialto, "Coburn's Show Pleases Many," 2.

129. Heap, *Slumming*, chaps. 5–6; Bean, "Black Minstrelsy and Double Inversion"; Roediger, *The Wages of Whiteness*.

130. Rialto, "Coburn's Show Pleases Many," 2.

131. May, "Middle-Class Morality," 160–62.

132. "Vermont Nominates His Minstrel Stars," 51.

133. Stanfield, *Body and Soul*, 114–15.

134. "Leary and Lee," 12.

135. Glick, *Materializing Queer Desire*, chap. 4.

136. "Opening of the Palatial Fairfax Theatre," 1.

137. "Amateur Minstrelsy Proved by the Elks," 4; "Fairfax Will Offer Bill of Amateurs," 2; "'Lasses' White Minstrel Good," 7.

138. Rose, *The Struggle for Black Freedom*, chap. 1.

139. Pharr, "Colored Town Section," 46.

140. Ibid.

141. "Lyric Theater, Miami, FLA.," 6.

142. "Stage Notes," 5.

143. Bean, "Black Minstrelsy and Double Inversion."

144. Chude-Sokei, *The Last "Darky."*

145. Bean, "Black Minstrelsy and Double Inversion," 180.

146. "Lyric Theater, Miami, FLA.," 6.

147. Smith, "No Good Man."

148. Chauncey, *Gay New York*, chap. 4.

149. Hurewitz, *Bohemian Los Angeles*, 44, chap. 1.

150. Gunter and Redmond, *A Florida Enchantment*, 55.

151. Drew, *A Florida Enchantment*.

152. Faderman and Timmons, *Gay L.A.*; Chauncey, *Gay New York*.

153. Drew, *A Florida Enchantment*.

154. Erenberg, *Steppin' Out*.

155. Drew, *A Florida Enchantment*.

156. Ibid.

157. Somerville, *Queering the Color Line*, chap. 2; Duggan, *Sapphic Slashers*.

158. "At Capital Theaters This Week," 15.

159. "Big Gaiety Company Decided Departure," 7.

160. Nelson, "Palm Trees, Public Relations, and Promoters."

161. Flinn, "Showmanship," 33.

162. "Smashing Window Displays Exploit 'Miami,'" 35–37.

163. "Don't Miss Bathing Girl Stunts," 45.

164. "Film House Reviews," 46.

165. "Arthur Knorr Stages Knockout," 8.

166. "New York Capitol," 45.

167. "Film House Reviews," 46.

168. Chauncey, *Gay New York*, chaps. 9, 11, 12; Heap, *Slumming*, 82–97, chap. 6.

169. "Evelyn Wilson," 62.

170. Heap, *Slumming*, chap. 5.

171. Boyd, *Wide-Open Town*, 35.

172. "Famous Minstrel Show Coming to City," 7; Hurewitz, *Bohemian Los Angeles*, 26–39.

173. "Coburn's Minstrels Open Up in Miami," 3.

174. "Bradenton Has Lasses White Show," 8. Also see "Coburn Minstrels Score Hit," 18.

175. Hurewitz, *Bohemian Los Angeles*, 34.

176. May, "White Lies and Stony Silence."

177. "Lasses White Minstrels to Come Nov. 3," 11.

178. Osborne, *Music in Ohio* 419; newspaper clipping, "Burnt Corkers Formed in Lancaster in 1941," Fairfield County Chapter of the Ohio Genealogical Society, Lancaster, OH.

179. "Minstrels to Entertain in Season Debut," 5.

180. Qtd. in Heap, *Slumming*, 34. Also see Clement, "From Sociability to Spectacle."

181. Advertisement: Capitol Theatre, 5; "Many Good Acts," 7.

182. "At White House Inn," 2.

183. Newspaper clipping, "Karl Denton, 64, Ex-Minstrel Man, Is Dead," May 9, 1957, box 13, Denton Family Collection, University of North Texas Special Collections, Denton, TX; 1930 United States Federal Census, Lancaster, Fairfield, OH, Roll 1791, 10A, ANC; "Longtime Minstrel Man Buried Today," 9.

184. Rose, *The Struggle for Black Freedom*, 23–29; Dunn, *Black Miami*, 143–58; Heap, *Slumming*, chap. 6.

185. "Taking It Over," 8.

186. Haskins, *Mabel Mercer*, 63.

187. Boyd, *Wide-Open Town*, 34–38.

CHAPTER FIVE

1. For more on this study, see Terry, *An American Obsession*, chap. 7.

2. Henry, *Sex Variants*, 465–77.

3. Ibid.

4. Ibid.

5. Ibid.

6. Chauncey, *Gay New York*, 88–89.

7. Terry, *An American Obsession*, chap. 7.

8. Henry, *Sex Variants*, 470, 474.

9. My gratitude to George Painter, whose earlier research helped me locate the cases pertinent to these shifts in Florida law. See Painter, "The Sensibilities of Our Forefathers."

10. Chauncey, *Gay New York*, chaps. 2, 4. Also see Boyd, *Wide-Open Town*, chap. 1; Johnson, "The Kids of Fairytown."

11. Boag, *Same-Sex Affairs*, chap. 1.

12. Ibid., 29–30; Chauncey, *Gay New York*, 89–95.

13. Terry, *An American Obsession*, 78–79.

14. Abelove, "Freud, Male Homosexuality," 61, 66.

15. Terry, *An American Obsession*, 55–62.

16. Abelove, "Freud, Male Homosexuality," 59–69.

17. "Vasile Is Acquitted," 14; General Index, binder G–M, MDCCA.

18. Rybczynski and Olin, *Vizcaya*, 106–7, 127–32.

19. Parks and Bennett, *Coconut Grove*, 91.

20. House Committee on Naval Affairs, *Estimates Submitted by the Secretary of the Navy*, 1002–3.

21. "Naval Air Station to Be Abandoned," 1.

22. "For Coconut Grove's Bank, Price Was Right."

23. Chauncey, *Gay New York*, 66–69; Boag, *Same-Sex Affairs*, chaps. 1–2.

24. Canaday, *The Straight State*, 57–58.

25. Chauncey, "Christian Brotherhood or Sexual Perversion?"

26. James Ray Harwell, Service No. 171-10-44, box 2, Florida Military Dept., World War I Navy Card Roster of Floridians, 1925, Series 1249, Florida Memory, State Library and Archives of Florida, https://www.floridamemory.com/.

27. Qtd. in Bérubé, *Coming Out under Fire*, 129–30.

28. James R. Harwell, Index to Atlanta Federal Penitentiary, Inmate Case Files, 1902–1921, NARA Southeast Region, 5780 Jonesboro Road, Morrow, GA, ANC.

29. Qtd. in Bérubé, *Coming Out under Fire*, 129–30.

30. "Who Stole My Girl?," *Friday Night*, Nov. 10, 1933, file 17, box 29, GDSC, SAF.

31. *Friday Night*, Nov. 10, 1933, file 17, box 29, GDSC, SAF.

32. Letter from Criminal Court of Record Judge William I. Metcalf to Board of Dade County Commissioners, July 21, 1908, Jail Conditions—Dade County, DCR, HM. See also Kunzel, *Criminal Intimacy*, 20–22.

33. Letter from Criminal Court of Record Judge William I. Metcalf to Board of Dade County Commissioners, July 21, 1908, Jail Conditions—Dade County, DCR, HM.

34. "Reasons Why Miami Should Have a Modern Y.M.C.A. Building," 2.

35. "Over $40,000 the First Day," 1–2; "YMCA Observing 40th Anniversary," 5B.

36. E. G. Wilson and I. B. Rhodes, "Some Suggestions for the Miami Young Men's Christian Association," Miami, 1938, YMCA National Level Research, Planning and Development: An Inventory of Miscellaneous Records, Kautz Family YMCA Archives, University of Minnesota, Archives and Special Collections, Minneapolis.

37. Gustav-Wrathall, *Take the Young Stranger by the Hand*. Also see Chauncey, *Gay New York*, chap. 6.

38. Chauncey, *Gay New York*, 156.

39. Henry, *Sex Variants*, 471.

40. Wilson and Rhodes, "Some Suggestions."

41. "Hotels Turning People Away," 1.

42. "YMCA Observing 40th Anniversary," 5B.

43. Capó, "'It's Not Queer to Be Gay,'" 88–89, 91–92; Bérubé, *Coming Out under Fire*, 109–10.

44. *Miami Life*, Oct. 22, 1933, file 17, box 29, GDSC, SAF.

45. "Segregated District and Home," 8.

46. Retzloff, "Cars and Bars," 228. Also see Howard, *Men Like That*, 100–101.

47. Fass, *The Damned and the Beautiful*.

48. "Segregated District and Home," 8.

49. Abraham, *Metropolitan Lovers*, 30.

50. "The Uses of the Loafer," 2.

51. Holmes, "What's the Tea," 56. Also see Liebow, *Tally's Corner*.

52. "Short Shrift," 27.

53. "The Rambler," Jan. 13, 1937, 4A.

54. "Some Town," *Friday Night*, Nov. 3, 1933, file 17, box 29, GDSC, SAF.

55. Ibid.

56. See "Things I'd Like to Know," *Miami Life*, Sept. 29, 1934, and March 2, 1935, JCPC.

57. "Long Masquerade as Woman Ends," 6.

58. Newspaper clipping, "Sheriff Raids 2 Night Clubs," box 1, RRTS, HM.

59. Newspaper clipping, "La Paloma 'Artists' Handed $25 Fines," box 1, RRTS, HM.

60. "Sheriff Raids 2 Night Clubs."

61. D'Emilio and Freedman, *Intimate Matters*, chap. 10; Abelove, "Freud, Male Homosexuality."

62. Canaday, *The Straight State*, chap. 1.

63. American Social Hygiene Association, *Social Hygiene*, 67, 72.

64. Snow, "Fight Planned," 4.

65. U.S. Interdepartmental Social Hygiene Board, "Appendix VIII," 71.

66. Snow, "Fight Planned," 4.

67. Laws of Fla. (1917), chap. 7361.

68. *Williams v. State*, 43 So. 431 (Fla. 1907); *Harris v. State*, 72 So. 520 (Fla. 1916).

69. *Blameuser v. State*, 142 So. 909 (Fla. 1932).

70. Laws of Fla. (1917), chaps. 7359 and 7360.

71. Ullman, *Sex Seen*, 66–67; Eskridge, *Dishonorable Passions*, 50.

72. Faderman and Timmons, *Gay L.A.*, 30.

73. McLaren, *The Trials of Masculinity*, 153.

74. Chauncey, *Gay New York*, 61.

75. *Lason v. State*, 12 So.2d 305 (Fla. 1943).

76. *Drawdy v. State*, 120 So. 844 (Fla. 1929); *Ephraim et al. v. State*, 89 So. 344 (Fla. 1921).

77. Laws of Fla. (1917), chap. 7361.

78. *Ephraim et al. v. State.*

79. U.S. Bureau of the Census, *U.S. Census of Population: 1950*, vol. 2.

80. Francis Brady to Gov. Sholtz, May 16, 1935, file 6, box 28, GDSC, SAF.

81. General Index, binders A–F, G–M, & N–Z, MDCCA.

82. General Index, binder G–M, MDCCA.

83. General Index, binder G–M, MDCCA.

84. Laws of Fla. (1868), chap. 11, §8.

85. General Index, binders G–M & N–Z, MDCCA.

86. Shah, *Stranger Intimacy*, 135–37; Robertson, "'Boys, of Course, Cannot Be Raped.'"

87. Laws of Fla. (1872), chap. 52, §8.

88. See *Medis and Hill v. State*, 27 Tex. App. 194 (1889).

89. Henry, *Sex Variants*, 474.

90. *Ephraim et al. v. State.*

91. Brief of plaintiff-in-error, *Blameuser v. State*, no. 7537, box 959, FSCCF, SAF.

92. Kofoed, "Boys in Girls' Clothes," 7B; "Miami Sex-Town," *Miami Life*, Feb. 2, 1935, 1, JCPC.

93. Cason, *Code of the City of Miami.*

94. Ibid., 217.

95. Cohen, "Negro Involuntary Servitude in the South."

96. Chauncey, *Gay New York*, 65.

97. General Index, binders A–F & G–M, MDCCA.

98. Florida Division of Corrections, Compiled Register, 1875–1959: D–I, Prisoner Registers, RG 670, box 2, Prisoner Registers, 1875–1972, no. S 500, SAF; 1920 United States Federal Census, Raiford, Bradford, FL, Roll T625_214, 5A, Enumeration District 44, Image 924, ANC; General Index, binder A–F, MDCCA. Also see Miller, *Hard Labor and Hard Time.*

99. U.S. Census Bureau, *Fourteenth Census of the United States, 1920*, 760–61.

100. Fairchild, *Greek Immigration*, 260; Ellis, "American Sponge Fisheries," 260.

101. Bernard, "Kalymnos," 291–307.

102. O'Mahen Malcom, "Greek Immigrant Experience," 232–34.

103. Fairchild, *Greek Immigration*, 206.

104. "Convicted Slayer of Greek Spongers," 14.

105. "Greek Sponge Fishers Face Miami Battle," 9.

106. Cram, *Old Seaport Towns of the South*, 218.

107. Henry, *Sex Variants*, 471.

108. Green, *Cassell's Dictionary of Slang*, 645.

109. "Things I'd Like to Know," *Miami Life*, Sept. 29, 1934, 1, JCPC.

110. Halperin, *One Hundred Years of Homosexuality*.

111. Boag, *Same-Sex Affairs*, chap. 2.

112. Mangold, *The Challenge of Saint Louis*, 42, 44.

113. Fairchild, *Greek Immigration*, 38–39.

114. Stedman, "Some of the Medical Aspects of Immigration," 978.

115. Canaday, *The Straight State*, 39.

116. Wilson, "Medical Examination of Immigrants," 505–6.

117. Stedman, "Some of the Medical Aspects of Immigration," 978.

118. Jacobson, *Whiteness of a Different Color*; Barrett and Roediger, "Inbetween Peoples,"3–44; Roediger, *Working toward Whiteness*.

119. Charteris, *The Saint in Miami*, 101.

120. General Index, binder G–M, MDCCA; 1910 United States Federal Census, West Tampa, Hillsborough, FL, Roll T624_161, 3B, Enumeration District 37, ANC.

121. "Many Defendants Enter Pleas at Court's Session," 4.

122. "Convicted Slayer of Greek Spongers," 14.

123. Barkan, *A Nation of Peoples*, 250.

124. Bernard, "Kalymnos," 295–96.

125. Gilmore, *Manhood in the Making*, 12. Also see Cram, *Old Seaport Towns of the South*, 216–22; Boag, *Same-Sex Affairs*, 19.

126. Freedman, *Redefining Rape*, 182; Sutton, "Greeks of Kalymnos," 421–22.

127. Bernard, "Kalymnos," 295–307; Sutton, "Greeks of Kalymnos."

128. *Ex Parte Joe L. Earman*, 95 So. 755 (Fla. 1923).

129. Cecil A. Turner to Gov. Sholtz, July 11, 1935, file 6, box 28, GDSC, SAF; *Miami Retreat Foundation v. Ervin*, 66 So. 2d 748 (Fla. 1952).

130. Nelson, "'More of a Prison than an Asylum,'" 75.

131. Noll, *Feeble-Minded in Our Midst*, 93–95, 123.

132. Noll, "Care and Control of the Feeble-Minded," 71–72.

133. "Abraham Goldman," file 11, box 123, FSHMR, SAF.

134. See "Elizabeth Collins," file 1, box 123, FSHMR, SAF; "A. B. Anderson," box 2, FSHCR, SAF.

135. "Clyde Caswell," file 12, box 89, FSHMR, SAF.

136. Qtd. in Larson, *Sex, Race, and Science*, 74.

137. Noll, *Feeble-Minded in Our Midst*, 65.

138. Ibid., 74–75.

139. Ibid., 74–78. Also see Kline, *Building a Better Race*, chap. 2.

140. "E. S. Strong," file 42, box 23, FSHMR, SAF.

141. "Walter General," file 150, box 23, FSHMR, SAF.

142. "William Birdsong," file 93, box 23, FSHMR, SAF; "William Birdsong," box 7, FSHCR, SAF.

143. "Israel Saunders," file 30, box 23, FSHMR, SAF.

144. "George Simmonet," file 56, box 122, FSHMR, SAF.

145. "Fred Anthom," box 2, FSHCR, SAF.

146. "Pearl Anthom," box 2, FSHCR, SAF.

147. "Vienna Joseph," file 4, box 8, FSHMR, SAF.

148. In emphasizing immigration from eastern and southern Europe, Steven Noll notes that institutions in the U.S. South "did not concern themselves" with "the relationship between mental deficiency and national origins." Shifting attention to the Caribbean, however, suggests otherwise. See Noll, *Feeble-Minded in Our Midst*, 121–22.

149. Qtd. in Kline, *Building a Better Race*, 54–55.

150. "Mamie Baxton," file 67, box 8, FSHMR, SAF. Also see "Sarah Wilson," file 32, box 123, FSHMR, SAF; MacLaren, "Clinical Lecture," 1–3.

151. "Mamie Coleman," file 81, box 8, FSHMR, SAF.

152. "Tislane Russell," file 34, box 123, FSHRM, SAF.

153. "L. C. Atkinson," box 2, FSHCR, SAF.

154. "Irving Young," box 95, FSHCR, SAF.

155. Qtd. in Noll, *Feeble-Minded in Our Midst*, 120–21, 197–98n63.

156. "Adele Galy," file 8, box 120, FSHMR, SAF.

157. Gualtieri, "Becoming 'White.'"

158. *Jackson v. State*, 94 So. 505 (Fla. 1922).

159. *Drawdy v. State*.

160. *Blameuser v. State*.

161. *English v. State*, 164 So. 848 (Fla. 1935).

162. Boag, *Same-Sex Affairs*, chaps. 1–2; Chauncey, *Gay New York*; Boyd, *Wide-Open Town*, chap. 1; Johnson, "The Kids of Fairytown."

163. Robertson, "'Boys, of Course, Cannot Be Raped,'" 358.

164. Laws of Fla. (1901), chaps. 4964 and 4965.

165. Robertson, "'Boys, of Course, Cannot Be Raped,'" 365.

166. Ibid., 371.

167. Transcript of record, *English v. State*, no. 10688, box 1382, FSCCF, SAF.

168. Transcript of record, *Ephraim et al. v. State*, no. 661, Loose Cases, FSCCF, SAF; Shah, *Stranger Intimacy*, 136–38.

169. Transcript of record, *Blameuser v. State*, no. 7537, box 959, FSCCF, SAF.

170. Motion in arrest of judgment, *English v. State*, no. 10688, box 1382, FSCCF, SAF.

171. *Franklin v. State*, 257 So. 2d 21 (Fla. 1971).

172. Brief of plaintiff-in-error, *English v. State*, no. 10688, box 1382, FSCCF, SAF.

173. Brief for the State, *English v. State*, no. 10688, box 1382, FSCCF, SAF.

174. *English v. State*.

175. Brief of plaintiff-in-error, *English v. State*.

176. J. Walter Kehoe to Gov. Sholtz, Nov. 9, 1936, file 7, box 28, GDSC, SAF; "J. Walter Kehoe," 32.

177. Transcript of record, *English v. State*, no. 10688, box 1382, FSCCF, SAF.

178. Brockley, "Martyred Mothers and Merciful Fathers," 294.

179. Transcript of record, *English v. State*, no. 10688, box 1382, FSCCF, SAF.

180. Connolly, *A World More Concrete*.

181. Transcript of record and brief of plaintiff-in-error, *Blameuser v. State*, no. 7537, box 959, FSCCF, SAF.

182. *Blameuser v. State.*

CHAPTER SIX

1. Kincannon, "Florida Haven of Happiness," 38.

2. "Amateur Minstrelsy Proved by the Elks," 4; Kincannon, "Florida Haven of Happiness," 38.

3. Kincannon, "Florida Haven of Happiness," 38.

4. Cott, "Passionlessness," 219–36; Lystra, *Searching the Heart.*

5. Jabour, *Marriage in the Early Republic*; Kerber, "Separate Spheres"; Cott, *The Bonds of Womanhood.*

6. Faderman, *Surpassing the Love of Men.*

7. Tweed, "An Emerging Protestant Establishment." Miami did, however, house Miss Harris's School, which offered young and adolescent girls intimate homosocial spaces and prepared many for college (although boys could also be admitted to the Day School). The boarding school, which opened in 1914, emphasized Miami's tropical climate and the salubrity that offered young girls. It catered to residents and long-term tourists alike through the twelfth grade. Sargent, *A Handbook of American Private Schools*, 210, 766.

8. Newton, "The Mythic Mannish Lesbian," 561–62.

9. Hansen, "'No Kisses Is Like Youres'"; Jones, *Labor of Love*; Lerner, "The Lady and the Mill Girl."

10. Woolson, "Felipa," 702.

11. "Miss Woolson's 'Rodman the Keeper.'"

12. "Bills Recommended by the Legislative Committee," 17.

13. "Dade County Is Voted Dry," 1.

14. "Commissioners Count Election Returns," 1.

15. Taylor, "The Woman Suffrage Movement in Florida."

16. Douglas, "State Suffrage Convention in Miami," 3.

17. "Suffrage League Members Agree," 5.

18. Thompson, *Woman*, 114.

19. "26 Out of 92 Votes Were Cast by Women," 1.

20. Rose, *The Struggle for Black Freedom*, 34–35.

21. Shell-Weiss, "Coming North to the South," 95–96; Craton and Saunders, *Islanders in the Stream*, 256–57.

22. Johnson, *The Quiet Revolution in the Bahamas.*

23. Sneider, *Suffragists in an Imperial Age*; Burton, *Burdens of History.*

24. "The Nassau Negro Problem," 4.

25. Ibid.

26. Meyerowitz, *Women Adrift*; Mjagkij and Spratt, *Men and Women Adrift.*

27. Shell-Weiss, *Coming to Miami*, 68–71.

28. Smiley, *The Whistles Were Blowing*, 3–20.

29. "Miami's Y.W.C.A.," 14; "At Nassau Hard Times Party," 14.

30. Qtd. in Smiley, *The Whistles Were Blowing*, 7–8, 10.

31. Pierson, "Vilona P. Cutler," 54–55.

32. Smiley, *The Whistles Were Blowing*, 14–16.

33. Qtd. in ibid., 16.

34. 1920 United States Federal Census, Miami, FL, Roll T625_216, 22B, ANC.

35. York, *Some Adventures of Two Vagabonds*.

36. Reitman, *Sister of the Road*.

37. Davis, *Everglades Providence*, 96; Douglas, *Marjory Stoneman Douglas*, 70–71.

38. Qtd. in Davis, *Everglades Providence*, 154.

39. Douglas, *Marjory Stoneman Douglas*, 85.

40. Ibid., 89.

41. Ibid., 101–24.

42. Davis, *Everglades Providence*, 656, fn3.

43. Douglas, "Japanese Costume Ball," 12.

44. McCarthy, *Nine Florida Stories*, ix–x.

45. Douglas, "He-Man," 51.

46. Duval, "Some Sex Cases," 169–70.

47. Douglas, "He-Man," 50–51.

48. Ibid., 52.

49. Ibid., 57; my emphasis.

50. Ibid., 61.

51. Ibid., 58–59.

52. Chauncey, *Gay New York*, 3, 64.

53. Perry, "Lotus Spell Cast on Visitors," 10.

54. Cason, *Code of the City of Miami*, 217.

55. Newton, "The Mythic Mannish Lesbian."

56. Smith-Rosenberg, *Disorderly Conduct*, 281–85; Terry, *An American Obsession*, 97–100.

57. Duggan, *Sapphic Slashers*, 26–29.

58. "Wearies of Waiting a Comstock Arrest," 7.

59. "'September Morn' Can't Be Seen in Magic City," 1; 1910 United States Federal Census, Miami, Dade, FL, Roll, T624_158, 19A & 25A, ANC.

60. Kendrick, *The Secret Museum*, 143.

61. "'September Morn' Can't Be Seen in Magic City," 1.

62. Katz, *The Invention of Heterosexuality*, chap. 2.

63. Holmes, "The Public Pulse, July 15, 1913," 4C.

64. Stahl, "The Public Pulse, July 17, 1913," 4C.

65. See "Oh, You September Morn," 4; "September Morn and the Press," 6; "State Press Comment," 4.

66. Kleinberg, "The Censorship Flap of '13," 4C.

67. "'September Morn' Can't Be Seen in Magic City," 1.

68. Holmes, "The Public Pulse, July 15, 1913," 4C.

69. D'Emilio and Freedman, *Intimate Matters*, chaps. 10–11.

70. Nelson, "Palm Trees, Public Relations, and Promoters."

71. "Entertainment Variety Listed at Showplaces," 10.

72. "Where to Find Entertainment in Miami Area," April 28, 1927, 12.

73. Faderman and Timmons, *Gay L.A.*

74. "Where to Find Entertainment in Miami Area," April 19, 1927, 10.

75. Reprinted in "Turn About," 2.

76. "Thingumbobs," 4.

77. Simmons, "Companionate Marriage and the Lesbian Threat," 54–59; Katz, *The Invention of Heterosexuality.*

78. Erenberg, *Steppin' Out*; Peiss, *Cheap Amusements*; Peiss, *Hope in a Jar*; Simmons, *Making Marriage Modern.*

79. Vandenberg-Daves, "The Manly Pursuit of a Partnership."

80. "Gleanings from the Press," 2A. Also see "Menace of Companionate Marriage," 6.

81. Davis, "'Not Marriage at All'"; Simmons, *Making Marriage Modern.*

82. Bailey, *From Front Porch to Back Seat*; D'Emilio and Freedman, *Intimate Matters*, chaps. 10–11.

83. Tribune Society Department, "Family Album," 4. Consumer Price Inflation Calculator, U.S. Department of Labor, Bureau of Labor Statistics, http://data.bls.gov/cgi-bin/cpicalc.pl (accessed March 23, 2017).

84. Fass, *The Damned and the Beautiful*, chap. 6.

85. Tribune Society Department, "Family Album," 4.

86. Retzloff, "Cars and Bars."

87. Perry, "Lotus Spell Cast on Visitors," 10.

88. Lardner, "Lardner Observes Miami Mermaids," 26.

89. *Miami–Palm Beach–Havana Gimlet*, Season of 1929–30, XC2002.11.4.218, VGLC, WFIU.

90. "Miami Beach Censorless," 14.

91. Chauncey, *Gay New York*, 126.

92. "Miami Beach Censorless," 14.

93. Roberts, "Tropical Growth," 80.

94. "These Mermaids Add to Lures," 23.

95. Neil, "Miami Mermaid Retains Title," 2B.

96. Fisher, *Fabulous Hoosier*, 128.

97. Warner, *When the Girls Came Out to Play*, 79.

98. Fisher, *Fabulous Hoosier*, 128–29.

99. Ibid., 129.

100. Bramson, *Sunshine*, 139–40.

101. Ruark, "Steve Hannagan," 25.

102. Carl Fisher to O. W. Kennedy, June 13, 1927; O. W. Kennedy to Carl Fisher, June 27, 1927, Miami Beach—Advertising (Correspondence), box 10, CGFP, HM.

103. "Steve Hannagan's Girls," 18–22.

104. U.S. Census Bureau, "Table 18," *Fifteenth Census of the United States: 1930*, 412.

105. *Chevrolet Leader News* 2, no. 1 (1936), https://archive.org/details/Chevrole1936 (accessed Oct. 17, 2016).

106. Porter, "Anything Goes."

107. Custen, "Too Darn Hot."

108. Library of Congress, U.S. Copyright Office, *Catalogue of Copyright Entries*, part 3, *Musical Compositions*, vols. 26, 27, 28, 30, 31.

109. F. W. Vandersloot (music) and Ray Sherwood (lyric), "Dreamy Havana Moon Song," c. 1926, XC2002.11.4.145, VGLC, WFIU; Norman Spencer (music) and Joe McKiernan (lyric), "Cuban Moon," c.1920, XC2002.11.4.156, VGLC, WFIU.

110. R. Roy Coats (music and lyric), "I'm Going Down to Old Havana Town," c. 1921, XC2002.11.4.154, VGLC, WFIU.

111. Pérez, "Between Encounter and Experience," 178.

112. Roberts, *Sun Hunting*, 183–84.

113. Peiss, *Cheap Amusements*.

114. Remus, "Tippling Ladies," 753.

115. Cohen, *A Consumers' Republic*, chap. 1.

116. "Latest in Resort Modes," 3.

117. "Styles Observed in the Southland," X10.

118. Foster, "Miami to Set Winter Fashions for Milady," 10.

119. Clemente, "Made in Miami," 138.

120. Shell-Weiss, *Coming to Miami*, 140.

121. *Chevrolet Leader News* 2, no. 1.

122. "Vacation Days in the Bahamas," 15.

123. "Women in Trousers," 1, 4.

124. Globe Tours, Inc., *Havana Tours Brochure*, c. 1925, XC2002.11.4.13, VGLC, WFIU.

125. Davis Tours, Inc., *Havana Guidebook*, c. 1930, XC2002.11.4.219, VGLC WFIU.

126. Schwartz, *Pleasure Island*, 70.

127. Briggs, *Reproducing Empire*, chap. 3. Also see Kline, *Building a Better Race*.

128. Hernández and Piñero, *Historia del humor gráfico en Cuba*, 77–78.

129. Pérez, *On Becoming Cuban*, 315.

130. See *Carteles*, June 30, 1934, June 21, 1936, Sept. 13, 1936, June 6, 1937, and May 8, 1938.

131. Hernández Catá, *El placer de sufrir*, 32; my translation.

132. Ibid., 42–43; my translation.

133. Ibid., 45; my translation.

134. Pérez, "Between Encounter and Experience," 175–79.

135. Rodríguez, "The Architectural Avant-Garde," 255–63.

136. "It's Just an 'Old Spanish Custom,'" *Condé Nast Travel Directory*, Jan. 1931, XC2002.11.4.260, VGLC, WFIU.

137. Ibid. Also see "Havana a Second, Almost a Gayer, Riviera."

138. Pérez, *Cuba in the American Imagination*, chap. 2.

139. *Miami–Palm Beach–Havana Gimlet*.

140. Sippial, *Prostitution*, chap. 5.

141. Stoner, *From the House to the Streets*, 46–53.

142. Ibid., 113.

143. Pérez, *On Becoming Cuban*, 312–16.

144. "Miami Beach Censorless," 14.

145. Ibid.

146. Stearns, *Fat History*, chap. 4.

147. "Miami Beach Censorless," 14.

148. Cocks, *Tropical Whites*, 110–23; Peiss, *Hope in a Jar*, chap. 5; Warner, *When the Girls Came Out to Play*, chap. 4.

149. Bederman, *Manliness and Civilization*, 149.

150. Cocks, *Tropical Whites*, 112.

151. Qtd. in Peiss, *Hope in a Jar*, chap. 5.

152. Cocks, *Tropical Whites*, 118.

153. "Miami Beach Censorless," 14.

154. Roberts, *Sun Hunting*, 184.

155. "Miami Beach Censorless," 14.

156. "Florida Anglers Now Hook Pretty Mermaids," 1.

157. Postcard from Miami, FL, to Paducah, KY, June 1941, author's collection.

158. Peiss, *Hope in a Jar*; Davis, "'Not Marriage at All.'"

159. Qtd. in Lavender, *Miami Beach in 1920*, 107.

160. "Latest in Resort Modes."

161. Cocks, *Tropical Whites*, 119.

162. Tribune Society Dept., "Family Album," 4.

163. Bederman, *Manliness and Civilization*; Heap, *Slumming*.

164. Tribune Society Dept., "Family Album," 4.

165. Kline, *Building a Better Race*, 59.

166. Simmons, *Making Marriage Modern*, 143.

167. White, *The First Sexual Revolution*, 167.

168. Tribune Society Dept., "Family Album," 4.

169. Davis, "'Not Marriage at All,'" 1138–39; Heap, *Slumming*.

170. "The People's Forum," 4.

171. Chase, "Not Censoring Bathers' Dress," 4.

172. "Miami Beach Censorless," 14.

173. "Freedom for Bathers," 4.

174. Fisher, *Fabulous Hoosier*, 128–29.

175. "Forecast for Next Week," *Miami Life*, April 13, 1935, 2, JCPV.

CHAPTER SEVEN

1. "Club Klan Raided Closed Down," 1A; newspaper clipping, "La Paloma Ban Asked by State," box 1, RRTS, HM; Kelly's Torch Club newspaper advertisement, n.d., author's collection. I am grateful to Miami Spring Memories for originally posting the ad and allowing me to use it. See https://www.facebook.com/MiamiSpringsMemories/.

2. "Club Klan Raided Closed Down," 1A.

3. Ibid., 1A–2A.

4. For the voyeurism of civilian-led surveillance, see Fronc, *New York Undercover*.

5. "Club Klan Raided Closed Down," 1A–2A.

6. "County Night Spots Closed by Sheriff," 1A.

7. Newspaper clipping, "La Paloma Club Reopens," box 1, RRTS, HM.

8. Eastman, Scott & Company Summer Campaign, file 3, box 4, GDSC, SAF; newspaper clipping, "Florida to Make Strong Bid for Summer Tourists," file 3, box 4, GDSC, SAF.

9. Muir, *Miami, U.S.A.*; Bachin and James, "Miami Beach, Florida," 175–82.

10. Shell-Weiss, *Coming to Miami*, 104; Moore, *To the Golden Cities*.

11. *El Mundo*, May 30, 1936, qtd. in Maribona, *Turismo y ciudadanía*, 311, G155. C9M3, CHC, UM; my translation.

12. Chauncey, *Gay New York*, chap. 12.

13. Heap, *Slumming*, 89–94.

14. Boyd, *Wide-Open Town*, 47–48.

15. Dorman, "Miami Bootlegger Is a Businessman," 11.

16. "$28,000,000 Voted to Aid Prohibition," 25; Buchanan, "Miami's Bootleg Boom," 13.

17. Sáenz Rovner, "La prohibición norteamericana y el contrabando."

18. "Florida Gulf Coast Is Called Paradise for Bootleggers," 1.

19. "The Bootlegger's Bad Ways," 34.

20. Carter, "Florida and Rumrunning," 49.

21. Buchanan, "Miami's Bootleg Boom: A Decade of Prohibition," 29.

22. Buchanan, "Miami's Bootleg Boom"; George, "Bootleggers," 34–41.

23. "The Bootlegger's Bad Ways," 31–32.

24. Schwartz, *Pleasure Island*, 40, 45.

25. Irving Berlin (music and lyric), "I'll See You in C-U-B-A," 1920, Item 45, box 78, Lester S. Levy Sheet Music Collection, Johns Hopkins University, Sheridan Libraries, Special Collections, Baltimore, MD, http://levysheetmusic.mse.jhu.edu/.

26. Halsey K. Mohr (music) and William Tracey (lyric), "It Will Never Be Dry Down in Havana," c. 1920, XC2002.11.4.144, VGLC, WFIU.

27. Program for *Pagan Lady*, Nixon Theatre, Oct. 1930, author's collection.

28. Dillon, *The Pagan Lady*.

29. Stuart, "Constructing Identity," 33.

30. Maribona, *Turismo y ciudadanía*, 95; my translation.

31. López Lima, *Turismo y urbanismo*, 11–15, G155.C9L6, CHC, UM; my translation. Also see Corporación Nacional del Turismo, "Boletín," Dec. 1935, file 1, box 27, GDSC, SAF.

32. López Lima, *Turismo y urbanismo*, 116–17.

33. Maribona, *Turismo y ciudadanía*, 296–97; my translation.

34. Ibid., 206; my translation.

35. *Avance*, Sept. 29, 1935, qtd. in Maribona, *Turismo y ciudadanía*, 135–37; my translation.

36. Ibid.; my translation. In some circles in Cuba today, the word *cuadro* can also refer to group sex that may be exhibitionist or performed for entertainment purposes. While its usage in Cuba during the 1930s certainly implied sexual exhibitionism, it is uncertain if the term referred to group sex. Thank you to Annet Sanchez for helping me make this distinction.

37. Pérez, *Cuba in the American Imagination*, 235–37.

38. Maribona, *Turismo y ciudadanía*, 320; my translation.

39. Ibid.; my translation.

40. Ibid., 296; my translation.

41. De la Fuente, *A Nation for All*; Dur and Gilcrease, "US Diplomacy and the Downfall of a Cuban Dictator."

42. James Carson, "The Ifs and Ands of Race Track Gambling in Florida," April 1929, RFP, HM.

43. *Committee of One Hundred Newsletter*, May 4, 1934, 20, box 20, COHN, HM.

44. *El Mundo*, May 30, 1936, qtd. in Maribona, *Turismo y ciudadanía*, 311; my translation.

45. Stuart, "Constructing Identity," 37.

46. Walter J. Matherly, "Primary Functions of Florida Advertising," file 4, box 4, GDSC, SAF; "Millions Are Being Spent to Take Business Away from Florida," file 4, box 4, GDSC, SAF.

47. Qtd. in Carter, "Florida and Rumrunning," 56.

48. House Committee on the Judiciary, *Hearings on the Prohibition Amendment*, 730–31.

49. B. Angus to Gov. Sholtz, Feb. 27, 1933, file 8, box 4, GDSC, SAF.

50. Kofoed, "Miami," 673.

51. Qtd. in newspaper clipping, "Greater Miami, World Resort," RFP, HM.

52. Sheriff Hardie to Gov. Sholtz, Jan. 30, 1933, file 2, box 30, GDSC, SAF; Schwartz, *Pleasure Island*.

53. "Excerpt from WQAM News Program," Feb. 29, 1936, file 7, box 28, GDSC, SAF.

54. Bergreen, *Capone*, 78–81.

55. Leslie, "The Great Depression in Miami Beach," 44.

56. *Committee of One Hundred Newsletter*, April 1941, 6, box 21, COHN, HM.

57. "Clayton Sedgwick Cooper," 4.

58. *Committee of One Hundred Newsletter*, Jan. 1, 1934, 10, box 20, COHN, HM; "Miami Women Raise Carrie Nation Banner," 5.

59. *Committee of One Hundred Newsletter*, Jan. 30, 1932, 17, COHN, B20, HM.

60. City of Miami Beach Council Minutes, Jan. 14, 1931, CMB.

61. *Committee of One Hundred Newsletter*, Feb. 28, 1934, 15–16, box 20, COHN, HM.

62. Qtd. in Edmonds, *The Prohibition Question*, 48.

63. "92 Arrested in Miami War on Petty Vice," 1.

64. Dulles, *America Learns to Play*, 308–19; Aron, *Working at Play*, 156–236.

65. Scrapbook, "The History of Our TCT," 1946, box 2, TCTWR, SAF; Hurley, *Diners, Bowling Alleys and Trailer Parks*, 195–206.

66. Maribona, *Turismo y ciudadanía*, 8, 71–72.

67. *Trailer News*, Dec. 1936/Jan. 1937, file 5, box 1, TCTWR, SAF.

68. "Where Motor Tourists Spend Their Vacations in Florida" and Florida State Chamber of Commerce release, June 22, 1935, file 4, box 4, GDSC, SAF.

69. Newspaper clippings, "Trailer Tintypes," file 5, box 1, TCTWR, SAF.

70. Scrapbook, "The History of Our TCT"; Constitution and By-Laws of Tin Can Tourists of the World, Inc., file 1, box 1, TCTWR, SAF.

71. *Friday Night*, Nov. 3, 1933, file 17, box 29, GDSC, SAF.

72. "Former Mayor Lang Tells Miami Tin Can Tourists 'Undesirable,'" 5.

73. Newspaper clipping, "Molester Arrested 4th Time," box 1, RRTS, HM.

74. "Miami District Unites against Capone Menace," 1.

75. "City Commission Adopts New Vagrancy Ordinance," 1.

76. "Miami's Vagrancy Drive Ordinance Becomes Law," 14.

77. "Negro Vagrant Drive Started in Miami Area," 4.

78. Bousquet, "The Gangster in Our Midst," 298–304.

79. "Fisher Testifies," 1, 4.

80. Bousquet, "The Gangster in Our Midst," 306–9.

81. *Sky Talk*, "Florida and the Gamblers," May 25, 1929, RFP, HM.

82. Greater Miami Ministerial Association to Gov. Sholtz, July 14, 1933, file 15, box 29, GDSC, SAF.

83. Clipsheet, "Florida and the Gamblers," April 1, 1929, RFP, HM.

84. Statement issued by Ministerial Association of Greater Miami, Jan. 1927, RFP, HM.

85. Newspaper clipping, "Sheriff Allen Replies to Botts' Statement," RFP, HM.

86. Ibid.

87. Newspaper clipping, "Miami Is Wide Open Again," RFP, HM.

88. P. L. Dodge to Gov. Sholtz, Nov. 10, 1933, file 17, box 29, GDSC, SAF.

89. Anonymous to L. R. Railey, Feb. 25, 1931, RFP, HM.

90. James Carson, "The Ifs and Ands of Race Track Gambling in Florida," April 1929, RFP, HM.

91. *Sky Talk*, "Florida and the Gamblers," May 25, 1929.

92. Ortiz, *Emancipation Betrayed*.

93. Dunn, *Black Miami*, 117–24.

94. MacLean, *Behind the Mask of Chivalry*, xiii, 98–99.

95. Reprinted 1908 advertisement: Dan Hardie, Candidate for Sheriff, 4C.

96. In the Matter of the Suspension of Dan Hardie, n.d., file 2, box 30, GDSC, SAF.

97. Leslie, "The Great Depression in Miami Beach," 42.

98. Miami WCTU to Gov. Sholtz, May 24, 1933, file 15, box 29, GDSC, SAF; Dade County League of Democratic Women Voters to Gov. Sholtz, Nov. 2, 1933, file 17, box 29, GDSC, SAF; S278, B29, FF17; Committee of One Hundred to Gov. Sholtz, March 31, 1933, file 2, box 30, GDSC, SAF.

99. J. R. B. Clemons to Gov. Sholtz, Nov. 3, 1933, file 17, box 29, GDSC, SAF.

100. "The New Deal," *Miami Rote*, April 5, 1933, file 2, box 30, GDSC, SAF.

101. Herbert Myers to Gov. Sholtz, Oct. 28, 1933, file 17, box 29, GDSC, SAF.

102. Nelson, "Florida Crackers," 55–58; Cox, "David Sholtz," 142–52.

103. Signed petition, Feb. 18, 1935, file 6, box 29, GDSC, SAF.

104. *Miami Mirror* to Gov. Sholtz, Feb. 21, 1935, file 6, box 29, GDSC, SAF.

105. Confidential Resolution by Labor's Citizenship Committee, Oct. 26, 1933, file 17, box 29, GDSC, SAF.

106. Kent Watson and Frank Fildes to Gov. Sholtz, Jan. 25, 1935, file 6, box 29, GDSC, SAF.

107. MacLean, *Behind the Mark of Chivalry*, chap. 3.

108. Stuart, "Constructing Identity," 38–39.

109. City of Miami Beach Council Minutes, Jan. 16, 1931, CMB.

110. Disposition of the Cases *The State of Florida v. Fred Pine*, file 8, box 30, GDSC, SAF.

111. "La Paloma Ban Asked by State."

112. "Life Sentences for Robbery Pair Asked," 4.

113. Miller, "The Life and Crimes of Harry Sitamore."

114. Sheriff Coleman to Gov. Sholtz, April 19, 1933, file 16, box 27, GDSC, SAF.

115. U.S. Department of State to Gov. Sholtz, March 27, 1933, file 16, box 27, GDSC, SAF.

116. Pérez, "Between Encounter and Experience," 179.

117. "Large Sum Bet," 2.

118. Kleinberg, "Hialeah: Prairie to Pari-Mutuels," 4C; Bauer, "Sarasota: Hardship and Tourism in the 1930s," 141.

119. Bell, "O'er the Sports Desk," 10.

120. Sheriff Hardie to Gov. Sholtz, Jan. 30, 1932, file 2, box 30, GDSC, SAF.

121. Walters, *Audition*, 34–35; "Bill Dwyer Dies," 32.

122. "Irving Young," C-17584, box 95, FSHMR.

123. Henry, *Sex Variants*, 474.

124. Grant, "Crime over Miami," 83–89.

125. Reitman, *Sister of the Road*, 79–80, 184–85.

126. Newspaper clipping, "Colorful Crowd Sees Program of Six Races," RFP, HM.

127. Anonymous letter to L. R. Railey, Nov. 20, 1928, RFP, HM.

128. *Friday Night*, Oct. 20, 1933, file 17, box 29, GDSC, SAF.

129. Porter, "Plea of Cubans Exiled Here," E1.

130. Stuart, "Constructing Identity."

131. Newspaper clipping, "Ultimatum to Race-Track Gamblers," RFP, HM.

132. Guthrie, "Rekindling the Spirits," 23–39; Guthrie, *Keepers of the Spirits*.

133. "Night Clubs," *Friday Night*, Oct. 20, 1933, file 17, box 29, GDSC, SAF.

134. Durante and Kofoed, *Night Clubs*, 184, 245.

135. "Mary Kirk Brown Weds Miami Beach Youth," 16.

136. Brigham, "'Mother Kelly' Gives Up Night Club," 16.

137. "Walter Winchell on Broadway," 4.

138. "Good Season."

139. Mother Kelly's matchbook covers, n.d., author's collection.

140. Ibid.; Mother Kelly's postcard, n.d., author's collection.

141. Henry, *Sex Variants*, 346; Grant, "Crime over Miami," 83; Harnell and Skutch, *Counterpoint*, 50–51.

142. *Committee of One Hundred Newsletter*, May 4, 1934, 20, box 20, COHN, HM.

143. *Sky Talk*, "Florida and the Gamblers," May 25, 1929, RFP, HM.

144. Arnaz, *A Book*, 23–63; Abreu, *Rhythms of Race*.

145. Kofoed, *Moon over Miami*, 229–31.

146. *Committee of One Hundred Newsletter*, Aug. 31, 1933, 9, box 20, COHN, HM.

147. Guthrie, "Hard Times," 441.

148. McGirr, *The War on Alcohol*.

149. Laws of Fla. (1933), chap. 16087.

150. Henry Hanson (Florida State Board of Health) to Gov. Sholtz, May 19, 1934, file 7, box 4, GDSC, SAF.

151. Anonymous to Gov. Sholtz, May 10, 1935, file 6, box 28, GDSC, SAF; "Welcome Back Bootleggers," *Miami Life*, Nov. 10, 1934, 1, JCPC.

152. Laws of Fla. (1933), chap. 15884.

153. Leslie, "The Great Depression in Miami Beach," 66–69; "Main Items of New Liquor Ordinance," *Miami Life*, Dec. 1, 1934, 1, JCPC.

154. Testimony of Percy Hunter, 1936, file 7, box 28, GDSC, SAF.

155. V. Clinton to Gov. Sholtz, Feb. 24, 1935, file 6, box 28, GDSC, SAF.

156. Kofoed, *Moon over Miami*, 226.

157. Anonymous to Gov. Sholtz, March 3, 1934, file 9, box 28, GDSC, SAF.

158. Sheriff Coleman to Gov. Sholtz, Feb. 5, 1934, file 9, box 28, GDSC, SAF.

159. John Brozzo to Gov. Sholtz, Jan. 20, 1934, file 9, box 28, GDSC, SAF.

160. "Protect the Morals of Children," file 7, box 28, GDSC, SAF. "Miami Girl Murder," 1.

161. Newspaper clipping, "Fight over Hialeah 'Hot Spot' Averted," box 1, RRTS, HM; Barnhill, "Once Lawless Hialeah," 8.

162. "Night Spot Closing Order Is Modified," 1, 4.

163. "Illegal or Legal Liquor," *Friday Night*, Nov. 10, 1933, file 17, box 29, GDSC, SAF.

164. Grant, "Crime over Miami," 62.

165. Laws of Fla. (1937), chap. 17833; "Zoning Regulations in County Discussed."

166. T. L. Bowers to Gov. Sholtz, June 27, 1936, file 7, box 28, GDSC, SAF.

167. Boyd, *Wide-Open Town*, 52–56, 73–83.

168. Telegram from KKK to Gov. Sholtz, May 14, 1935, file 7, box 30, GDSC, SAF.

169. Newspaper clipping, "Ku Klux Threatens Miami Cleanup," file 1, box 27, GDSC, SAF.

170. Kofoed, *Moon over Miami*, 229.

171. Newspaper clipping, "Torch Is Told to Clean Show or Close Club," box 1, RRTS, HM.

172. Kelly's Torch Club newspaper advertisement.

173. Charteris, *The Saint in Miami*, 140, 136–37.

174. Cross, "Race Plant at Tropical Park, Miami," 20.

175. "Irving Young," C-17584, box 95, FSHMR, SAF.

176. Connolly, *A World More Concrete*, 80–81.

177. Petit, "Bolita and Cuba Survive 'The Heat,'" 8D; Connolly, *A World More Concrete*, 80–81. Also see White et al., *Playing the Numbers*.

178. Sheriff Hardie to Gov. Sholtz, Jan. 30, 1932.

179. Grant, "Crime over Miami," 83–84.

180. Wheatley, *Murder off Miami*; Chauncey, "Christian Brotherhood or Sexual Perversion?"

181. King, *Murder Masks Miami*, 33, 58–60, 106, 156.

182. Jack Kofoed, "Boys in Girls' Clothes," 7B.

183. Heap, *Slumming*, 240.

184. Kofoed, "Boys in Girls' Clothes," 7B. Also see Butler, *Gender Trouble*, 175–93.

185. "Miami Club Must Change Its Songs," 16.

186. Kofoed, "Boys in Girls' Clothes," 7B.

187. "Torch Club Replies," *Miami Life*, Feb. 9, 1935, 1, JCPC.

188. Kofoed, "Boys in Girls' Clothes," 7B.

189. "Miami Sex-Town," *Miami Life*, Feb. 2, 1935, 1, JCPC.

190. Kofoed, "Boys in Girls' Clothes," 7B.

191. Newspaper clipping, "Sheriff Raids 2 Night Clubs," box 1, RRTS, HM.

192. For more on the employment of physical violence to defend queer spaces and people, see Kennedy and Davis, *Boots of Leather, Slippers of Gold*, chap. 3.

193. Newspaper clipping, "Trio Convicted in Club Brawl," box 1, RRTS, HM.

194. Newspaper clipping, "Club Brawl Jails Three," box 1, RRTS, HM.

195. Newspaper clipping, "La Paloma 'Artists' Handed $25 Fines," box 1, RRTS, HM.

196. "Torch Club Replies," 1.

197. "Sheriff Raids 2 Night Clubs"; "La Paloma 'Artists' Handed $25 Fines."

198. Kofoed, "Boys in Girls' Clothes," 7B.

199. "Sheriff Raids 2 Night Clubs."

200. "Things I'd Like to Know," *Miami Life*, March 23, 1935, 3, JCPC.

201. Noll, "Care and Control of the Feeble-Minded."

202. Dunn, *Black Miami*, 138–39. Also see Rose, *The Struggle for Black Freedom*, chap. 2.

203. Dunn, *Black Miami*, 138–39.

204. British Consulate General, New Orleans, to Gov. Sholtz, June 6, 1933, file 8, box 28, GDSC, SAF; Dade County Unemployed Citizens League to Gov. Sholtz, June 24, 1933, file 8, box 28, GDSC, SAF.

205. "Help Wanted," n.d., file 9, box 28, GDSC, SAF.

206. Geo. A. Kramer to Gov. Sholtz, April 20, 1935, file 6, box 28, GDSC, SAF.

207. "Klan Is Not Law," 5.

208. "Miami Night Life Loses 'Hot Spots,'" 2.

209. "Night Spot Closing Order Is Modified," 1, 4.

210. "Early Club Opening Is Seen by Manager," 9A.

211. Heap, *Slumming*, 89–94.

212. Chauncey, *Gay New York*, chap. 12.

213. Sullivan, "Broadway Characters," 20.

214. Killen, "Miami Night Clubs," 18. Also see "Good Season."

215. "Good Season."

216. Kelly's Torch Club newspaper advertisement.

217. Chauncey, *Gay New York*, 227–28.

218. Killen, "Miami Night Clubs," 18.

219. Chauncey, *Gay New York*, chap. 12.

220. "Sheriff Raids 2 Night Clubs."

221. Ibid.

222. Heap, *Slumming*, 52–53.

223. Patron, "Jackie Johnson," 10–11.

224. Newspaper clipping, "La Paloma Ban Asked by State," box 1, RRTS, HM.

225. "Sheriff Raids 2 Night Clubs."

226. Ibid. Also see "Two Miami Clubs Raided by Cops," 2.

227. McDermott, "Male Strip-Tease Act Too Raw," 13.

228. Kofoed, "Boys in Girls' Clothes," 7B.

229. McDermott, "Male Strip-Tease Act Too Raw," 13.

230. "Tonight's the Night"; Romesburg, "Longevity and Limits," 119–35.

231. Dunn, *Black Miami*, chap. 4.

232. Connolly, *A World More Concrete*, chap. 3.

233. Barnes, "Walter Barnes Finds Many Big Broadwayites," 20.

234. Sweeting, "Miami," 31; Sweeting, "Night Life in Miami," 97–98.

235. Baker, Burke, and Corelli, "Nuits de Miami."

236. Dunn, *Black Miami*, 150–51.

237. Coleman, "The Jewel Box Revue," 79–91.

238. Paulson and Simpson, *An Evening at the Garden of Allah*, chap. 5.

239. Newspaper clipping, file 179, box 8, CSPP, YU.

240. Souvenir program, *Danny and Doc's Jewel Box Revue*, c. 1951, author's collection.

241. Souvenir program, *The Jewel Box Revue: Show Sensation of the Nation*, n.d., author's collection.

242. J. D. Doyle, who was gifted Danny Brown's scrapbooks, has conducted prodigious research and uncovered significant findings that challenge much of the information presented in the souvenir programs distributed by the Jewel Box Revue. My analysis relies on this and several other sources. See http://queermusicheritage.com/jbr.html (accessed March 6, 2016).

243. "'Jewel Box' Opens at Embassy Hotel."

244. Jackie Johnson to Candida Scott Piel, Feb. 21, 1984, file 180, box 8, CSPP, YU; Coleman, "The Jewel Box Revue," 80; Drorbaugh, "Sliding Scales," 132; Patron, "Jackie Johnson," 10–11.

245. Souvenir program, *Danny and Doc's Jewel Box Revue*.

246. Coleman, "The Jewel Box Revue," 81.

247. Harnell and Skutch, *Counterpoint*, 50–51.

248. Kennedy and Davis, *Boots of Leather, Slippers of Gold*, xii, xixn4.

249. Dauphin, "'A Bit of Woman in Every Man,'" 1–16; Drorbaugh, "Sliding Scales."

250. Newspaper clipping, "Jewel Box Sets Road Show Dates," file 179, box 8, CSPP, YU.

251. "Season Open Early," 4–7; "Miami Launches Winter Season Early This Year," 10B.

252. Newspaper clipping, *Rochester Sun*, Aug. 30, 1951, file 179, box 8, CSPP, YU.

253. Boyd, *Wide-Open Town*, 54–56.

254. Program, *Jewel Box Revue*, n.d., file 179, box 8, CSPP, YU; souvenir program, *The Jewel Box Revue: Show Sensation of the Nation*.

255. Harnell and Skutch, *Counterpoint*, 50–51.

256. Patron, "Jackie Johnson," 10–11.

257. "Jewel Box Gets License"; "Bar Operator Declared Guilty."

258. "Bookies in Confusion after Surprise Raids," 1A–2A.

EPILOGUE

1. "Raiders Seize 19 in Pervert Roundup," 1A.

2. "Attorney Scores Miami Morals," 3.

3. "Government Opens Case against Pine," 5.

4. Brigham, "'Mother Kelly' Gives Up Night Club," 16.

5. "Court Rules City May License Club," 6B.

6. "Nightclub Loses Venetian Area Zoning Appeal."

7. Souvenir program, *Danny and Doc's Jewel Box Revue*, c. 1951, author's collection.

8. Coleman, "The Jewel Box Revue," 91.

9. Mormino, "Midas Returns," 11–12.

10. Bérubé, *Coming Out under Fire*, 6.

11. Shell-Weiss, *Coming to Miami*, 140.

12. Wolff, *Miami*; Mohl, "Changing Economic Patterns," 63–73; Beeber, "Dade Tops Florida Industry," 8C.

13. U.S. Census Bureau, "Table 4—Population of Urban Places," *U.S. Census of Population: 1950*, vol. 2; U.S. Census Bureau, "Table P-1," *U.S. Censuses of Population and Housing: 1960, Census Tracts.*

14. D'Emilio, *Sexual Politics, Sexual Communities*; Bérubé, *Coming Out under Fire*.

15. Capó, "'It's Not Queer to Be Gay,'" chaps. 2–3; Fejes, "Murder, Perversion, and Moral Panic"; Fejes, *Gay Rights and Moral Panic*; Sullivan, "Political Opportunism."

16. "Boy Admits FLA. Killing," 1.

17. "Teen-Ager Faces Murder Charges," 1.

18. "Whidden's House May Be Condemned," 1C; "El Portal Murder House Curios under Hammer," 6B.

19. Miami, FL, City Directory, 1944, U.S. City Directories, 1822–1989, ANC.

20. 1940 United States Federal Census, El Portal, Dade, FL, Roll T627_580, 4B, ANC.

21. Capó, "'It's Not Queer to Be Gay,'" chap. 3; Fejes, "Murder, Perversion, and Moral Panic"; Chauncey, "The Postwar Sex Crime Panic."

22. Ibid.

23. Johnson, *The Lavender Scare*; Braukman, *Communists and Perverts*.

24. Crispell, *Testing the Limits*, 5–8.

25. Lichtenstein, "In the Shade of the Lenin Oak."

26. "Anything Goes," 29.

27. Kofoed, *Moon over Miami*, 228.

28. Senate Special Committee to Investigate Organized Crime in Interstate Commerce, *Interim Report on Investigations in Florida and Preliminary General Conclusions*, 2–4.

29. Bousquet, "The Gangster in Our Midst," 309.

30. Robb, "Governor Warren Has the Floor," 15A.

31. Kefauver, *Crime in America*, 96. Also see Moore, *The Kefauver Committee.*

32. Strichartz, "Legal Aspects of Municipal Incorporation," 80–82.

33. Portes and Stepick, *City on the Edge*, 80–83.

34. *The Code of the City of Miami, 1945*, §72, 86–87. For more on how zoning variances were used to enforce racial segregation, see Connolly, *World More Concrete*, 168, 252.

35. "Nightclub Loses Venetian Area Zoning Appeal."

36. Portes and Stepick, *City on the Edge*, 80–81.

37. "3 New Miami Area Towns," 5.

38. "Dade Dealers Sue to Limit Liquor License," 2.

39. Mohl, "Shadows in the Sunshine"; Mohl, "Making the Second Ghetto"; Connolly, *A World More Concrete*, chaps. 3 and 8.

40. Mohl, "Shadows in the Sunshine," 72–76.

41. Connolly, *A World More Concrete*, 261.

42. Dunn, *Black Miami*, 157–58.

43. Pieze, "Good Morning Judge," Oct. 20, 1951, 4.

44. Pieze, "Good Morning Judge," Oct. 4, 1952, 3.

45. U.S. Census Bureau, "Table 19: Population of the 100 Largest Urban Places: 1960."

46. D'Emilio, *Sexual Politics, Sexual Communities*; Stein, *City of Sisterly and Brotherly Loves*; Boyd, *Wide-Open Town*; Johnson, *The Lavender Scare*; Gallo, *Different Daughters*.

47. For instance, see Howard, *Carryin' On*; Howard, *Men Like That*, chap. 6; Sears, *Lonely Hunters*; Sears, *Rebels, Rubyfruit, and Rhinestones*; Stein, *Rethinking*, chap. 2; and Chenault, Braukman, and Atlanta History Center, *Gay and Lesbian Atlanta*.

48. Capó, "'It's Not Queer to Be Gay,'" chap. 4; Sears, *Lonely Hunters*, 213.

49. Fuentes, *The Autobiography of Fidel Castro*, 153–55.

50. Pérez, *On Becoming Cuban*, 434.

51. Schwartz, *Pleasure Island*, chap. 10.

52. Kofoed, "Miami after Dark," 51–53.

53. García, *Havana USA*.

54. McGirr, *Suburban Warriors*; Frank, "'The Civil Rights of Parents.'"

55. Capó, "'It's Not Queer to Be Gay,'" chap. 5.

# Bibliography

ARCHIVES

Coral Gables, FL
    University of Miami, Otto Richter Library
        Cuban Heritage Collection
        Pan American World Airways Inc. Records
Denton, TX
    University of North Texas Special Collections
        Denton Family Collection
Lancaster, OH
    Fairfield County Chapter of the Ohio Genealogical Society
Miami, FL
    City of Miami Clerk's Office
        City of Miami Council Minutes
    HistoryMiami Museum Archives and Research Center
        Angus McGregor Papers
        Carl G. Fisher Papers
        *Committee of One Hundred Newsletter*, no. 2007-408
        Dade County Records, 1867–1944
        Railey Family Papers, no. 1986-307
        Robert R. Taylor Scrapbooks, no. 2010-235-1
        Selling Miami to the Tourist, Norman-Fennell Corp.
        Tamiami Trail Construction Papers, 1916–24
    Miami-Dade Clerk of the Court Archives
        General Index to Criminal Cases, Defendants Dade County, Prior 1929
    Vizcaya Museum and Gardens Archive
        James Maher Papers
            James Maher Archive Series IV, Interviews—1964–65
        Vizcaya Estate Records
            Correspondence Series
    Wolfsonian-Florida International University
        Vicki Gold Levi Collection
Minneapolis, MN
    University of Minnesota, Archives and Special Collections
        Kautz Family YMCA Archives
Nassau, New Providence, the Bahamas
    National Archives of the Bahamas
        Appendix, *Votes of the Honourable Legislative Council of the Bahama Islands*
        Colonial Office Records

New Haven, CT
    Yale University, Manuscript and Archives, Sterling Memorial Library
        Candida Scott Piel Papers, no. MS 1831
Tallahassee, FL
    State Archives of Florida
        Florida laws (for both Florida and U.S. Territory)
        Florida State Hospital Commitment Records, no. S 1062
        Florida State Hospital Medical Records, no. S 1063
        Florida Supreme Court Case Files, 1825–2013, no. S 49
        Governor David Sholtz Correspondence, no. S 278
        Prisoner Registers, 1875–1972, no. S 500
        Tin Can Tourists of the World Records, no. M93-2

### PRIVATE COLLECTION

Joe Clein Private Collection
    *Miami Life*

### DIGITAL ARCHIVES

Ancestry.com Online Database, http://www.ancestry.com/
City of Miami Beach Digital Archives, Miami Beach, FL, City of Miami Beach Council
    Minutes, http://docmgmt.miamibeachfl.gov/weblink/browse.aspx?dbid=0&cr=1
Consumer Price Inflation Calculator, U.S. Department of Labor, Bureau of Labor
    Statistics, http://data.bls.gov/cgi-bin/cpicalc.pl
Florida Memory, State Library and Archives of Florida, https://www.floridamemory
    .com/
The Lester S. Levy Sheet Music Collection, Johns Hopkins University, Sheridan
    Libraries, Special Collections, Baltimore, MD, http://levysheetmusic.mse.jhu.edu/
Metropolitan Museum of Art, New York, NY, www.metmusuem.org
Prelinger Archives, https://archive.org/details/prelinger

### COURT CASES

*Blameuser v. State*, 142 So. 909 (Fla. 1932)
*Drawdy v. State*, 120 So. 844 (Fla. 1929)
*English v. State*, 164 So. 848 (Fla. 1935)
*Ephraim et al. v. State*, 89 So. 344 (Fla. 1921)
*Ex Parte Joe L. Earman*, 95 So. 755 (Fla. 1923)
*Franklin v. State*, 257 So. 2d 21 (Fla. 1971)
*Gorey v. State*, 71 So. 328 (Fla. 1916)
*Harris v. State*, 72 So. 520 (Fla. 1916)
*Jackson v. State*, 94 So. 505 (Fla. 1922)
*Lason v. State*, 12 So. 2d 305 (Fla. 1943)
*Luster and Another v. State*, 2 So. 690 (Fla. 1887)
*Medis and Hill v. State*, 27 Tex. App. 194 (1889)
*Miami Retreat Foundation v. Ervin*, 66 So. 2d 748 (Fla. 1952)
*Williams v. State*, 43 So. 431 (Fla. 1907)

Abelove, Henry. "Freud, Male Homosexuality, and the Americans." *Dissent* 33, no. 1 (Winter 1985–86): 59–69.

"About Miami." *Evening Independent* (St. Petersburg, FL), October 20, 1927.

"About North Miami." *Miami Metropolis*, December 4, 1896.

Abraham, Julie. *Metropolitan Lovers: The Homosexuality of Cities*. Minneapolis: University of Minnesota Press, 2009.

Abrams, Kerry. "Polygamy, Prostitution, and the Federalization of Immigration Law." *Columbia Law Review* 105, no. 3 (April 2005): 641–716.

Abreu, Christina D. *Rhythms of Race: Cuban Musicians and the Making of Latino New York City and Miami, 1940–1960*. Chapel Hill: University of North Carolina Press, 2015.

Advertisement. *Miami Daily News*, December 21, 1930.

Advertisement. *Tribune* (Nassau), January 7, 1913.

Advertisement: A Night in Japan. *Miami Herald*, March 6, 1917.

Advertisement: Capitol Theatre. *New Castle (PA) News*, October 24, 1928.

Advertisement: LaFayette. *New York Age*, June 2, 1934.

Advertisement: Miami Beach Has the Ocean Front. *Miami Daily Metropolis*, December 7, 1922.

Advertisement: Office of Recruiting Committee. *Tribune* (Nassau), June 21, 1916.

"Alden Freeman Dies in Long Illness Here." *Miami Daily Metropolis*, December 30, 1937.

Allen, Jafari S. "Black/Queer/Diaspora at the Current Conjuncture." *GLQ: A Journal of Lesbian and Gay Studies* 18, no. 2–3 (2012): 211–48.

"Along the Color Line." *The Crisis*, April 1912.

"Amateur Minstrelsy Proved by the Elks to Be Not Lost Art." *Miami Daily Metropolis*, January 28, 1922.

American Social Hygiene Association. *Social Hygiene*, vol. 5. New York: American Social Hygiene Association, 1919.

"Among the Alumni." *Princeton Alumni Weekly*, January 12, 1934.

"Anchor of Ship Columbus Sailed Comes to Florida." *Evening Independent* (St. Petersburg, FL), November 14, 1930.

"Anything Goes." *Time*, April 17, 1950.

Arnaz, Desi. *A Book*. Cutchogue, NY: Buccaneer, 1976.

Aron, Cindy S. *Working at Play: A History of Vacations in the United States*. New York: Oxford University Press, 1999.

"Arrests for Foul Murder of Ed Kinsey." *Miami Herald*, February 23, 1917.

"Arthur Knorr Stages Knockout Capitol Show." *Film Daily*, February 18, 1929.

"At Capital Theaters This Week." *Washington Times*, December 10, 1911.

"At Nassau Hard Times Party." *Miami Daily News*, February 12, 1928.

"Attorney Scores Miami Morals." *Palm Beach Post*, July 23, 1941.

"At White House Inn." *Warren (PA) Times Mirror*, October 20, 1942.

Auer, John Jeffrey, IV. "Queerest Little City in the World: LGBTQ Reno." In *LGBTQ America: A Theme Study of Lesbian, Gay, Bisexual, Transgender, and Queer*

*History*, edited by Megan E. Springate, chap. 28. Washington, DC: National Park
Foundation, 2016.

"An Auto Trip to Florida." *Cape Girardeau Southeast Missourian*, March 23, 1922.

"Bachelor Builds a Palace Where He Lives the Simple Life." *Milwaukee Journal*,
October 4, 1917.

Bachin, Robin F., and F. Donnelly James. "Miami Beach, Florida." In *American
Tourism: Constructing a National Tradition*, edited by J. Mark Souther and
Nicholas Dagen Bloom, 175–82. Chicago: Center for American Places at Columbia
College, 2012.

Bagnall, Gaynor. "Performance and Performativity at Heritage Sites." *Museum and
Society* 1, no. 2 (July 2003): 87–103.

Bahamas Department of Statistics. *Demographic Aspects of the Bahamian
Population, 1901–1974*. Nassau: Bahamas Department of Statistics, 1976.

Bailey, Beth L. *From Front Porch to Back Seat: Courtship in Twentieth-Century
America*. Baltimore: Johns Hopkins University Press, 1988.

Baker, Joséphine (performer), Joe Burke (music), and Nita Corelli (lyric). "Nuits de
Miami." New York: Columbia, 1937.

Baldwin, Esther E. "A British Colony in War Times." *The Outlook: A Weekly
Newspaper* (New York), July 26, 1916.

Baptist, Edward E. *Creating an Old South: Middle Florida's Plantation Frontier
before the Civil War*. Chapel Hill: University of North Carolina Press, 2002.

"Baptist Ladies' Aid Yesterday Afternoon." *Miami Metropolis*, April 5, 1913.

"Bar Operator Declared Guilty." *Miami Daily News*, March 14, 1947.

Barbour, Dale. *Winnipeg Beach: Leisure and Courtship in a Resort Town, 1900–1967*.
Winnipeg: University of Manitoba Press, 2011.

Barkan, Elliott Robert. *A Nation of Peoples: A Sourcebook on America's Multicultural
Heritage*. Westport, CT: Greenwood, 1999.

Barker, Roger G. *Ecological Psychology: Concepts and Methods for Studying the
Environment of Human Behavior*. Stanford, CA: Stanford University Press, 1968.

Barnes, Walter. "Walter Barnes Finds Many Big Broadwayites Playing on the Beaches
in Miami." *Chicago Defender*, February 27, 1937.

Barrett, James R., and David Roediger. "Inbetween Peoples: Race, Nationality and
the 'New Immigrant' Working Class." *Journal of American Ethnic History* 16, no. 3
(Spring 1997): 3–44.

Barth, Gunther Paul. *Instant Cities: Urbanization and the Rise of San Francisco and
Denver*. New York: Oxford University Press, 1975.

Bauer, Ruthmary. "Sarasota: Hardship and Tourism in the 1930s." *Florida Historical
Quarterly* 76, no. 2 (Fall 1997): 135–51.

Bean, Annemarie. "Black Minstrelsy and Double Inversion, circa 1890." In *African
American Performance and Theater History: A Critical Reader*, edited by Harry J.
Elam Jr. and David Krasner, 171–91. New York: Oxford University Press, 2001.

Beard, George. "Neurasthenia, or Nervous Exhaustion." *Boston Medical and Surgical
Journal* 3, no. 18 (April 29, 1869): 217–21.

Becker, Phil. "Wall Is Acquitted on Morals Count." *Miami Daily News*, July 20, 1956.

Bederman, Gail. *Manliness and Civilization: A Cultural History of Gender and Race in the United States, 1880–1917*. Chicago: University of Chicago Press, 1995.

Beeber, Holland. "Dade Tops Florida Industry, 96 New Plants in 6 Months." *Miami Daily News*, January 21, 1958.

Beemyn, Genny. *A Queer Capital: A History of Gay Life in Washington*. New York: Routledge, 2015.

Bell, Jack. "O'er the Sports Desk." *Miami Daily News*, December 30, 1933.

Belmonte, Laura A., Mark Philip Bradley, Julio Capó Jr., Paul Farber, Shanon Fitzpatrick, Melani McAlister, David Minto, Michael Sherry, Naoko Shibusawa, and Penny Von Eschen. "Colloquy: Queering America and the World." *Diplomatic History* 40, no. 1 (2016): 19–80.

Bergreen, Laurence. *Capone: The Man and the Era*. New York: Simon & Schuster, 1994.

Bernard, H. Russell. "Kalymnos: The Island of the Sponge Fishermen." *Annals of the New York Academy of Sciences* 268 (February 10, 1976): 291–307.

Bérubé, Allan. *Coming Out under Fire: The History of Gay Men and Women in World War Two*. New York: Free Press, 1990.

"Big Gaiety Company Decided Departure." *Toronto World*, April 30, 1911.

"Bill Dwyer Dies; 'Bootlegger King.'" *New York Times*, December 11, 1946.

"Billingsley Gives Way to Judge Sanders Today." *Miami Metropolis*, May 12, 1917.

"Bills Recommended by the Legislative Committee, FFWC Adopted." *Miami Herald*, March 11, 1917.

"Birth of Another Newspaper." *Nassau Guardian*, March 3, 1920.

Bishop, Jim. "Jim Bishop: Reporter." *Lewiston (ME) Evening Journal*, February 20, 1961.

Blair, Cynthia M. *I've Got to Make My Livin': Black Women's Sex Work in Turn-of-the-Century Chicago*. Chicago: University of Chicago Press, 2010.

———. "African American Women's Sexuality." *Frontiers: A Journal of Women's Studies* 35, no. 1 (November 2014): 4–10.

Bleys, Rudi C. *The Geography of Perversion: Male-to-Male Sexual Behavior outside the West and the Ethnographic Imagination, 1750–1918*. New York: New York University Press, 1995.

Boag, Peter. *Re-dressing America's Frontier Past*. Berkeley: University of California Press, 2011.

———. *Same-Sex Affairs: Constructing and Controlling Homosexuality in the Pacific Northwest*. Berkeley: University of California Press, 2003.

"Bookies in Confusion after Surprise Raids." *Miami Daily News*, March 10, 1947.

"The Bootlegger's Bad Ways and Big Profits." *Literary Digest*, December 30, 1922.

Bousquet, Stephen C. "The Gangster in Our Midst: Al Capone in South Florida, 1930–1947." *Florida Historical Quarterly* 76, no. 3 (Winter 1998): 297–309.

"Boy Admits FLA. Killing." *Times-News* (Hendersonville, NC), March 7, 1952.

Boyd, Nan Alamilla. *Wide-Open Town: A History of Queer San Francisco to 1965.* Berkeley: University of California Press, 2003.

Boyle, Hal. "The Bahamas Are Fast Becoming a Vacation Paradise." *Fort Scott (KS) Tribune*, April 5, 1956.

"Boy Scouts Minstrel Success." *Miami Metropolis*, June 27, 1913.

"Bradenton Has Lasses White Show Tonight." *Sarasota (FL) Herald*, October 24, 1925.

Bramson, Seth H. *Sunshine, Stone Crabs and Cheesecake: The Story of Miami Beach.* Charleston, SC: History Press, 2009.

Braukman, Stacy. *Communists and Perverts under the Palms: The Johns Committee in Florida, 1956-1965.* Gainesville: University Press of Florida, 2012.

Briggs, Laura. *Reproducing Empire: Race, Sex, Science, and U.S. Imperialism in Puerto Rico.* Berkeley: University of California Press, 2002.

Brigham, Ruth. "'Mother Kelly' Gives Up Night Club." *Daily Times* (New Philadelphia, OH), December 24, 1947.

Brinton, Daniel G. *A Guide-Book of Florida and the South for Tourists, Invalids, and Emigrants, with a Map of the St. John River.* Philadelphia: G. Maclean, 1869.

Brockley, Janice A. "Martyred Mothers and Merciful Fathers: Exploring Disability and Motherhood in the Lives of Jerome Greenfield and Raymond Repouille." In *The New Disability History: American Perspectives*, edited by Paul K. Longmore and Lauri Umansky, 293-312. New York: New York University Press, 2001.

*Brooklyn Blue Book and Long Island Society Register.* New York: Brooklyn Life, 1920.

"A Brutal Murder." *Miami Metropolis*, July 29, 1898.

Buchanan, Patricia. "Miami's Bootleg Boom." *Tequesta* 30 (1970): 13-31.

———. "Miami's Bootleg Boom: A Decade of Prohibition." MA thesis, University of Miami, 1967.

Burke, Joe (music), and Edgar Leslie (lyric). "Moon over Miami." Irving Berlin Inc., 1935.

Burnham, Bradford. "Down the East Coast." *MotorBoating*, March 1913.

Burrelli, David F. "An Overview of the Debate on Homosexuals in the U.S. Military." In *Gays and Lesbians in the Military: Issues, Concerns, and Contrasts*, edited by Wilbur J. Scott and Sandra Carson Stanley, 17-32. New York: Aldine de Gruyter, 1994.

Burton, Antoinette. *Burdens of History: British Feminists, Indian Women, and Imperial Culture, 1865-1915.* Chapel Hill: University of North Carolina Press, 1994.

Burton, J. C. "A Promised Road to the Lands of Promise." *Motor Age*, November 4, 1915.

Bush, Gregory W. "'Playground of the USA': Miami and the Promotion of Spectacle." *Pacific Historical Review* 68, no. 2 (May 1999): 153-72.

"Busy Police Arrested 62 in 24 Hours." *Miami Herald*, March 5, 1917.

Butler, Jon. "Protestant Success in the New American City, 1870-1920." In *New Directions in American Religious History*, edited by Harry S. Stout and D. G. Hart, 296-333. New York: Oxford University Press, 1997.

Butler, Judith. *Bodies That Matter: On the Discursive Limits of "Sex."* New York: Routledge, 1993.

———. *Gender Trouble: Feminism and the Subversion of Identity.* New York: Routledge, 1990.

Cammack, Lucius Henry. *What about Florida?* Chicago: Laird & Lee, 1916.

Canaday, Margot. *The Straight State: Sexuality and Citizenship in Twentieth-Century America*. Princeton, NJ: Princeton University Press, 2009.

———. "Thinking Sex in the Transnational Turn: An Introduction." *American Historical Review* 114, no. 5 (2009): 1250–57.

Capó, Julio, Jr. "'It's Not Queer to Be Gay': Miami and the Emergence of the Gay Rights Movement, 1945–1995." PhD diss., Florida International University, 2011.

———. "Locating Miami's Queer History." In *LGBTQ America: A Theme Study of Lesbian, Gay, Bisexual, Transgender, and Queer History*, edited by Megan E. Springate, chap. 27. Washington, DC: National Park Foundation, 2016.

Capozzola, Christopher. "The Man Who Illuminated the Gilded Age?" *American Quarterly* 52, no. 3 (September 2000): 514–32.

Carpenter, Niles. *Immigrants and Their Children, 1920: A Study Based on Census Statistics Relative to the Foreign Born and the Native White of Foreign or Mixed Parentage*. Washington, DC: Government Printing Office, 1927.

*Carteles*, June 30, 1934.

*Carteles*, June 21, 1936.

*Carteles*, September 13, 1936.

*Carteles*, June 6, 1937.

*Carteles*, May 8, 1938.

Carter, James A., III. "Florida and Rumrunning during National Prohibition." *Florida Historical Quarterly* 48, no. 1 (July 1969): 47–56.

Cason, Fred W. *Code of the City of Miami*. Miami: R. C. Denicke, 1917.

Castillo, Thomas A. "Laboring in the Magic City: Workers in Miami, 1914–1941." PhD diss., University of Maryland, 2011.

———. "Miami's Hidden Labor History." *Florida Historical Quarterly* 82, no. 4 (Spring 2004): 438–67.

"Catches." *Palm Beach Daily News*, February 21, 1938.

Chapman, Arthur. "'Watch the Port of Miami.'" *Tequesta* 53 (1993): 7–30.

Charteris, Leslie. *The Saint in Miami*. Philadelphia: Triangle, 1944 [1940].

Chase, Charles W., Sr. "Not Censoring Bathers' Dress." *Miami Daily News*, October 17, 1928.

Chauncey, George. *Gay New York: Gender, Urban Culture, and the Making of the Gay Male World, 1890–1940*. New York: Basic Books, 1994.

———. "Christian Brotherhood or Sexual Perversion? Homosexual Identities and the Construction of Sexual Boundaries in the World War One Era." *Journal of Social History* 19, no. 2 (December 1985): 189–211.

———. "The Postwar Sex Crime Panic." In *True Stories from the American Past*, edited by William Graebner, 160–78. New York: McGraw-Hill, 1993.

Chenault, Wesley, Stacy Braukman, and Atlanta History Center. *Gay and Lesbian Atlanta*. Charleston, SC: Arcadia, 2008.

Child, Richard Washburn. "The Feminist." *Cosmopolitan*, February 1915.

———. "Shark." *Everybody's Magazine*, June 1910.

———. "Shark." In *The Man in the Shadow*. New York: Macmillan, 1911.

Chudacoff, Howard P. *The Age of the Bachelor: Creating an American Subculture*. Princeton, NJ: Princeton University Press, 1999.

Chude-Sokei, Louis. *The Last "Darky": Bert Williams, Black-on-Black Minstrelsy, and the African Diaspora*. Durham, NC: Duke University Press, 2005.

Churchill, David S. "Transnationalism and Homophile Political Culture in the Postwar Decades." *GLQ: A Journal of Lesbian and Gay Studies* 15, no. 1 (2008): 31–66.

"Circumcision for the Correction of Sexual Crimes among the Negro Race." *Maryland Medical Journal* 30, no. 16 (February 10, 1894): 345–46.

"City Commission Adopts New Vagrancy Ordinance, 3 to 1, with Labor Still Protesting." *Miami Daily News*, May 23, 1930.

"City Court Severe on Wife Beaters." *Miami Herald*, February 27, 1917.

Clancy, Jacqueline E. "Hell's Angel: Eleanor Kinzie Gordon's Wartime Summer of 1898." *Tequesta* 43 (2003): 37–61.

"Clarke Ship Aids Anglers." *Pittsburgh Press*, February 20, 1938.

"Clayton Sedgwick Cooper." *Miami Daily News*, October 14, 1936.

Clement, Elizabeth. "From Sociability to Spectacle: Interracial Sexuality and the Ideological Uses of Space in New York City, 1900–1930." *Journal of International Women's Studies* 6, no. 2 (June 2005): 24–43.

Clemente, Deirdre. "Made in Miami: The Development of the Sportswear Industry in South Florida, 1900–1960." *Journal of Social History* 41, no. 1 (Fall 2007): 127–48.

"Club Klan Raided Closed Down after Sheriff's Warning." *Miami Herald*, November 17, 1937.

"Coburn Is Glad to Be Back in Miami Again." *Miami Daily Metropolis*, January 15, 1923.

"Coburn Minstrels Score Hit." *Index-Journal* (Greenwood, SC), November 21, 1920.

"Coburn's Minstrels Open Up in Miami for Four-Day Run." *Miami Daily Metropolis*, January 16, 1922.

Cocks, Catherine. *Tropical Whites: The Rise of the Tourist South in the Americas*. Philadelphia: University of Pennsylvania Press, 2013.

*The Code of the City of Miami, Florida, 1945*. Charlottesville, VA: Michie, 1945.

Cohen, Cathy J. "Punks, Bulldaggers, and Welfare Queens: The Radical Potential of Queer Politics?" *GLQ: A Journal of Lesbian and Gay Studies* 3 (1997): 437–65.

Cohen, Isidor. *Historical Sketches and Sidelights of Miami, Florida*. Miami: Privately printed, 1925.

Cohen, Lizabeth. *A Consumers' Republic: The Politics of Mass Consumption in Postwar America*. New York: Alfred A. Knopf, 2003.

Cohen, William. "Negro Involuntary Servitude in the South, 1865–1940: A Preliminary Analysis." *Journal of Southern History* 42, no. 1 (February 1976): 31–60.

Colbert, Haines. "Beach Hails 'Near-Nude' Ban." *Miami Daily News*, September 21, 1950.

Cole, Catherine M. "American Ghetto Parties and Ghanaian Concert Parties: A Transnational Perspective on Blackface." In *Burnt Cork: Traditions and Legacies of Blackface Minstrelsy*, edited by Stephen Johnson, 223–57. Amherst: University of Massachusetts Press, 2012.

Coleman, Bud. "The Jewel Box Revue: America's Longest-Running, Touring Drag Show." *Theatre History Studies*, no. 17 (1997): 79–91.

Combs, Jerald A. *The History of American Foreign Policy*, vol. 1, *To 1920*. 3rd ed. New York: Routledge, 2015.

"Commissioners Count Election Returns." *Miami Daily Metropolis*, November 3, 1913.

Conklin, Oscar. "More than Thousand Bahama Islanders Reach Miami during Year." *Miami Metropolis*, June 12, 1909.

Connolly, N. D. B. *A World More Concrete: Real Estate and the Remaking of Jim Crow South Florida*. Chicago: University of Chicago Press, 2014.

"Consul Rescued after Floating in Plane 6 Hours." *Daily Capital Journal* (Salem, OR), February 3, 1931.

"Convicted Slayer of Greek Spongers Is Given Parole." *Evening Independent* (St. Petersburg, FL), August 8, 1944.

Cooper, Frederic Taber. "The Clothing of Thoughts and Some Recent Novels." *Bookman*, December 1911.

Cooper, Helen A. *Winslow Homer Watercolors*. New Haven, CT: Yale University Press, 1986.

Corliss, Carlton J. "Building the Overseas Railway to Key West." *Tequesta* 13 (1953): 3–21.

Cott, Nancy F. *The Bonds of Womanhood: "Women's Sphere' in New England, 1780–1835*. New Haven, CT: Yale University Press, 1977.

———. "Passionlessness: An Interpretation of Victorian Sexual Ideology, 1790–1850." *Signs* 4, no. 2 (Winter 1978): 219–36.

"County Night Spots Closed by Sheriff." *Miami Herald*, November 19, 1937.

"Court Rules City May License Club." *Miami Daily News*, December 21, 1947.

Cowie, Jefferson. *Capital Moves: RCA's Seventy-Year Quest for Cheap Labor*. Ithaca, NY: Cornell University Press, 1999.

Cox, Merlin G. "David Sholtz: New Deal Governor of Florida." *Florida Historical Quarterly* 43, no. 2 (October 1964): 142–52.

Cram, Mildred. *Old Seaport Towns of the South*. New York: Dodd, Mead, 1917.

Craton, Michael, and Gail Saunders. *Islanders in the Stream: A History of the Bahamian People*, vol. 2, *From the Ending of Slavery to the Twenty-First Century*. Athens: University of Georgia Press, 1998.

Crispell, Brian Lewis. *Testing the Limits: George Armistead Smathers and Cold War America*. Athens: University of Georgia Press, 1999.

Cronon, William. *Nature's Metropolis: Chicago and the Great West*. New York: W. W. Norton, 1992.

Cross, Austin F. "Race Plant at Tropical Park, Miami." *Ottawa (ONT) Evening Citizen*, April 13, 1936.

"Current Fiction." *The Nation*, February 1, 1912.

Custen, George F. "Too Darn Hot: Hollywood, Popular Media and the Construction of Sexuality in the Life of Cole Porter." *Radical History Review* 59 (1994): 142–71.

"Dade County Is Voted Dry." *Miami Daily Metropolis*, October 30, 1913.

"Dade County Young Men Flock to Registration Booths." *Miami Daily Metropolis*, June 5, 1917.

"Dade Dealers Sue to Limit Liquor License." *Sarasota (FL) Herald-Tribune*, November 17, 1948.

Dauphin, Mara. "'A Bit of Woman in Every Man': Creating Queer Community in Female Impersonation." *Valley Humanities Review* (Spring 2012): 1–16.

Davis, Jack E. *Everglades Providence: Marjory Stoneman Douglas and the American Environmental Century*. Athens: University of Georgia Press, 2009.

Davis, Rebecca I. "'Not Marriage at All, but Simple Harlotry': The Companionate Marriage Controversy." *Journal of American History* 94, no. 4 (March 2008): 1137–63.

de la Fuente, Alejandro. *A Nation for All: Race, Inequality, and Politics in Twentieth-Century Cuba*. Chapel Hill: University of North Carolina Press, 2001.

"Dealing with Vagrants." *Weekly Miami Metropolis*, November 23, 1906.

"Death of Edith E. Hanan." *Shoe and Leather Facts* 32, no. 1 (January 1920): 20.

Decena, Carlos Ulises. *Tacit Subjects: Belonging and Same-Sex Desire among Dominican Immigrant Men*. Durham, NC: Duke University Press, 2011.

D'Emilio, John. "Capitalism and Gay Identity." In *Powers of Desire: The Politics of Sexuality*, edited by Ann Barr Snitow, Christine Stansell, and Sharon Thompson, 100–113. New York: Monthly Review Press, 1983.

———. *Sexual Politics, Sexual Communities: The Making of a Homosexual Minority in the United States, 1940–1970*. Chicago: University of Chicago Press, 1983.

D'Emilio, John, and Estelle B. Freedman. *Intimate Matters: A History of Sexuality in America*. New York: Harper & Row, 1988.

Derby, Lauren. *The Dictator's Seduction: Politics and the Popular Imagination in the Era of Trujillo*. Durham, NC: Duke University Press, 2009.

"Dewing Woodward Active in Art despite Her Years." *Miami Daily News*, November 30, 1941.

Dillon, John Francis. Director. *The Pagan Lady*. Columbia Pictures, 1931.

Dodge, Charles Richards. "Subtropical Florida." *Scribner's Magazine*, March 1894.

Doherty, Phil. *The Miami Police Worksheet*. Bloomington, IN: Xlibris, 2012.

"Don't Miss Bathing Girl Stunts." *Exhibitors Trade Review*, June 21, 1924.

Dorman, Bob. "Miami Bootlegger Is a Businessman." *Bluefield (WV) Daily Telegraph*, December 14, 1924.

Dorn, J. K. "Reflections of Early Miami." *Tequesta* 9 (1949): 43–59.

Douglas, Marjory Stoneman. "He-Man." In *Nine Florida Stories by Marjory Stoneman Douglas*, edited by Kevin M. McCarthy, 49–73. Jacksonville: University of North Florida Press, 1990.

———. "Japanese Costume Ball Great Financial Success." *Miami Herald*, March 9, 1917.

———. "Japanese Costume Dance as Planned by Mr. Hanan Was Superb Social Event." *Miami Herald*, March 9, 1917.

———. *Marjory Stoneman Douglas: Voice of the River*. Englewood, FL: Pineapple, 1987.

————. "State Suffrage Convention in Miami March 15 and 16 of National Importance." *Miami Herald*, March 6, 1917.

Drew, Sidney, dir. *A Florida Enchantment*. Vitagraph Studios, 1914.

Drorbaugh, Elizabeth. "Sliding Scales: Notes on Stormé DeLarverié and the Jewel Box Revue, the Cross-Dressed Woman on the Contemporary Stage, and the Invert." In *Crossing the Stage: Controversies on Cross-Dressing*, edited by Lesley Ferris, 131–52. London: Routledge, 1993.

Duany, Jorge. *Blurred Borders: Transnational Migration between the Hispanic Caribbean and the United States*. Chapel Hill: University of North Carolina Press, 2011.

Dubler, Ariela R. "From *McLaughlin v. Florida* to *Lawrence v. Texas*: Sexual Freedom and the Road to Marriage." *Columbia Law Review* 106, no. 5 (2006): 1165.

"Duckett Gets His Man." *Miami Metropolis*, October 16, 1896.

Duggan, Lisa. *Sapphic Slashers: Sex, Violence, and American Modernity*. Durham, NC: Duke University Press, 2000.

Duis, Perry. *The Saloon: Public Drinking in Chicago and Boston, 1880–1920*. Urbana: University of Illinois Press, 1983.

Dulles, Foster Rhea. *America Learns to Play: A History of Popular Recreation, 1607–1940*. New York: D. Appleton-Century, 1940.

Dunn, George M. "Headquarters Department of Cuba, Office of the Judge-Advocate, Havana, July 16, 1901." In *Annual Report of Major General Leonard Wood, U.S.V., Commanding Department of Cuba*, Havana, 1901.

Dunn, Marvin. *Black Miami in the Twentieth Century*. Gainesville: University Press of Florida, 1997.

Dur, Philip, and Christopher Gilcrease. "US Diplomacy and the Downfall of a Cuban Dictator: Machado in 1933." *Journal of Latin American Studies* 34, no. 2 (May 2002): 255–82.

Durant, Will, and Ariel Durant. *A Dual Autobiography*. New York: Simon and Schuster, 1977.

Durante, James Francis, and Jack Kofoed. *Night Clubs*. New York: Alfred A. Knopf, 1931.

Duval, L. E. "Some Sex Cases." *Urologic and Cutaneous Review* 22, no. 3 (1918): 169–70.

Early, Eleanor. *Ports of the Sun*. Boston: Houghton Mifflin, 1937.

"Early Club Opening Is Seen by Manager." *Miami Herald*, November 18, 1937.

Edmonds, Richard H. *The Prohibition Question Viewed from the Economic and Moral Standpoint*. Baltimore: Manufacturers Record, 1922.

Ellis, Leonara Beck. "American Sponge Fisheries Worked by Greeks." *Popular Mechanics*, February 1914.

"El Portal Murder House Curios under Hammer." *Miami Daily News*, October 15, 1953.

*The Encyclopedia Britannica: A Dictionary of Arts, Sciences, Literature and General Information*. 11th ed., vol. 28. Cambridge: Cambridge University Press, 1911.

"Entertainment Variety Listed at Showplaces." *Miami Daily News and Metropolis*, January 7, 1927.

Erenberg, Lewis A. *Steppin' Out: New York Nightlife and the Transformation of American Culture, 1890–1930*. Chicago: University of Chicago Press, 1981.

"Escapes the Heat, Has Warm Debate over Scanty Garb." *Milwaukee Journal*, July 10, 1931.

Eskridge, William N., Jr. *Dishonorable Passions: Sodomy Laws in America, 1861–2003*. New York: Viking, 2008.

Esten, John. *John Singer Sargent: The Male Nudes*. New York: Universe, 1999.

"Evelyn Wilson." *Brooklyn Daily Eagle*, September 22, 1929.

"The Exodus to Florida." *Tribune* (Nassau), January 11, 1913.

Faderman, Lillian. *Surpassing the Love of Men: Romantic Friendship and Love between Women from the Renaissance to the Present*. New York: Morrow, 1981.

Faderman, Lillian, and Stuart Timmons. *Gay L.A.: A History of Sexual Outlaws, Power Politics, and Lipstick Lesbians*. New York: Basic Books, 2006.

Fairbrother, Trevor. *John Singer Sargent*. New York: Harry N. Abrams, 1994.

———. *John Singer Sargent: The Sensualist*. New Haven, CT: Yale University Press, 2000.

Fairchild, Henry Pratt. *Greek Immigration to the United States*. New Haven, CT: Yale University Press, 1911.

"Fairfax Will Offer Bill of Amateurs." *Miami Daily Metropolis*, September 15, 1922.

"Famous Minstrel Show Coming to City." *St. Petersburg (FL) Times*, October 5, 1924.

Faris, John T. *Seeing the Sunny South*. Philadelphia: J. B. Lippincott, 1921.

Fass, Paula S. *The Damned and the Beautiful: American Youth in the 1920s*. New York: Oxford University Press, 1977.

Fejes, Fred. *Gay Rights and Moral Panic: The Origins of America's Debate on Homosexuality*. 1st ed. New York: Palgrave Macmillan, 2008.

———. "Murder, Perversion, and Moral Panic: The 1954 Media Campaign against Miami's Homosexuals and the Discourse of Civic Betterment." *Journal of the History of Sexuality* 9, no. 3 (July 2000): 305–47.

Ferrer, Ada. *Insurgent Cuba: Race, Nation, and Revolution, 1868–1898*. Chapel Hill: University of North Carolina Press, 1999.

"Fiendish Assault Attempted at Cocoanut Grove Wednesday Night." *Miami Metropolis*, December 22, 1905.

"Fifty Cases on Docket of the Criminal Court." *Miami Metropolis*, January 5, 1918.

"Film House Reviews." *Variety*, February 13, 1929.

Fisher, Jane. *Fabulous Hoosier: A Story of American Achievement*. Chicago: Harry Coleman, 1947.

"Fisher Testifies That Capone Presence Makes Beach Citizens Fearful, Cuts Property Values." *Miami Daily News*, May 16, 1930.

Fleischmann, Thomas F. "'Watch Miami': The Miami Metropolis and the Spanish-American War." *Tequesta*, no. 47 (1987): 31–48.

"Flights & Flyers." *Time*, February 16, 1931.

Flinn, John C. "Showmanship." *Exhibitors Trade Review*, February 16, 1924.

"Florida Anglers Now Hook Pretty Mermaids." *Milwaukee Journal*, January 4, 1937.

"Florida Counties Put Millions in Highways." *Dependable Highways*, October 1916.

"Florida Gulf Coast Is Called Paradise for Bootleggers." *Evening Independent* (St. Petersburg, FL), July 10, 1923.

"Florida, Impressions of a Visitor." *Tribune* (Nassau), December 2, 1911.

"Florida Not Destroyed." *Bradford County Telegraph* (Starke, FL), April 19, 1895.

"Florida Realizing Dreams of Wealth." *New York Times*, March 22, 1925.

Florida State Planning Board. *A Guide to Miami and Dade County*. Northsport, NY: Bacon, Percy & Daggett, 1941.

Flynt, Josiah. "Homosexuality among Tramps." In *Studies in the Psychology of Sex: Sexual Inversion*, 2nd ed., vol. 2, edited by Havelock Ellis, 219–24. Philadelphia: F. A. Davis, 1906.

Forbes, B. C. "Ex-Sailor Who Wouldn't Be Licked Founds 'Ideal' City." *Milwaukee Sentinel*, January 23, 1926.

"The Forbidden City." *Chicago Defender*, October 2, 1926.

"For Coconut Grove's Bank, Price Was Right." *Miami News*, April 10, 1966.

Ford, Clellan S., and Frank A. Beach. *Patterns of Sexual Behavior*. New York: Harper & Brothers, 1951.

"Former Mayor Lang Tells Miami Tin Can Tourists 'Undesirable.'" *Evening Independent* (St. Petersburg, FL), January 4, 1921.

"Forty Years Old." *Sarasota (FL) Herald*, August 3, 1936.

Foster, Lydia. "Miami to Set Winter Fashions for Milady." *Miami Daily News*, September 20, 1925.

Foster, Thomas A. "The Sexual Abuse of Black Men under American Slavery." *Journal of the History of Sexuality* 20, no. 3 (September 2011): 445–64.

Foucault, Michel. *The History of Sexuality*, vol. 1, *An Introduction*. Translated by Robert Hurley. New York: Vintage, 1990 [1976].

Fowler, Peter N. "Adult Adoption: A 'New' Legal Tool for Lesbians and Gay Men." *Golden Gate University Law Review* 14, no. 3 (1984): 1–42.

Frank, Andrew K. "Taking the State Out: Seminoles and Creeks in Late Eighteenth-Century Florida." *Florida Historical Quarterly* 84, no. 1 (Summer 2005): 10–27.

Frank, Gillian. "'The Civil Rights of Parents': Race and Conservative Politics in Anita Bryant's Campaign against Gay Rights in 1970s Florida." *Journal of the History of Sexuality* 22, no. 1 (January 2013): 126–60.

Freedman, Estelle B. *Redefining Rape: Sexual Violence in the Era of Suffrage and Segregation*. Cambridge, MA: Harvard University Press, 2013.

———. "'Uncontrolled Desires': The Response to the Sexual Psychopath, 1920–1960." *Journal of American History* 74, no. 1 (1987): 83–106.

"Freedom for Bathers." *Miami Daily News*, October 14, 1928.

"Freeman, Alden, Author and Political Reformer." In *American Biography: A New Cyclopedia*, vol. 4, 44–50. New York: American Historical Society, 1918.

"From Our Northern Sister." *Miami Metropolis*, May 15, 1896.

Fronc, Jennifer. *New York Undercover: Private Surveillance in the Progressive Era*. Chicago: University of Chicago Press, 2009.

Fuentes, Norberto. *The Autobiography of Fidel Castro*. Translated by Anna Kushner. New York: W. W. Norton, 2010.

Funnell, Charles E. *By the Beautiful Sea: The Rise and High Times of That Great American Resort, Atlantic City*. New York: Alfred A. Knopf, 1975.

Gallo, Marcia M. *Different Daughters: A History of the Daughters of Bilitis and the Rights of the Lesbian Rights Movement*. New York: Carroll & Graf, 2006.

Gambino, Matthew Joseph. "Mental Health and Ideals of Citizenship: Patient Care at St. Elizabeth's Hospital in Washington, D.C., 1903–1962." PhD diss., University of Illinois at Urbana-Champaign, 2010.

"Gang of Negroes Try to Revive Old Conditions in North Miami." *Miami Metropolis*, April 6, 1909.

García, María Cristina. *Havana USA: Cuban Exiles and Cuban Americans in South Florida, 1959–1994*. Berkeley: University of California Press, 1996.

Gardner, John A. "Wickedest City in World Is Havana; U.S. Intervention Near, Press Man Says." *Cleveland Press*, January 27, 1911.

Gassan, Richard H. "Fear, Commercialism, Reform, and Antebellum Tourism to New York City." *Journal of Urban History* 41, no. 6 (November 2015): 1077–90.

General Assembly of the Bahama Islands. *Bahamas: Acts Passed in the Fourteenth and Fifteenth Years of the Reign of His Majesty King George V*. Nassau: Office of the Nassau Guardian, 1924.

———. *The Statute Law of the Bahamas*, vol. 2. London: Henry Sweet Law, 1868.

George, Paul S. "Bootleggers, Prohibitionists and Police: The Temperance Movement in Miami, 1896–1920." *Tequesta* 39 (1979): 34–41.

———. "Colored Town: Miami's Black Community, 1896–1930." *Florida Historical Quarterly* 56, no. 4 (April 1978): 432–47.

———. "A Cyclone Hits Miami: Carrie Nation's Visit to 'The Wicked City.'" *Florida Historical Quarterly* 58, no. 2 (October 1979): 150–59.

———. "The Evolution of Miami and Dade County's Judiciary, 1896–1930." *Tequesta* 1, no. 36 (1976): 28–42.

———. "Policing Miami's Black Community, 1896–1930." *Florida Historical Quarterly* 57, no. 4 (April 1979): 434–50.

Gilfoyle, Timothy J. *City of Eros: New York City, Prostitution, and the Commercialization of Sex, 1790–1920*. New York: W. W. Norton, 1992.

Gilmore, David D. *Manhood in the Making: Cultural Concepts of Masculinity*. New Haven, CT: Yale University Press, 1990.

"Gleanings from the Press." *Evening Independent* (St. Petersburg, FL), March 19, 1930.

Gleijeses, Piero. "1898: The Opposition to the Spanish-American War." *Journal of Latin American Studies* 35, no. 4 (November 2003): 681–719.

Glick, Elisa. *Materializing Queer Desire: Oscar Wilde to Andy Warhol*. Albany: State University of New York Press, 2009.

"A Go Ahead Suburb." *Miami Metropolis*, May 15, 1896.

Goldman, Emma. *Living My Life*, vol. 1. New York: Alfred A. Knopf, 1931.

"Good Season." *Time*, March 17, 1941.

"Government Opens Case against Pine." *Palm Beach Post*, April 8, 1942.

"Grand Jury Is Reconvened to Hear Evidence in Assault Case." *Miami Daily Metropolis*, July 31, 1920.

Grant, Maxwell. "Crime over Miami." In *The Shadow*, vol. 83, 58–111. San Antonio: Sanctum, 2014 [1940].

Grapho. "In Florida: The Tide of Tourists in Summer Land." *Congregationalist and Christian World*, March 11, 1915.

"Greater Miami Approved by Residents of Suburb." *Miami Daily Metropolis*, February 22, 1913.

"Greek Sponge Fishers Face Miami Battle." *Miami Daily News*, December 23, 1928.

Green, James N. *Beyond Carnival: Male Homosexuality in Twentieth-Century Brazil*. Chicago: University of Chicago Press, 1999.

Green, Jonathon. *Cassell's Dictionary of Slang*. 2nd ed. London: Weidenfeld & Nicolson, 2005.

Gualtieri, Sarah. "Becoming 'White': Race, Religion and the Foundations of Syrian/ Lebanese Ethnicity in the United States." *Journal of American Ethnic History* 20, no. 4 (Summer 2001): 29–58.

"Guardsmen Called Out When Negroes Threaten Uprising." *Meriden (CT) Morning Record*, August 3, 1920.

Gunter, Archibald Clavering, and Fergus Redmond. *A Florida Enchantment: A Novel*. New York: Home, 1892.

Gustav-Wrathall, John Donald. *Take the Young Stranger by the Hand: Same-Sex Relations and the YMCA*. Chicago: University of Chicago, 1998.

Guthrie, John J., Jr. "Hard Times, Hard Liquor, and Hard Luck: Selective Enforcement of Prohibition in North Florida, 1928–1933." *Florida Historical Quarterly* 72, no. 4 (April 1994): 435–52.

———. *Keepers of the Spirits: The Judicial Response to Prohibition Enforcement in Florida, 1885–1935*. Westport, CT: Greenwood, 1998.

———. "Rekindling the Spirits: From National Prohibition to Local Option in Florida, 1928–1935." *Florida Historical Quarterly* 74, no. 1 (Summer 1995): 23–39.

Gutiérrez, Ramón A. *When Jesus Came, the Corn Mothers Went Away: Marriage, Sexuality, and Power in New Mexico, 1500–1846*. Stanford, CA: Stanford University Press, 1991.

Haight, Walter L. *Racine County in the World War: A History*. Racine, WI: Western Printing & Lithographing, 1920.

Halberstam, Judith. *In a Queer Time and Place: Transgender Bodies, Subcultural Lives*. New York: New York University Press, 2004.

Haldrup, Michael, and Jonas Larsen. "Material Cultures of Tourism." *Leisure Studies* 25, no. 3 (July 2006): 275–89.

Halperin, David M. *One Hundred Years of Homosexuality and Other Essays on Greek Love*. New York: Routledge, 1990.

Hamer, David. *New Towns in the New World: Images and Perceptions of the Nineteenth-Century Urban Frontier*. New York: Columbia University Press, 1990.

Hansen, Karen V. "'No Kisses Is Like Youres': An Erotic Friendship between Two African-American Women during the Mid-nineteenth Century." *Gender & History* 7, no. 2 (August 1995): 153–82.

Harnell, Joe, and Ira Skutch. *Counterpoint: The Journey of a Music Man*. Bloomington, IN: Xlibris, 2000.

Harris, LaShawn. *Sex Workers, Psychics, and Numbers Runners: Black Women in New York City's Underground Economy*. Urbana: University of Illinois Press, 2016.

Haskins, James. *Mabel Mercer: A Life*. New York: Atheneum, 1987.

"Havana a Second, Almost a Gayer, Riviera." *New York Tribune*, January 23, 1916.

Havard, Valery. "Headquarters Department of Cuba, Office of the Chief Surgeon, Havana, 22 July 1901." In *Annual Report of Major General Leonard Wood, U.S.V., Commanding Department of Cuba*, Havana,1901.

"Have the Saloon Men Made Good?" *Miami Metropolis*, March 13, 1908.

Heap, Chad. *Slumming: Sexual and Racial Encounters in American Nightlife, 1885–1940*. Chicago: University of Chicago Press, 2009.

"He Fought in 'Battle of Miami.'" *Miami Daily News*, August 28, 1957.

Henry, George W. *Sex Variants: A Study of Homosexual Patterns*, vol. 1. New York: Paul B. Hoeber, 1941.

Herdrich, Stephanie L., and H. Barbara Weinberg. *American Drawings and Watercolors in the Metropolitan Museum of Art: John Singer Sargent*. New Haven, CT: Yale University Press, 2000.

Hernández, Arístides, and Jorge Piñero. *Historia del humor gráfico en Cuba*. Lleida, Spain: Milenio, 2007.

Hernández Catá, Alfonso. *El placer de sufrir*. Madrid: Helénica, 1920.

"Hialeah to Open Beautiful Racing Plant Tomorrow." *Evening Independent* (St. Petersburg, FL), January 13, 1932.

"A Hint to the Lawyers." *Trenton (NJ) Evening Times*, May 25, 1909.

History Project. *Improper Bostonians: Lesbian and Gay History from the Puritans to Playland*. Boston: Beacon, 1998.

Hobson, Emily K. *Lavender and Red: Liberation and Solidarity in the Gay and Lesbian Left*. Oakland: University of California Press, 2016.

Hoffman, Paul E. *Florida's Frontiers*. Bloomington: Indiana University Press, 2002.

Hoffman, F. Burrall, Jr., and Paul Chalfin. "The Mechanism of a Great Estate: 'Vizcaya' at Miami, Fla." *Architecture and Building* 49, no. 8 (August 1917).

Hoganson, Kristin L. *Fighting for American Manhood: How Gender Politics Provoked the Spanish-American and Philippine-American Wars*. New Haven, CT: Yale University Press, 1998.

Holmes, A. G. "The Public Pulse, July 15, 1913." *Miami News*, January 15, 1983.

Holmes, Kwame. "What's the Tea: Gossip and the Production of Black Gay Social History." *Radical History Review* 122 (May 2015): 55–69.

"Honeymooners at the Beach." *Miami News-Metropolis*, February 28, 1924.

"Hotels Turning People Away, More Rooms Needed." *Miami Daily Metropolis*, February 11, 1916.

Howard, John. *Men Like That: A Southern Queer History*. Chicago: University of Chicago Press, 1999.

Howard, John, ed. *Carryin' on in the Lesbian and Gay South*. New York: New York University Press, 1997.

"Hull to Get Report on Haitian Incident." *Miami Daily News*, December 5, 1939.

Huneker, Diana. "Portrait Drawings by Dewing Woodward." *International Studio*, July 1917.

Hurewitz, Daniel. *Bohemian Los Angeles and the Making of Modern Politics.* Berkeley: University of California Press, 2007.

Hurley, Andrew. *Diners, Bowling Alleys and Trailer Parks: Chasing the American Dream in the Postwar Consumer Culture.* New York: Basic Books, 2001.

Hurston, Zora. "Dance Songs and Tales from the Bahamas." *Journal of American Folklore* 43, no. 169 (September 1930): 294–312.

"Incorporating North Miami." *Miami Metropolis,* July 16, 1897.

"Indian Arrested While Trying to Sell His Egrets." *Weekly Miami Metropolis,* June 14, 1912.

Ingram, Tammy. *Dixie Highway: Road Building and the Making of the Modern South, 1900–1930.* Chapel Hill: University of North Carolina Press, 2014.

"An Isolated Plant at Nassau, Bahama Islands." *Electrical World and Engineer* 37, no. 22 (June 1, 1901): 914–16.

Jabour, Anya. *Marriage in the Early Republic: Elizabeth and William Wirt and the Companionate Ideal.* Baltimore: Johns Hopkins University Press, 1998.

Jackson, Kenneth T. *Crabgrass Frontier: The Suburbanization of the United States.* New York: Oxford University Press, 1985.

Jacobson, Matthew Frye. *Barbarian Virtues: The United States Encounters Foreign Peoples at Home and Abroad, 1876–1917.* New York: Hill and Wang, 2000.

———. *Whiteness of a Different Color: European Immigrants and the Alchemy of Race.* Cambridge, MA: Harvard University Press, 1998.

James, Lawrence. *The Golden Warrior: The Life and Legend of Lawrence of Arabia.* New York: Skyhorse, 1990.

Jervis, Rick. "Stylish Life, Brutal Death." *Miami Herald,* July 16, 1997.

"Jewel Box Gets License." *Miami Daily News,* February 21, 1947.

"'Jewel Box' Opens at Embassy Hotel." *Miami Daily News,* December 11, 1936.

Johns, Elizabeth. *Winslow Homer: The Nature of Observation.* Berkeley: University of California Press, 2002.

Johnson, Colin R. *Just Queer Folks: Gender and Sexuality in Rural America.* Philadelphia: Temple University Press, 2013.

Johnson, David K. "The Kids of Fairytown: Gay Male Culture on Chicago's Near North Side in the 1930s." In *Creating a Space for Ourselves: Lesbian, Gay, and Bisexual Community Histories,* edited by Brett Beemyn, 97–118. New York: Routledge, 1997.

———. *The Lavender Scare: The Cold War Persecution of Gays and Lesbians in the Federal Government.* Chicago: University of Chicago Press, 2004.

Johnson, Doris L. *The Quiet Revolution in the Bahamas.* Nassau: Family Islands, 1972.

Johnson, Howard. "Bahamian Labor Migration to Florida in the Late Nineteenth and Early Twentieth Centuries." *International Migration Review* 22, no. 1 (Spring 1988): 84–103.

Johnson, John J. *Latin America in Caricature.* Austin: University of Texas Press, 1980.

Johnson, Louise. "Letter to the Editor: The Blue Dome Fellowship." *Miami Daily News,* December 29, 1940.

Jones, Jacqueline. *Labor of Love, Labor of Sorrow: Black Women, Work, and the Family from Slavery to the Present*. New York: Basic Books, 1985.

"The Joy of Beauty and the American Renaissance." *Price's Carpet and Rug News*, November 1917.

"Judge Dismisses Disorderly Case against Bouldin." *Miami Daily Metropolis*, July 15, 1920.

Judicial Committee of the Privy Council. "Joint Responsibility for Murder (*Farquharson v. The Queen*)." *Journal of Criminal Law* 37, no. 3 (September 1973): 206–7.

"Just an Incident in Which Five Miami Boys Were Led Astray." *Miami Metropolis*, October 4, 1907.

"J. Walter Kehoe." *New York Times*, August 21, 1938.

Katz, Jonathan Ned. *Gay American History: Lesbians and Gay Men in the U.S.A.: A Documentary*. Rev. ed. New York: Meridian, 1976.

———. *The Invention of Heterosexuality*. New York: Dutton, 1995.

Keene, Jennifer D. *World War I*. Westport, CT: Greenwood, 2003.

Kefauver, Estes. *Crime in America*. 1st ed. Garden City, NY: Doubleday, 1951.

Keire, Mara Laura. *For Business and Pleasure: Red-Light Districts and the Regulation of Vice in the United States, 1890–1933*. Baltimore: Johns Hopkins University Press, 2010.

Kendrick, Walter M. *The Secret Museum: Pornography in Modern Culture*. Berkeley: University of California Press, 1987.

Kennedy, Elizabeth Lapovsky, and Madeline D. Davis. *Boots of Leather, Slippers of Gold: The History of a Lesbian Community*. 2nd ed. New York: Routledge, 2014 [1993].

Kennedy, Kathleen, and Sharon Ullman. "Introduction: Sex on the Borderlands." In *Sexual Borderlands: Constructing an American Sexual Past*, xi–xvi. Columbus: Ohio State University Press, 2003.

Kerber, Linda K. "Separate Spheres, Female Worlds, Woman's Place: The Rhetoric of Women's History." *Journal of American History* 75, no. 1 (June 1988): 9–39.

Killen, James L. "Miami Night Clubs Drawing the Spenders." *Hammond (IN) Times*, January 19, 1940.

Kincannon, Oliver. "Florida Haven of Happiness for Women Declares New York Woman Lawyer Visiting Jacksonville." In *All Florida*, edited by Bureau of Immigration and Department of Agriculture. Tallahassee: Record Company, 1926.

King, Rufus. *Murder Masks Miami*. New York: Popular Library, 1939.

Kissack, Terence. *Free Comrades: Anarchism and Homosexuality in the United States, 1895–1917*. Oakland, CA: AK, 2008.

"Klan Is Not Law." *Miami Herald*, November 17, 1937.

Kleinberg, Howard. "The Censorship Flap of '13." *Miami News*, January 15, 1983.

———. "Backed Up Tough Talk." *Miami News*, August 10, 1985.

———. "History of the *Miami News*, 1896–1987." *Tequesta* 57 (1987): 5–29.

———. "Hialeah: Prairie to Pari-Mutuels." *Miami News*, March 26, 1983.

———. "The Real Beginning of South Beach." *Miami News*, November 26, 1988.

———. "Smith's Casino Was a Top Attraction." *Miami News*, December 3, 1988.

Kline, Wendy. *Building a Better Race: Gender, Sexuality, and Eugenics from the Turn of the Century to the Baby Boom.* Berkeley: University of California Press, 2005.

Knowles, Leonard J. *Elements of Bahamian Law.* Nassau: Business & Law, 1978.

Kofoed, Jack. "Boys in Girls' Clothes Open Another Problem." *Miami Daily News,* March 22, 1939.

———. "Miami." *North American Review* 228, no. 6 (December 1929): 670–73.

———. "Miami after Dark." *Real,* December 1952, 51–53.

———. *Moon over Miami.* New York: Random House, 1955.

Krahulik, Karen Christel. *Provincetown: From Pilgrim Landing to Gay Resort.* New York: New York University Press, 2005.

Kramer, Paul A. "Power and Connection: Imperial Histories of the United States in the World." *American Historical Review* 116, no. 5 (December 2011): 1348–91.

Kraut, Alan M. *Silent Travelers: Germs, Genes, and the Immigrant Menace.* Baltimore: Johns Hopkins University Press, 1995.

Krolikowski, Christopher, and Graham Brown. "The Structure and Form of Urban Tourism Precincts: Setting the Stage for Tourist Performances." In *City Spaces–Tourist Places: Urban Tourism Precincts,* edited by Bruce Hayllar, Tony Griffin, and Deborah Edwards, 127–49. Oxford: Butterworth-Heinemann, 2008.

Kunzel, Regina. *Criminal Intimacy: Prison and the Uneven History of Modern American Sexuality.* Chicago: University of Chicago Press, 2008.

LaMonaca, Caesar (music), and Teresa Conner (lyric). "Miami, Playground of the U.S.A." Miami Beach, 1929.

Landers, Jane. *Black Society in Spanish Florida.* Urbana: University of Illinois Press, 1999.

Lane, Jill. *Blackface Cuba, 1840–1895.* Philadelphia: University of Pennsylvania Press, 2005.

Lardner, Ring W. "Lardner Observes Miami Mermaids." *El Paso Herald*, March 3, 1923.

"Large Sum Bet during Hialeah Racing Program." *St. Petersburg (FL) Times*, March 15, 1933.

Larson, Edward J. *Sex, Race, and Science: Eugenics in the Deep South.* Baltimore: Johns Hopkins University Press, 1995.

"Lasses White Brings Great Minstrel Show." *Miami Daily News and Metropolis,* November 12, 1926.

"'Lasses' White Minstrel Good." *Miami Daily News and Metropolis,* November 11, 1927.

"Lasses White Minstrels to Come Nov. 3." *Sarasota (FL) Herald,* October 31, 1926.

"Latest in Resort Modes Described by Local Store Executives Back from Miami Beach Fashion Parade." *Evening Independent* (St. Petersburg, FL), January 28, 1935.

Lavender, Abraham D. *Miami Beach in 1920: The Making of a Winter Resort.* Charleston, SC: Arcadia, 2002.

Lears, T. J. Jackson. *Rebirth of a Nation.* New York: HarperCollins, 2009.

———. "Reconstructing Nature: The Rise and Fall and Rise of the American Sublime, 1820–1920." In *Sargent: The Late Landscapes,* edited by Hilliard T.

Goldfarb, Erica E Hirshler, and T. J. Jackson Lears. Hanover, NH: University Press of New England, 1999.

"Leary and Lee." *Miami Daily News and Metropolis*, April 2, 1925.

"Left False Teeth as He Made Hurried Exit from Gambling Dive Raided by Sheriff Hardie." *Miami Daily Metropolis*, March 25, 1912.

Lente, Frederick D. *Florida as a Health-Resort*. New York: D. Appleton, 1876.

Lerner, Gerda. "The Lady and the Mill Girl: Changes in the Status of Women in the Age of Jackson." *Midcontinent American Studies Journal* 10 (Spring 1969): 5–15.

Leslie, Vernon M. "The Great Depression in Miami Beach." MA thesis, Florida Atlantic University, 1980.

"Letter to the Editor: Emigration." *Nassau Guardian*, April 28, 1920.

"Letter to the Editor from Twist Black." *Tribune* (Nassau), January 19, 1911.

"Letter to the Editor: Out Island Development." *Nassau Guardian*, January 28, 1920.

Library of Congress, U.S. Copyright Office. *Catalog of Copyright Entries*, part 3, *Musical Compositions*, vol. 26. Washington, DC: Government Printing Office, 1931.

———. *Catalog of Copyright Entries*, part 3, *Musical Compositions*, vol. 27. Washington, DC: Government Printing Office, 1932.

———. *Catalog of Copyright Entries*, part 3, *Musical Compositions*, vol. 28. Washington, DC: Government Printing Office, 1933.

———. *Catalog of Copyright Entries*, part 3, *Musical Compositions*, vol. 30. Washington, DC: Government Printing Office, 1935.

———. *Catalog of Copyright Entries*, part 3, *Musical Compositions*, vol. 31. Washington, DC: Government Printing Office, 1937.

Lichtenstein, Alex. "In the Shade of the Lenin Oak: 'Colonel' Raymond Robins, Senator Claude Pepper, and the Cold War." *American Communist History* 3, no. 2 (2004): 185–214.

———. *Twice the Work of Free Labor: The Political Economy of Convict Labor in the New South*. London: Verso, 1996.

Liebow, Elliot. *Tally's Corner: A Study of Negro Streetcorner Men*. Boston: Little, Brown, 1967.

"Life Sentences for Robbery Pair Asked." *Miami Daily News*, March 20, 1936.

"The Life That's Lived in Books." *New York Times*, January 7, 1912.

"Liquor Petitioners Warned." *Miami Metropolis*, August 14, 1896.

Livingston, Grant. "The Annexation of the City of Coconut Grove." *Tequesta* 1, no. 60 (2000): 32–55.

"Long Masquerade as Woman Ends." *Pittsburgh Press*, January 4, 1946.

"Longtime Minstrel Man Buried Today." *Lancaster (OH) Eagle-Gazette*, February 18, 1963.

López Lima, Reinaldo. *Turismo y urbanismo*. Havana, 1949.

"Loud and Sporty Clothes Proper at Miami Beach." *Milwaukee Journal*, December 14, 1941.

Love, Richard H., and Carl William Peters. *Carl W. Peters: American Scene Painter from Rochester to Rockport*. Rochester, NY: University of Rochester Press, 1999.

Luibhéid, Eithne. *Entry Denied: Controlling Sexuality at the Border*. Minneapolis: University of Minnesota Press, 2002.

Lydston, G. Frank. *The Diseases of Society: The Vice and Crime Problem*. Philadelphia: J. B. Lippincott, 1904.

"Lyric Theater, Miami, FLA." *Freeman* (Indianapolis, IN), March 22, 1913.

Lystra, Karen. *Searching the Heart: Women, Men, and Romantic Love in Nineteenth-Century America*. New York: Oxford University Press, 1989.

MacDowell, Wanda. "Miami Music and Musicians." *Miami Daily News*, July 25, 1937.

Macías-González, Víctor M. "The Transnational Homophile Movement and the Development of Domesticity in Mexico City's Homosexual Community, 1930–70." *Gender & History* 26, no. 3 (November 2014): 519–44.

Mackay, Gordon. "The Story of the House That James Deering Built." *Miami Daily Metropolis*, December 21, 1916.

Mackintosh, J. A. "Pellagra in the Bahamas." In *Transactions of the National Association for the Study of Pellagra: Second Triennial Meeting at Columbia, South Carolina, 3, 4 Oct. 1912*, 199–200. Columbia, SC: R. L. Bryan, 1914.

MacLaren, Archibald. "Clinical Lecture." *Northwestern Lancet* 20 (1900): 1–3.

MacLean, Nancy. *Behind the Mask of Chivalry: The Making of the Second Ku Klux Klan*. New York: Oxford University Press, 1994.

Manalansan, Martin F., IV. "The 'Stuff' of Archives: Mess, Migration, and Queer Lives." *Radical History Review*, no. 120 (Fall 2014): 94–107.

Mangold, George Benjamin. *The Challenge of Saint Louis*. New York: Missionary Education Movement of the United States and Canada, 1917.

"Manufacturers' Exhibit Given New Additions." *Miami Daily News*, February 22, 1931.

"Many Defendants Enter Pleas at Court's Session." *Evening Independent* (St. Petersburg, FL), October 11, 1933.

"Many Good Acts." *Times Recorder* (Zanesville, OH), October 11, 1935.

"Many Improvements for Beach Casino Planned by Owner." *Miami Metropolis*, March 30, 1921.

Marchand, Roland. *Advertising the American Dream: Making Way for Modernity, 1920–1940*. Berkeley: University of California Press, 1985.

Maribona, Armando. *Turismo y ciudadanía*. Havana: Editorial Alrededor de América, 1942.

Marshall, Daniel, Kevin P. Murphy, and Zeb Tortorici. "Editors' Introduction: Queering Archives: Historical Unravelings." *Radical History Review*, no. 120 (Fall 2014): 1–11.

———. "Editors' Introduction: Queering Archives: Intimate Tracings." *Radical History Review*, no. 122 (May 2015): 1–10.

Martin, Jill E. "'The Greatest Evil': Interpretations of Indian Prohibition Laws, 1832–1953." *Great Plains Quarterly*, no. 23 (Winter 2003): 35–53.

"Mary Garden Craze Led Girl to Suicide." *New York Times*, February 18, 1913.

"Mary Garden Will Arrive Here Today." *Miami Daily News*, February 11, 1931.

"Mary Kirk Brown Weds Miami Beach Youth." *Palm Beach Post*, December 25, 1938.

May, Heather. "Middle-Class Morality and Blackwashed Beauties: Francis Leon and

the Rise of the Prima Donna in the Post-war Minstrel Show." PhD diss., Indiana
     University, 2007.

———. "White Lies and Stony Silence: Reconstruction in the Personal Narrative of
     America's Most Popular Female Impersonator on the Minstrel Stage." *Performing
     Arts Resources* 28 (2011): 217–24, 349–50.

"May Cut Out Passports on Travel to Bahamas." *Miami Metropolis*, March 11, 1920.

Mayer, Gordon E. "A Cruise to Nassau from Miami." *Rudder*, February 1922.

McCarthy, Kevin M., ed. *Nine Florida Stories by Marjory Stoneman Douglas.*
     Jacksonville: University of North Florida Press, 1990.

McDermott, John B. "Male Strip-Tease Act Too Raw." *St. Petersburg (FL) Times*,
     March 24, 1944.

McElory, Jerome L., and Klaus de Albuquerque. "Migration Transition in Small
     Northern and Eastern Caribbean States." *International Migration Review* 22,
     no. 3 (Autumn 1988): 30–58.

McGirr, Lisa. *Suburban Warriors: The Origins of the New American Right.* Princeton,
     NJ: Princeton University Press, 2001.

———. *The War on Alcohol: Prohibition and the Rise of the American State.* New
     York: W. W. Norton, 2016.

McGuire, Hunter, and G. Frank Lydston. "Sexual Crimes among the Southern
     Negroes—Scientifically Considered; An Open Correspondence." *Western Medical
     Reporter* 15, no. 6 (June 1893): 121–27.

McIntyre, O. O. "New York Day by Day." *Miami Daily News*, February 10, 1932.

McLaren, Angus. *The Trials of Masculinity: Policing Sexual Boundaries, 1870–1930.*
     Chicago: University of Chicago Press, 1997.

"Menace of Companionate Marriage." *Miami Daily News and Metropolis*, December
     29, 1927.

Meriam, Annie Lund. "Woman's Present Position in the Teaching World." *Western
     Journal of Education* 10 (August 1905): 639–44.

Merrick, George E. "Pre-Flagler Influences on the Lower Florida East Coast."
     *Tequesta* 1, no. 1 (March 1941): 1–10.

"A Message from Miami, Florida." *Commoner* (Lincoln, NE), February 1, 1916.

Meyerowitz, Joanne. "Transnational Sex and U.S. History." *American Historical
     Review* 114, no. 5 (2009): 1273–86.

———. *Women Adrift: Independent Wage Earners in Chicago, 1880–1930.* Chicago:
     University of Chicago Press, 1988.

"Miamian Receives Psychopathic Care." *Miami Daily News*, July 18, 1936.

"Miami Art Leader, Painter Succumbs." *Sarasota (FL) Herald-Tribune*, July 13, 1950.

"Miami Beach by-the-Sea." *Miami News-Metropolis*, February 28, 1924.

"Miami Beach Casino Is Popular Indeed for Dances and Swimming." *Miami
     Metropolis*, January 8, 1919.

"Miami Beach Censorless; Bathers Set Own Styles." *Scranton (PA) Republican*,
     February 2, 1924.

"Miami Club Must Change Its Songs." *Palm Beach Post*, July 21, 1939.

"Miami District Unites against Capone Menace." *Miami Daily News*, June 28, 1928.

"Miami Girl Murder Brings Nightclub Employment Probe." *Sarasota (FL) Herald-Tribune*, August 14, 1939.

"Miami Incorporated." *Miami Metropolis*, July 31, 1896.

"Miami in Paragraph." *Miami Metropolis*, August 28, 1914.

"Miami Launches Winter Season Early This Year." *Brooklyn Daily Eagle*, November 7, 1937.

"Miami Mince Meat." *Miami Metropolis*, November 20, 1896.

"Miami Mince Meat." *Miami Metropolis*, March 12, 1897.

"Miami Mince Meat." *Miami Metropolis*, July 29, 1898.

"Miami Night Life Loses 'Hot Spots.'" *New York Times*, November 22, 1937.

"Miami Observes 39th Birthday." *Sarasota (FL) Herald*, July 28, 1935.

"Miami Physician Flies to Havana." *Miami Daily News*, December 18, 1929.

"Miami's Gallows." *Miami Herald*, June 6, 2014.http://www.miamiherald.com/2014/06/06/4163492/in-1906-miami-hanged-him-for-a.html.

"Miami's Negro Problem." *Miami Metropolis*, August 22, 1913.

"Miami to Have Liquor." *Miami Metropolis*, March 5, 1897.

"Miami's Unconquerable Soul." *Miami Tribune*, September 19, 1926.

"Miami's Vagrancy Drive Ordinance Becomes Law." *Lewiston (ME) Daily Sun*, May 24, 1930.

"Miami's Y.W.C.A. Has Become a Real Community Center." *Miami Metropolis*, March 5, 1921.

"Miami Women Raise Carrie Nation Banner." *New York Times*, February 23, 1931.

"Miami, World's 'Winter Play City.'" *Brooklyn Daily Eagle*, September 20, 1926.

Miller, Vivien. "The Life and Crimes of Harry Sitamore, New York 'Prince of Thieves' and the 'Raffles' of Miami." *Florida Historical Quarterly* 87, no. 3 (Winter 2009): 378–403.

Miller, Vivien M. L. *Hard Labor and Hard Time: Florida's "Sunshine Prison" and Chain Gangs*. Gainesville: University Press of Florida, 2012.

———. *Crime, Sexual Violence, and Clemency: Florida's Pardon Board and Penal System in the Progressive Era*. Gainesville: University Press of Florida, 2000.

Minian, Ana Raquel. *Undocumented Lives: A History of Mexican Migration to the United States*. Cambridge, MA: Harvard University Press, forthcoming.

"Minstrel Show's Rehearsal Set." *Miami Daily News and Metropolis*, July 15, 1929.

"Minstrels to Entertain in Season Debut." *Sarasota (FL) Herald*, November 3, 1926.

"Miss Woolson's 'Rodman the Keeper.'" *Scribner's Monthly*, August 1880.

Mitchell, Pablo. *Coyote Nation: Sexuality, Race, and Conquest in Modernizing New Mexico, 1880–1920*. Chicago: University of Chicago Press, 2005.

Mjagkij, Nina, and Margaret Ann Spratt, eds. *Men and Women Adrift: The YMCA and the YWCA in the City*. New York: New York University Press, 1997.

Moffett, Samuel E. "Henry Morrison Flagler." *Cosmopolitan*, August 1902.

Mohl, Raymond A. "Black Immigrants: Bahamians in Early Twentieth-Century Miami." *Florida Historical Quarterly* 65, no. 3 (January 1987): 271–97.

———. "Changing Economic Patterns in the Miami Metropolitan Area, 1940–1980." *Tequesta* 42 (1982): 63–73.

―――. "Making the Second Ghetto in Metropolitan Miami, 1940–1960." *Journal of Urban History* 21, no. 3 (March 1995): 395–427.

―――. "Miami: The Ethnic Cauldron." In *Sunbelt Cities: Politics and Growth since World War II*, edited by Richard M. Bernard and Bradley R. Rice, 58–99. Austin: University of Texas Press, 1983.

―――. "The Origins of Miami's Liberty City." *Florida Environmental and Urban Issues* 12 (July 1985): 9–12.

―――. "Shadows in the Sunshine: Race and Ethnicity in Miami." *Tequesta* 49 (1989): 63–80.

―――. *South of the South: Jewish Activists and the Civil Rights Movement in Miami, 1945–1960*. Gainesville: University Press of Florida, 2004.

Monroe, Mary Barr. "Pioneer Women of Dade County." *Tequesta* 1, no. 3 (July 1943): 49–56.

Moore, Deborah Dash. *To the Golden Cities: Pursuing the American Jewish Dream in Miami and L.A.* Cambridge, MA: Harvard University Press, 1994.

Moore, William Howard. *The Kefauver Committee and the Politics of Crime, 1950–1952*. Columbia: University of Missouri Press, 1974.

"Moral Collapse of Miami." *Philadelphia Record*, October 25, 1933.

Morgan, Edward M. "Court-Martial Jurisdiction over Non-military Persons under the Articles of War." *Minnesota Law Review* 4, no. 2 (January 1920): 79–116.

Morgan, Jennifer L. "'Some Could Suckle over Their Shoulder': Male Travelers, Female Bodies, and the Gendering of Racial Ideology, 1500–1770." *William and Mary Quarterly* 54, no. 1 (January 1997): 167–92.

Mormino, Gary R. "Midas Returns: Miami Goes to War, 1941–1945." *Tequesta* 57 (1997): 5–51.

Mormino, Gary R., and George E. Pozzetta. *The Immigrant World of Ybor City: Italians and Their Latin Neighbors in Tampa, 1885–1985*. Gainesville: University Press of Florida, 1998.

Morris, Charles Smith, ed. *The Imperial Reference Library*. Philadelphia: Syndicate, 1898.

"Mrs. Dora Suggs, of Cocoanut Grove Assaulted and Fouly Murdered at an Early Hour Monday Night." *Miami Metropolis*, December 22, 1905.

"Mrs. Nation Summoned before Solicitor to Tell Her Troubles." *Miami Metropolis*, March 13, 1908.

"Mrs. Nation Will Lecture Next Week." *Miami Metropolis*, March 7, 1908.

Muir, Helen. *Miami, U.S.A.* Expanded ed. Gainesville: University Press of Florida, 1953.

Mumford, Kevin J. *Interzones: Black/White Sex Districts in Chicago and New York in the Early Twentieth Century*. New York: Columbia University Press, 1997.

Muñoz, José Esteban. *Disidentifications: Queers of Color and the Performance of Politics*. Minneapolis: University of Minnesota Press, 1999.

Murphy, Kevin P. *Political Manhood: Red Bloods, Mollycoddles, and the Politics of Progressive Era Reform*. New York: Columbia University Press, 2008.

"Mystery Surrounds the Wrecked V-832." *Miami Daily Metropolis*, August 29, 1921.

"Nan Britton's Girl to Get Trust Fund." *Pittsburgh Press*, March 12, 1932.

"The Nassau Negro Problem." *Miami Daily Metropolis*, June 10, 1912.

"National Association for the Advancement of Colored People." *The Crisis*, June 1917.

"Naval Air Station to Be Abandoned within 2 Months." *Miami Daily Metropolis*, August 27, 1919.

"Negro's 'Stage' Career Stopped When Cast Flees." *Miami Daily News*, August 23, 1925.

"Negro Vagrant Drive Started in Miami Area." *Miami Daily News*, March 20, 1936.

Neil, Edward J. "Miami Mermaid Retains Title in Medley Race." *St. Petersburg (FL) Times*, July 21, 1935.

Nelson, Dave. "'More of a Prison than an Asylum': Florida Hospital for the Indigent Insane during the Progressive Era." *Southern Studies: An Interdisciplinary Journal of the South* 14, no. 2 (Fall/Winter 2009): 68–85.

Nelson, David J. "Florida Crackers and Yankee Tourists: The Civilian Conservation Corps, the Florida Park Service and the Emergence of Modern Florida Tourism." PhD diss., Florida State University, 2008.

Nelson, Richard Alan. "Palm Trees, Public Relations, and Promoters: Boosting Southeast Florida as Motion Picture Empire, 1910–1930." *Florida Historical Quarterly* 61, no. 4 (April 1983): 383–403.

"New Bath House Will Have 450 Rooms and Large Free Pavilion." *Miami Daily Metropolis*, July 16, 1921.

"New England Group Has Haitian Night." *Miami Daily News*, March 20, 1935.

Newton, Esther. *Cherry Grove, Fire Island: Sixty Years in America's First Gay and Lesbian Town*. Boston: Beacon, 1993.

———. *Mother Camp: Female Impersonators in America*. Chicago: University of Chicago Press, 1972.

———. "The Mythic Mannish Lesbian: Radclyffe Hall and the New Woman." *Signs* 9, no. 4 (Summer 1984): 557–75.

"New York Capitol." *Exhibitors Herald-World*, February 23, 1929.

Ngai, Mae M. *Impossible Subjects: Illegal Aliens and the Making of Modern America*. Princeton, NJ: Princeton University Press, 2004.

"Nightclub Loses Venetian Area Zoning Appeal." *Miami Daily News*, August 15, 1950.

"Night Spot Closing Order Is Modified." *Miami Herald*, November 20, 1937.

Nijman, Jan. *Miami: Mistress of the Americas*. Philadelphia: University of Pennsylvania Press, 2011.

"92 Arrested in Miami War on Petty Vice." *Miami Daily News*, May 13, 1929.

"No Eskimo Story in This Flight." *Spokane (WA) Daily Chronicle*, July 13, 1931.

Noll, Steven. "Care and Control of the Feeble-Minded: Florida Farm Colony, 1920–1945." *Florida Historical Quarterly* 69, no. 1 (July 1990): 57–80.

———. *Feeble-Minded in Our Midst: Institutions for the Mentally Retarded in the South, 1900–1940*. Chapel Hill: University of North Carolina Press, 1995.

"Noted Soprano Gives Concert Here Tonight." *Miami Daily News*, January 4, 1931.

"Nothing but Prosperity and Progress Is in Store for Miami and Dade County." *Miami Daily Metropolis*, November 1, 1913.

"Oh, You September Morn." *Miami Metropolis*, July 22, 1913.

"Old Settlers Who Took Part in Incorporation of Miami Tell of the Birth of the Magic City." *Miami Daily Metropolis*, July 28, 1917.

O'Mahen Malcom, Allison. "Greek Immigrant Experience, Early 20th Century." In *Anti-immigration in the United States: A–R*, edited by Kathleen R. Arnold, 232–34. Santa Barbara, CA: ABC-CLIO, 2011.

"On Air Trip to Havana." *Miami Daily News*, June 23, 1929.

"100 Carolinians Be in Miami Thursday Night." *Miami Daily Metropolis*, March 17, 1914.

"On the Straight Road." *Miami Metropolis*, July 17, 1896.

"Only Two Cases before Judge Phillips Today." *Miami Metropolis*, June 5, 1915.

"Opening of Big Bridge Across Bay Celebrated." *Miami Daily Metropolis*, June 13, 1913.

"Opening of the Palatial Fairfax Theatre an Important Event in Miami History." *Miami Daily Metropolis*, January 20, 1922.

"Ornate Palace at Miami Beach Has New Owner." *Miami Daily News*, April 9, 1939.

Ortiz, Paul. *Emancipation Betrayed: The Hidden History of Black Organizing and White Violence in Florida from Reconstruction to the Bloody Election of 1920.* Berkeley: University of California Press, 2005.

Osborne, William. *Music in Ohio.* Kent, OH: Kent State University Press, 2004.

"Our Business Interests." *Miami Metropolis*, May 15, 1896.

"Over $40,000 the First Day for Miami Y.M.C.A. Building." *Miami Daily Metropolis*, February 11, 1916.

Painter, George. "The Sensibilities of Our Forefathers: The History of Sodomy Laws in the United States, Florida," https://www.glapn.org/sodomylaws/sensibilities /florida.htm (accessed March 26, 2017).

Parks, Arva Moore, and Bo Bennett. *Coconut Grove.* Charleston, SC: Arcadia, 2010.

Parsons, Alan. *A Winter in Paradise.* London: A. M. Philpot, 1926.

"Part of Phantom Estate Claimed by Nan Britton." *Evening Independent* (St. Petersburg, FL), August 24, 1938.

"Passenger Steamer Takes Up Run between Miami and Nassau, N.P." *Miami Daily Metropolis*, June 27, 1910.

Patron, Eugene J. "Jackie Johnson: The Life and Times of a Dixie Belle." *Weekly News* (Miami, FL), October 12, 1994.

Paulson, Don, and Roger Simpson. *An Evening at the Garden of Allah: A Gay Cabaret in Seattle.* New York: Columbia University Press, 1996.

"'Peculiar' Alden Freeman." *Trenton (NJ) Evening Times*, May 24, 1909.

Peiss, Kathy. *Cheap Amusements: Working Women and Leisure in Turn-of-the-Century New York.* Philadelphia: Temple University Press, 1986.

———. *Hope in a Jar: The Making of America's Beauty Culture.* Philadelphia: University of Pennsylvania Press, 1998.

"The People's Forum." *Miami Daily News and Metropolis*, October 17, 1928.

Pérez, Louis A., Jr. "Between Encounter and Experience: Florida in the Cuban Imagination." *Florida Historical Quarterly* 82, no. 2 (Fall 2003): 170–90.

———. *Cuba in the American Imagination: Metaphor and the Imperial Ethos.* Chapel Hill: University of North Carolina Press, 2008.

———. *On Becoming Cuban: Identity, Nationality, and Culture*. Chapel Hill: University of North Carolina Press, 1999.

———. *The War of 1898: The United States and Cuba in History and Historiography*. Chapel Hill: University of North Carolina Press, 1998.

Perrine, M. C. L. "The Tropic Home." *Tropic Magazine*, April 1914.

Perry, Burroughs F. "Lotus Spell Cast on Visitors by Bewitching Magic of Miami." *Miami Daily News*, September 22, 1929.

Petit, Don. "Bolita and Cuba Survive 'The Heat.'" *Miami Daily News*, August 10, 1952.

Pharr, Kelsey Leroy. "Colored Town Section of the City of Miami Is a Thriving Community." *Miami Metropolis*, October 16, 1915.

Pierson, Gregory N. "Vilona P. Cutler: Humanitarian, Activist, and Educator." *Chronicles of Oklahoma* 90, no. 1 (2012): 52–67.

Pieze, Elliott J. "Good Morning Judge." *Miami Times*, October 20, 1951.

———. "Good Morning Judge." *Miami Times*, October 4, 1952.

Pleck, Elizabeth H. *Not Just Roommates: Cohabitation after the Sexual Revolution*. Chicago: University of Chicago Press, 2012.

"Police Department Again." *Miami Metropolis*, March 25, 1910.

Pollack, Deborah C. *Visual Art and the Urban Evolution of the New South*. Columbia: University of South Carolina, 2015.

Polyné, Millery. *From Douglass to Duvalier: U.S. African Americans, Haiti, and Pan Americanism, 1870–1964*. Gainesville: University Press of Florida, 2010.

Porter, Cole (music and lyric). "Anything Goes." New York: Harms, 1934.

Porter, Russell B. "Plea of Cubans Exiled Here Stems Anti-American Tide." *New York Times*, September 17, 1933.

Portes, Alejandro, and Alex Stepick. *City on the Edge: The Transformation of Miami*. Berkeley: University of California Press, 1993.

Poyo, Gerald Eugene. *With All, and for the Good of All: The Emergence of Popular Nationalism in the Cuban Communities of the United States, 1848–1898*. Durham, NC: Duke University Press, 1989.

"Prohibition Given a Boost." *Miami Metropolis*, March 13, 1908.

Putnam, Lara. *Radical Moves: Caribbean Migrants and the Politics of Race in the Jazz Age*. Chapel Hill: University of North Carolina Press, 2013.

*The Raab Collection, Catalog 71*, March 2012, www.raabcollection.com/sites/default /files/pdf/Catalog-71.pdf.

"Raiders Seize 19 in Pervert Roundup." *Miami Daily News*, August 14, 1954.

Rainbolt, Victor. *The Town That Climate Built: The Story of the Rise of a City in the American Tropics*. Miami: Parker Art Printing Association, 1925.

"The Rambler." *Evening Independent* (St. Petersburg, FL), January 13, 1937.

"The Rambler." *Evening Independent* (St. Petersburg, FL), March 20, 1941.

Ramsey, Kate. *The Spirits and the Law: Vodou and Power in Haiti*. Chicago: University of Chicago Press, 2011.

"Reasons Why Miami Should Have a Modern Y.M.C.A. Building." *Miami Daily Metropolis*, February 11, 1916.

Reck, Alfred P. "Plan Air Line to Buenos Aires." *Pittsburgh Press*, November 20, 1928.

"The Red Cross Fund." *New York Times*, September 27, 1928.

Rees, Ralph. "The Search for Dewing Woodward: Revealing a Life and the Difficulty of Documenting That Life." *Bucknell World* 15 (November 1991): 14–15.

"Reformer Held for Observation." *Bradford (PA) Evening Star and Daily Record*, July 18, 1936.

Reid, Ira De Augustine. *The Negro Immigrant: His Background, Characteristics, and Social Adjustment, 1899–1937*. New York: Columbia University Press, 1939.

Reitman, Ben L. *Sister of the Road: The Autobiography of Box Car Bertha*. Oakland, CA: AK, 2002 [1937].

Remus, Emily A. "Tippling Ladies and the Making of Consumer Culture: Gender and Public Space in Fin-de-Siècle Chicago." *Journal of American History* 101, no. 3 (December 2014): 751–77.

Renda, Mary A. *Taking Haiti: Military Occupation and the Culture of U.S. Imperialism, 1915–1940*. Chapel Hill: University of North Carolina Press, 2001.

Reprinted 1908 advertisement: Dan Hardie, Candidate for Sheriff. *Miami News*, August 10, 1985.

Reprinted 1932 advertisement: Dan Hardie, Candidate for Sheriff. *Miami News*, August 10, 1985.

Retzloff, Tim. "Cars and Bars: Assembling Gay Men in Postwar Flint, Michigan." In *Creating a Space for Ourselves: Lesbian, Gay, and Bisexual Community Histories*, edited by Brett Beemyn, 227–52. New York: Routledge, 1997.

Rialto, Ben. "Coburn's Show Pleases Many." *St. Petersburg (FL) Times*, December 27, 1921.

Richardson, Riché. *Black Masculinity and the U.S. South: From Uncle Tom to Gangsta*. Athens: University of Georgia Press, 2007.

Robb, Inez. "Governor Warren Has the Floor." *Miami Daily News*, November 14, 1950.

Roberts, Jack. "A Salute to Caesar LaMonaca, Miami Music Man for 48 Years." *Miami News*, January 12, 1977.

Roberts, Kenneth L. *Sun Hunting*. New York: Curtis, 1922.

———. "Tropical Growth." *Saturday Evening Post*, April 29, 1922.

Roberts, Wilbur Edwards. "A Riviera 'Conch.'" Interview by Veronica D. Huss. Transcript, November 14, 1936. Washington, DC: U.S. Work Projects Administration, Federal Writers' Project, Library of Congress.

Robertson, Stephen. "'Boys, of Course, Cannot Be Raped': Age, Homosexuality and the Redefinition of Sexual Violence in New York City, 1880–1955." *Gender & History* 18, no. 2 (August 2006): 357–79.

Robinson, Charles Frank. *Dangerous Liaisons: Sex and Love in the Segregated South*. Fayetteville: University of Arkansas Press, 2003.

Robinson, John Bunyan. "Florida." In *Epic Ballads of the Land of Flowers*. DeLand, FL: News Publishing, 1905.

Robinson, Louie. "The Expanding World of Sidney Poitier." *Ebony*, November 1971.

Rodgers, Daniel T. *Atlantic Crossings: Social Politics in a Progressive Age*. Cambridge, MA: Harvard University Press, 1998.

Rodríguez, Eduardo Luis. "The Architectural Avant-Garde: From Art Deco to

Modern Regionalism." *Journal of Decorative and Propaganda Arts* 22 (1996): 254–77.

Roediger, David R. *The Wages of Whiteness: Race and the Making of the American Working Class*. New York: Verso, 1999.

———. *Working toward Whiteness: How America's Immigrants Became White: The Strange Journey from Ellis Island to the Suburbs*. New York: Basic Books, 2005.

Romesburg, Don. "Longevity and Limits in Rae Bourbon's Life in Motion." In *Transgender Migrations: The Bodies, Borders, and Politics of Transition*, edited by Trystan T. Cotten, 119–35. New York: Routledge, 2012.

Roscoe, Will. *Changing Ones: Third and Fourth Genders in Native North Americans*. New York: St. Martin's, 1998.

Rose, Chanelle N. *The Struggle for Black Freedom in Miami: Civil Rights and America's Tourist Paradise, 1896–1968*. Baton Rouge: Louisiana State University Press, 2015.

Rosen, Deborah A. *Border Law: The First Seminole War and American Nationhood*. Cambridge, MA: Harvard University Press, 2015.

Rotundo, E. Anthony. *American Manhood: Transformations in Masculinity from the Revolution to the Modern Era*. New York: Basic Books, 1993.

Ruark, Robert C. "Steve Hannagan." *Pittsburgh Press*, March 17, 1953.

Ruiz, Jason. *Americans in the Treasure House: Travel to Porfirian Mexico and the Culture Politics of Empire*. Austin: University of Texas Press, 2014.

Rupp, Leila J. "The Persistence of Transnational Organizing: The Case of the Homophile Movement." *American Historical Review* 116, no. 4 (2011): 1014–39.

Rybczynski, Witold, and Laurie Olin. *Vizcaya: An American Villa and Its Makers*. Philadelphia: University of Pennsylvania Press, 2007.

"The Sad Case of Mr. Freeman." *Brooklyn Daily Eagle*, May 31, 1909.

Sáenz Rovner, Eduardo. "La prohibición norteamericana y el contrabando entre Cuba y los Estados Unidos durante los años veinte y treinta." *Innovar: Revista de Ciencias Administrativas y Sociales*, no. 23 (June 2004): 147–57.

Saillant, John. "The Black Body Erotic and the Republican Body Politic, 1790–1820." *Journal of the History of Sexuality* 5, no. 3 (January 1995): 403–28.

Sandoval-Strausz, A. K. "Latino Landscapes: Postwar Cities and the Transnational Origins of a New Urban America." *Journal of American History* 101, no. 3 (December 2014): 804–31.

Sargent, Porter. *A Handbook of American Private Schools: An Annual Survey*. 7th ed. Boston: Porter Sargent, 1922.

Schafer, Daniel L. "'A Class of People Neither Freemen nor Slaves': From Spanish to American Race Relations in Florida, 1821–1861." *Journal of Social History* 26, no. 3 (Spring 1993): 587–609.

Schellings, William J. "The Advent of the Spanish-American War in Florida, 1898." *Florida Historical Quarterly* 39, no. 4 (April 1961): 311–29.

———. "Soldiers in Miami, 1898." *Tequesta*, no. 17 (1957): 69–76.

Schmidt, Hans. *The United States Occupation of Haiti, 1915–1934*. 2nd ed. New Brunswick, NJ: Rutgers University Press, 1995 [1971].

Schneider, Dorothee. *Crossing Borders: Migration and Citizenship in the Twentieth-Century United States*. Cambridge: Harvard University Press, 2011.

"School Notes." *International Studio*, April 1916.

Schwartz, Rosalie. *Pleasure Island: Tourism and Temptation in Cuba*. Lincoln: University of Nebraska Press, 1997.

"Seaboard Air Line Ry. Changes." *New York Times*, December 8, 1901.

Sears, Clare. "All That Glitters: Trans-ing California's Gold Rush Migrations." *GLQ: A Journal of Lesbian and Gay Studies* 14, no. 2 (2008): 383–402.

———. *Arresting Dress: Cross-Dressing, Law, and Fascination in Nineteenth-Century San Francisco*. Durham, NC: Duke University Press, 2014.

Sears, James T. *Lonely Hunters: An Oral History of Lesbian and Gay Southern Life, 1948–1968*. Boulder, CO: Westview, 1997.

———. *Rebels, Rubyfruit, and Rhinestones: Queering Space in the Stonewall South*. New Brunswick, NJ: Rutgers University Press, 2001.

"Season Open Early." *Cincinnati Enquirer*, November 27, 1938.

Sedgwick, Eve Kosofsky. *Epistemology of the Closet*. Berkeley: University of California Press, 1990.

"Segregated District and Home for Disorderly Women Urged by Grand Jury in Presentment." *Miami Metropolis*, November 30, 1918.

Seligmann, C. G. "Sexual Inversion among Primitive Races." *Alienist and Neurologist* 23 (1902): 11–15.

"Selling Liquor in Miami." *Miami Metropolis*, September 4, 1896.

"Seminole Indians Master Alligators in Wrestling Bout." *Cincinnati Enquirer*, July 13, 1930.

"The Seminole Still Savage." *Miami Metropolis*, December 11, 1896.

"September Morn and the Press." *Miami Metropolis*, July 26, 1913.

"'September Morn' Can't Be Seen in Magic City." *Miami Daily Metropolis*, July 14, 1913.

Sessa, Frank B. "Miami in 1926." *Tequesta* 16 (1956): 15–36.

Sewell, John. *John Sewell's Memoirs and History of Miami, Florida*. Miami: Franklin, 1933.

Shah, Nayan. *Contagious Divides: Epidemics and Race in San Francisco's Chinatown*. Berkeley: University of California Press, 2001.

———. *Stranger Intimacy: Contesting Race, Sexuality, and the Law in the North American West*. Berkeley: University of California Press, 2011.

Shappee, Nathan D. "Flagler's Undertaking in Miami in 1897." *Tequesta* 1, no. 19 (1959): 3–13.

"Shave Is Needed as Well as Good Cleanup by City." *Miami Metropolis*, September 21, 1916.

Shell-Weiss, Melanie. "Coming North to the South: Migration, Labor and City-Building in Twentieth-Century Miami." *Florida Historical Quarterly* 84, no. 1 (Summer 2005): 79–99.

———. *Coming to Miami: A Social History*. Gainesville: University Press of Florida, 2009.

Sheller, Mimi. "Mobility History and Caribbean Tourism." *Mobility in History* 6 (2015): 143–49.

———. "Natural Hedonism: The Invention of Caribbean Islands as Tropical Playgrounds." In *Tourism in the Caribbean: Trends, Development, Prospects*, edited by David Timothy Duval, 23–38. New York: Routledge, 2004.

Sherry, Michael S. *Gay Artists in Modern American Culture: An Imagined Conspiracy*. Chapel Hill: University of North Carolina Press, 2007.

Sherwin, Vernon C. "The Other Side of Paradise." *American Spectator*, August 1933.

"Ship Lines Are Obliged to Increase Service to Jamaica." *Pittsburgh Press*, January 17, 1937.

Shire, Laurel Clark. *The Threshold of Manifest Destiny: Gender and National Expansion in Florida*. Philadelphia: University of Pennsylvania Press, 2016.

"Short Shrift: Men's Swim-Suits Down to Trunks as No-Shirt Movement Goes to Sea." *Literary Digest*, June 12, 1937.

Sieminski, Mary. "Willamsport's Bold Vagabond Artist." *Williamsport (PA) Sun-Gazette*, June 9, 2013.

Simmons, Christina. "Companionate Marriage and the Lesbian Threat." *Frontiers: A Journal of Women's Studies* 4, no. 3 (Autumn 1979): 54–59.

———. *Making Marriage Modern: Women's Sexuality from the Progressive Era to World War II*. New York: Oxford University Press, 2009.

Simon, Bryant. *Boardwalk of Dreams: Atlantic City and the Fate of Urban America*. Oxford: Oxford University Press, 2004.

Sippial, Tiffany A. *Prostitution, Modernity, and the Making of the Cuban Republic, 1840–1920*. Chapel Hill: University of North Carolina Press, 2013.

"Slogans Are Numerous but Beach Governors Uncertain." *Miami Daily Metropolis*, December 24, 1921.

"Small War over in Colored Town." *Miami Metropolis*, November 29, 1918.

"Smashing Window Displays Exploit 'Miami.'" *Exhibitors Trade Review*, June 21, 1924.

Smiley, Nixon. *The Whistles Were Blowing: Miami YWCA*. Miami: YWCA, 1967.

Smith, Trixie (performer). "No Good Man." *Trixie Smith*, vol. 2, *1925–1939*. Document Records. Compact disc.

Smith-Rosenberg, Carroll. *Disorderly Conduct: Visions of Gender in Victorian America*. New York: Alfred A. Knopf, 1985.

Sneider, Allison. *Suffragists in an Imperial Age: U.S. Expansion and the Woman Question, 1870–1929*. New York: Oxford University Press, 2008.

Snow, Major William F., MRC. "Fight Planned on Insidious Foe of Armies in Camp." *Miami Metropolis*, March 5, 1918.

"Some Attractive Homes of Well Known People." *Architect and Engineer of California* 51, no. 1 (October 1917): 63–67.

Somerville, Siobhan B. *Queering the Color Line: Race and the Invention of Homosexuality in American Culture*. Durham, NC: Duke University Press, 2000.

"Sons Oust Alden Freeman." *The (NY) Sun*, June 6, 1909.

"Stage Notes." *Freeman* (Indianapolis, IN), May 23, 1914.

Stahl, Eugene C. "The Public Pulse, July 17, 1913." *Miami News*, January 15, 1983.

Stanfield, Peter. *Body and Soul: Jazz and Blues in American Film, 1927–63*. Urbana: University of Illinois Press, 2005.

"State Press Comment." *Miami Metropolis*, August 5, 1913.

Stearns, Peter N. *Fat History: Bodies and Beauty in the Modern West*. New York: New York University Press, 1997.

Stedman, Thomas. "Some of the Medical Aspects of Immigration." *Medical Record* (November 11, 1911): 978.

Steele, Rufus. "Miami, an Air Capital." *Miami Daily News*, May 13, 1929.

Stein, Marc. *City of Sisterly and Brotherly Loves: Lesbian and Gay Philadelphia, 1945–1972*. Chicago: University of Chicago Press, 2000.

———. *Rethinking the Gay and Lesbian Movement*. New York: Routledge, 2012.

———. "Introduction: U.S. Homophile Internationalism." *Journal of Homosexuality* (forthcoming).

Taylor, Elizabeth A. "The Woman Suffrage Movement in Florida." *Florida Historical Quarterly* 36, no. 1 (July 1957): 42–60.

Stepick, Alex. "The Refugees Nobody Wants: Haitians in Miami." In *Miami Now! Immigration, Ethnicity, and Social Change*, 57–82. Gainesville: University Press of Florida, 1992.

Stepick, Alex, Guillermo Grenier, Max Castro, and Marvin Dunn. *This Land Is Our Land: Immigrants and Power in Miami*. Berkeley: University of California Press, 2003.

"Steve Hannagan's Girls." *LIFE*, November 30, 1936.

Stewart-Winter, Timothy. *Queer Clout: Chicago and the Rise of Gay Politics*. Philadelphia: University of Pennsylvania Press, 2016.

Stoler, Ann Laura, ed. *Haunted by Empire: Geographies of Intimacy in North American History*. Durham, NC: Duke University Press, 2006.

Stone, Isabel. "Expect Shipping Activity at Nassau Harbor, Bahamas." *Evening Independent* (St. Petersburg, FL), August 29, 1925.

Stoner, K. Lynn. *From the House to the Streets: The Cuban Woman's Movement for Legal Reform, 1898–1940*. Durham, NC: Duke University Press, 1991.

Stowe, Harriet Beecher. *Palmetto Leaves*. Boston: J. R. Osgood, 1873.

Strichartz, Richard. "Legal Aspects of Municipal Incorporation in Florida." *University of Miami Law Review* (1949): 78–97.

Stuart, John A. "Constructing Identity: Building and Place in New Deal South Florida." In *The New Deal in South Florida: Design, Policy, and Community Building, 1933–1940*, edited by John A. Stuart and John F. Stack Jr., 31–70. Gainesville: University Press of Florida, 2008.

"Styles Observed in the Southland." *New York Times*, January 27, 1924.

Sueyoshi, Amy. *Queer Compulsions: Race, Nation, and Sexuality in the Affairs of Yone Noguchi*. Honolulu: University of Hawai'i Press, 2012.

"Suffrage League Members Agree That Dress Should Be Changed." *Miami Metropolis*, August 21, 1917.

Sullivan, Ed. "Broadway Characters." *Harrisburg (PA) Telegraph*, February 11, 1937.

Sullivan, Gerard. "Political Opportunism and the Harassment of Homosexuals in Florida, 1952–1965." *Journal of Homosexuality* 37, no. 4 (1999): 57–81.

Summers, Claude J., ed. *The Queer Encyclopedia of the Visual Arts*. San Francisco: Cleis, 2004.

Sutton, David E. "Greeks of Kalymnos." In *Encyclopedia of Sex and Gender: Men and Women in the World's Cultures*, edited by Carol R. Ember and Melvin Ember, 417–24. New York: Klower Academic, 2003.

Sweeting, Stanley Ivern. "Miami." *New York Amsterdam News*, December 18, 1948.

———. "Night Life in Miami." *The Crisis*, March 1942.

"Swift Justice Meeted Out to Vagrants and Prostitutes by Judge." *Miami Metropolis*, June 25, 1917.

"Taking It Over." *Pittsburgh Courier*, April 9, 1949.

"Talk about War." *Miami Metropolis*, March 18, 1898.

Tatum, B. B. "What Shall Be Done?" *Miami Metropolis*, January 23, 1903.

Taylor, Elizabeth A. "The Woman Suffrage Movement in Florida." *Florida Historical Quarterly* 36, no. 1 (July 1957): 42–60.

Taylor, Frank Fonda. *To Hell with Paradise: History of the Jamaican Tourist Industry*. Pittsburgh: University of Pittsburgh Press, 1993.

"Teen-Ager Faces Murder Charges." *Spokane (WA) Daily Chronicle*, March 8, 1952.

Terry, Jennifer. *An American Obsession: Science, Medicine, and Homosexuality in Modern Society*. Chicago: University of Chicago Press, 1999.

"These Mermaids Add to Lures of Sunny Miami Beach Shores." *Miami Daily News*, February 3, 1925.

"Thingumbobs." *Miami Daily News*, June 2, 1932.

Thomas, Donna. "'Camp Hell': Miami during the Spanish-American War." *Florida Historical Quarterly* 2, no. 57 (October 1978): 141–56.

Thompson, Brock. *The Un-natural State: Arkansas and the Queer South*. Fayetteville: University of Arkansas Press, 2010.

Thompson, J. F. *Locomotive Engineers' Monthly Journal*, December 1902.

Thompson, Vance. *Woman*. New York: E. P. Dutton, 1917.

"3 New Miami Area Towns Find Their Troubles Multiplying over Liquor." *Sarasota (FL) Herald-Tribune*, August 13, 1948.

"Three Thousand Bath Rooms for the Approaching Season." *Miami Daily Metropolis*, September 26, 1921.

Tiemeyer, Phil. *Plane Queer: Labor, Sexuality, and AIDS in the History of Male Flight Attendants*. Berkeley: University of California Press, 2013.

Ting, Jennifer. "Bachelor Society: Deviant Heterosexuality and Asian American Historiography." In *Privileging Positions: The Sites of Asian American Studies*, edited by Gary Y. Okihiro, Marilyn Alquizola, Dorothy Fujita Rony, and K. Scott Wong, 271–79. Pullman: Washington State University Press, 1995.

Toll, Robert C. *Blacking Up: The Minstrel Show in Nineteenth-Century America*. New York: Oxford University Press, 1974.

"Tolls Be Now Charged to Cross Bay Bridge." *Miami Daily Metropolis*, June 13, 1913.

"Tonight's the Night." *Miami Daily News*, December 24, 1941.

"Topics of the Times." *New York Times*, August 23, 1921.

Treasury Department, Bureau of Public Health and Marine-Hospital Service. *Book*

*of Instructions for the Medical Inspection of Immigrants*. Washington, DC:
Government Printing Office, 1903.

Tribune Society Department. "Family Album Shows Startling Changes in Cost of
Young Peoples' Fun in Miami." *Miami Tribune*, October 12, 1924.

"Triumphant Florida." *New York Times*, March 15, 1925.

Trouillot, Michel-Rolph. *Haiti, State against Nation: The Origins and Legacy of
Duvalierism*. New York: Monthly Review Press, 1990.

————. *Silencing the Past: Power and the Production of History*. Boston: Beacon,
1995.

"Turn About." *Evening Independent* (St. Petersburg, FL), October 20, 1927.

Turner, Frederick Jackson. "The Significance of the Frontier in American History
(1893)." In *Rereading Frederick Jackson Turner: "The Significance of the Frontier
in American History" and Other Essays*, edited by John Mack Faragher, 31–60.
New York: Henry Holt, 1994.

Turner, Jackson. "King Faustin of Haitian Isle Is Expected as Miami Visitor." *Miami
Daily News and Metropolis*, September 3, 1929.

Twa, Lindsay J. *Visualizing Haiti in U.S. Culture, 1910–1950*. Burlington, VT: Ashgate,
2014.

Tweed, Thomas A. "An Emerging Protestant Establishment: Religious Affiliation and
Public Power on the Urban Frontier in Miami, 1896–1904." *Church History* 64,
no. 3 (September 1995): 412–37.

"$28,000,000 Voted to Aid Prohibition." *New York Times*, February 15, 1928.

"26 Out of 92 Votes Were Cast by Women in Today's Election." *Miami Daily
Metropolis*, October 16, 1919.

"Two Miami Clubs Raided by Cops." *Evening Independent* (St. Petersburg, FL),
March 23, 1939.

"Two More Martyrs to Miami's Fame." *Daily Picayune* (New Orleans, LA), August 8,
1898.

Ullman, Sharon R. *Sex Seen: The Emergence of Modern Sexuality in America*.
Berkeley: University of California Press, 1997.

Unrau, William E. *Man's Wicked Water: The Alcohol Trade and Prohibition in Indian
Country, 1802–1892*. Lawrence: University Press of Kansas, 1996.

"The Uses of the Loafer." *Evening Independent* (St. Petersburg, FL), July 4, 1912.

U.S. Census Bureau. *Fifteenth Census of the United States, 1930, Population*, vol. 3,
part 1. Washington, DC, 1932.

————. *Fourteenth Census of the United States, 1920, Population*, vol. 2. Washington,
DC, 1922.

————. "Table 19: Population of the 100 Largest Urban Places: 1960," https://www
.census.gov/population/www/documentation/twps0027/tab19.txt (accessed
November 26, 2016).

————. *U.S. Censuses of Population and Housing: 1960, Census Tracts*. Final Report
PHC(1)-90. Washington, DC: Government Printing Office, 1962.

————. *U.S. Census of Population: 1950*, vol. 2, *Characteristics of the Population*, part
10, *Florida*. Washington, DC: Government Printing Office, 1952.

U.S. Congress. House of Representatives. Committee on the Judiciary. *Hearings on the Prohibition Amendment*, part 2, 71st Cong., 2nd sess. Washington, DC: Government Printing Office, 1930.

———. Committee on Naval Affairs. *Hearings before Committee on Naval Affairs of the House of Representatives on Estimates Submitted by the Secretary of the Navy.* 66th Cong. Washington, DC: Government Printing Office, 1919.

U.S. Congress. Senate. Committee on Immigration. *Emergency Immigration Legislation: Hearing before Committee on Immigration, H.R. 14461, part 1, United States Senate.* 66th Cong., 3rd sess. Washington, DC: Government Printing Office, 1921.

———. Special Committee to Investigate Organized Crime in Interstate Commerce. *Interim Report on Investigations in Florida and Preliminary General Conclusions, Senate Report No. 2370.* 81st Cong., 2d sess. Washington, DC: Government Printing Office, 1950.

U.S. Department of Labor. Bureau of Immigration. *Annual Report of the Commissioner General of Immigration to the Secretary of Labor.* Washington, DC: Government Printing Office, 1916.

U.S. Interdepartmental Social Hygiene Board. "Appendix VIII: Local Financial Support to Anti-venereal Campaign." In *Manual for the Various Agents*, 71–74. Washington, DC: Government Printing Office, 1920.

"U.S. Marine Is Ruler of Haiti Kingdom." *Tyrone (PA) Daily Herald*, October 19, 1929.

"Vacation Days in the Bahamas." *Hide and Leather: The International Weekly* (Chicago), March 25, 1922.

Vandenberg-Daves, Jodi. "The Manly Pursuit of a Partnership between the Sexes: The Debate over YMCA Programs for Women and Girls, 1914–1933." *Journal of American History* 78, no. 4 (March 1992): 1324–46.

Vanderblue, Homer B. "The Florida Land Boom." *Journal of Land & Public Utility Economics* 3, no. 2 (May 1927): 113–31.

———. "The Florida Land Boom II." *Journal of Land & Public Utility Economics* 3, no. 3 (August 1927): 252–69.

Vanderwood, Paul J. *Satan's Playground: Mobsters and Movie Stars at America's Greatest Gaming Resort.* Durham, NC: Duke University Press, 2010.

Van Ness, Thomas. "Florida, New and Old." *Christian Register*, March 28, 1912.

"Vasile Is Acquitted in the Criminal Court." *Miami Metropolis*, November 15, 1918.

"Vermont Nominates His Minstrel Stars." *Billboard*, March 18, 1950.

Viglucci, Andres. "Intense Mediation Leads to Agreement on Historic Tequesta Site in Downtown Miami." *Miami Herald*, March 20, 2014.

Villard, Oswald Garrison. "Florida Flamboyant." *The Nation*, March 13, 1935.

"Villa Vizcaya, Miami, Florida." *Harper's Bazaar*, July 1917.

Wade, Richard C. *The Urban Frontier: The Rise of Western Cities, 1790–1830.* Cambridge, MA: Harvard University Press, 1959.

Walters, Barbara. *Audition: A Memoir.* 1st Vintage Books ed. New York: Vintage, 2009.

"Walter Winchell on Broadway." *Burlington (NC) Daily Times-News*, December 31, 1938.

Walton, John K. "Seaside Tourism in Europe: Business, Urban and Comparative History." *Business History* 53, no. 6 (October 2011): 900–916.

Warner, Michael. *Publics and Counterpublics*. New York: Zone, 2002.

Warner, Patricia Campbell. *When the Girls Came Out to Play: The Birth of American Sportswear*. Amherst: University of Massachusetts Press, 2006.

Warren, Harry, Harry M. Snodgrass, Walter Hirsch, and Abe Olman. "Along Miami Shore." Chicago: Manlowe Music, 1926.

"Washington Society Has a Gay Round." *Milwaukee Journal*, January 23, 1927.

"Wearies of Waiting a Comstock Arrest." *New York Times*, May 15, 1913.

Weber, David J. *The Spanish Frontier in North America*. New Haven, CT: Yale University Press, 1992.

Weede, Fred L. "Publicity and Palm Trees." *Judicious Advertising* 19, no. 12 (January 1922): 61–64.

"West Indian Contingent Committee." *Tribune* (Nassau), February 1, 1916.

Wheatley, Dennis. *Murder off Miami*. London: Hutchinson, 1936.

"Where to Find Entertainment in Miami Area." *Miami Daily News*, April 19, 1927.

"Where to Find Entertainment in Miami Area." *Miami Daily News and Metropolis*, April 28, 1927.

"Whidden's House May Be Condemned." *Miami Daily News*, March 12, 1952.

"Whiskey Dealers Warned Not to Sell Ardent to Indians." *Miami Metropolis*, June 12, 1909.

White, Kevin. *The First Sexual Revolution: The Emergence of Male Heterosexuality in Modern America*. New York: New York University Press, 1993.

White, Le Roy "Lasses." "Nigger Blues." Dallas: Bush & Gerts, 1913.

White, Shane, Stephen Garton, Stephen Robertson, and Graham White. *Playing the Numbers: Gambling in Harlem between the Wars*. Cambridge, MA: Harvard University Press, 2010.

Wilbanks, William, and Paul S. George. "Re-evaluating the 'Good Old Days': A Study of Dade County Homocides, 1917–1982." *American Journal of Criminal Justice* 8, no. 2 (March 1984): 232–44.

Williams, Jay. "Henry Salem Hubbell's 'The Building of the House': A Boom-Era Symbol of Optimism and Growth." *SECAC Review* 13, no. 4 (1999): 419–20.

Willis, Lee. *Southern Prohibition: Race, Reform, and Public Life in Middle Florida, 1821–1920*. Athens: University of Georgia Press, 2011.

"Will Names Harding 'Daughter.'" *Miami Daily News*, August 24, 1938.

Willsie, Honoré. "Migration of Peoples as Related to National Solidarity and Sovereignty." In *The World's Moral Problems: Addresses at the Third World's Christian Citizenship Conference*, 184–90. Pittsburgh: National Reform Association, 1920.

Wilson, F. Page. "Miami: From Frontier to Metropolis—An Appraisal." *Tequesta* 14 (1954): 25–49.

Wilson, J. G. "Medical Examination of Immigrants." In *A Reference Handbook of the Medical Sciences*, vol. 5, edited by Thomas Stedman, 3rd ed., 503–8. New York: William Wood, 1915.

Wing, Grace. "Flamingo Chicks Safely Hatched." *Miami Daily News*, July 15, 1945.

Wolff, Reinhold P. *Miami: Economic Patterns of a Resort Area*. Coral Gables, FL: University of Miami, Inc., 1945.

"Women in Trousers." *Tribune* (Nassau), November 2, 1916.

Wood, Elizabeth. "Sapphonics." In *Queering the Pitch: The New Gay and Lesbian Musicology*, edited by Philip Brett, Elizabeth Wood, and Gary C. Thomas. New York: Routledge, 2006.

Woolner, Cookie. "'Woman Slain in Queer Love Brawl': African American Women, Same-Sex Desire, and Violence in the Urban North, 1920–1929." *Journal of African American History* 100, no. 3 (Summer 2015): 406–27.

Woolson, Constance Fenimore. "Felipa." *Lippincott's Magazine*, June 1876.

"YMCA Observing 40th Anniversary of Service to Greater Miami." *Miami News*, May 11, 1958.

York, Wealthy Ann. *Some Adventures of Two Vagabonds: By One of 'Em*. New York: Broadway, 1908.

"Zoning Regulations in County Discussed." *Miami Herald*, November 18, 1937.

# Index

*Page numbers in italics refer to illustrations.*

White slavery, 277
Wilde, Oscar, 107
Williams, Bert, 151
Wilson, Evelyn, 155
Winnipeg Beach, (Manitoba), Canada, 8
Wirkus, Faustin, 121–22
*Woman* (Thompson), 202
Woman's Club, 203
Women's Christian Temperance Union
    (WCTU), 53, 54, 251
Women's suffrage, 145, 202, 210, 224
Woodward, Dewing, 114–17, *115*, 204–5
Woolson, Constance Fenimore, 29, 30,
    201
Woon, Basil, 243
Works Progress Administration (WPA),
    117. *See also* New Deal

World War I, 44, 67, 74, 164–65, 172, 182,
    205, 220
World War II, 17, 278–79

Ybor City, Fla., 65
Young, Irving, 189, 254, 264
Young, Joseph W., Jr., 4
Young Men's Christian Association
    (YMCA), 167–68, 172, 182, 212
Young Women's Christian Association
    (YWCA), 203–4, 212
Youst, Al, 232, 233, 252, 269, 277–78,
    281, 282, 283

Zangara, Giuseppe, 252
Zoning, 24–26, 57–59, 283